American Furniture

AMERICAN FURNITURE 1993

Edited by Luke Beckerdite

Published by the CHIPSTONE FOUNDATION

Distributed by University Press of New England

Hanover and London

Cover Illustration: Arm of a ceremonial chair made for the South Carolina State House in Charleston, ca. 1756. (All rights reserved, McKissick Museum, University of South Carolina.)

Cover Design: Wynne Patterson
Photography: Gavin Ashworth, New York, New York

Published by the Chipstone Foundation
Distributed by University Press of New England, Hanover, NH 03755

Printed in the United States of America 5 4 3 2 1
ISSN 1069–4188
ISBN 0–87451–648–X

Contents

Editorial Statement

American Furniture is an interdisciplinary journal dedicated to advancing knowledge of furniture made or used in the Americas from the seventeenth century to the present. Authors are encouraged to submit articles on any aspect of furniture history, essays on conservation and historic technology, reproductions or transcripts of documents, such as account books and inventories, annotated photographs of new furniture discoveries, and book and exhibition reviews. References for compiling an annual bibliography also are welcome.

Manuscripts must be typed, double-spaced, illustrated with 8″ × 10″ black-and-white prints or transparencies, and prepared in accordance with the *Chicago Manual of Style*. Computer disk copy is requested but not required. The Chipstone Foundation will offer significant honoraria for manuscripts accepted for publication and reimburse authors for all photography approved in writing by the editor.

Luke Beckerdite

Preface

The Chipstone Foundation was organized in 1965 by Stanley Stone and Polly Mariner Stone of Fox Point, Wisconsin. Representing the culmination of their shared experiences in collecting American furniture, American historical prints, and early English pottery, the foundation was created with the dual purpose of preserving and interpreting their collection and stimulating research and education in the decorative arts.

The Stones began collecting American decorative arts in 1946, and by 1964 it became apparent to them that provisions should be made to deal with their collection. With the counsel of their friend Charles Montgomery, the Stones decided that their collection should be published and exhibited.

Following Stanley Stone's death in 1987, the foundation was activated by an initial endowment provided by Mrs. Stone. This generous bequest allowed the foundation to institute its research and grant programs, begin work on three collection catalogues, and launch an important new journal, *American Furniture*.

Allen M. Taylor

Introduction

Luke Beckerdite

American furniture studies have changed dramatically since the publication in 1891 of Irving W. Lyon's *Colonial Furniture of New England*. Lyon, Esther Singleton, and Luke Vincent Lockwood were the first scholars to systematically study the English and Continental origins of American furniture and to develop a terminology and chronology for different furniture forms. Their books and the large pictorial works of the 1920s and 1930s—for instance, Wallace Nutting's *Furniture of the Pilgrim Century* (1921) and *Furniture Treasury* (1928)—generated intense interest in American furniture.

Following the publication of William Macpherson Hornor's *Blue Book, Philadelphia Furniture* (1935), regionalism became a major focus of furniture historians. Today, the best books of this genre examine the cultural and socioeconomic factors that influenced furniture styles and use. Representative examples are Robert Trent's *Hearts &. Crowns: Folk Chairs of the Connecticut Coast* (1977), Robert Blair St. George's *Wrought Covenant: Source Material for the Study of Craftsmen and Community in Southeastern New England, 1620–1700* (1979), the Wadsworth Atheneum's *Great River: Art &. Society of the Connecticut Valley, 1635–1820* (1985), John Bivins's *Furniture of Coastal North Carolina, 1700–1820* (1988), and Brock Jobe's *Portsmouth Furniture: Masterworks from the New Hampshire Seacoast* (1993). Related to these are regional-ethnic studies, such as Lonn Taylor and Dessa Bokides, *New Mexican Furniture, 1600–1940* (1987), that examine the historical context and meaning of furniture.

Most of the early scholarship focused on the eighteenth century, and it was not until the 1960s that serious studies of nineteenth-century furniture began. Such stylistic surveys as *Classical America, 1815–1845* (1963), *The Arts in America: The Nineteenth Century* (1969), and *19th-Century America: Furniture and Other Decorative Arts* (1970) kindled popular interest in nineteenth-century furniture and laid the groundwork for more specific studies of late neoclassical, revival, art nouveaux, and arts and crafts styles. Recently publications have focused on specific cabinetmaking firms, the furniture industry in large cities, the furniture of regional and ethnic groups, the influence of mechanization and technology, the transmission and diffusion of design, the development of tastes, and on furniture as a form of nonverbal communication.

As furniture studies have broadened, so have perspectives. Philip Zimmerman's "Methodological Study in the Identification of Some Important Philadelphia Chippendale Furniture" in *Winterthur Portfolio* 13 and

Ben Hewitt's *Work of Many Hands: Card Tables in Federal America, 1790–1820* represent significant efforts to bring scientific methods and objectivity to connoisseurship. Hewitt's book also contains an essay titled "'Avarice and Conviviality': Card Playing in Federal America," one of several excellent works by Gerald W. R. Ward that examine furniture and social interaction.

Studies of historic technology also have expanded our knowledge of American furniture. Charles Hummel's *With Hammer in Hand: The Dominy Craftsmen of East Hampton, New York* (1968) graphically depicts life in a cabinet shop by examining surviving tools, patterns, and furniture, whereas Wallace Gusler's *Furniture of Williamsburg and Eastern Virginia, 1710–1790* (1979) and Benno Forman's *American Seating Furniture, 1630–1730* (1988) demonstrate the importance of understanding style and technology in international and regional contexts. Since the founding of the Wood Artifacts Group of the American Institute for Conservation of Historic and Artistic Works (AIC) in the late 1970s, conservators have been instrumental in rediscovering and writing about historic techniques. Representative contributions are in *Upholstery in America & Europe from the Seventeenth Century to World War I* (1987), *Gilded Wood: Conservation and History* (1991), and AIC and American Conservation Consortium preprints.

The scholarly study of twentieth-century furniture is scarcely more than a decade old, yet such significant publications as Karen Davies's *At Home in Manhattan* (1982) and Derek Ostergard's *Bentwood and Metal Furniture: 1850–1946* (1987) have focused considerable attention on the art deco and art moderne styles. Woodworking and craft magazines and books such as Michael Stone's *Contemporary American Woodworkers* (1986) are responsible for much of today's interest in contemporary furniture making. Perhaps the most important scholarly study in this area is Edward S. Cooke's *New American Furniture: The Second Generation of Studio Furnituremakers* (1989). Cooke's discussion of the philosophical and technical foundations of first- and second-generation studio furniture making and his excellent catalogue entries demonstrate that new chapters in American furniture history are being written in wood and other materials every day.

The publications mentioned in this introduction represent only a fraction of the scholarship of the last century, but they clearly show that American furniture history has been a vital, evolving, and increasingly popular area of inquiry. Although many excellent books and catalogues have been published, only a few magazines and journals have emerged to provide a consistent forum for articles and essays on American furniture: *The Magazine Antiques* (1922–), *The Antiquarian* (1923–1933), *The American Collector* (1933–1948), *Winterthur Portfolio: A Journal of American Material Culture* (1964–), and the *Journal of Early Southern Decorative Arts* (1977–).

At a pivotal seminar at the National Gallery of Art in 1987, several scholars began an ongoing discussion about forming a journal devoted solely to American furniture. Inspired by their dialogue, the Chipstone Foundation sponsored a planning meeting at Yale University in 1988 and subsequently assembled an editorial advisory board and made a long-term commitment to publishing *American Furniture*. This inaugural issue represents the combined efforts of the Chipstone Foundation's board of directors, the editorial advisory board, the authors, and University Press of New England and attests to the foundation's commitment to encouraging research and education in the decorative arts.

If the past century of scholarship is any indication, *American Furniture* has an exciting future. By seeking out and encouraging new research and new methodologies, we intend to play an active role in shaping the future of American furniture history. Articles in *American Furniture* will identify artisans, shops, and regional schools; examine technology, industry, and the business of furniture making; and address such critical issues as stylistic influences, consumerism, patronage, and furniture use. We also will publish broad interdisciplinary studies that examine the social, economic, and political contexts of furniture making and show how furniture and other artistic objects offer insights into behavior, thought, and belief. Articles on furniture conservation will keep subscribers informed of the latest techniques and theories, while annual bibliographies and book reviews will critique and survey recent publications in the field. In short, our goal is to make *American Furniture* the journal of record for its subject.

American Furniture

Figure 1 Design for a state bed in Daniel Marot, *Second Livre d'Apartments*, ca. 1702. (Dumbarton Oaks, Trustees for Harvard University.)

Linda Baumgarten

Protective Covers for Furniture and Its Contents

▼ IN MANY ways, the finest textiles and furnishings of the seventeenth and eighteenth centuries functioned more for display than use. Yet householders were keenly aware of the destructive effects of sunlight, dust, and wear on their textiles, furniture, and domestic goods. To mitigate the problem, they frequently turned to less costly materials to cover their expensive furnishings, sometimes carrying protection to the extreme of encasing these objects entirely and removing the covers only for formal occasions. The concept of protecting material goods ranged from objects as small as the contents of a desk to those as large as entire beds and room-size carpets.

Decorative floors and carpets often had protective covers. Although leather covers occasionally were used to protect patterned wood floors, woolen textiles were preferred for covering carpets, probably because leather would more easily tear from a shoe heel sinking into the resilient carpet beneath. Baize and serge frequently were used for covers in the eighteenth century. The "Elegant Turkey carpet" in Aaron Burr's New York residence was protected by "a Carpet of Blue Bays." Sir Lawrence Dundas had in the front room of his London townhouse, "A large Carpet, [and] A green baize cover to do." In England and her colonies, both patrons and tradesmen realized that covers were essential to protect expensive carpets from wear and fading. When Ninian Horne wrote to Chippendale, Haig and Company about a carpet, he insisted that "there must be a covering for it of green serge." Thomas Sheraton summed up the practice of covering carpets in his *Cabinet Dictionary* (1803) noting that "bays" was used "to cover over carpets, and made to fit round the room, to save them." Where loose carpets had loose covers, wall-to-wall carpets often had specially fitted covers that could be attached to the floor. On January 10, 1778, Chippendale charged Sir Gilbert Heathcote £1.2.0 for "Thread and piecing out the Serge Carpet in [the] Breakfast room to fit the floor, making Eyelet holes in do and laying down with studs Compleat."[1]

Furnishings as large as beds also were slipcovered. Daniel Marot's early-eighteenth-century designs for state beds included several with an outside compass rod for curtains that could be drawn around the bed to enclose it and prevent the decorative curtains from fading (fig. 1). The red and gold state bed at Dyrham Park originally had case curtains, and the upper frame has holes where rods for these curtains were fastened. Late-seventeenth-century inventories for Ham House near London list "case curtains" for most of the important tall post beds. These were made

Figure 2 Cover for a side chair, plate printed in England by Robert Jones, Old Ford, 1761–1780. Cotton with wool and cotton fringe. (Colonial Williamsburg Foundation, acc. 1963-36, 12.)

Figure 3 Cushion cover for an easy chair, plate printed in England by Robert Jones, Old Ford, 1761–1780. Cotton with wool and linen binding over the seams and cotton and wool fringe. (Colonial Williamsburg Foundation, acc. 1963-36, 10.)

out of white "plading" (wool), white serge (wool), yellow "sarsnet" (silk), and India silk.[2]

The use of loose, often wrinkled, slipcovers on upholstered chairs and sofas is well documented in original records, print sources, and surviving examples (figs. 2, 3).[3] Wool serge cases were gradually superseded during the second half of the eighteenth century by washable linens or cottons, usually of a color or pattern to match the rest of the furnishings in the room. Checks and stripes were preferred for public rooms such as libraries or parlors, whereas printed cottons were favored for bedchambers where the slipcovers often matched the bed hangings. The plate-printed covers illustrated in figures 2 and 3 were once part of matching textile furnishings for a bedchamber that included a tall post bed, an easy chair, and several side chairs. Virginian Robert Beverley, who ordered many of his furnishings directly from England, wanted all the furnishings of his parlor, including the case covers, to be en suite with the wallpaper. On July 16, 1771, he ordered:

> 3 yellow Damask window Curtains of Stuff worstit with Pullies to draw up to the Top of the Window, 11 Feet high & 4 Feet six Inches wide, the Colour to be the same as the ground of the rich yellow Paper wch I described 12 neat plain mahogany Chairs, with yellow worstit Stuff Damask Bottoms like the Curtains, & spare loose Cases of yellow & white Check to tie over them. The Bottoms all to be loose & not nailed with brass Nails, wch I dislike much & the Covering of the Hair [stuffing], with wch the Bottoms are filled to be of thick strong Canvas, & not the thin coarse stuff with wch Chairs are coverd, because they are soon set out. N B all the Chairs to be done in this Manner.[4]

Figure 4 Side chair, Philadelphia, 1769–1770. Mahogany with white cedar. H. 37″, W. 24″, D. 24″. (Colonial Williamsburg Foundation, acc. 1964-680.)

From the description, it is clear that Beverley preferred chairs with slip seats or "loose bottoms" as he called them. If one assumes that the "cases of yellow & white check" were to be tied over the slip seats rather than to the stiles, Beverley intended to have slipcovers that could be tied on over the damask before the seats were placed in the chair frame. Beverley probably reserved the yellow wool damask covers for formal occasions.[5] Occasionally owners had chairs finished "in linen" until permanent upholstery was nailed on or a slipcover was made to match the room furnishings. Thomas Chippendale finished chairs in linen for Sir Edward Knatchbull of Mersham-le-Hatch, Kent, while the intended needlework was being completed by his wife. In his recommendation for case material Chippendale recognized that the wool serge commonly used was out of keeping with the light painted Chinese wallpaper Knatchbull had chosen: "as the Chairs can only at present be finishd in Linnen We should be glad to know what kind of Covers you would please to have for them—Serge is most commonly usd but as the room is hung with India paper, perhaps you might Chuse some sort of Cotton—suppose a green Stripe Cotton which at this is fashionable." John Cadwalader's accounts with Philadelphia upholsterers Plunket Fleeson and John Webster provide a contemporary parallel from the colonies. Between October 8, 1770, and January 28, 1771, Fleeson charged John Cadwalader £33.3.10 for labor and materials for thirty-two chairs, three sofas, and an easy chair, all of which he "finish'd in Canvis." In January 1772, Webster made silk cases for the sofas and twenty chairs with fabric that Cadwalader ordered from a London firm, Rushton and Beachcroft, in the summer of 1771. In the interim, Fleeson fitted the chairs with "fine Saxon blue" check cases with blue and white fringe. Although Webster's bill was somewhat vague, a February 12, 1772, entry in John Cadwalader's waste book recorded that he was paid £18.17.10 for "making Curtains in front &. back Rooms, Covers to Settee's & Covers to Chairs in front &. back Rooms." The side chair illustrated in figure 4 may have been one of those in the front room. If so, it almost certainly had a "Rich Blue Silk Damask" cover with narrow blue silk fringe.[6] The silks used for Cadwalader's furniture covers were en suite with the curtain fabrics in the front and back parlors of his house.

Easy chairs often had loose cases. The Massachusetts chair illustrated in figure 5 has its original foundation upholstery. The absence of nail holes for an outer textile proves that the chair was always fitted with a removable cover (figs. 6, 7). Such covers could be tightly fitted to follow the contours of the chair, or they could be constructed simply to drape over the frame. The Rhode Island easy chair illustrated in figure 8 probably had an informal, loosely fitted cover. Made around 1790, it has a removable slip seat (not shown) that covers a hole for a chamber pot.

Scholars traditionally have assumed that case covers were intended to protect textile upholstery, but covers were as often used to protect the wooden elements of furniture. This was especially true of gilt and inlaid surfaces that were particularly susceptible to abrasion or light. It is difficult to envision expensive pieces of furniture shrouded in case covers,

Figure 5 Easy chair, Massachusetts, 1760–1770. Mahogany with maple; linen foundation upholstery. H. 47½", W. 34", D. 26". (Chipstone Foundation, acc. 1991. 2; photo, Hans Lorenz.)

Figure 6 Detail of the upholstery evidence on the easy chair illustrated in fig. 5. (Chipstone Foundation; photo, Hans Lorenz.) The only period tack evidence on the stiles and seat rails is for the linen cover. During conservation, an eighteenth-century pin was found between the inner back and side panels. The loose cover may have been pinned temporarily in this area.

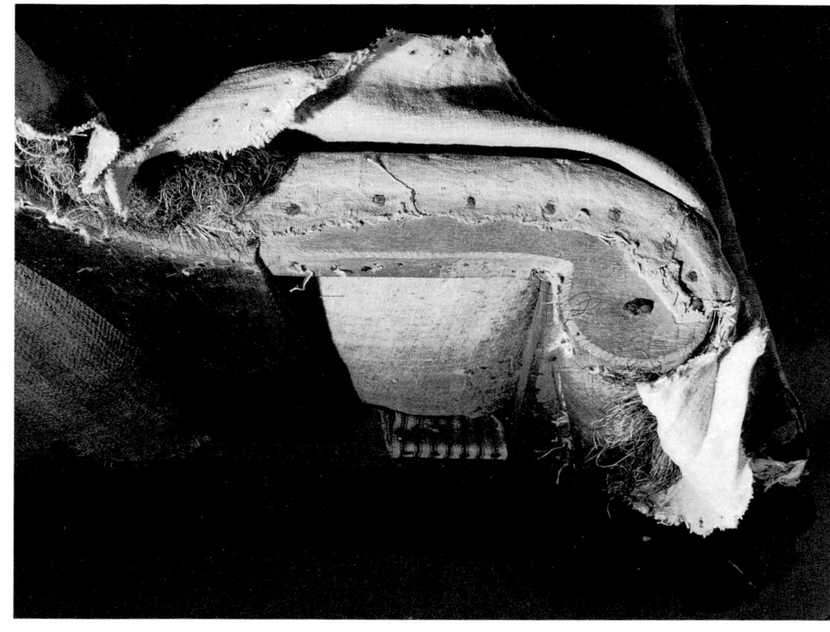

Figure 7 Detail of the arm of the easy chair illustrated in fig. 5. (Chipstone Foundation; photo, Hans Lorenz.) This view shows the original grass roll, curled horsehair stuffing, and linen cover (pulled back). The tack holes in the cover match those on the arm; there is no tack or nail evidence or stitching in the arm area that would indicate fixed upholstery.

Figure 8 Easy chair, Rhode Island, 1785–1795. Cherry with maple and white pine; linen foundation upholstery. H. 46″, W. 30″, D. 26½″. (Colonial Williamsburg Foundation, gift of Mrs. Eleanor G. Sargent, acc. 1977-215.)

Figure 9 Cover for the back of an armchair, England, 1680–1700. Embossed leather. H. 30″, W. 26″. (Colonial Williamsburg Foundation, acc. 1954-985.)

but that was exactly the situation in the seventeenth and eighteenth centuries. The elaborate set of chairs and sofas made for Sir Lawrence Dundas's London house were among Thomas Chippendale's most expensive seating furniture. The chairs cost Dundas £20 each not counting the cost of the damask and were described by Chippendale as "exceeding Richly Carv'd in the Antick manner & Gilt in oil Gold." They were double the price of the most luxurious chairs (which had serge covers) Chippendale provided for Harewood House. Because of their opulence, Dundas's chairs and sofas had two sets of cases, one of crimson check and one of leather lined with flannel. The leather cases may have resembled the embossed or "damask leather" fragment illustrated in figure 9. Undoubtedly made for the back of a large armchair, the sides of this cover were cut to fit around the arms, and the top was shaped to accommodate a carved wooden crest. Internal evidence indicates that the cover once was sewn to a back piece (now lost). The cover has a tradition of use in Ham House, although it does not fit any of the furniture now surviving there.[7]

The inventories for Ham House, dating from the last quarter of the seventeenth century, also list leather covers for billiard tables, for oval cedar tables, for five different sets of tables and stands, and for a portion of an inlaid floor. Two leather tabletop covers with a history of use at Ham House may have been among those inventoried, although, like the chair cover, they do not fit any furniture now at Ham. One is an oval of patterned leather approximately 28″ × 40″ with an overhang of about 1½″. The other cover is circular, about 27″ in diameter, and stamped with a small floral pattern typical of seventeenth-century design (fig. 10). Although no American examples of leather furniture covers are known to have survived, they occasionally were listed in seventeenth- and early-eighteenth-century inventories. An appraisal of the estate of Thomas Notley of St. Mary's County, Maryland, in April 1679 listed "3 Leather Carpetts" and a "Table with Leather Carpett." "One painted leather Coverlid for a large Table old" and "2 stampt Leather Coverlids for tables" were included in the effects of James Phillips of Baltimore County in 1724.[8]

The practice of protecting tables with leather continued well into the following century. Elaborate covers were made to protect the pair of carved and gilt console tables designed by Robert Adam and executed by France and Bradbury for Dundas in 1765. The table used in Dundas's drawing room came with "a Brown Leather Cover lin'd with flannel with a fall to hang quite to the floor welted and bound with Gilt Leather." An inventory taken three years later noted that the leather cover was still on the table in that room. The tables have pedestals carved with rams heads, husks, and swags, but this elaborate carved-and-gilded decoration was hidden by the leather that hung "quite to the floor."[9] Dundas had spent an enormous amount of money on his furnishings, and he took every precaution to protect them.

The cost of covers was minimal in comparison to the textiles and furniture they protected. The magnificent "Diana and Minerva" commode

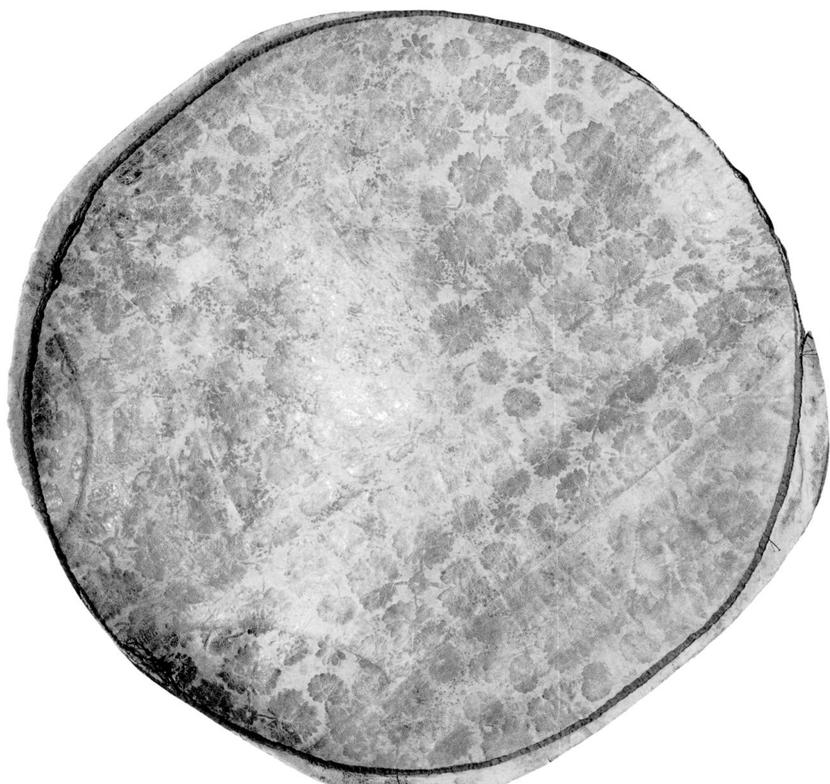

Figure 10 Cover for a table, England, 1675–1700. Embossed leather. H. 1½", D. 27". (Colonial Williamsburg Foundation, acc. 1966-415, 2.)

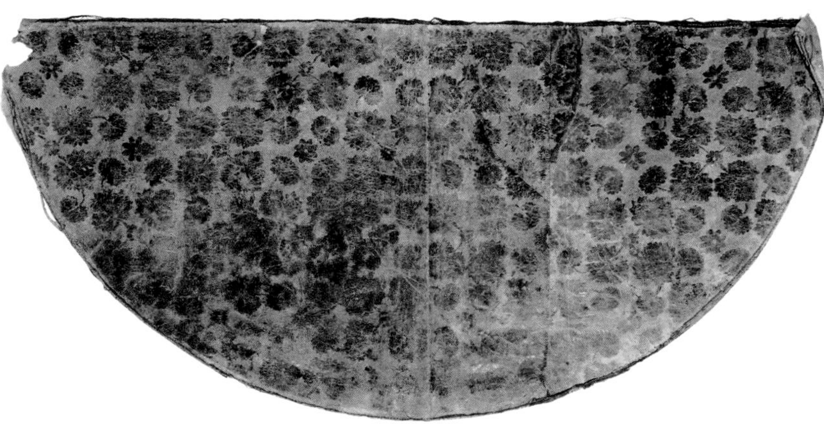

Figure 11 Commode cover, England, 1765–1775. Embossed leather. Dimensions not recorded. (Museum of Leathercraft; photo, Victoria and Albert Museum.)

that Chippendale made for Harewood House at a cost of £86.0.0 was accompanied by a damask leather cover for which he charged £1.0.0.[10] Designed to protect the elaborate marquetry top, this cover probably resembled the one illustrated in figure 11.

The practice of covering commodes and other highly finished pieces of furniture continued in the early nineteenth century. In his *Cabinet Dictionary*, Sheraton described "Covers for pier tables, made of stamped

Figure 12 Clothespress attributed to Giles Grendey, London, 1735–1745. Mahogany with oak and deal. H. 65¼″, W. 52½″, D. 27½″. (Colonial Williamsburg Foundation, acc. 1956-298.)

leather and glazed, lined with flannel to save the varnish of such table tops." He also advocated newly introduced painted canvas (similar to later oilcloth) that he deemed superior to leather.[11]

Just as covers were used to protect furniture, textiles were used to protect the items stored within the furniture. Several of Thomas Chippendale's invoices mention "bays aprons" among the materials for making clothespresses. One of the earliest surviving bills of Chippendale's firm, dated January 29, 1757, listed "A mahogany Cloaths-press wt sliding shelves £6 6—[and] Bayes tape tacks &c. £0:10:0." The clothespress for the "Little Room" or closet next to the State bedchamber at Nostell Priory was invoiced in Chippendale's bills as "A Cloaths Press very neatly Japan'd green and Gold with folding doors and drawers under, Sliding Shelves lin'd with marble paper and bays Aprons £24." An examination of the interior of this clothespress in 1981 revealed the drawers had their original marble paper and pieces of loosely woven green napped wool trapped beneath nailed-down tape at the front of each drawer—remnants of the "bays Aprons" invoiced with the press. Chippendale explained the use of baize aprons in the first edition of *The Gentleman and Cabinet-Maker's Director* (1754). For the clothespress in plate 126, he specified sliding shelves "which should be covered with green baize to cover the clothes." The soft wool covers protected the piles of clothing, preventing abrasion and snagging on the shelf above. To remove the clothing, a householder or servant drew back the covers and simply allowed them to

Figure 13 Interior of the clothespress in fig. 12 showing sliding trays with nail holes and fragments of tape trapping green baize. (Photo, Colonial Williamsburg Foundation.)

Figure 14 Detail of the green baize trapped beneath nail heads on the sliding trays of the clothespress in figs. 12, 13. (Photo, Colonial Williamsburg Foundation.)

hang down from the front of the drawer, much like an apron. A clothespress attributed to London cabinetmaker Giles Grendey also shows evidence of baize aprons; at the front edges of the sliding drawers are remnants of green napped wool trapped beneath ½″ wool twill tape, nailed down at 3½″ intervals (figs. 12–14). Baize aprons continued to be used in the nineteenth century. In *The Cabinet Dictionary*, Sheraton stated that "bays, or baize" as "used by cabinet-makers, to tack behind clothes press shelves, to throw over the clothes." In connection with a wardrobe illustrated in the third edition of his *Cabinet-Maker and Upholsterer's Drawing-Book* (1793, revised ed., 1802), he wrote: "The upper middle part contains six or seven clothes press shelves, generally made about six, or six inches and an half deep, with green baize tacked to the inside of the front to cover the clothes with."[12]

The fabric named "bays" or "baize" was made of plain weave wool, woven rather loosely, and usually napped to give it a soft, shaggy surface. Sheraton defined it as "a sort of open woolen stuff, having a long nap, sometimes frized, and sometimes not. This stuff is without wale, and is wrought in a loom with two treadles like flannel." In addition to being used for carpet and clothing covers, this soft, napped fabric was used across service doors to buffer the noise of kitchen wings from the principal rooms of large houses. Chippendale also used it to line a plate closet at Harewood House, probably to keep the silver stored inside free of scratches.[13]

Long associated with the green wool fabric used on card tables and writing surfaces, baize is a familiar word to most furniture historians. Yet the use of the name "baize" for this textile is erroneous in an eighteenth-century context. Chippendale and Sheraton consistently used the term "cloth" (usually green) for the writing surfaces of desks and for the tops of billiard tables. For example, Sheraton suggested that the fall or writing part on the gentleman's secretary illustrated in figure 15 be "lined with green cloth."[14]

Both "baize" and "cloth" were made of wool and were often dyed green, but they were very different textiles. Where baize was woven loosely and the nap generally left long, cloth was a more expensive textile that was woven closely, fulled or shrunk after weaving to give it a dense texture, with a nap shorn close after weaving, resulting in a velvety, mat surface resembling felt. Cloth often was woven in very wide widths on two-man looms, hence the term "broadcloth." After years of use, the nap of cloth often wears away, allowing the tabby weave construction to show, but when new the velvety surface of the short nap obscured the woven structure. Smooth, dense, and slightly cushioned, cloth made an excellent writing surface for quill pens. The shaggy, open surface of true eighteenth-century baize would have allowed the pen to pierce the paper. By the early nineteenth century the terminology and perhaps the character of the textiles began to change. In 1809, Philip Ludwell Grymes of Virginia had "1 Mahogany writing Table, covered with green Baize," and in 1839 William Blathwayt of Dyrham Park near Bath, England, had a "Large Mahogany Library Table with Baize Top."[15] For the eighteenth century, however, "cloth" was the material used to top writing surfaces and card tables.

Protective liners and covers clearly were both functional and decorative. The gathered fabric curtains shown on the upper doors of Sheraton's gentleman's secretary were to protect the books from dust and light (or perhaps camouflage a messy interior) and to provide a colorful, patterned

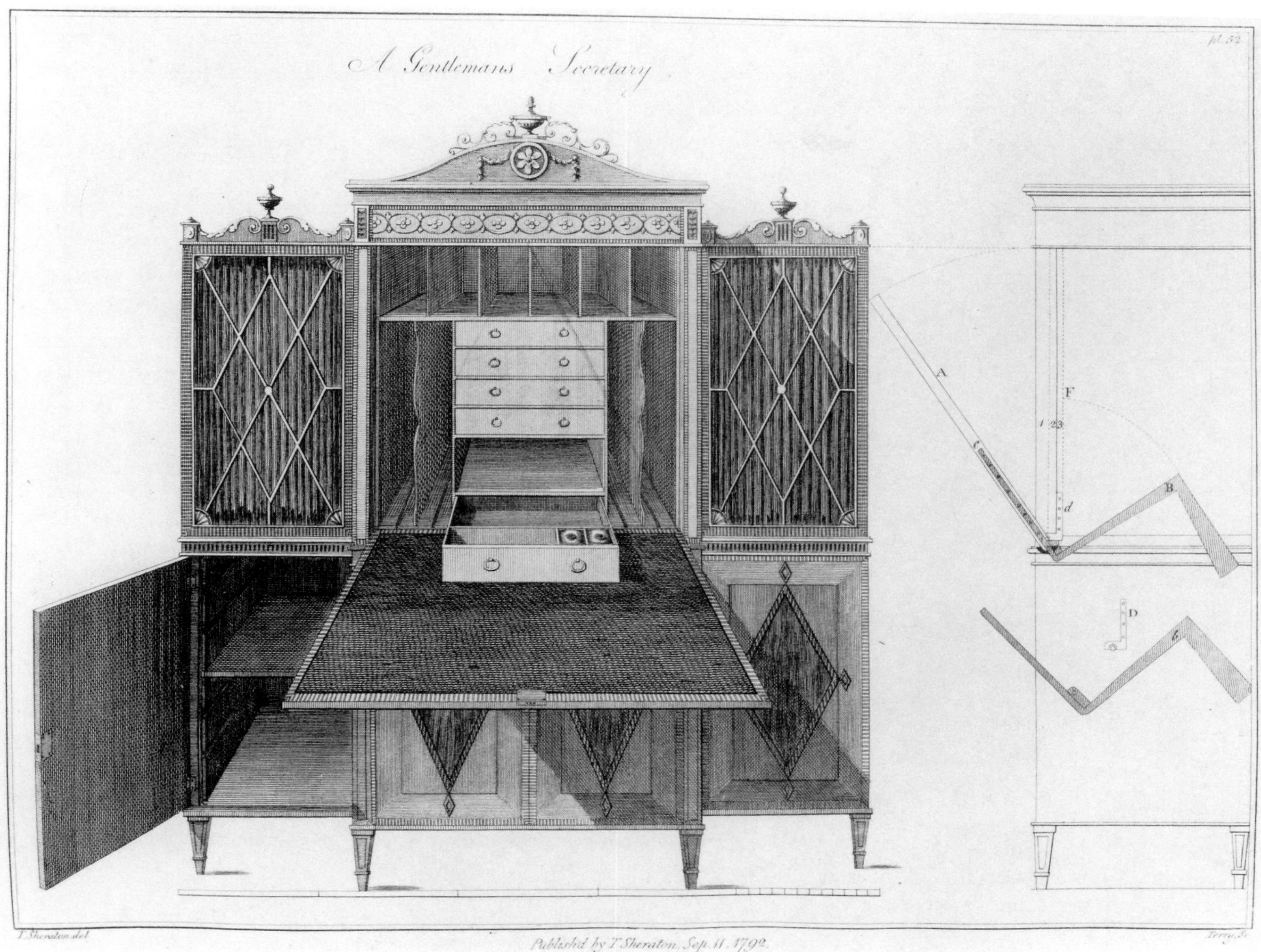

Figure 15 "A Gentleman's Secretary" from Thomas Sheraton's *The Cabinet-Maker and Upholsterer's Drawing-Book* (1802). (Courtesy, The Winterthur Library: Printed Books and Periodical Collection.)

(from the gathers) background for the muntins (fig. 15). Silk almost invariably was used for curtains, and here, too, the color green predominated. In 1760, Thomas Chippendale billed a customer for "Sewing Silk brass pins & making 4 silk curtains for your bookcase" and "7 yds Green Lutstring" for the purpose. Ince and Mayhew's 1762 book of designs illustrated a ladies' secretary described as having a "green Silk Curtain" over the open shelves. More than thirty years later Sheraton recommended the same color silk for several bookcases illustrated in his *Drawing Book*.[16]

In some instances the cabinetmaker tacked the curtains to the doors. For example, Sheraton wrote that a silk curtain with drapery ornamentation at the top was made by first assembling the silk pieces, after which "both are tacked into a rabbet together." Both plain and ornamental curtains were used in the colonies. A Williamsburg desk-and-bookcase has eighteenth-century tack holes on the stiles and upper and lower rails of each door indicating that it originally was fitted with curtains (fig. 16). Strips of wool tape, leather, or wooden nailers may have been used occasionally to hold the curtain fabric and prevent it from tearing. George Smith instructed that his bookcase doors "may be used with or without

Figure 16 Desk-and-bookcase attributed to the Anthony Hay shop, Williamsburg, 1765–1770. Walnut with yellow pine and walnut. H. 95½″, W. 39⅛″, D. 21⅜″. The silk curtains are reproductions. (Colonial Williamsburg Foundation, acc. 1978-9.)

glass in the pannels, at pleasure; the doors having curtains of silk, to slide on rods, as occasion may require." A brocaded silk curtain (later dyed green) was used in front of a built-in corner cupboard in the Jonathan Sayward House in York, Maine. The fabric was shirred on a string from a narrow casing.[17] Built-in bookcases also were fitted with curtains, as an amusing satirical print from the 1760s indicates (fig. 17).

Protective textiles originally used with furniture often have perished, whereas the more sturdy wooden elements have survived. However, the frames retain evidence of their use—telltale nail or screw holes—waiting to be "read" by those literate in the visual language of original construction methods. More importantly, the use of ephemeral but important slipcovers may have been instrumental in the very survival of the furniture itself.

1. Rodris Roth, *Floor Coverings in Eighteenth-Century America* (Washington: Smithsonian Press, 1967), p. 28. Inventory, 19 Arlington Street, London, 1768, as quoted in Anthony Coleridge, "Sir Lawrence Dundas and Chippendale," *Apollo* 86, no. 67 (September 1967): 195. Ninan Horne to Chippendale, Haig and Company, June 20, 1789, quoted in Karin M. Walton and Christopher Gilbert, "Chippendale's Upholstery Branch," *Leeds Art Calendar*, no. 74 (1974): 26. For more on carpet covers, see Christopher Gilbert, *The Life and Work of Thomas Chippendale*, 2 vols. (London: Studio Vista, 1978), 1: 209, 216–17, 219, 251, 265. Thomas Sheraton, *The Cabinet Dictionary* (London, 1803), annotated reprint, Wilford P. Cole and Charles F. Montgomery, eds. (New York: Praeger Publishers, 1970), 1: 40. Gilbert, *Chippendale*, 1: 251.

2. Daniel Marot, *Das Ornamentwerk des Daniel Marot* (ca. 1702), ed. P. Jessen (Berlin: Wasmuth, 1892). The author examined the Dyrham bed on July 21, 1981. The bed was published in John Cornforth and John Fowler, *English Decoration in the Eighteenth Century* (London: Barrie and Jenkins, 1974), pl. 10, pp. 89–90. Reproduction case curtains were installed based on the evidence on the upper frame. Peter Thornton and Maurice Tomlin, *The Furnishing and Decoration of Ham House* (London: Furniture History Society, 1980), pp. 55, 73, 102, 112, 116, 144, 156, 169.

3. For information about the use of slipcovers, see Florence Montgomery, "Room Furnishings as Seen in British Prints from the Lewis Walpole Library," *Antiques* 105, no. 3 (March 1974): 522–31; Florence Montgomery, *Printed Textiles* (New York: Viking, 1970), pp. 78–82; Florence Montgomery, *Textiles in America, 1650–1870* (New York: Norton, 1984), pp. 123–27; Linda Baumgarten, "Curtains, Covers, and Cases: Upholstery Documents at Colonial Williamsburg," and Susan B. Swan, "An Analysis of Original Slip Covers, Window, and Bed Furnishings at Winterthur Museum," both in Mark A. Williams et al., eds., *Upholstery Conservation* (East Kingston, N.H.: American Conservation Consortium, 1990), pp. 160–217.

4. Robert Beverley to Samuel Athawes, July 16, 1771, Robert Beverley Letterbook, 1761–1775, Library of Congress (microfilm M-3, Foundation Library, Colonial Williamsburg).

5. This method is useful when restoring chairs with slip seats without using nails for the outer upholstery. Care must be taken that the textile is not so thick that it strains the chair frame.

6. Chippendale, Haig and Company to Sir Edward Knatchbull, May 7, 1773, as quoted in Gilbert, *Chippendale*, 1: 226. Chinese wallpaper often was referred to as "India Paper," as it was imported by the East India Company. The bills from Fleeson, from Rushton and Beachcroft, and from Webster are reproduced in Nicholas B. Wainwright, *Colonial Grandeur in Philadelphia: The House and Furniture of General John Cadwalader* (Philadelphia: Historical Society of Pennsylvania, 1964), pp. 40–41, 51, 69. Household Furniture, February 12, 1772, p. 94, John Cadwalader waste book, Cadwalader Collection, Historical Society of Pennsylvania. This entry is important in establishing the location of Cadwalader's chairs and in revealing that they were fitted with two sets of loose covers. The formal silk covers were blue (for the chairs in the front parlor) and yellow (for those in the rear parlor) and made of the same fabric as the window curtains. The covers probably also had narrow fringe

Figure 17 A Pleasing Method of Rouzing the Doctor, printed for Bowles and Carver, London, 1765–1775. Mezzotint. 10½″ × 8½″. (Colonial Williamsburg Foundation, acc. 1941-230.)

to match the larger fringe on the curtains. The materials are listed in the Rushton and Beachcroft bill. The "Inventory of Contents Remaining in Cadwalader['s] House," taken on April 1, 1786, listed "1 blue damask settee cover," "10 chair do do," and ten yellow damask chair "bottoms" (transcribed in Wainwright, *Colonial Grandeur*, pp. 72–73). The author thanks Luke Beckerdite for the Cadwalader references.

7. Gilbert, *Chippendale*, 1: 157, 160 and 2: figs. 176, 357; check cases for a set of fourteen mahogany elbow chairs "Cover'd & brass nailed the Elbows and fronts of the seats richly carv'd & scrold feet 7 castors" made for the Earl of Dumfries in 1759 are cited in 1: 137. The leather case fragment was purchased in 1954 from S. W. Wolsey who reported that it came from Ham House. Maurice Tomlin determined that the case does not fit any of the surviving furniture from Ham House (Maurice Tomlin, Department of Furniture and Woodwork, Victoria and Albert Museum to Mildred Lanier, March 26, 1970, Colonial Williamsburg, acc. 1966-415, 2).

8. Thornton and Tomlin, *Ham House*, pp. 39, 45, 50, 88, 107, 114, 147. Inventories and Accounts, 1679, 6: 576–96 and Inventories, 1724, 10: 177, Maryland Perogative Court (transcripts from microfilm, Museum of Early Southern Decorative Arts). The author thanks Frank Horton for these references.

9. Anthony Coleridge, "Some Rococo Cabinet-Makers and Sir Lawrence Dundas," *Apollo* 86, no. 67 (September 1967): 214–15. The tables were sold at Christie's in 1934; their locations were unknown to Coleridge when he wrote the article.

10. Gilbert, *Chippendale*, 1: 197, 207 and 2: figs. 232–34. For more on leather covers furnished by Chippendale, see 1: 184, 188, 192, 206, 209, 214.

11. Sheraton, *Dictionary*, 2: 336.

12. Gilbert, *Chippendale*, 1: 128, 191 and 2: figs. 239–40; for more on baize aprons furnished by Chippendale, see 1: 138–39, 145, 159, 184–86, 191, 228, 231, 255, 274, 279. Thomas Chippendale, *The Gentleman and Cabinet-Maker's Director*, 1st ed. (London, 1754). Sheraton, *Dictionary*, 1: 40. Thomas Sheraton, *The Cabinet-Maker and Upholsterer's Drawing-Book*, Wilford P. Cole and Charles F. Montgomery, eds. (London, 1793, 3d. revised ed. 1802; reprint, New York: Praeger, 1970), app., p. 13, pl. 8.

13. Sheraton, *Dictionary*, 1: 40. Sheraton evidently copied the definition of baize in Samuel Johnson's *Dictionary of the English Language* (London, 1755; reprint, New York: Arno Press, 1979): "BAYZE—See Baize. BAIZE. n.f. A kind of coarse open cloth stuff, having a long nap; sometimes frized on one side, and sometimes not frized, according to the use it is intended for. This stuff is without wale, being wrought on a loom with two treddles, like flannel." Gilbert, *Chippendale*, 1: 215–16, 247–48, 212.

14. For more on cloth writing surfaces, see Gilbert, *Chippendale*, 1: 138, 142, 146, 160, 180, 183, 185, 189, 231, 245, 247, and 273–75; and Sheraton, *Drawing-Book*, pp. 356, 373, 378, 392, 395, 396, 409, 437, and appendix 21. For more on the secretary, see Sheraton, *Drawing-Book*, p. 409 and pl. 52.

15. Ephriam Chambers, *Cyclopaedia* (London: printed for D. Midwinter, A. Bettesworth, &. C. Hitch, 1738) and *Encyclopedia Britannica* (Edinburgh: printed for A. Bell &. C. MacFarquhar, 1771) gave lengthy descriptions for making cloth. They outlined the steps in weaving, fulling, napping, and shearing. Philip Ludwell Grymes Inventory, Middlesex County, Va., 1809, Middlesex County Courthouse; William Blathwayt, Esq. Inventory, Dyrham Park, Gloucester, England, March, 1839 (photocopy, Research File, Department of Collections, Colonial Williamsburg Foundation).

16. Invoice, Thomas Chippendale to Sir William Robinson, July 7, 1760, as quoted in Gilbert, *Chippendale*, 1: 143. "Lutstring" or lustring was a crisp, thin silk (Montgomery, *Textiles in America*, p. 283). William Ince and John Mayhew, *The Universal System of Household Furniture*, Ralph Edwards, ed. (London, 1762; reprint, London: Alec Tiranti, 1960), pl. 18. Sheraton, *Drawing-Book*, pp. 399, 404; supp. pp. 7, 56, 60. Other colors may have been added to the palette early in the nineteenth century. Sheraton recommended green, white, or pink silk, fluted behind the wire doors of commodes (Sheraton, *Dictionary*, 1: 172, and 2: 332–33).

17. Sheraton, *Drawing-Book*, p. 404, pl. 48. George Smith, *A Collection of Designs for Household Furniture and Interior Decoration*, annotated reprint, Constance V. Hershey, Charles F. Montgomery, and Benno M. Forman, eds. (London, 1808; New York: Praeger Publishers, 1970), p. 19, pls. 106–7 The curtain was made from a woman's dress, later cut up and dyed green. It was in the cupboard and described as a "long damask curtain" in 1869 (Richard Nylander, "The Johnathan Sayward House, York, Maine," *Antiques* 116, no. 3 [September 1979]: 571–77).

Luke Beckerdite

Origins of the Rococo Style in New York Furniture and Interior Architecture

▼ DURING the third quarter of the eighteenth century the rococo style emerged in New York furniture and architectural carving. Like many British designers of the mid-1740s, New York cabinetmakers, carvers, and master builders were slow to accept the rococo style. Although rococo details are discernible in New York carving from the early 1750s, they typically are restrained and confined within a classical framework. This modified style was particularly well-suited to New York's Anglo-European aristocracy who were accustomed to the strong architectural overtones of baroque classicism.[1] The rococo style matured during the mid-1750s, coincident with the publication of British design books such as Thomas Chippendale's *The Gentleman and Cabinet-Maker's Director* (1754). Several examples of New York furniture and architectural carving were based on published designs and some appear to have been executed almost immediately after the corresponding patterns were issued. The finest work reflects an awareness of London fashions and a level of technical competence that was rarely equaled in colonial America.

As in every colonial city, artisans in New York were dependent on a wealthy style-conscious patronage. The origins of this aristocratic society can be traced to the Dutch West India Company's establishment in 1629 of large land grants called patroonships. The patroons, or owners, were given land on the condition that they settle at least fifty persons at their own expense. Although only one patroonship survived the period of Dutch rule (1609–1664), the British, following their conquest of New Netherland, introduced a manorial system based on large land holdings. Like the earlier patroonships, the manorial system created a pronounced social hierarchy that gave the landlords wealth, prestige, and a considerable measure of political power.[2]

European-born colonists like the Philipses were among the most successful and influential land owners under the British system. In return for political allegiance, Frederick Philipse received a patent granting manorial status to his estate in 1693. Through land speculation, slave trading, and two financially advantageous marriages, he amassed a fortune that enabled him to maintain residences at Philipseburg Manor and in Manhattan. In 1716, Frederick Philipse II became the second lord of Philipseburg Manor. Educated in England, he pursued a legal career culminating in his appointment to the New York Supreme Court in 1755. His principal residence was a grand country house built (or enlarged from an earlier structure) on his estate during the second quarter of the

Figure 1 First-floor southeast parlor, Philipse Manor, Yonkers, New York, 1745–1755. (New York State Office of Parks, Recreation, and Historic Preservation; photo, Gavin Ashworth.)

eighteenth century. With its hipped roof and five-bay brick facade, Philipse Manor is one of the most important New York houses of the colonial period. It reflects a series of ambitious building campaigns culminating in the installation of a luxurious interior about 1750.[3]

The southeast parlor on the first floor has a stucco and papier-mâché ceiling and a monumental chimneypiece flanked by engaged stop-fluted ionic columns and doors with classical entablatures (fig. 1). Recalling the style of Palladian architects, such as William Kent, the chimneypiece has a compressed broken-scroll pediment with bold floral rosettes, carved moldings and frets, and a swelled oak-leaf frieze with a central tablet depicting Diana (figs. 2–5). The side brackets are incorrect, late nineteenth-century replacements based on those in the southeast parlor on the second floor. The original brackets had additional acanthus inside the S scrolls and heavy husk (bellflower) drops rather than garlands (fig. 3).[4]

The corresponding parlor on the second floor is even more detailed. Although the architectural arrangement of the two parlors is basically the same, the chimneypiece on the second floor is flanked by fluted pilasters and doors with pitched pediments, carved frieze appliqués, and central ornaments (figs. 6–12). As fig. 7 shows, the ornaments of the door pediments have been missing since the late nineteenth century; however, surviving fragments of the carving indicate that they were large birds perched on the crest of a rococo plinth (fig. 10). They may well have been more sculptural renditions of the small bird in the frieze appliqué of the chimneypiece (fig. 11) or prospect door of the desk-and-bookcase illus-

Figure 2 Detail of the chimneypiece illustrated in fig. 1. (Photo, Gavin Ashworth.)

Figure 3 Engraving of the first-floor southeast parlor, Philipse Manor, from *Frank Leslie's Illustrated Newspaper* (1882). (Collection of the Hudson River Museum of Westchester, Yonkers, New York; photo, John Kennedy.)

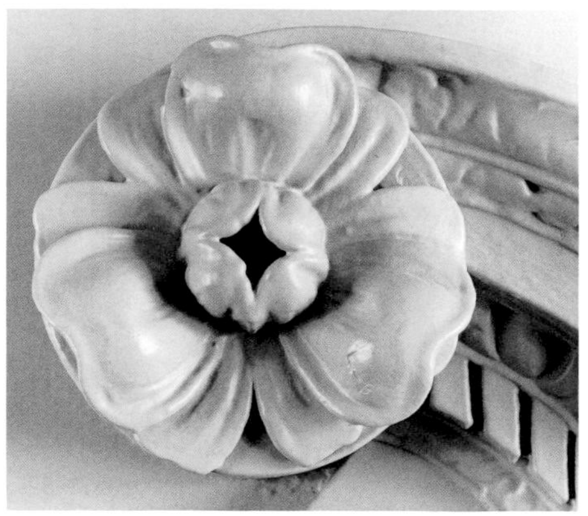

Figure 4 Detail of the rosette of the chimneypiece illustrated in fig. 1. (Photo, Gavin Ashworth.)

Figure 5 Detail of the tablet of Diana on the chimneypiece illustrated in fig. 1. (Photo, Gavin Ashworth.)

Figure 6 Second-floor southeast parlor, Philipse Manor. (Photo, Gavin Ashworth.)

Figure 7 Engraving of the second-floor southeast parlor, Philipse Manor, from *Frank Leslie's Illustrated Newspaper* (1882). (Collection of the Hudson River Museum of Westchester, Yonkers, New York; photo, John Kennedy.)

trated in figure 19 later in this article. Together with the abstract shells of the door friezes and playful asymmetrical scrollwork framing the small bird on the overmantle frieze, these ornaments are among the earliest manifestations of the rococo style in America (figs. 10, 11).[5]

Although tremendously important as documents of an emerging style, these ornaments appear almost as intrusions in the classical fabric of Philipse Manor. Colonial conservatism was not entirely the reason for Philipse's tenuous embrace of the rococo style. As late as 1759, architects in England also were looking back to the designs of first generation Palladians. In his *Treatise on Civil Architecture*, Sir William Chambers wrote: "I believe we may justly consider Inigo Jones as the first who arrived at any great degree of perfection [in the design of chimneypieces]. . . . Others of our Architects, since his time, have wrought upon his ideas; and some of them, particularly the late Mr. Kent, have furnished good inventions of their own."[6]

The artisan who executed the carving in Philipse Manor probably trained in London (or another large urban center in England) during the 1730s or early 1740s when architects, such as James Gibbs, Batty Langley, and William Kent, published their designs and executed important commissions. A marble chimneypiece designed by Kent for the dining room in Houghton Hall, Norfolk, has a central tablet with a bust and garlands with large clusters of grapes and grape leaves that closely resemble those on the chimneypieces in Philipse Manor. The scale and the sculptural quality of the carving in Philipse Manor suggests that the artisan intended his work to resemble stone.[7]

During the Palladian era (1715–1745), architects and cabinetmakers often

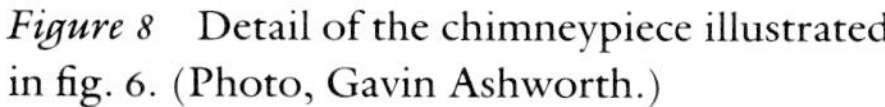

Figure 8 Detail of the chimneypiece illustrated in fig. 6. (Photo, Gavin Ashworth.)

designed furniture to complement interior architecture. A New York desk-and-bookcase made about 1750 has carved details that are virtually en suite with those in Philipse Manor (fig. 13). The bookcase has a low, broken-scroll pediment with bold floral rosettes and intricate moldings like the overmantle in the first-floor parlor (figs. 2, 4, 14). Similarities in the design and execution of the major carved elements indicate that they are by the same hand. Except for differences in size, the rosettes are practically interchangeable. Each has four small petals closed in the center,

Figure 9 Detail of the left side bracket of the chimneypiece illustrated in fig. 6. (Photo, Gavin Ashworth.)

three large convex petals with deeply fluted and veined depressions, and flat half-petals in the background (figs. 4, 14).

Although much of the detail in the architectural carving is obscured by layers of paint, the carver clearly used similar techniques to outline and model the scrolling leaves on the cove molding of the bookcase and the acanthus on the overmantle fret and stair brackets (figs. 2, 12, 15). Deep vertical cuts made with large flat gouges created strong shadow lines and (with minimal modeling) multiple levels that simplified the shading process. Nearly all the leaves and flowers of the scrollboard appliqué were duplicated in the bracket garlands in the second-floor parlor (figs. 9, 15, 16). The roses have laminated centers and flat, overlapping petals that the carver shaded with short gouge cuts made within larger flutes. Similar shading cuts are on the tattered shells in the door friezes (fig. 10) and the body of the bird illustrated in figures 11 and 19. Many aspects of this carver's style are individualistic, but none are more distinctive than his veining and shading. He used a very small gouge or veiner (U-shaped

Figure 10 Detail of the frieze appliqué and ornament of the right door in fig. 6. (Photo, Gavin Ashworth.)

Figure 11 Detail of the frieze appliqué of the chimneypiece illustrated in fig. 6. (Photo, Gavin Ashworth.)

Figure 12 Detail of a carved stair bracket, Philipse Manor. (Photo, Luke Beckerdite.)

Figure 13 Desk-and-bookcase with carving attributed to Henry Hardcastle, New York, 1745–1755. Mahogany with tulip poplar and gum. H. 99½″, W. 45½″, D. 25″. (Chipstone Foundation, acc. 1991.5; photo, Gavin Ashworth.)

Figure 14 Detail of the pediment of the desk-and-bookcase illustrated in fig. 13. (Photo, Gavin Ashworth.) The heron, plinth, and applied carving flanking the outermost roses (approx. 6″) were restored based on the carving in Philipse Manor.

Figure 15 Detail of the appliqué on the pediment of the desk-and-bookcase illustrated in fig. 13. (Photo, Gavin Ashworth.)

gouge) to cut shallow diverging flutes on the serrated leaves in the bookcase appliqué and on the small flat leaves and grape leaves in the frieze appliqués and bracket garlands in Philipse Manor (figs. 9–11, 15, 16). Most eighteenth-century carving is representational rather than sculptural, but the grape leaves, fruit, and large blooms carved by this artisan are naturalistic and botanically accurate. He used diverging and converging flutes to shade the large acanthus leaves on the feet and scrollboard of the desk-and-bookcase and the side brackets in the second-floor parlor (figs. 9, 16, 17). He also occasionally used perpendicular fluting, or cross-cutting (cuts made perpendicular to the overall flow of the design), on curled leaf ends and on broad convex surfaces.[8]

Another desk-and-bookcase, this one with a history of ownership by

Figure 16 Detail of the appliqué on the pediment of the desk-and-bookcase illustrated in fig. 13. (Photo, Gavin Ashworth.)

Figure 17 Detail of left front foot and base molding of the desk-and-bookcase illustrated in fig. 13. (Photo, Gavin Ashworth.)

Peter and Margaret (Livingston) Stuyvesant, appears to be by the same cabinetmaker and carver (fig. 18).[9] It has mirrored doors with double ogee-shaped rails, a writing compartment with a central prospect door flanked by tiers of serpentine blocked drawers and pigeonholes with shaped brackets, and a cyma reversa base molding. The relief-carved bird on the prospect door of the Stuyvesant desk-and-bookcase compares closely to the bird in the overmantle appliqué in Philipse Manor (figs. 11, 19). Both have prominent crests, slightly curled beaks, and protruding eyes. To carve the body feathers, the carver used a small gouge to cut short paired flutes within a larger shallow flute. The long tail feathers were simply rough modeled with gouges and chisels.

The construction of the two desks-and-bookcases is consistent with New York work of the mid-eighteenth century. Both pieces have large drawers with fully paneled bottoms and interior drawers with rabbeted bottoms and serpentine fronts that are splayed on the top and side edges. Paneled-drawer construction occurs frequently on New York furniture made between 1700 and 1770. The desk illustrated in figure 13 has thin dustboards with broad beveled edges (front and sides) that are set into grooves ploughed in the drawer blades and drawer runners. In typical early New York fashion, the runners are notched and nailed to the sides. Because nailed runners restrict the movement of case sides, causing the wood to split, London cabinetmakers began using full-bottom dustboards (dustboards that are the full thickness of the drawer blades and that are dadoed to the case sides) during the early 1720s. By the late 1730s, progressive cabinetmakers like Giles Grendey used thin dustboards that they wedged into the dadoes with strips of wood whose grain ran in the same direction as the dustboards. This produced a strong, dust-proof case that could respond to changes in humidity. In contrast, although the dustboards of figure 13 are thin and able to expand and contract, the case sides are rigidly bound by the nailed runners. Slightly later in the century, New York cabinetmakers improved this system significantly by making the runners out of oak and by dadoing them to the case sides.

The technological advances in case construction made by New York cabinetmakers during the early 1750s coincided with a shift to a more mature rococo style. A bedstead with hairy-paw feet, knees ornamented with ruffled C scrolls and vines, balusters with finely detailed acanthus, and basket-capitals with fruit and flowers attests to New York artisans' and patrons' style consciousness (fig. 20). The original owner is not known; however, the bedstead has a nineteenth-century Massachusetts history in the Cambridge-based family of Ersastus Forbes Brigham (b. 1807) and his wife Sophia De Wolf Homer Brigham (d. 1881), who married in Troy, New York, in 1832.[10]

Although certain elements of the carving are rooted in baroque design, the abstract panels and whimsical vines on the side rails and tattered foliage on the knees are clearly rococo (figs. 21, 22). The small carved bells capping the diapered reserves above the knees appear to be a concession to Chinese fancy. It would be difficult to find a closer parallel between

Figure 18 Desk-and-bookcase with carving attributed to Henry Hardcastle, New York, 1745–1755. Mahogany with tulip poplar, gum, oak, and mahogany. Dimensions not recorded. (Private collection; courtesy, Walton Antiques.)

Figure 19 Detail of the prospect door of the desk-and-bookcase illustrated in fig. 18. (Private collection; courtesy, Walton Antiques.)

Figure 20 Bedstead with carving attributed to Henry Hardcastle, New York, 1750–1755. Mahogany with red oak and white pine (nineteenth-century lath frame and headboard). H. 89⅛", W. 54⅛", D. 78". (Courtesy, The Society for the Preservation of New England Antiquities, bequest of Janet M. Agnew, acc. 1975.152; photo, Richard Cheek.) During the late nineteenth or early twentieth century, the bedstead was reduced in width by 4–6 inches.

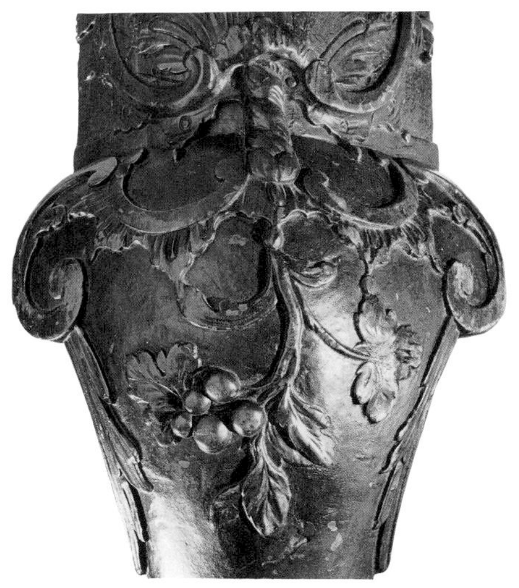

Figure 21 Detail of the knee carving on the bedstead illustrated in fig. 20. (Courtesy, Museum of Early Southern Decorative Arts.)

Figure 22 Detail of the carving on a side rail of the bedstead illustrated in fig. 20. (Courtesy, Museum of Early Southern Decorative Arts.)

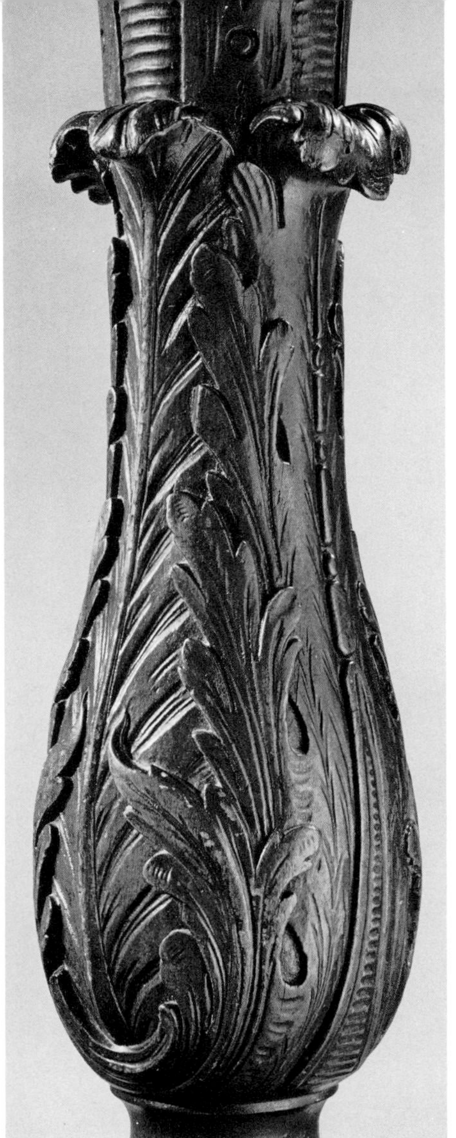

furniture and architectural carving than the acanthus on the balusters of the bedstead, on the feet and scrollboard of the desk-and-bookcase, and on the side brackets and frieze appliqués in the second-floor parlor of Philipse Manor (figs. 9–11, 15–17, 23). All of these leaves have similar profiles, converging and diverging veining flutes, and perpendicular crosscuts in the same contexts. In virtually every instance, the carver used a very small gouge (approximately equivalent to a modern 2-mm #8 or #9) to execute the veining. On the grape leaves in the bracket garlands and on the capitals and knees of the bedstead, the flutes are so delicate that they are barely discernible (figs. 9, 24). The carver used large "quarter-round" gouges to rough out the toes and pad segments of the feet (figs. 25–27). To carve the fetlocks, he used relatively small gouges to make angled converging cuts that removed crescent-shaped sections of wood

Figure 23 Detail of the urn acanthus on a footpost of the bedstead illustrated in fig. 20. (Courtesy, Museum of Early Southern Decorative Arts.)

Figure 24 Detail of a basket capital on the bedstead illustrated in fig. 20. (Courtesy, Museum of Early Southern Decorative Arts.)

and delineated the individual tufts. After contouring the surfaces with inverted or backbent gouges, he fluted the tufts to accentuate the downward spiral and make the hair appear to roll over against the leg. These techniques are essentially the same as those used to carve the hair of Diana in Philipse Manor (fig. 5).

The footposts of the bedstead are made in two sections and joined with a round mortise and tenon between the stop-fluted and spiral elements. Each post has two cloak pin holes indicating that the bedstead had festooned curtains and a tester frame with pulleys similar to those on a bedstead illustrated in the first edition of the *Director* (fig. 28). The original curtains probably were nailed to the tester frame and raised with a cord that passed through the pulleys and tied off on the cloak pins. The present headboard and tester frame are nineteenth-century replacements. The original headboard may have been intricately carved or rough modeled and covered with fabric.

Evidence for the form and attachment of the base valences is sketchy; however, they possibly hung beneath the rails so the carving could remain visible. Unlike many bedsteads that have bed bolts to tighten the mortise-and-tenon joints, the Brigham family bedstead has a key-and-eye system. The tenons were locked into the mortises by a large two-pronged key (now missing) that fit into the eyes of wrought iron staples on the rails. Although the rails are altered (shortened at the ends), remnants of wooden pins in the rabbeted edges indicate that the bedstead had a canvas or "sacking" bottom.

The foot rail and lower sections of the footposts are all that survives of the bedstead illustrated in figure 29; however, the two-part post construction, knee carving, and bold hairy-paw feet associate it with the Brigham example. On both objects, the feet have toes with three distinct joints, spiraling fetlocks, and hair that is carved in essentially the same fashion (figs. 25–27, 30–32). In relying on sculptural form rather than

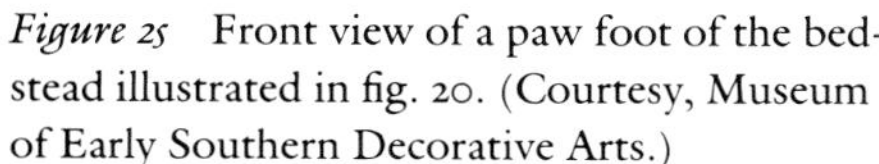

Figure 25 Front view of a paw foot of the bedstead illustrated in fig. 20. (Courtesy, Museum of Early Southern Decorative Arts.)

Figure 26 Side view of a paw foot of the bedstead illustrated in fig. 20. (Courtesy, Museum of Early Southern Decorative Arts.)

Figure 27 Back view of a paw foot of the bedstead illustrated in fig. 20. (Courtesy, Museum of Early Southern Decorative Arts.)

Figure 28 Plate 27 from Thomas Chippendale's *The Gentleman and Cabinet-Maker's Director* (1754, 1755). (Courtesy, Museum of Early Southern Decorative Arts.)

surface detail, these resemble smooth-paw feet more than conventional hairy-paw feet. It is difficult to determine whether the feet of these bedsteads are by the same hand or simply products of the same shop (or school). Those of figure 29 are laminated rather than cut from the solid and are less competently carved than the Brigham examples; however, this discrepancy may have been the result of time constraints or cost.[11]

An early serpentine card table with an oral tradition of descent in the Vreeland and Gautier families of New Jersey and New York has carving from the same shop as the preceding pieces (fig. 33). Although it predates the vast majority of New York serpentine card tables by nearly a decade, its construction and carved details are remarkably sophisticated. The rails are dovetailed together and slip-tenoned to the legs at the front corners. The fluted and gadrooned molding glued beneath the rails and rabbeted onto the knees is virtually identical to that on the first desk-and-bookcase (figs. 17, 34). On both, the gadrooning is broad and flat, and the flutes have precisely cut fillets terminated with a gouge cut just short of the molding edge. Several of the elements of the knee carving on the card

Figure 29 Fragment of a footpost with carving attributed to the shop of Henry Hardcastle, New York, 1745–1755. Mahogany. H. 44¼″. (Private collection; photo, Luke Beckerdite.)

table are also on the cove molding of the desk-and-bookcase, on the overmantle fret and stair brackets in Philipse Manor, and on the feet of a commode chest of drawers that descended in the Van Rensselaer family of New York (figs. 2, 12, 15, 34–36).[12]

Many sophisticated examples of rococo furniture survive with histories of ownership in the Beekman, Van Cortlandt, and Van Rensselaer families, but none reflects modish London style more clearly than the chest of drawers illustrated in figure 34. Commode (serpentine or "swelled") forms became popular in England during the late 1740s and remained so throughout the eighteenth century. Chippendale, for example, illustrated a variety of commode chests, dressing tables, and clothespresses in rococo and neoclassical styles in all three editions of the *Director* (1754, 1755, 1762). The Van Rensselaer chest appears to have been made about 1755, one of the earliest completely rococo American case pieces. The sole concession to New York style is fluted and gadrooned molding between the front feet. While the molding is virtually identical to that of the desk-and-bookcase and card table, it is unusual in being nailed directly under the case rather than to a base molding. The case and foot construction also match that of the desk-and-bookcase. On both examples the feet are supported by large vertical blocks that were shaped with gouges and nailed to the bottom of the case.

A pair of footposts by the same carver as the preceding pieces are the most sophisticated American examples in the rococo style (fig. 37). The posts have cascading vines with leaves, fruit, and a variety of naturalistic blooms that literally quote elements on the side brackets in Philipse Manor, knees and "basket capitals" of the Brigham bedstead, and appli-

Figures 30 to 32 Side, front, and back views of the paw foot of the footpost illustrated in fig. 29. (Private collection; photo, Luke Beckerdite.)

Figure 33 Card table with carving attributed to the shop of Henry Hardcastle, New York, 1750–1755. Mahogany with yellow pine. H. 28″, W. 30″, D. 15″ (closed). (Chipstone Foundation, acc. 1965.5; photo, Gavin Ashworth.)

Figure 34 Detail of the knee carving and fluted and gadrooned molding of the card table illustrated in fig. 33. (Photo, Gavin Ashworth.)

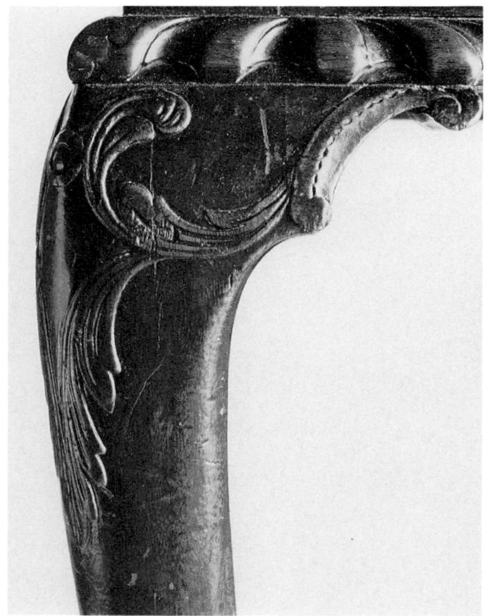

Figure 35 Chest of drawers with carving attributed to the shop of Henry Hardcastle, New York, 1750–1755. Mahogany with tulip poplar. H. 33", W. 35½", D. 20¾". (Courtesy, Winterthur Museum, acc. G54.86.)

Figure 36 Detail of the left foot carving and fluted and gadrooned molding on the chest of drawers illustrated in fig. 35. (Courtesy, Winterthur Museum.)

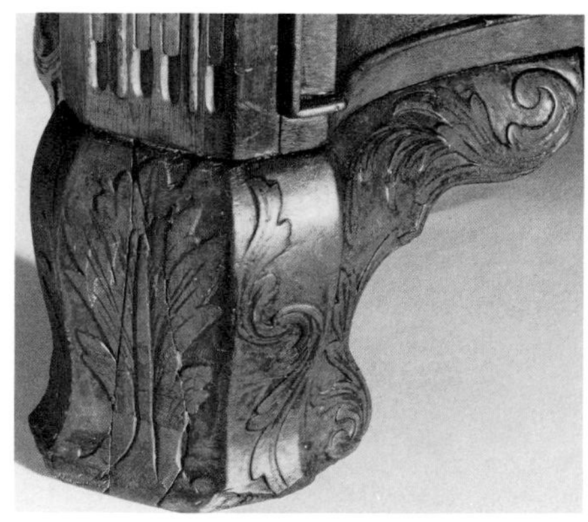

qué of the first desk-and-bookcase (figs. 9, 14–16, 21, 24, 38, 39). In all, relatively simple ornaments like flat chip-carved flowers and leaves are juxtaposed with fully rendered blooms and foliage. Several of the more detailed leaves have diverging veining and deep offsets to create a strong shadow line and divide the surface into two planes for easy fluting. Although many artisans used gigs for fluting and reeding, this carver cut the reeding entirely by hand, a laborious process, particularly in the areas around the leaves and flowers.

The design of the posts appears to derive from a bedstead illustrated in the first edition of the *Director* or a style that was current at that time (fig. 40). The bedstead probably had an ornate carved cornice, perhaps

Figure 37 Footposts of a bedstead with carving attributed to Henry Hardcastle, New York, 1750–1755. Mahogany. H. 94". (Chipstone Foundation, acc. 1991.4; photo, Gavin Ashworth.)

Figures 38 and 39 Details of the carving on the footposts illustrated in fig. 37. (Photo, Gavin Ashworth.)

Figure 40 Plate 31 from Thomas Chippendale's *The Gentleman and Cabinet-Maker's Director* (1754, 1755). (Courtesy, Museum of Early Southern Decorative Arts.)

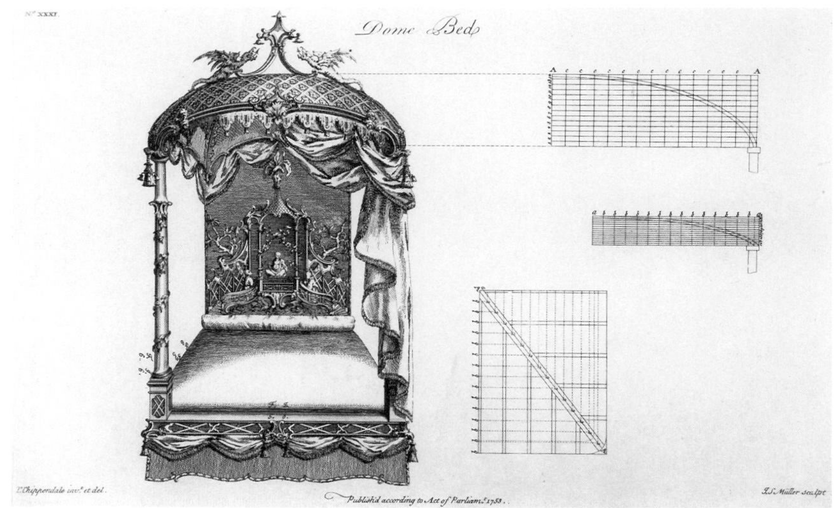

Figure 41 Detail of the mortises for a rail and spring rod on the footposts illustrated in fig. 37. (Photo, Gavin Ashworth.)

even a domed example similar to the *Director* engraving. Unfortunately, the posts retain only partial evidence of how the bedstead was hung. Although the absence of cloak pin holes on the footposts suggests that the curtains were straight-hung from a "compass rod" or from the cornice, the evidence is not conclusive. In the eighteenth century there were intricate pulley systems for drapery curtains that were tied off at the headposts, thus eliminating the need for cloak pins at the foot. Such a system would allow the curtains on a bedstead like this to be "tied up in drapery," as Chippendale described them.[13] Unlike the Brigham bedstead, on which the carved rails were apparently left exposed, the rails of this example were completely covered by the base valences. The bases were suspended from a flexible spring rod that mortised into the legs just above the rails (fig. 41).

An imposing ceremonial armchair made for the State House in Charleston, South Carolina (built 1752–1756), provides strong circumstantial evidence for attributing all of the above-mentioned carving to the shop of Henry Hardcastle, the only New York carver known to have moved to Charleston before the Revolution (fig. 42). As mentioned in reference to the carving in Philipse Manor, Hardcastle probably trained in London. Although there is no documentation for his arrival in New York, he was listed as a freeman there in 1751. On June 30, 1755, the *New York Mercury* printed a notice by Hardcastle for a runaway apprentice named Stephen Dwight. That Dwight established his own business the following month suggests that the term of Dwight's indenture had nearly expired or that Hardcastle was no longer in the city and able to contest his apprentice's actions. Hardcastle apparently moved to Charleston sometime between July 1755 and his death in October 1756.[14]

Hardcastle's move coincided with the completion and furnishing of Charleston's first State House. Shortly before moving into the new State House, the Commons House of Assembly appointed a committee to "provide such furniture as will be necessary for the service of [the] House."

Figure 42 Armchair with carving attributed to the shop of Henry Hardcastle, Charleston, South Carolina, 1755–1756. Mahogany with sweet gum. H. 53⅜″, W. 37⅝″ (at arms). (Collection of the McKissick Museum University of South Carolina; photo courtesy, Museum of Early Southern Decorative Arts.)

On March 13, 1756, the House resolved to appropriate funds for "such furniture as his Exty. the Governor &. His Majty's Council shall think fit to order for . . . the New Council Chamber." The committee apparently wasted little time in placing orders. On July 6, 1756, the Commons House directed the public treasurer to advance "as much money as will be sufficient to pay the Tradesmen's Bills for . . . Furniture." Although the journals of the upper and lower houses fail to identify these artisans or describe their work, the armchair, which most likely served as the royal governor's chair during sessions of the Commons House of Assembly, may have been one of the first items commissioned for use in the State House.[15]

To create a sense of majesty and formality, the governor's chair probably was placed on a plinth and draped with a canopy similar to the throne of George II in B. Coles's engraving, *A View of the House of Peers*. Like the king's throne, the stance and seat height mandated the use of a footstool. Although the stool for the royal governor's chair does not survive,

Figure 43 Detail of the knee carving on the armchair illustrated in fig. 42. (Courtesy, Museum of Early Southern Decorative Arts.)

Figure 44 Front view of a paw foot of the armchair illustrated in fig. 42. (Courtesy, Museum of Early Southern Decorative Arts.)

Figure 45 Side view of a paw foot of the armchair illustrated in fig. 42 (Courtesy, Museum of Early Southern Decorative Arts.)

it undoubtedly was made en suite with the chair. A royal coat of arms may have been mounted on the crest rail of the governor's chair. Mortises and screw holes there indicate that it was secured with three wooden or wrought iron braces.[16]

The carving on the chair is closely related to that of the bedsteads and probably represents the work of a journeyman associated with Hardcastle in Charleston. Like the Brigham bedstead, the chair has C scrolls with tattered leaves and trailing vines of fruit and flowers on the knees. Both designs feature overlapping flowers, grape leaves with diverging veining, and curled leaves with short, perpendicular shading cuts (figs. 21, 43). The feet of the chair are less competently carved than those of the bedsteads. However, they clearly emerge from the same shop tradition: they have fetlocks with thick, spiraling tufts of hair, toes with three distinct knuckles, and outward-flaring pad segments (figs. 25–27, 30–32, 44–46). The patterns of gouge and chisel cuts used to outline and rough-model the pad segments on the feet of the chair and bedstead are also remarkably similar. So is the basic approach to fluting the hair and carving the retracted claws.

Although the royal governor's chair is a keystone for understanding the development of the rococo style in New York, it has almost no relation to extant Charleston work. Hardcastle's career in Charleston lasted scarcely a year; thus it is doubtful that he significantly influenced local styles. When he died he left a meager estate valued at £84.10.0, including two silver watches, a pair of silver buckles, a gold ring, a crosscut saw, a musket, clothing, a lot of books and "1 Gross & half of Carving Tools with Grindstone."[17]

Figure 46 Rear view of a paw foot of the armchair illustrated in fig. 42. (Courtesy, Museum of Early Southern Decorative Arts.)

The architecture and furniture associated with Hardcastle exemplifies forces that governed stylistic change in eighteenth-century New York. The convergence of European and English culture is reflected in the transformation of Philipse Manor from a modest Anglo-European baroque dwelling to an aspiring country seat marked by Palladian interior details and ornate architectural carving. Its owners epitomize the New Yorkers of English and European descent who looked to Britain for the latest customs and fashions. The stylistically advanced carving that can now be attributed to Hardcastle attests to New Yorkers' acute awareness of the flow of British design. As in the earliest rococo designs of William Kent, there are strong baroque overtones in much of Hardcastle's work. This is particularly true of the carving in Philipse Manor and on the two desks-and-bookcases and two paw-foot bedsteads where large-scale, naturalistic ornaments embellish architectural elements and furniture of classical form. The commode card table, chest of drawers, and *Director*-inspired bed posts (fig. 37) represent a purer interpretation of the rococo style. On these pieces, Hardcastle had successfully integrated rococo form and ornament five to ten years before the style emerged in most other American urban centers. Hardcastle was clearly a pioneer in the early development of the rococo style in New York. However, his shop could not have flourished without parallel advances in the cabinet trade and wealthy, style-conscious patrons.

ACKNOWLEDGMENTS For assistance with this article the author thanks Gavin Ashworth, Deborah Gordon, Morrie Heckscher, Ned Hipp, Frank Horton, George and Linda Kaufman, Joe Kindig, Joe Lionetti, Alan Miller, Sumpter Priddy, Brad Rauschenberg, Karol Schmiegel, Peggy Scholley, Cindy Siebels, Wes Stewart, and Joseph Tanenbaum.

1. In both the Anglo and continental European furniture traditions, strong baroque details persisted well into the 1750s. For mid-eighteenth-century furniture with classical baroque details, see Dean F. Failey, *Long Island Is My Nation: The Decorative Arts & Craftsmen, 1640–1830* (Setauket, N.Y.: Society for the Preservation of Long Island Antiquities, 1976), pp. 123, 127, 128, 131. Illustrated on these pages are a cabriole-leg high chest with fluted chamfered corners capped with heavy baroque shells, dating from 1740–1760; a corner cupboard from the 1725–1745 period, with engaged pilasters, arched doors, a stylized carved interior shell and geometric raised panels (multiplicity of panels being a baroque characteristic); a slightly later corner cupboard (1725–1750) with a carved shell; and a desk-and-bookcase with a double arched head dating from 1740–1760. With their bold architectural cornices and baroque proportions (approx. 1:1 height to width), New York *kasten* document the taste for early classical details in the Continental traditions. During the seventeenth century,

immigrants came from the provinces of North Holland, Gelderland, Utrecht, South Holland, Friesland, and at least eleven provinces of the United Province. They also came from Germany (East Friesland and Oldenburg), Belgium (both the Walloon and Flemish provinces), France, the Schleswig-Holstein region, Norway, Sweden, and Denmark. See Nan A. Rothschild, *New York City Neighborhoods: The Eighteenth Century* (New York: Academic Press, 1990).

2. For a discussion of Dutch settlement in America, New Netherland's role as a commercial colony, and landholding systems, see Roderic H. Blackburn and Ruth Piwonka, *Remembrance of Patria: Dutch Arts and Culture in America, 1609–1776* (New York: Albany Institute of History and Art, 1988), pp. 35–41, 43, 63–69.

3. Frederick Philipse I. (also "Ffrerick Vlypse" and "Flypsen") was born in Friesland. See John T. Faris, *Historic Shrines of America* (New York: George H. Doran Co., 1918), pp. 91–94 and Esther Singleton, *Dutch New York* (1909, reprinted, New York: Benjamin Blom, 1968), p. 46. For more on the Philipse family, see Harold Donaldson Eberlein, *The Manors and Historic Homes of the Hudson Valley* (Philadelphia: Lippincott, 1928), pp. 82–98. The renovations and additions are discussed in John G. Waite, *The Stabilization of an Eighteenth Century Plaster Ceiling at Philipse Manor* (New York: New York State Historical Trust, 1972), pp. 1–16.

4. Several of the ceiling ornaments and the gadrooned molding around the perimeter of the ceiling are closely related to the carving. It is quite possible that the carver made several of the molds for the stucco and papier-mâché ornaments.

5. The carving on the overmantle in the Hampton Room in the Winterthur Museum also appears to be by the same hand. Although the museum files date it ca. 1761, there is no supporting documentation. The author thanks Morrison Heckscher for this reference.

6. As quoted in Alastair Laing, "The Eighteenth-Century English Chimneypiece," in Gervase Jackson-Stops, Gordon J. Schochet, Lena Cowen Orlin, and Elisabeth Blair MacDougall, eds., *The Fashioning and Functioning of the British Country House*, Studies in the History of Art, vol. 25 (Hanover, N.H.: distributed by University Press of New England for the National Gallery of Art, 1989), p. 241.

7. See, for example, the chimneypiece designed by Kent for the dining room in Houghton Hall, Norfolk, in Mark Girourard, *Life in the English Country House* (New Haven: Yale University Press, 1978), p. 162. This carver occasionally divided leaf surfaces into two levels. After making a deep vertical cut in the center of a leaf, he used a flat gouge to lower the surface on one side. This created a strong shadow line in the center and divided the surface into two planes for easy fluting. This technique was used frequently by stone cutters and steel engravers and suggests that this artisan also may have worked in stone.

8. The desk-and-bookcase was conserved by Alan Miller of Quakertown, Pennsylvania. The restored areas of the carving are identified in the caption for figure 14.

9. Advertisement of John Walton, *Antiques* 85, no. 4 (April 1964): 356.

10. For more on the history of the bedstead, see Brock Jobe and Myrna Kaye, *New England Furniture, the Colonial Era: Selections from the Society for the Preservation of New England Antiquities* (Boston: Houghton Mifflin, 1984), pp. 442–44. Museum of Early Southern Decorative Arts Research File S-13758.

11. This bedstead had a sacking bottom, but it was nailed into a rabbet rather than being suspended from wooden pins. It also appears to have had a brace between the head and foot rail. The brace probably was curved to drop below the sacking. Unlike the Brigham bedstead, this example had joints secured with bed bolts.

12. Chipstone Foundation acc. file 1965.5. Oswaldo Rodriguez Roque, *American Furniture at Chipstone* (Madison: University of Wisconsin Press, 1984), p. 316. Charles F. Hummel, *A Winterthur Guide to American Chippendale Furniture: Middle Atlantic and Southern Colonies* (New York: Crown, 1976), pp. 26–27.

13. A Boston bedstead in the Chipstone Collection (acc. 1990.4) has evidence for this type of pulley system. The author thanks Linda Baumgarten for her corroborating analysis of the Boston and New York bedsteads.

14. *The Dictionary of English Furniture Makers* lists only two eighteenth-century furniture makers named Hardcastle—Aaron, a cabinetmaker and joiner in Fewston, Harrowgate, York (1724–1755) and Robert, a carver "on the sunny side of Westminster Bridge," London (1763). All other furniture makers by that name were nineteenth-century tradesmen from Yorkshire (Geoffrey Beard and Christopher Gilbert, eds., *Dictionary of English Furniture Makers, 1660–1840* [Leeds: Furniture History Society and W. S. Maney &. Son, 1986], p. 395).

In execution, the carving resembles work associated with the shop of William Hallett (d. 1781) (see *The Samuel Messer Collection of English Furniture, Clocks and Barometers*, December 5, 1991 [London: Christie's, 1991], lot 63). The author thanks Morrison Heckscher for the reference to Hardcastle's inclusion in the list of freemen. In 1754 Hardcastle sued Thomas Davis for assault. In his petition to the court, Hardcastle described himself as a carver from New York (*Henry Hardcastle vs. Thomas Davis*, Court of Common Pleas of the City and County of New York, January 22, 1754, Municipal Archives of the City and County of New York). The advertisements by Hardcastle and Dwight are cited in Rita S. Gottesman, *The Arts and Crafts in New York, 1726–1776* (1938, reprinted, New York: Da Capo Press, 1970), p. 127. Hardcastle was buried in Charleston on October 20, 1756 (D. E. Huger Smith and A. S. Salley, Jr., eds., *Register of St. Philip's Parish, Charles Town, or Charleston, S.C., 1754–1810* [Columbia: University of South Carolina Press, 1971], p. 282). The author currently is researching a group of architectural carving that may be by Dwight or another apprentice or journeyman associated with Hardcastle.

15. Bradford L. Rauschenberg, "The Royal Governor's Chair: Evidence of the Furnishing of South Carolina's First State House," *Journal of Early Southern Decorative Arts* 6, no. 2 (November 1980): 6. The Journal of the Commons House of Assembly (Lower House), July 6, 1756, p. 232 (microfilm, Museum of Early Southern Decorative Arts). In his article, Rauschenberg attributed the royal governor's chair to the cabinet firm of Elfe and Hutchinson based on a March 14, 1758, entry in the Journal of the Commons House of Assembly, which recorded their bill for "Furniture for the Council Chamber amo £728.2.6" and Act 874 of the 1758 Statutes at Large of South Carolina, which noted that the firm's "Extraordinary" charge was for chairs and tables for the Council Chamber (Rauschenberg, "Royal Governor's Chair," pp. 8–9). This bill does not mention the governor's chair and probably referred to chairs and tables for the members of the Upper House of Assembly. Although Elfe and Hutchinson's charges initially appear "extraordinary," the exchange rate for Charleston and English currency was approximately 7:1 in 1758, compared to 1.7:1 in New York and 1.6:1 in Pennsylvania (John J. McCusker, *Money and Exchange in Europe and America, 1600–1775* [Chapel Hill: University of North Carolina Press, 1978]). Although the governor's chair is not described in any contemporary document, it seems more likely that it was ordered in 1756. This theory is supported by the treasurer's advance to pay tradesmens' bills for furniture on July 6 and by Hardcastle's working dates in Charleston. A mace for the governor, robes for the speaker, and a gown for the clerk were ordered from London in March 1756 (Rauschenberg, "Royal Governor's Chair," pp. 7, 30). The author thanks Mr. Rauschenberg for sharing his excellent research on the chair.

16. The use and display of the chair are detailed in Rauschenberg, "Royal Governor's Chair," pp. 15, 16, 26.

17. Smith and Salley, *Register of St. Philip's Parish*, p. 282. Transcript of Charleston County, S.C. Wills, et cetera, 1756–1758, 84: 54.

Figure 1 View of Walnut Street Between Third and Fourth Streets, Philadelphia, 1830–1840. Watercolor on paper. 18¾″ × 33½″. (Courtesy, Library Company of Philadelphia.) Hancock's rented four-story brick wareroom is shown on the left corner. An insurance survey indicated that building was 31′ × 43′ and that the middle two floors were partitioned into two rooms. The building was centrally located in Philadelphia's commerical district, directly opposite the merchants' Exchange and close to the waterfront.

David H. Conradsen

The Stock-in-Trade of John Hancock and Company

▼ THE FIRM John Hancock and Company opened "Upholstery Furnishing Rooms" at the southwest corner of Third and Walnut streets in Philadelphia in May 1830. When the proprietor John Hancock died in 1835, the stock-in-trade and debts to the estate totaled over $24,000. The probate documents—will, executor's account, and an extensive shop inventory (see appendix)—which record the stock, materials, tools, and trade of a large upholstery and furnishing business of the 1830s, are an invaluable source to both cultural and decorative arts historians.[1]

John Hancock (born 1803, Brookline, Mass.) was one of four ambitious and entrepreneurial brothers who entered the furniture trade. Two brothers remained in Boston—Henry (born 1788, Roxbury, Mass.), a chairmaker and cabinetmaker from 1816 to 1851, and William (born 1794, Roxbury), an upholsterer from 1819 to 1849. A third brother, Belcher (born 1800, Brookline), was an upholsterer and moved with John to Philadelphia (fig. 1). The executor's account demonstrates that John Hancock and Company was the Philadelphia branch of an extensive upholstery and decorating business. John owned a one-fourth interest in his firm; William probably supplied the rest of the capital and materials.[2]

The inventory of the stock-in-trade of John Hancock and Company sheds light on the size and scope of Hancock's enterprise and the upholstery trade during the early nineteenth century. The firm produced a variety of expensive seating and bed and window furniture. By 1835 the stock included more than 200 chairs and sofas that were retailed directly through the wareroom. The proportion of unupholstered frames to upholstered chairs suggests that the firm maintained a smaller number of finished goods and numerous frames, which were upholstered to order from a variety of fabrics and trims.

Rocking chairs represented more than half of the stock of seating furniture. Eighty-six were spring-seat rockers made of mahogany, walnut, or less expensive woods such as maple, painted to simulate rosewood or curled maple. The firm also kept in stock 150 inexpensive maple rocking chairs without upholstery, variously described as "scroll seat"; "nurse" ("high" and "low back," "small," "scroll seat," "best quality," and "inferior kind"); "[New?] York Pattern"; and "common."

Fifty rosewood-grained rocking chairs outnumbered all other types, and references in Philadelphia household inventories from 1830 to 1845 attest to the popularity of these fancy rocking chairs with plush covers. Guillema Evans, for example, had "one Elastic Spring Seat Rocking Chair

Figure 2 Rocking chair, labeled "John Hancock & Co.," Philadelphia, 1831–1840. Maple, mahogany, and pine H. 41″, W. 24″, D. 27″. (Courtesy, Winterthur Museum, acc. 90.82.) A roll of curled hair forms a headrest, a thin padding of hair sandwiched between two pieces of fabric and twined to the spindles forms the back upholstery, and two pieces of fabric padded with hair form the arm panels. The replaced burlap cover of the left arm has been removed, revealing the curled hair and tow stuffing. The perimeter of the finish cover had a matching gimp and closely spaced brass nails.

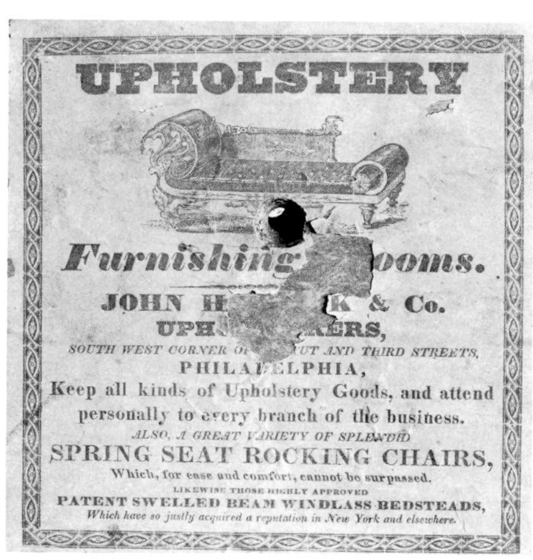

Figure 3 Label on the underside of the rocking chair seat illustrated in fig. 2. (Photo, Winterthur Museum.) The firm remained at Walnut and Third streets until 1840.

Figure 4 Campeche chair, Philadelphia, 1810–1820. Mahogany, satinwood inlay. H. 37½", W. 23⅞", D. 30½". (Private collection; photo, Winterthur Museum.) The original owner of this chair was Franklin Bache (1797–1864), Benjamin Franklin's great grandson.

covered with green velvet."[3] One surviving "Im[ita]t[ion] Rosewood Rocking Chair" has its original spring seat and curled hair and tow foundation (figs. 2, 3). The cushion has five helical iron wire springs that are secured to a plank deck and twined in place.

Hancock and Company sold Spanish arm- and rocking chairs, based on late-eighteenth-century campeche chairs (fig. 4), in both black walnut and mahogany and probably finished them in morocco (a goatskin leather with a grained surface), plush (a woolen velvetlike fabric, with a long pile), and haircloth (a fabric with a horsehair weft). Henry C. Carey, who owed Hancock's estate $118 in 1835, had two types of Spanish chairs in his library and may well have purchased them from Hancock's firm (figs. 5–7).

Smaller quantities of stylistically innovative or patent furniture were in stock. Among these were "Groove Arm Chairs" that may have resembled Louis XV chairs with molded or reeded backs. The "Self-Acting Chairs," or "London Recumbent Chair," which the firm advertised in 1833,

Figure 5 George Bacon Wood, Jr., *Interior of the Library of Henry C. Carey*, Philadelphia, 1879. 14" × 20¼". (Courtesy, Pennsylvania Academy of the Arts, Philadelphia. Gift of the artist.)

is illustrated by a reclining chair sold by William Hancock. The design of this chair, with a sliding footrest beneath the front rail and a ratchet-and-hinge system that allows the arms to slide and the back to recline, may have been inspired by London cabinetmaker William Pocock's design for a "Reclining Patent Chair" published in Rudolf Ackermann's *Repository of Arts* in 1813.[4]

The firm's printed label suggests that "easy chair" referred to any chair with upholstered arms and back. The inventory included two easy chairs, fourteen easy chair frames, and a loose cover for an easy chair. The reference to "Tin Chair Pans" indicates that at least some of Hancock's easy chairs were fitted as close stools.

Like eighteenth-century upholsterers, Hancock and Company probably made to order much of its bedding and bed and window hangings.

Figure 6 Detail of the Spanish rocking chair in the left foreground of the painting in fig. 5. The chair appears to have been upholstered in green plush. (Courtesy, Pennsylvania Academy of the Arts, Philadelphia. Gift of the artist.)

Figure 7 Detail of the Spanish arm chair in the right foreground of the painting in fig. 5. The chair also appears to have been upholstered in green plush. (Courtesy, Pennsylvania Academy of the Arts, Philadelphia. Gift of the artist.)

Although the firm maintained a substantial stock of curtain fabrics, trims, and fixtures, only five completed sets of bed hangings and a set of window curtains were in the wareroom. The appraisers found one-half dozen ready-made hair mattresses, one spring mattress, and twenty-six feather pillows and also inventoried seventy-nine ticks for beds, bolsters, and pillows, and seventy-nine yards of ticking. Feathers were processed in a kiln, and four hundred pounds of feathers were on hand. One "rattan palias" is the only mattress stuffed with cheap plant fiber; "cane shavings" were substituted for the more commonly used Spanish moss, cattail, or chaff.[5]

In a span of five years, John Hancock, with the financial and material support of his brothers, built the largest upholstery and decorating firm in Philadelphia. The company produced a relatively small line of innovative spring-seated chairs, sofas, and stools, which they finished to suit a range of customers. In part their success was linked to this flexibility, to aggressive advertising and marketing, and to the existence of a growing urban middle class of consumers. The inventory, which catalogues the stock, tools, and materials used by John Hancock and Company, sheds light on an important entrepreneurial venture of the 1830s. It is a rich document that provides a key to further interpretation of this period in American history.

1. John Hancock Will, 1835:172, City and County of Philadelphia Wills and Administrations, microfilm copy in Joseph Downs Collection of Manuscripts and Printed Ephemera, Winterthur Museum Library. For more on John Hancock and Company and the upholstery trade in early-nineteenth-century Philadelphia, see David H. Conradsen, "'Chairs of Every Description Constantly on Hand': John Hancock and Company, 1830–1840." Master's thesis, University of Delaware, 1993.

2. Page Talbott, "Boston Empire Furniture, Part II," *Antiques* 109, no. 5 (May 1976): 1006–7. After John's death Belcher managed the firm with a fifth sibling, James B. Hancock (born 1810, Brookline), until 1840. Inward Coastal Manifests, 1830–1835, National Archives, Washington, D.C. From 1830 to 1833, manifests for thirty vessels record more than sixty-six shipments amounting to 158 chairs, 379 packages and 68 bundles of chairs, 69 boxes and 26 bales of merchandise, 100 pounds and 4 bags of "hare," and other goods.

3. Guillema Evans Will, 1833:76, City and County of Philadelphia Wills and Administrations, microfilm, Joseph Downs Collection of Manuscripts and Printed Ephemera, Winterthur Library. The appraisers of Evans's estate quoted in full the trade name by which Hancock advertised his fancy rocking chairs.

4. *United States Gazette*, April 6, 1833. A labeled example by William is illustrated in *Nineteenth-Century America: Furniture and Other Decorative Arts* (New York: Metropolitan Museum of Art, 1970), no. 66. Pauline Agius, *Ackermann's Furniture and Regency Interiors* (Marlborough, England: Crowood Press, 1984), p. 72.

5. William Hancock sent six bales of rattan shavings on July 16, 1830. Inward Coastal Manifests.

Appendix

Inventory of John Hancock & Co. Stock Philad. 1835

1 Crimson Plush Sofa	90.00
1 Spanish Chair in Blue Chints	12.00
1 Self Acting Chair in Blue Morocco	45.00
1 Rocking Chair in Blue Leather	45.00
1 Rocking Chair in Crimson Plush	17.00
1 Do Do " Yellow Do	17.00
1 Do Do " Salmon Do	19.00
1 Do Do " Green Morocco	17.00
1 Easy Chair in French Chints	18.00
1 Doz Parlour Chairs Hair Cloth Seats	60.00
1 Doz Parlour French without Seats	68.00
11 Parlour Chairs Hair Cloth Seats	60.00
1 Doz. Parlour Chairs H.C. Seats	60.00
12 Parlour Chairs Carved Backs H.C. Seats	144.00
3 Patton Chairs	18.00
1 Lounge in Chints	10.00
25 Common Arm Chairs @ $3.25	81.25
2 Venetion Blinds & 4 Transparant Blinds	18.00
2 Fire Boards in Blue Muslin	3.00
1 Pair Bellows	.50
2 Groove Arm Chairs in Green & Maroon Leather	68.00
1 Sofa in Hair Cloth	45.00
1 Bed Sofa in worsted Damask	40.00
2 Mahogany Arm Chair in Hair Cloth $16.	32.00
1 Recumbent Chair (2d Hand)	20.00
1 Spring Mattress	25.00
1 Air Mattress	27.00
1 Easy Chair in Sheeting	14.00
1 Common Rocking Chair in Yellow Plush	12.00
2 Hair Cushions in Sheeting	2.00
Curtains, Drapery, Fixtures &c. [ ] Windows	50.00
1 Large & 2 Small Venetion Blinds	8.00
1 French Ornament for Bed	8.00
2 Brass Rings for Do	2.00
	1156.28

8 High Back Nurse R. Chairs 2 with Cushions $2.50	20.00
15 Scroll Seat Rocking Chairs @ $2.50	37.50
10 Small Nurse R.C. Inferior Kind @ $1.50	15.00
8 Do Do R.C. Best Quality $2.25	16.00
6 Common R.C. with Arms ___ $1.75 ¢	10.00
3 Pair Bellows _ 1 India Rubber Do	4.00
7 Single French Bedsteads Mahogany & Maple	42.00
2 Single Do Mahogany (Better Quality)	22.00
1 Double Do French Do	16.00
1 Black walnut Spanish Frame Rocking Chair	16.00
1 Mahogany Recumbent Do Do Do	16.00
2 Do Highly Finished Carving &c R.C. $28.	56.00
1 Do Spanish Frame Rocking Chair	16.00
4 Do Dolphin Do Do	32.00
1 Do Rocking Chair Frame (Carving Work)	16.00
1 Do Arm Chair Do (Do Do)	16.00
1 Do Spanish Frame	16.00
1 Rose wood Music Stool Frame	8.00
2 Mahogany Do Do Do	10.00
2 Do Wooden Screws Do	10.00
1 Do with Back Do	11.00
5 Pair Foot Stool Frames Mahogany Border	14.00
5 Imt Rose wood Rocking Chair Frames $5.00	25.00
1 Mahogany Do	7.00
1 Single Rattan Palias 1 Feather Pillow	8.00
1 Spring Seat Cushion in Green Plush	3.00
1 Do Do Do in Maroon Leather	2.00
1 Green Moreen Cushion	1.50
11 Scroll Seat Rocking Chairs @ $3	33.00
1 Rocking Chair in Black Worsted Damask	10.00
1 Nurse Rocking Chair in Crimson Moreen	5.00
4 Mahogany Music Stools in Hair Cloth	32.00
3 Do Do Do in Maroon Leather	24.00
	572.50

4 Mahogany Music Stool Frames @ $6.	24.00
1 Do Rocking Chair in Hair Cloth	17.00
1 Rocking Chair in H.C. Imt Maple	10.00
1 Mahogany Parlour Chair H.C. Seat	5.00
1 Mahogany Water Closet	8.00
1 Rocking Chair in Green Moreen	10.00
1 Do Do in Hair Cloth	10.00
9 Velvet Air Cushions @ $3	27.00
4 Drilling Do Do " " 2.50	10.00
4 Do Do Pillows	9.00
1 Mahogany Arm Chair in Hair Cloth (2d hand)	10.00
11 Yankee Made Blinds @ 50 ¢	5.50
16 Canton Window Shades @ 50 ¢	8.00
22 Transparencies @ $3.	66.00
1 Hand Saw	2.25
10 lbs Cut Nails @ 70 ¢	.70
1 Mahogany R.C. in Plush	17.00
2 Maple Frame R.C. @ $7.	14.00

35 Imt Rose wood Frames R.C. @ $5	175.00
8 Mahogany R.C. Frames @ $7.	56.00
2 Do Arm Chair Do @ $16	32.00
4 Do Self Acting Arm Chair Frames @ $16	64.00
1 Do Groove Seat Frame	9.00
19 Scroll Seat R. Chairs @ $2.50	47.50
1 Mahogany R.C. Frame	8.00
9 High Back Nurse S. S. R.C. @ $2.25 ¢	20.25
5 Low Back Do Do Do @ $2.25 ¢	11.25
5 Do Common Do @ $1.25 ¢	7.50
2 Mahogany Sofa Frames @ $26.	56.00
Embossing Blocks	60.00
1 Canton Chair (2d Hand)	8.00
Set Bed Curtains	60.00
72 Scroll Seat R.C. @ $2.50	180.00
10 Imt Rose wood R.C. Frames @ $5	50.00
	1097.95

16 Small Nurse R.C. Best Quality	@ $2.25 ¢	36.00
14 Do " Inferior Kind Do	@ $1.50 ¢	21.00
4 Easy Chair Frames @ $4.75		19.00
40 ½ Yds. Bell Line @ 8 ¢		3.24
9 Groce Blind Cord Various Colours	@ $1.87½ ¢	16.88
25 Yds Orange Bell Line	@ 8 ¢	2.80
40 ½ Do Green Do Do	@ 10 ¢	4.05
40 Do Drab Do Do	@ 10 ¢	4.00
99 ½ Do C & Yellow Raisd Gimp	@ 12 ¢	12.34
Lot of Cord diffrant Colours		20.00
80 Yds Blue Raisd Gimp	@ 12½ ¢	10.00
50 Do Various Colours	@ 12½ ¢	6.25
70 Do Black Raised Gimp	@ 12½ ¢	8.75
80 Do Crimson Do Do	@ 12½ ¢	10.00
80 Do Maroon Do Do	@ 12½¢	10.00
50 Do Green & Orange Do Do	@ 12½ ¢	6.25
25 Do Yellow & Green Do Do	@ 12½ ¢	3.12
6 Groce Crimson Cord	@ $2.25 ¢	13.50
12 Do Green Do	@ $1.50 ¢	18.00
3 Do Drab Do	@ $1.50 ¢	4.50
6 Do Blue Silk Lace	@ $9	54.00
21 Do Bed Lace	@ $1.25 ¢	26.25
4 Doz Belham Tassels	@ $2.75	11.00
5 Groce Worsted Binding	@ $2.	10.00
2 Pieces Crimson Worsted Damask @ $18.		36.00
2 Do Worsted Fringe 37 Yds each @ 30 ¢		22.20
10 Pair Cornice Ends No 2678	@ $4.50	45.00
7 Do Do Do " 5044	@ $3.	21.00
6 Do Do Do " 5215	@ $3.	18.00
5 Do Do Do " 5644	@ $3.50	17.50
6 Do Do Do " 3749	@ $2.25	13.50
4 Do Do Do " 2679	@ $3.25	13.00
12 Do Do Do " 2288	@ $2.25	27.00
3 Do Do Do " 3327	@ 33 ¢	.99
		545.12

7 Pair Cornice Ends No 3287 @ 33¢	2.31
8 Do Do Do " 3090 @ $1.35 ¢	10.80
13 Do Do Do " 3023 @ $1.10 ¢	14.30
10 Do Do " 3022 @ 72 ¢	7.20
12 Do Do " 3052 @ 88 ¢	10.56
10 Do Do " 3090 @ $1.35 ¢	13.50
3 Do Do " 2975 @ $1.85 ¢	5.55
4 Do Do " 2995 @ $1.85 ¢	7.40
4 Sets Casters @ $1.25 ¢	5.00
17 Do Do @ $1 25 ¢	21.25
7 Brass Centre Ornaments @ 50 ¢	3.50
50 Pair Brass Brackets @ 75 ¢	37.50
2 Brass Racks for Writing Desks @ $2.75	5.50
3 Bronze Lamp Sockets @ $2.	6.00
5 Brass Do Do @ $2.	10.00
11 Wooden Wreaths @ $2.	22.00
15 Pair Curtain Bands @ $1.12½ ¢	16.88
34 Sets Casters @ $1.25 a Set	42.50
28 Doz Cornice Rings @ $2.	56.00
6 Do Blind Furniture @ $2.80	16.80
6 Do Rack Pulleys @ $1.50	9.00
2 Brass Ornaments @ 50 ¢	1.00
1 Doz Do @ 33 ¢	3.96
10 Brass Do @ 50 ¢	5.00
10 Do Do @ 45 ¢	4.50
8 Do Do @ 37 ¢	2.96
7 Do Do @ 25 ¢	1.75
10 Bell Handles @ 37½ ¢	3.75
12 Sets Roller Ends	2.80
2 Doz Pulley Hooks @ 10 ¢ apiece	2.40
12 Brass Hooks @ 10 ¢ "	1.20
24 Do Knobs @ 90 ¢ a Doz	1.80
10 M 14 oz Flemish Tacks @ 45 ¢ pr M	4.50
6 Doz Rack Pulleys @ ¢2.	12.00
	371.17

4 Groce Brass Rings @ $1.25	5.00
8 Doz Sets Iron Blind Pulleys @ 8 ¢/a St	7.68
3 Doz Glass Knobs @ $1.37 ¢	4.11
2 Do Do Do @ 90 ¢	1.80
56 Yds Crimson & Drab French Chints @ 60 ¢	33.60
11 Do Blue & Yellow Do Do @ 60 ¢	6.60
78 Do White Cotton Fringe @ 25 ¢	19.50
7 lbs White Worsted @ $2	14.00
7 lbs Various Colours @ $1.50	10.50
3 Groce French Cord @ $2.	6.00
1½ Do. White Venetion Binding @ $3.25	4.85
75 Yds Green & Orange Flat Gimp @ 8 ¢	6.00
124 do Blk Raisd Gimp @ 12½ ¢	15.50
124 do Do Do Do @ 12½ ¢	15.50
163 Do Do Do Do @ 12½ ¢	20.39
166 Do Do Do Do @ 12½ ¢	20.76
156 Do Do Do Do @ 12½ ¢	19.50

146 Do Flat Black Gimp @ 8 ¢	11.68
2 Doz C & Yellow worsted Tassels @ 33 ¢	7.92
1 Do B & Yellow Do Do @ 33 ¢	3.96
1½ Do G & Yellow Do Do @ 33 ¢	5.94
4 Do C & White Silk & Worsted Tassels @ $1.25 ¢	5.00
2 Doz C & White worsted Tassels @ 33	7.92
3½ lbs Patent Thread @ $1 12½ ¢	3.93
6 French Ornaments No 5408 @ $1.20 ¢	7.20
6 Do Do " 5416 @ $1.66 ¢	4.98
6 Do Do " 1392 @ $1.	6.00
6 Do Do " 5410 @ $1.20 ¢	3.60
6 Do Do " 1388 @ $1.	6.00
6 Do Do " 5423 @ 25 ¢	1.50
6 Do Do " 5403 @ 50 ¢	3.00
6 Do Do " 1396 @ 80 ¢	4.80
Lot English Wire Springs	3.00
9 Cotton Ticks for Mattresses & Feather Beds $4	36.00
	333.75

2 Cotton Ticks for Pillows @ 50	1.00
27 Cotton & Linen Ticks for Mattresses & F. B. $3.50	94.50
29 Do Tick Pillow Cases & Bolsters @ 62	17.98
8 Pair Bellows @ 30 ¢	2.40
4 Leather Embd Piano Covers @ $5	20.00
9 Tin Chair Pans @ 40 ¢	3.60
19 Cotton Tick Pillow Cases @ 50 ¢	9.50
8 Do Do for Mattresses, Feather Beds @ $3.50	28.00
10 Groce Drapery Web No 10 @ $3.50	35.00
6 Do Do Do " 9 @ $3.	18.00
1 Pair Foot Stools Mahogany Border	3.00
1 Stool Mahogany Border	6.00
23 Iron Screws for Piano Stools @ 72 ¢	16.56
4 Sacking Bottoms @ 87 ¢	3.48
4 M Clout Nails @ 45 ¢	1.80
5 Groce Wood Screws @ $2	10.00
6 Do Iron Do @ $1.88	11.28
69 Iron Fixtures for Windows @ 3 ¢	2.07
8 lbs Green & White Worsted @ $1.62	10.96
Lot Carpeting	10.00
135 M 3 oz Tacks @ 8 ¢	10.80
110 Do 1 oz Do @ 8 ¢	8.80
104 Do 6 oz Do @ 8 ¢	8.32
137 Do 8 oz Do @ 8 ¢	10.96
172 Do 2½ oz Do @ 8 ¢	13.76
Lot Screws, Hooks, and Clout Nails	5.00
6 Rules @ 62 ¢	3.75
4 lbs Black Pins @ $2.	8.00
15 M 2½ oz Tacks @ 8 ¢	1.20
16 M 14 oz Flemish Tacks @ 45	7.20
6 Groce Screws @ 50 ¢	3.00
1 Paper Brass Nails	.83
3 M Flemish Tacks @ 45 ¢	1.35
Cuts of Various Patterns	10.00
	398.30

1 Groce Rings	1.25
Cord of Various Colours	3.00
4 Sets Large French Curtains for Beds @ $2.	8.00
5 Do Pattern Roller Caster @ $1.75	8.75
1 Do Common Do	1.25
1 Do Common Do	1.25
11 Bell Handles @ 30 ¢	3.30
8 Sets Pattern Roller Casters @ $1.75	14.00
7 Do Common Do @ $2	14.00
3 Do Pattern Roller Do @ $1.75	5.25
6 Do Common Trencher Do @ 90 ¢	5.40
3 Do Do Socket Casters @ $1.20	3.60
6 Groce Curtain Rings @ 50 ¢	3.00
2 Doz Fancy Ornaments @ 50	1.00
3 Sets Patent Roller Blind Fixtures @ $2.	6.00
Remnants of Silk & worsted Damask, Moreen &c	10.00
1 lb Sewing Silk Various Colours	8.00
1 lb Worsted Yearn	1.00
6 Set Sofa Casters @ $1.20	7.20
Twine & Spring Cord	10.00
26 Pieces of Silk Damask @ $26. apiece	676.00
34 Do Worsted Damask @ $18. do	512.00
20 Yds C & White Silk Drapery Cord @ $1	20.00
24 Doz Small Shade Tassels @ $1.	24.00
14 pairs Crimson & Yellow Bracelets @ $2.25 a pair	31.50
12 Do Do " Do French Ornaments @ $2.50	30.00
12 Do Blue " Do Do Do @ $2.25	27.00
24 Large Silk French Tassels @ $2.	48.00
3 Pair Bracelets @ $2.25	6.75
80 Yds Maroon Flat Gimp @ 8 ¢	6.40
60 do Black Do Do @ 8 ¢	4.80
50 Do Crimson Do Do @ 10 ¢	5.00
60 Do Blue Do Do @ 8 ¢	4.80
70 Do Green Do Do @ 8 ¢	5.60
	1517.10

110 Yds Flat Gimp Various Colours @ 8 ¢	8.80
100 Do Do Green & Orange Lace @ 13 ¢	13.00
Remnants Lace Various Colours	20.00
3 Pieces B & Yellow Lace 16 Yds. E. @ 20 ¢	36.00
70 Yds C & Yellow Do @ 25 ¢	17.50
200 Do C & Yellow Do @ 18 ¢	36.00
180 Do C & Yellow Do @ 25 ¢	45.00
9 Pieces 15 Yds Each @ $2.25 ¢	20.25
16 Do Do @ 70 ¢	11.20
15 Do Do Various Colours	60.00
1 Do C & Yellow Lace 25 Yds. @ 30 ¢	7.50
70 Yds C & Yellow Bell Lace @ 37½ ¢	26.25
12 Do Blue & Bluff Do Do @ 37½ ¢	4.50
2½ Groce Pearl Binding @ $3.25	8.13
3 Do Fancy Do @ $1.25 ¢	3.75
3½ Do Silk Binding @ $10	35.00
18 Worsted Rosets @ 12 ¢	2.16

100 Yds German Lace @ 12 ¢	12.00
34 Pieces of Moreens, Various Colours @ $10 apiece	340.00
3 Hair Matresses @ $14.	42.00
17 Feather Pillows @ $1.25 ¢	21.25
23 Chair Cushions @ $1.50 ¢	34.50
4 Pieces Cotton Tick 40 Yds Each @ 23 ¢	36.80
1 Pair Ottomans in Blue Plush	12.00
1 Foot Stool Mahogany Border Morocco Top	5.00
2 Sets Drab Figured Sofa & Chair Covers @ $120.	240.00
2 Hair Cloth Pillows @ $3.	6.00
5 Feather Pillows @ $2.25	11.25
3 Morocco Foot Stools	6.00
2 Crimson Silk Foot Stools @$4	8.00
1 Pair Foot Stools in Carpet	4.00
4 Leather Covers for Music Stools @ 75 ¢	3.00
4 Pair Curtain Bands @ $2.	8.00
1 Pair Cornice Ends	1.00
	1145.84

1 Wooden Wreath	1.00
2 Pair Curtain Bands @ $2.	4.00
4 Doz Cornice Rings @ $2.75	11.00
1 Pair Cornice Ends	2.50
12 Doz Wooden Cornice Rings @ $2.50	30.00
8 Bracelets @ 30 ¢	2.40
16 Cornice Poles 5½ Feet @ 70 ¢	61.60
1 Pair Large Cornice Ends	3.00
3 Large Bell Pulls @ $9.	27.00
1 Pair Lace Bell Pulls	3.50
1 Doz Do Do Do @ 75 ¢	9.00
1 Pair Linen Shades	5.00
40 Yds Buff Linen @ 68 ¢	27.20
20 Pair Curtain Bands @ $2.25	45.00
34 Do Cornice Ends @ $2.50	85.00
56 Curtain Pins @ 50 ¢	28.00
12 pair Cornice Ends @ $1	12.00
8 Do Glass Curtain Pins @ 75	6.00
1 Doz Brass Centre Ornaments @ 27 ¢	3.24
8 Cut Glass Knobs @ 25 ¢	2.00
2½ Doz Bras Ornaments @ 50 ¢ apiece	15.50
7 Brass Lamp Sockets @ $2.	14.00
12 Do Ornaments @ 50 ¢	6.00
3 Wreaths @ 2.50	7.50
3 Lamp Sockets @ $2	6.00
20 Ornaments @ 75 ¢	15.00
14 Centre Ornaments @ 37½	5.25
1 Pair Cornice Ends	.75
1 Wooden Centre Ornament	1.50
3 Large Glas Knobs @ 37½ ¢	1.12
1 Leather Foot Stool	2.00
1 Pair French Foot Stools	3.00
5 Pair Wooden Cornice Ends @ $1.50	7.00
5 Do Cornice Ends @ $3.50	17.50
	470.56

Item	Rate	Amount
1 Brass Rack for Writing Desk		2.75
1 Bundle Pins		.70
2 Brass Ornaments		.75
6 Doz Spike Ornaments	@ $1.25	7.50
1½ Do Do Do	@ $1.25	1.87
2 Do Do Do	@ $2	4.00
Stair Rods & Fixtures		4.00
3 Curtain Bands @ $2. apair		3.00
1 Feather Duster		.50
1 Crimson & White Silk Tassel		1.00
3 Pieces Worsted Damask 90 Yds. E. @ 65 ¢		58.50
2 Pieces Silk Damask @ $27.		54.00
½ Yd Large Fringe		4.00
1 Pair Ottoman Frames		14.00
1 Square Do Stool		1.00
2 Bell Pulls @ 75 ¢		1.50
7¼ Yds C & Yellow Fringe	@ 88 ¢	6.38
37½ do Crimson S.B. Fringe	@ $1	37.50
20 Do Do " " Do	@ 50 ¢	10.00
37 Do Crimson & Yellow Do	@ 62½ ¢	22.94
28 Do Blue & Yellow Do	@ 87½	24.50
37½ Do Do & Do Do	@ 37½	14.05
40 Do Crimson & Yellow Do	@ 25 ¢	10.00
16 Do Do "Do Do	@ $1.	16.00
11 Do Do "Do Do	@ 75 ¢	8.25
37½ Do Do "Do Do	@ 37½ ¢	14.05
10 Do Do "Do Do	@ 87½ ¢	8.75
37½ Do Do "Do Do	@ 87½ ¢	32.81
50 Do Various Colours	@ 75 ¢	37.50
40 Do Worsted Ball Do	@ 33 ¢	13.20
20 Do Gimp Headed Fringe	@ 25 ¢	5.00
36 Do Scarlet Do Do	@ 25 ¢	9.00
36 Do Black Do Do	@ 20 ¢	7.20
36 Do Green Do Do	@ 20 ¢	7.20
		443.40

Item	Rate	Amount
14 Yds Plain Green Fringe	@ 14 ¢	1.96
10 Do Do Black Do	@ 14 ¢	1.40
5 Black Silk Tassels	@ 50 ¢	2.50
11 Crimson Silk Do	@ 50	5.50
6 Green Worsted Do	@ 37½ ¢	2.25
9 Yds Crimson Fringe	@ $1.50 ¢	13.50
16 Crimson Silk Tassels	@ 62 ¢	9.92
20 Worsted —— Do	@ 37½ ¢	7.50
20 Large Size Tassels Various Colours	@ $1.75	35.00
12 Embd Chair Covers @ $4.50		54.00
10 Pieces English Chints @ $8.25		82.50
1 Piece Brown Holland		7.80
18 Yds Silk Velvet	@ $2.75	49.50
12 Do Cotton Scarlet Do	@ $1.25	15.00
10 Do Purple Do Do	@ 30 ¢	3.00
8 Do Green Do Do	@ 30 ¢	2.40
19½ Yds Crimson & Drab French Chints	@ 55 ¢	10.75

17 Do Do Do Do @ 65 ¢	11.05
10 Do Blue & Yellow Do Do @ 65 ¢	6.50
Remnants of Cotton Sofa & Chair Covers	40.00
50 Yds Cotton Trimmings @ 6 ¢	3.00
18 Pieces Moreen Various Colours @ $7.50	135.00
4 Do Crimson & White Lace 31 Yds E. @ 30 ¢	37.20
8 Groce Worsted Binding @ $1.50	12.00
2 Do Common Venetion Do @ $3.25	6.50
1 Do Blue Silk Do	10.00
3 Do Common Bed Lace Do @ $1	3.00
1 Do Dimity Binding	1.00
24 Small Silk Tassels Differant Colours @ 50 ¢	12.00
16 Doz French Silk Tags of Differant Kinds @ $3.	48.00
2 Doz Do Do Do Do @ $6.	12.00
1 Brass Rod 5 Ft ½ Long @ 70 ¢	3.85
6 Doz Common Silk Tassels @ $2.50	15.00
2 Doz Crimson & Yellow Tags @ $6	12.00
	692.58

11 Brass Rod 4½	3.15
2 Hair Mattresses @ $20.	40.00
3 Doz Maroon Goat Skins @ $20.	60.00
3 Do Do Do Do @ $18.	54.00
2 Pieces Russia Sheeting @ $10.	20.00
9 Doz Common Pole Rings @ $2.50	22.50
4 Pair Cornice Ends @ $3.	12.00
6 Do Do Do @ $2	12.00
3 Pieces Black Muslin 30 Yds Each @ 8 ¢	7.20
1 Spring Seat	3.00
2 Pieces Cotton Check 30 Yds E. @ 18 ¢	10.80
2 Pair Curtain Bands @ $3.	6.00
1 Bed Chair	7.00
3 Feather Pillows @ $2.	6.00
25 Yds C & Drab French Chints @ 50 ¢	12.50
10 Groce Buttons @ 40 ¢	4.00
22 Do Brass Rings @ 35 ¢	7.70
½ Groce Knobs @ $2 a groce	1.00
Pins	.35
18 Brass Handles @ 25 ¢	4.50
Lot Brass Hooks	3.00
2 Doz Set Blind Fixtures @ $2.80 ¢	5.60
7 Do Rack Pulleys @ $1.	7.00
6 Do Iron Do @ 8 ¢	.48
2 Doz Knobs @ $1.50	3.00
3 lbs Sewing Thread @ $1 12½ ¢	3.38
64 rosets @ 8 ¢	5.12
7 Doz Shade Tassels @ $1	7.00
16 Large Worsted Tassels various Colours @ 25 ¢	4.00
6 Doz Shade Tassels @ $1	6.00
Pins	.25
22 Yds Crimson Silk Cord @ 12½ ¢	2.75
13 Pieces French Cord, various Colours @ 50 ¢	6.50
Remnants of Cord Various Colours	2.50
	350.28

Tape Cord & Braid &c	2.00
Lot of Tools	5.00
8 Doz Worsted Tassels Various Colours $2.75	22.00
Lot of Fringes Various Colours	20.00
100 Yds of Do Do Do @ 10 ¢	10.00
12½ Yds of 22 Inch Hair Cloth @ 98 ¢	12.24
4½ do 14 do Do Do @ 38 ¢	1.71
7 Do 26 do Do Do @ $1.32	9.24
1 Do 14 do Do Do @ 38 ¢	.38
1 Do 22 do Do Do	1.10
22¼ Do 24 Do Do Do @ $1.12½ ¢	25.03
24½ Do 22 Do Figured H. C. @ $1.65 ¢	40.43
29¾ Do 18 Do Do Do Do @ $1.15 ¢	34.21
21¾ Do 29 Do Hair Cloth (Plain) @ $1.40 ¢	30.45
15 Do 16 Do Do Do —— @ 47	7.04
15½ Do 25 Do Figured Do Do @ $1.62	25.11
1⅔ Do 26 Do Do Do Do @ $1.62	2.70
6⅓ Do 22 Do Do Do Do @ $1.50	9.50
13⅓ Do 20 Do Do Do Do @ $1.12½ ¢	15.00
4¾ Do 18 Do Do Do Do @ $1.15 ¢	4.46
3⅓d Do 23 Do Do Do Do @ $1.62 ¢	6.48
4 Do 18 Do Do Do Do @ $1.15	4.60
10¾ Do 25 Do Do Do Do @ $2.	21.50
7 Pieces Embd Curtain Muslin @ $10	70.00
1 Do Plain Do Do	3.50
12 Yds Crape Sisle @ 80 ¢	9.60
3 Pieces Green Muslin 12 Yds Each @ 30 ¢	10.80
2 Do Common Chints 33 Yds Each @ 12½ ¢	8.25
400 Yds Cotton Trimmings @ 4 ¢	16.00
1 Chince Chair Cover	3.00
1 Piece Crimson Muslin 33 Yds @ 14 ¢	4.62
4 Chair & 2 Sofa French Chintz Covers @ $2.	8.00
1 Easy Chair Cover	3.00
30 Yds Wide Yellow Muslin @ 25 ¢	7.50
	454.45

Remnants of Ratinett	3.00
10 Yds White Cotton Cloth @ 14 ¢	1.40
Remnants of Muslin	3.00
28 Large Size Silk Tassels @ $2	56.00
83 Yds Orange & Silk Lace @ 25 ¢	20.75
72 Do Crimson Do Do @ 12½ ¢	9.00
41 Do Crimson Orace Do @ 25 ¢	10.25
41 Do Do Do Do @ 18¢	7.38
125 Do Blue & Drab Do Do @ 25 ¢	3.00
11 Groce Carpet Bindings @ $3 a Groce	33.00
21 Yds Plain Blue Silk Lace @ 25 ¢	5.25
20 Do Crimson & Yellow Do @ 25 ¢	5.00
10 Do Crimson & Yellow Worsted Do @ 25 ¢	2.50
10 Do Blue Do Do @ 25 ¢	2.50
6 Do Blue & Yellow Do Do @ 25 ¢	1.50
20 Do Crimson & White Do Do @ 20 ¢	4.00
5 Do Yellow Do Do Do @ 25 ¢	1.25

10 Do Crimson & Yellow Do Do @ 25 ¢	2.50
1 Piece White Sarcenet	21.00
12 Yds Gold Coloured Silk Damask $1.87	22.44
2 Pieces English Chints 33 Yds E. @ 33 ¢	21.78
4 Do Yellow Sarcenets @ $25.	100.00
5 Doz Brass Drapery Rings @ $2.50 ¢	12.50
11 Pair Brass Brackets @ 75 ¢ pr pair	8.25
2 Groce Brass Ornaments @ $3	6.00
2 Doz Pulley Ends @ $1.50	3.00
75 Tin Screw Eyes @ 2 ¢	1.50
1 Piece Green Plush	85.00
1 Do Purple Do	85.00
2 Do C & Yellow Fringe 37½ Yds E. @ 35 ¢	26.25
2 Do " " Do Do 37½ do E. @ 28 ¢	21.00
3 Do Do Do Do 37½ do E. @ 18 ¢	20.25
1 Do Do Blue & Yellow 37½ do E. @ 35 ¢	13.13
2 Do Common Tick 35 Yds Each @ 12½ ¢	8.75
	627.13

5 Feather Dusters @ 50 ¢	2.50
1 Piece Plain Mill Muslin	3.50
23 Pieces Embd Curtain Muslin @ $10	230.00
2 Sofa Frames	43.00
2 Hair Mattresses @ $22.	44.00
1 Rocking Chair	3.50
25 Yds Crimson Damask Cotton @ $1.15 ¢	28.75
12 Do Fawn Do Do @ 68 ¢	8.16
29 Do Crimson Cashmarine @ 87 ¢	25.23
37½ Do Blue Plush @ $2.37 ¢	88.88
12 Do Crimson Do @ $2.75 ¢	33.00
40 Do Blue Cotton Damask @ 68 ¢	27.20
6 Wire Shades @ $4	24.00
Wheelbarrow & Hand Barrow	12.00
Awning for Front Store	20.00
Kiln for Drying Feathers	75.00
1 Scale Beam with Weights	10.00
2 Centre Lamps	6.00
10 Shop Lamps	2.00
Brace & Bitt	7.00
1 Stove & Pipe	20.00
1 Small Do in Varnish Room	4.00
1 Large Stove & pipe	20.00
Coal Scuttle & Shovels	3.00
1 Mahogany Desk	10.00
1 Cherry Do	20.00
Floor Cloths for 2 Rooms	30.00
2 Tailors Irons	1.00
2 Blocks for Making Springs	10.00
4 Lamp Stands	3.00
1 Cloths Basket	2.00
7 Work Benches	20.00
2 Tables @ $5.	10.00
4 Small Stools	2.00
	848.72

Lots of Bags	5.00
3 Step Ladders	6.00
3 Frames for Prints	3.00
Lot Shop Bills, Cards &c	4.00
Shelves, Cases & Store Fixtures	250.00
All the Signes outside	200.00
4 Large Linen Shades in Windows @ $3.	12.00
Lots of Tools	20.00
1 Patent Lamp	3.50
Oil Can & 5 Gallons Oil	5.00
10 Easy Chair Frames @ $4.33 ¢	43.30
400 lbs Feathers @ 50	200.00
50 Large Size Springs @ 12½ ¢	6.25
200 lbs Cane Shavings @ 6 ¢	12.00
6 Cot Bedsteads	6.00
4 Pieces White Sarcenets @ $21	84.00
3 Pieces Cotton Shirting 37½ Yds E. @ 14 ¢	15.75
5 Tones Coal @ $6.	30.00
Wrapping Paper	1.00
8 Sofa Frames @ $21.	168.00
1 Do Do	10.00
4 Rocking Chair Frames @ $4	16.00
3 Single Mahogany French Bedsteads @ $14.	42.00
8 Pair Mahogany Stool Frames @ $2.	16.00
400 lbs Curled Hair @ 30 ¢	120.00
100 Wire Springs @ 8 ¢	8.00
6 Stone Iron Wire @ $1.20 a stone	7.20
1 Russet Side	20.00
4 Doz Russet Sheepskins @ $5.	20.00
1 Doz Morocco Goat Skins	18.00
2 Sofa Frames @ $20.	40.00
100 Yds Burlaps @ 12 ¢	12.00
60 Do Narrow Do @ 8 ¢	4.80
6 Cutting Boards @ $1.50	9.00
	1407.80

12 Tassels	12.00
3 Linen Ticks @ $6	18.00
2 Bolsters & 4 Pillows @ $1	6.00
2 Green Cases for Cushions @ $2.	4.00
Screws & Tacks	2.00
Carpet on Floor	5.00
14 Common Chairs @ 50 ¢	7.00
13 Rocking Chairs (York Pattern) $6.	78.00
5 Brass Rods 5 ft ½ Long @ 70 ¢ pr ft	19.25
5 Do Do 4 ft ½ Long @ 70 ¢ " "	15.75
	167.00

	1156.25
	572.50
	1097.95
	545.12
	371.17
	333.75
	398.30
	1517.10
	1145.84
	470.56
	443.40
	692.58
	350.28
	454.45
	627.13
	848.72
	1407.80
Valued by the Undersigned	$12599.90

Thos. Cook
H. Duhring

Edward S. Cooke, Jr.

Scandinavian Modern Furniture in the Arts and Crafts Period: The Collaboration of the Greenes and the Halls

▼ FURNITURE designed by Pasadena, California, architects Charles Sumner Greene (1868–1957) and Henry Mather Greene (1870–1954) has attracted the attention of many arts and crafts enthusiasts. The Greenes' concern with the inherent beauty of wood, incorporation of visible joinery, reliance on local materials or imagery for decoration, and commitment to the integration of interior furnishings with architecture resulted in what many writers have described as the ultimate in arts and crafts furniture. Scholars have often attributed the success of the brothers' furniture to their knowledge of and affinity with the materials and processes. Both of the Greenes took woodworking courses at Calvin Milton Woodward's Manual Training School in St. Louis before enrolling in the architecture program at the Massachusetts Institute of Technology. Charles, in particular, enjoyed woodworking: he possessed enough skill to make a table as a wedding present for his wife in 1900 (fig. 1); carved wooden furniture and architectural elements throughout his career; and eagerly visited the shop where furniture makers executed his designs.[1] An examination of Greene-designed furniture, however, reveals the critical role of the professional craftsmen who contributed to the look of Greene and Greene furniture.

The Greenes first demonstrated an interest in the interior furnishings of the houses they designed in 1902. Charles's exposure to the English arts and crafts movement during his honeymoon there in 1901 and the publication of the first issue of *The Craftsman* in the fall of the same year inspired them to integrate movable furniture with architectural fabric. Initially they relied upon commercially available products such as Gustav Stickley furniture, Rookwood and Tiffany ceramics, and Navajo rugs.[2]

For two commissions in 1904, the Jennie Reeve and the Adelaide Tichenor houses in Long Beach, the Greenes began to design custom furniture. The Reeve bureau (fig. 2) and the Tichenor desk (fig. 3), for example, manifest a direct craftsman influence. The two slab sides with a fall-front writing surface over heavily battened doors resemble one of Stickley's earliest desk designs. The Greenes drew from Stickley's formal vocabulary and duplicated his structural decorative conventions such as the butterfly splines on the side of the desk and the projecting through-tenons of the bureau. Although the Greenes added a few new Asian motifs, such as the lift in the drawer pull and the setback along the front edge of the sides, their work of this period remained very much within the Anglo-based craftsman tradition: severely rectilinear, overengineered forms made from thick-dimensioned stock; surface decoration reliant on the figure of ring-porous native hardwoods such as oak and ash; and visible joinery that stressed handcraftsmanship.[3]

It is not known who built the Greene-designed furniture of this period. Several firms in Pasadena could have produced such work. Carl Enos Nash advertised himself in 1904 as a "builder of fine furniture and mantels" and in 1906 as a "designer of furniture." Another possibility was Ye Arts and Crafts Company, manufacturers of "artistic furniture," which William L. Leishman purchased in 1905 and renamed Crown City Man-

Figure 1 Table, designed and made by Charles Sumner Greene, Pasadena, 1900. Wood. (Private collection; photo, Marvin Rand.)

Figure 2 Bureau, designed by Charles Sumner Greene and Henry Mather Greene for the Jennie Reeve house, Long Beach, California, probably Pasadena, ca. 1904. Oak and cedar. (Private collection; photo, Marvin Rand.)

Figure 3 Desk, designed by Charles Sumner Greene and Henry Mather Greene for the Adelaide Tichenor house, Long Beach, California, probably Pasadena, ca. 1904. Ash. (Private collection; photo, Marvin Rand.)

ufacturing Company. The new firm specialized in planing and milling but also advertised "mission furniture" in 1906. A third possibility was Pasadena Manufacturing Company, a large shop that offered doors, sash, blinds, and moldings.[4]

It is more likely that the Greenes turned to one of the two millwork firms than to an individual like Nash. Since the 1870s millwork shops, particularly those that offered stairbuilding and mantels, had worked closely with architects. These firms offered particular advantages to designers: they worked according to estimates and specified budgets, they could produce a quantity of related furniture, and they were used to following the specifications of a designer rather than introducing their own style. As Chicago architect Elmer Gray, who also worked in Pasadena,

Figure 4 Entry hall in the Henry Robinson house, Pasadena, 1906–1907. (Photo, Documents Collection, College of Environmental Design, University of California, Berkeley.)

Figure 5 Library table, designed by Charles Sumner Greene and Henry Mather Greene for the Henry Robinson house, Pasadena, 1906–1907. (Private collection; photo, Marvin Rand.)

wrote in 1907: "The architect must be at the head in all attempts to bring his work and that of craftsmen closer together. All such attempts should begin on the working basis of the cooperation of an architect's office with a practical (but not visionary) craftsman's shop." Millwork shops, rather than small cabinetmaking shops, were ideally pliant and efficient manufacturers who would suppress their own aesthetics.[5]

For the Greenes 1906 proved to be a pivotal year. Whereas in some commissions, such as the Caroline DeForest house and the Josephine van Rossem house, the Greenes retained many of the same craftsman woodworking conventions, some of the furniture they designed for the Henry Robinson house in the last half of 1906 reflected a new direction. Echoing the constructional and aesthetic conventions of the Tichenor and Reeve work were the oak and cedar woods and pinned through-tenon construction of the entry-hall shoe bench (fig. 4); the Voysey-inspired shape, stretcher with wedged through-tenons, and inlaid splines of the library table (fig. 5); and the pinned- and wedged through-tenons of the birch hall table (fig. 6). But the furniture and fittings of the dining room (figs. 7, 8) and part of the living room (fig. 9) were dramatically different in form, materials, and technique. The designs were based on historical examples such as Chinese chairs of the Ming period, neoclassical sideboards, and leafed pedestal tables. This historical grace was underlined

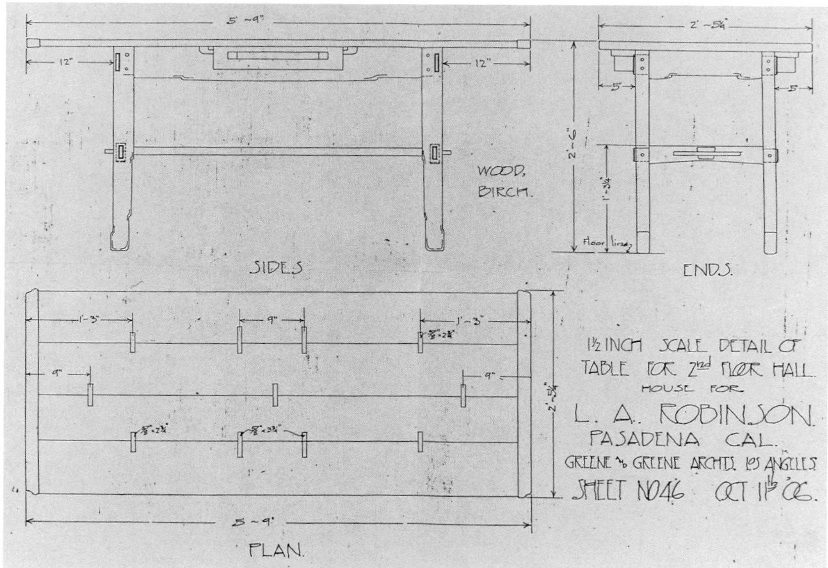

Figure 6 Drawing of a hall table in the Henry Robinson house, Pasadena, 1906–1907. (Photo, Drawings and Archives, Avery Architectural & Fine Arts Library, Columbia University.)

Figure 7 Dining-room furniture, designed by Charles Sumner Greene and Henry Mather Greene and made by the Hall shop for the Henry Robinson house, Pasadena, 1906–1907 (in recreated setting). Mahogany. (Huntington Library, Art Collections, and Botanical Gardens; photo, Marvin Rand.)

Figure 8 Sideboard, designed by Charles Sumner Greene and Henry Mather Greene and made by the Hall shop for the Henry Robinson house, Pasadena, 1906–1907. Mahogany. (Huntington Library, Art Collections, and Botanical Gardens; photo, Marvin Rand.)

Figure 9 Desk, designed by Charles Sumner Greene and Henry Mather Greene and made by the Hall shop for the Henry Robinson house, Pasadena, 1906–1907. Mahogany. (Huntington Library, Art Collections, and Botanical Gardens; photo, Marvin Rand.)

by thin-dimensioned verticals and softened, modeled edges. This furniture was executed in mahogany, a material preferred by cabinetmakers for its good weight-strength ratio, few imperfections, consistent grain structure, workability, and capacity to take an even finish. The joinery in this furniture also betrays the Greenes' more technically sophisticated approach: the dining-room armchairs feature splined miter joints at the juncture of the arms and front posts; the living-room desk features a carcass assembled with miter joints and well-fit doors and drawers; the weight boxes in the dining-room chandelier feature finger joints; and all the furniture has rounded edges and smooth surfaces with no visible tool marks. The base of this technical system was accomplished cabinetmaking rather than self-conscious "craftsmanship."[6]

Many scholars have attributed the change in approach so evident in the Robinson dining and living rooms to the continued developments and refinements of the Greenes' own vision. Evolving aesthetics, however, do not account for the extent of changes. The Robinson furniture embodies a whole new approach to furniture. It is different from the inside out, from the structure of the design, to the technical means to carry out the design, to the final appearance. Such a dramatic change raises the question: What caused the new direction? The answer can be found more on the shop floor than on the drawing board: the Robinson house was the first new construction on which the Greenes worked with Pasadena contractor Peter Hall (1867–1939) and his brother John Hall (1864–1940).

John and Peter Hall had been born in Stockholm, Sweden, but had immigrated to Illinois by 1872. Peter moved to Pasadena in 1886 and gained a reputation as a master stairbuilder. He worked in Seattle, Washington, and Port Townsend, Oregon, from 1889 through 1891, then returned to Pasadena and worked for the millwork firm known as Pasadena Manufacturing Company. John also worked for this firm in the 1890s. Although Peter left the company in 1900 and set up his own contracting firm in 1902, John remained in the employ of the company. With a reputation for fine workmanship, John became a foreman in 1899 and remained so into 1906.[7]

The Greenes had initially worked with Peter Hall on the renovations to the Todd Ford house in 1905 and must have been impressed with his expertise and ability to work according to their designs. With the confidence of the Greenes ensuring business, Hall took out a building permit to erect a one-story carpentry shop on South Raymond Avenue on June 15, 1906, just as construction on the Robinson house began. In the next month, they also began work on the William Bolton house. Although construction of the houses commenced in the summer of 1906, the furniture came later. Traditionally scholars have dated the Robinson furniture at 1906, but three pieces of circumstantial evidence suggest that it was built in 1907. First, John Hall was still listed as a foreman at the Pasadena Manufacturing Company in the Pasadena Directory of 1906, compiled in the summer and published in September of that year. Second, drawings for the Robinson hall table, which preceded actual production, were dated October 1906. Finally, according to oral history Peter Hall did not expand the space, machinery, and personnel of his shop until 1907. Simultaneous production of architectural fittings—doors, sashes, paneling, and trim—and furniture would have necessitated these additions.[8]

The furniture for the Robinson and Bolton houses embodies a distinctive wood system characterized by millwork preparation and joinery and handwork fitting, decorating, and finishing. Furniture made for the David Gamble house and the Robert Blacker house suggests that this system was further refined in 1908 and 1909. Close analysis of several pieces of furniture reveals the details of the woodworking system.[9]

The chiffonier for the Gamble master bedroom (fig. 10) features carcass joinery typical of the Halls' work.[10] The Halls cut, shaped, scraped, and sanded the rails, stiles, and panels first; then cut the joints and assembled

Figure 10 Chiffonier, designed by Charles Sumner Greene and Henry Mather Greene and made by the Hall shop for the master bedroom of the David Gamble house, Pasadena, 1908–1909. Mahogany, ebony, and oak; fruitwood inlay. (The Gamble House; photo, Marvin Rand.)

the components. In the process of assembly they did not fit intersecting parts in the same flush plane but used the offset joints to provide surface variety. Although they did not use the time-consuming practice of paring the joints to be flush, they did take the time to cope or house many of the joints. The decorative treatment of the chiffonier also reflects where they focused labor-intensive work: softly modeled drawer pulls, smoothed square ebony plugs for decorative rhythm, and the asymmetrical inlay and sword-guard appliqué inspired by Japanese design. These details provided the visual link between the various other furniture forms of the room.

The drawer construction of the chiffonier (fig. 11) is particularly noteworthy. The front corners are joined with finger joints that the Halls cut with a table saw or multiple dado cutters. After cutting the fingers the craftsman smoothed the edges and end grain and then screwed the parts together with countersunk screws that were concealed by modeled ebony plugs. The backs of these drawers were simply butted against the inside surface of the drawer sides and screwed in place. An ebony cover strip with a dovetailed joint at the corner was screwed to the top of the drawer linings, and even this detail was produced with machinery. One large ebony board had a dovetail key cut with a shaper, whereas another had a dovetail pin cut with a matching shaper blade. The craftsman then used a table saw to saw off several different thin strips. For the bottoms of these drawers, plywood was floated in machine-cut grooves along the inside of the drawer front and sides. These boards were screwed to the underside of the drawer back. An oak center strip was screwed to the underside of the drawer and slid within a matching rabbeted strip along the upper surface of the full-depth dust panels. This center guide ensured the proper action of the drawer even if the opening was oversize or the drawer out of square.

Figure 11 Detail of drawer construction of the chiffonier in fig. 10. (Photo, Marvin Rand.)

Figure 12 Dressing table, designed by Charles Sumner Greene and Henry Mather Greene and made by the Hall shop for the guest room of the David Gamble house, Pasadena, 1908–1909. Maple, ebony, and oak; silver and ivory inlay. (The Gamble House; photo, Marvin Rand.)

The dressing table in the guest room of the Gamble house reveals a second type of drawer construction used by the Hall shop (figs. 12, 13). The drawer fronts are secured to the sides with blind tongue and groove joints that were easily and tightly cut on a table saw or a shaper.

The drawer construction seen on these two pieces of Gamble house furniture is unparalleled in American furniture and is more typical of Scandinavian modern work.[11] And the expedient preparation and joinery on

Figure 13 Detail of drawer construction of the table in fig. 12. (Photo, Marvin Rand.)

Figure 14 Armchair, designed by Charles Sumner Greene and Henry Mather Greene and made by the Hall shop for the Robert Blacker house, Pasadena, 1908–1909. Mahogany, ebony; fruitwood, silver, and copper inlay. (Los Angeles County Museum of Art, gift of Max Palevsky, acc. M.89.151.4.)

each contrasts with the time-consuming inlay, detailing, scraping, sanding, and finishing.

Close analysis and X rays of several objects from the Blacker house also provide valuable information about the Hall shop. On the living-room armchair (fig. 14), X rays of the joints where the splat is attached to the rear seat rail (fig. 15) and to the crest rail (fig. 16) reveal that the mortises were chopped out very roughly before the splat was finished. Once finished, the splat then served as a pattern to scribe tight fitting, housed mor-

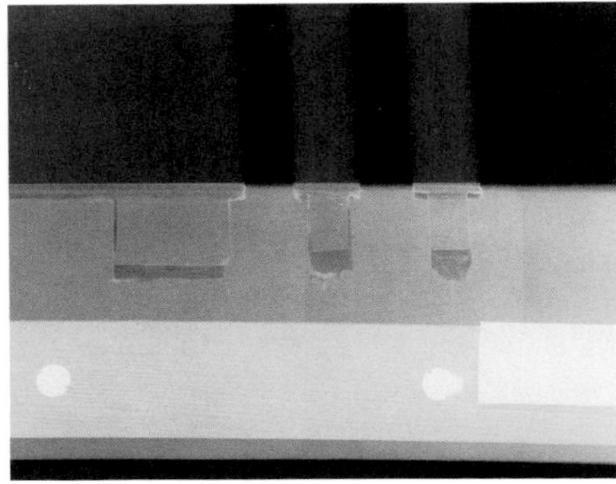

Figure 15 Photograph of X ray of detail where the splat is joined to the rear seat rail of the chair in fig. 14. (Photo, Los Angeles County Museum of Art.)

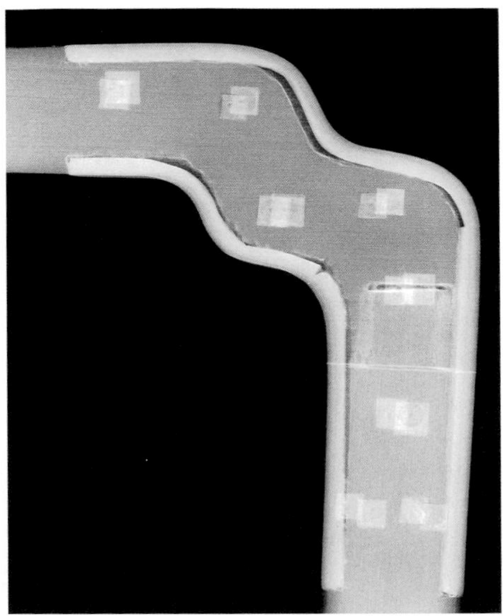

Figure 17 Photograph of X ray of detail where the arm is secured to the front post of the chair in fig. 14. (Photo, Los Angeles County Museum of Art.)

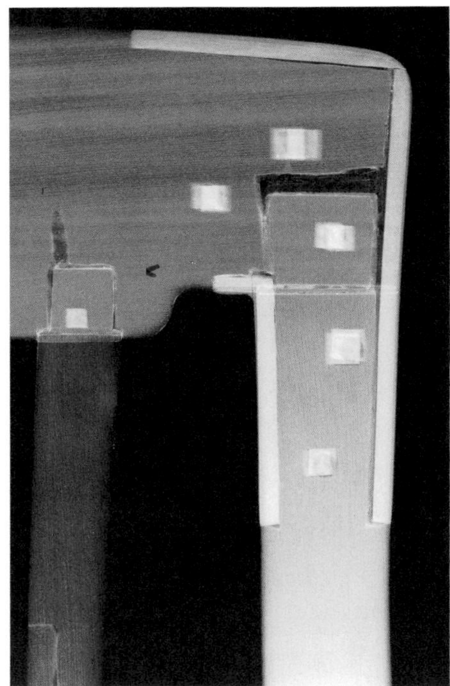

Figure 16 Photograph of X ray of detail where the splat is joined to the crest rail of the chair in fig. 14. (Photo, Los Angeles County Museum of Art.)

Figure 18 Bench, designed by Charles Sumner Greene and Henry Mather Greene and made by the Hall shop for the Robert Blacker house, Pasadena, 1908–1909. Mahogany, ebony, oak. (Museum of Fine Arts, Boston, Harriet Otis Cruft Fund, acc. 1982.407.)

Figure 19 Photograph of X ray of detail where the batten is secured to the top board of the bench in fig. 18. View is from above the seating surface. (X ray by Museum of Fine Arts, Boston; photo, Edward S. Cooke.)

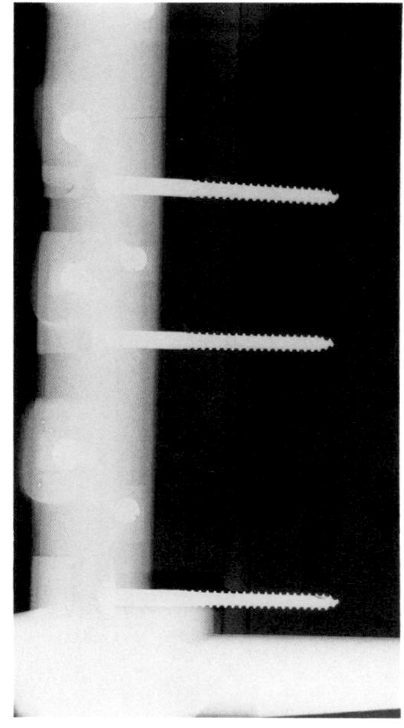

tises in the seat and crest rails. The same approach characterizes the joints that secure the crest rail to the rear post rail (fig. 16) and the arm to the front post (fig. 17). In the former the mortise in the crest rail is overcut but presumably has tight-fitting cheeks since there is no evidence of a pin or screw securing the joint. The groove for the ebony beading ensured this tight fit; an X ray indicates that the maker chopped from the groove into the mortise, the thickness of the former determining that of the latter. The rough depth and undercut ends of the groove also demonstrate how the maker worked expediently yet accomplished a finished look. The beading fits tightly, adds some strength to the joint, and provides a contrasting detail to detract one's eye from the joint line. Along the front-arm joint a tight-cheeked tenon is glued into a deeply cut mortise with width determined by the groove, applied decorative ebony plugs are set into holes that had been pilot-drilled and squared off with a chisel, and an ebony beading is pieced and bent along a groove extending beyond the joint, all further demonstrations of the same conventions.

The top of a bench (fig. 18) also demonstrates how the Halls constructed the tops of their case furniture and tables to prevent warping and to allow for the movement of the wood. A wide mahogany surface had a tongue cut on each end that fit into a groove cut along the inside of a batten. Two screws through the end of the batten into the wide board secured the middle of the board, but two screws placed near the outside edges of the batten were fit with slotted washers in oversized mortises (fig. 19). Ebony plugs conceal all four countersunk screws on each batten.

Figure 20 Detail of underside of the bench in fig. 18. (Photo, Museum of Fine Arts, Boston.)

Figure 21 Photograph of X ray of detail where the knee bracket and rail are secured to the front leg of the bench in fig. 18. (X ray by Museum of Fine Arts, Boston; photo, Edward S. Cooke.)

Figure 22 Cabinet, designed and made by Gottlob Karl Lapple, Pasadena, 1915–1930. Oak, ebony, and yellow poplar. (Private collection; photo, Edward S. Cooke.)

Figure 23 Detail of drawer from the cabinet in fig. 22. (Photo, Edward S. Cooke.)

The batten was then housed over the top of the frame and secured with ebony-covered, countersunk screws. The slotted washers allowed the large board to expand and contract as humidity changed. The Halls also made allowance for across-the-grain wood movement by using metal buttons with slotted holes to secure the top board to the frame (fig. 20). X rays of the joints where the frame was secured to the legs also reveal that they employed housed mortises. The maker secured the brackets to the rail with screws and chopped deep mortises in the legs, an approach presumably dictated by the sequence of assembly (fig. 21).

Such a concern with machine production, wood expansion, and modeled surfaces is not typical of American work in the 1900–1910 era and is often associated with Scandinavian furniture produced in the early twentieth century. The Scandinavian basis of this woodworking tradition is given additional credence by examination of the woodworkers in the Hall shop (see appendix). The majority of the skilled positions were held by Scandinavians. Some had immigrated in the 1890s, but two, David Swanson and Bror Krohn, the men responsible for the Gamble house bedroom and guest-room suites, had arrived more recently. Fellow Swedes Erik Peterson and George Nelson were the premier chairmakers who produced prototypes that others in the Hall shop then copied. The identification of a specific Scandinavian approach is also born out by Swanson's reference to the blind tongue-and-groove drawer joint as a "Swedish joint."[12]

The dominance of the Scandinavian system is apparent in furniture produced by Gottlob Karl Lapple, a German-trained craftsman who worked for Hall from 1908 until about 1913. In furniture he made for his own family (fig. 22), Lapple employed modeled drawer pulls, softened edges, and square plugs of ebony to conceal screwed construction, but he relied on a different drawer system. He dovetailed the corners and let the solid bottoms into rabbets cut along the bottom edges of the drawer fronts and sides, securing them with strips that he screwed in from the sides (fig. 23). (Although trained in the dovetailed tradition and reliant on it when working on his own, Lapple never used it in the Hall shop. None of the Halls' furniture has dovetailed drawers.)

Between 1907 and 1913, the Halls made about 400 pieces of furniture while working almost exclusively for the Greenes. The furniture for the other "ultimate bungalows" designed by the Greenes—the Charles Pratt house in Ojai and the William Thorsen house in Berkeley (both designed in 1909)—reveal the same woodworking conventions found on the Gamble and Blacker work. The Thorsen furniture is said to have been made by a Scandinavian craftsman from the Hall shop (fig. 24).[13] For the Cordelia Culbertson house in Pasadena (designed in 1911), the Halls built more historic forms (fig. 25) but retained the joinery systems, exquisite inlay, and fine oil finishes of their earlier work.

A simpler form without inlay from this same period was a sideboar made in late 1912 and early 1913 for Charles Sumner Greene himself (fig. 26). Its bill survives and indicates the favored materials and costs involved in a plainer piece of furniture:[14]

Figure 24 Sideboard, designed by Charles Sumner Greene and Henry Mather Greene and made by the Hall shop for the William Thorsen house, Berkeley, California, 1909–1910. Mahogany and ebony; fruitwood and mother-of-pearl inlay. (Huntington Library, Art Collections, and Botanical Gardens; photo, Marvin Rand.)

Figure 25 Dining room in the Cordelia Culbertson house, Pasadena, 1911–1913. Furniture designed by Charles Sumner Greene and Henry Mather Greene and made by the Hall shop. (Photo from original in the Greene and Greene Library, Huntington Library, Art Collections, and Botanical Gardens.)

Figure 26 Sideboard, designed by Charles Sumner Greene and Henry Mather Greene and made by the Hall shop for the Charles Sumner Greene house, Pasadena, 1912–1913. Mahogany and oak. (Private collection; photo, Marvin Rand.)

186¾ hr. @ 50	93.37
128 ft. Mahg. @ 25	32.00
oak	.30
33 ft. 5 ply @ 29	9.57
Hardware	4.07
Plating	1.25
Express	.50
	141.06

Figure 27 Box, Hall Manufacturing Company, Pasadena, 1918–1921. Redwood. (Private collection; photo, Edward S. Cooke.)

The maker used mahogany for the carcass and drawer linings; plywood for the drawer bottoms, carcass back, and bottom; and oak for the center guides of the drawers. Nevertheless the maker's time accounted for two-thirds of the cost of this basic sideboard.

Sometime toward the end of 1913, the furniture business declined. The Halls had worked almost exclusively for the Greenes for seven years and were affected by the sudden decrease in commissions for the architects' integrated bungalows and houses. At this point many key employees left the Halls. Swanson and Anton Erikson moved to the Binderheim Studios, an interior decoration firm that offered individuals complete mural, upholstery, and fine furniture-making services. Its cabinetmaking shop featured "various machines of the latest and best designs"—including a jointer, table saw, thickness planer, and shaper—and a bench room for fine handwork. Sven Carlson went to Crown City Manufacturing, and by 1919 Lapple had joined him.[15] Others may also have left the Halls; however the directories for these years do not consistently specify the places of employment.

John Hall continued making furniture for the Greenes, and in 1917 he was working on a commission for Mrs. Dudley Allen. Charles Sumner Greene had moved to Carmel, California, but his father kept him apprised of business with Hall by mail.[16]

As the furniture business began to decrease, the Halls used their machinery for different purposes. By 1918 their men were using table saws and shapers to mass-produce distinctive redwood boxes—with finger-joint corners, shaper-produced moldings, and smooth finish—for dried fruits (figs. 27, 28). This venture ended in 1921 when a fire destroyed the 200-foot long, one-story frame structure. Among the losses totalling $20,000 were "thousands of boxes in various stages of completion, as well as many thousands of feet of seasoned redwood and valuable machinery."[17]

After the fire the Halls did not rebuild their shop. Peter focused upon his contracting business, building St. Paul's Cathedral in Los Angeles in 1923, St. Alden's Chapel in Westwood, and many homes in the Pasadena and Los Angeles area. John, always in the background, continued to work as a finish carpenter and cabinetmaker in the Pasadena area, often with his brother. The furniture Charles Sumner Greene designed for the Mortimer Fleishhacker house in Woodside (1923) suggests that John Hall con-

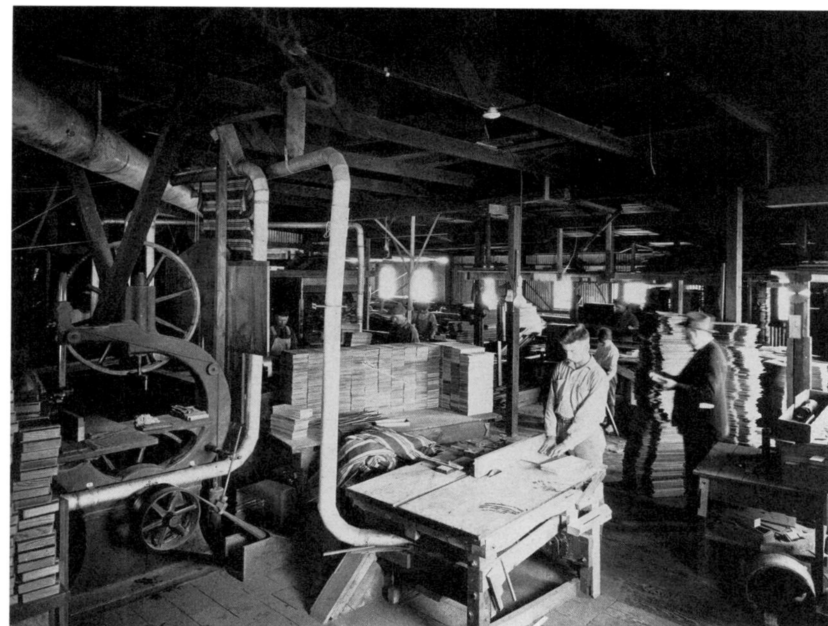

Figure 28 Interior of the Hall Manufacturing Company, Pasadena, 1918–1921. (Photo from original in the Greene and Greene Library, Huntington Library, Art Collections, and Botanical Gardens.)

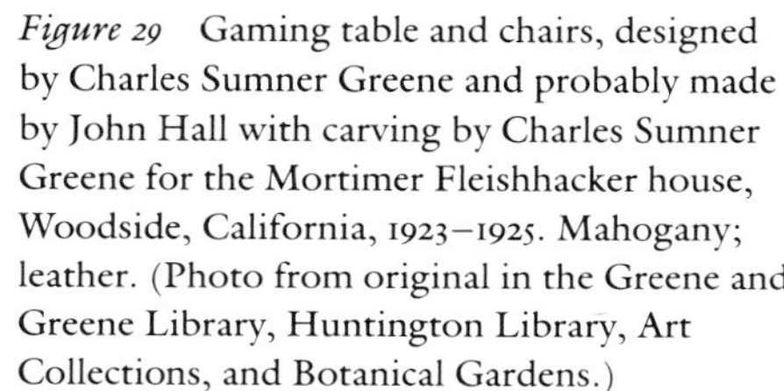

Figure 29 Gaming table and chairs, designed by Charles Sumner Greene and probably made by John Hall with carving by Charles Sumner Greene for the Mortimer Fleishhacker house, Woodside, California, 1923–1925. Mahogany; leather. (Photo from original in the Greene and Greene Library, Huntington Library, Art Collections, and Botanical Gardens.)

tinued to do occasional work for Greene. Although tradition maintains that Greene designed and made this furniture by himself in his own shop, the structural conception and the joinery on the game table and chairs suggest a professional hand and share many features with the Halls' work (fig. 29). It is a bit more simplified than the work of the 1908 to 1913 period but such a change may be due to Hall working without the specialized help of the full shop yet drawing from the approaches and techniques of that period. Greene may have done all the carving, but it is unlikely that he could have built the entire suite by himself.[18]

The Halls' withdrawal from furniture making was completely tied to the collapse of the Greene commissions for interior furnishings. Opportunities for skilled millwork cabinetmakers continued in Pasadena. Swanson and Erikson's firm and its successor, Swanson and Peterson, emerged as one of the specialty firms that catered to the new demands for office and domestic furniture. They offered a broad range of services: "jobbing, manufacturing, contracting and trading in lumber, wood-work, building supplies, cabinet work, store and office fixtures, stairwork, wood-carving, wood-turning, mill and factory work; furniture, office, store and cabinet polishing and finishing; construction and installation of store fronts and interiors; glazing, and all necessary, convenient and connected supplies." Walter Gripton, who took over Pasadena Manufacturing Company in 1916, offered many of the same services.[19]

Examination of the furniture built by the Halls' shop demonstrates how important the craftsmen and specialists were to the final product. The Halls and their employees played an integral role in the development and final appearance of the Greene and Greene style. In terms of American twentieth-century furniture history, the furniture is also important as the first true example of Scandinavian modern furniture design. The fit to the period and the combination of machined production with handworked finish has provided the enduring legacy of the furniture.

ACKNOWLEDGMENTS For assistance in the gathering of information and the analysis of the furniture, I thank the following: Randell Makinson and Ted Bosley of the Gamble House in Pasadena; Tim Gregory and Susan Coffman at Pasadena Historical Society; Doris Gertmenian at Greene and Greene Library; the staff of the Pasadena Public Library; Leslie Bowman and the Conservation Center at the Los Angeles County Museum of Art; Robert Walker, Letitia Stevens, Steve Stvenstrom, Richard Newman, and Kate Duffy at the Museum of Fine Arts, Boston; Brian Kelly of the North Bennett Street School; Lewis and Roy Gray; Kathryn Swanson; Marilyn Zeiss; Hank Gilpin; Cheryl Robertson; Lee Macneil; and Carol Warner.

1. The emphasis on the Greenes' role can be found in Robert Judson Clark, ed., *The Arts and Crafts Movement in America 1876–1916* (Princeton: Princeton University Press, 1972), pp. 83–86; and Randell Makinson, *Greene & Greene: Furniture and Related Designs* (Salt Lake City, Utah: Peregrine Smith, 1979).

2. On these early beginnings, see Makinson, *Greene & Greene Furniture*, pp. 12–19; and Randell Makinson, *Greene & Greene: Architecture as Fine Art* (Salt Lake City, Utah: Peregrine Smith, 1977), pp. 58–81.

3. Makinson, *Greene & Greene Furniture*, pp. 22–33; and Robert Edwards and Stephen Gray, eds., *Collected Works of Gustav Stickley* (New York: Turn of the Century Editions, 1981).

4. *Thurston's Pasadena City Directory* for 1904 and 1906–1907. On Crown City Manufacturing Company and Pasadena Manufacturing Company, see J. W. Wood, *Pasadena: Historical and Personal* (Pasadena: author, 1917), pp. 483–84 and 487.

5. Sharon Darling, *Chicago Furniture: Art, Craft, & Industry, 1833–1983* (New York: Norton, 1984), pp. 197–200; and Elmer Gray, "The Architect and the Arts and Crafts," *Architectural Record* 21, no. 6 (June 1907): 132–33.

6. Makinson, *Greene & Greene Furniture*, pp. 36–43; and personal study of several Robin-

son examples. On the advantages of mahogany, see Bruce Hoadley, *Understanding Wood: A Craftsman's Guide to Wood Technology* (Newton, Conn.: Taunton Press, 1980).

7. Makinson, *Greene & Greene Furniture*, pp. 34–35; Makinson, *Greene & Greene Architecture*, p. 118; recollection of R. Donald Hall, son of Peter Hall, Greene and Greene Library, Huntington Library, Art Collections, and Botanical Gardens in San Marino, Calif.; Pasadena city directories from 1895–1906.

8. *Thurston's Pasadena City Directory* for 1906–1907; Makinson, *Greene & Greene Furniture*, pp. 36, 56.

9. Alan Marks was the first person to closely examine the inner workings of Greene-designed furniture. This present study builds on his pioneering work, yet revises many aspects of it and integrates a variety of documents: "Greene and Greene: A Study in Functional Design," *Fine Woodworking* 12 (September 1978): 40–45. The dating of the Gamble and Blacker furniture is derived from an August 9, 1909, letter from Peter Hall to Charles Sumner Greene. Hall informed Greene, who was then in London, that the Gamble house furniture was "almost completed," the Blacker house furniture "well underway," and the Thorsen house pianos "underway," Gamble House Craftsman file, Greene and Greene Library.

10. Throughout this study I refer to the Halls' work rather than a specific company name since the firm went through several names. *Thurston's Pasadena City Directory* of 1908–1909 simply refers to the firm as Peter Hall. On the plate of an upright piano originally owned by a brother, The Reverend Albert Hall, was cast the name "Hall and Hall." This piano is similar to that made for the Gamble house in 1908 and suggests that, for some time in 1908 or 1909, they referred to themselves as Hall and Hall. In 1911 they incorporated. Peter Hall's granddaughter owns a seal dated 1911 with the name Hall Manufacturing Company, the name that appears in the 1912 city directory. Evidence drawn from city directories, recollections of relatives, and federal census records reveals that within the firm Peter was the head and primarily a contractor, whereas John ran the mill and served as the head cabinetmaker.

11. The form of drawer construction is discussed by Tage Frid, "How to Make Drawers," *Fine Woodworking* 45 (March/April 1984): 32–38. Frid trained in Denmark in the 1920s. On the table-saw joinery of these techniques, see Frid, *Tage Frid Teaches Woodworking—Joinery: Tools and Techniques* (Newtown, Conn.: Taunton Press, 1979), esp. pp. 60–62, 90–91, and 135–36.

12. Conversations with Katherine Swanson, March 1992; and Gamble House Craftsman file, Greene and Greene Library.

13. For an estimate of the total number, see Randell Makinson, *Greene & Greene and the American Arts and Crafts Movement* (San Marino, Calif.: Huntington Library, Art Collections, and Botanical Gardens, 1991), p. 5. On the Thorsen house furniture, see Makinson, *Greene & Greene Architecture*, pp. 174–78; Makinson, *Greene & Greene Furniture*, pp. 88–93; and Clark, *Arts and Crafts*, p. 83.

14. Bill of January 8, 1913, Gamble House Craftsman file, Greene and Greene Library.

15. Pamphlet of the Binderheim Studios, about 1915, privately owned by a descendant of David Swanson; *Thurston's Pasadena City Directory* of 1913–1914; and recollections of Martha Gray, daughter of Gottlob Karl Lapple, Gamble House Craftsman file, Greene and Green Library.

16. Charles Sumner Greene to his father, June 27, 1917, and September 17, 1917, Gamble House Craftsman file, Greene and Greene Library.

17. *Thurston's Pasadena City Directory* of 1919–1920; newspaper clippings, Gamble House Craftsman file, Greene and Greene Library. There was no mention of furniture making in the newspaper articles about the fire. According to descendants of Peter Hall and David Swanson, some large mahogany boards were saved from the fire but eight upright pianos made a decade or so earlier were lost.

18. Recollections of R. Donald Hall; and Makinson, *Greene & Greene Furniture*, pp. 126–27.

19. 1922 Articles of Co-partnership between David Swanson and Erik Peterson, privately owned by a descendant of David Swanson. On Gripton, see Makinson, *Greene & Greene Furniture*, p. 52; and *Pasadena and Pasadenans* (Pasadena: Hopkins-Smith, 1924), p. 38.

Appendix

Personnel for Hall and Hall

John T. Ball (1867–1943). Michigan-born Ball was listed as a benchman for the Pasadena Manufacturing Company in 1907 and a cabinetmaker for Peter Hall beginning in 1908, remaining with Hall and his brother until 1913–1914. He is listed without a company in directories from 1914 through 1918. In 1919 he was listed as a cabinetmaker for the Crown City Manufacturing Company. *Sources:* Pasadena City Directories; 1910 Federal Population Census, volume 54, enumeration district 305, family number 108; and *Pasadena Star News*, December 6, 1943.

Ralph Beal. Beal is identified as an apprentice for Peter Hall in the 1908–1909 Directory and as a cabinetmaker for Hall in the 1911 Directory and for Hall Manufacturing Company in the 1913–1914 Directory. Thereafter he was listed simply as a cabinetmaker or carpenter. A search through federal census records provided no additional information. *Sources:* Pasadena City Directories.

Frank Boynton (1861–?). Born in Maine or Vermont, Boynton had been listed in directories as an independent cabinetmaker/carpenter before 1908–1909, when he is identified as a cabinetmaker with Peter Hall. According to oral history, he worked on the Gamble house furniture in 1908. After 1909, he was not specifically associated with any firm but maintained a reputation as an inveterate woodworker. *Sources:* Pasadena City Directories; Gamble House Craftsman file (Greene and Greene Library); *Pasadena Star News*, September 25, 1916; and 1910 Federal Population Census, volume 53, enumeration district 285, family 238.

Sven Carlson (1872–1949). A Swede who arrived in 1889, Carlson worked as a cabinetmaker for James Baker in 1906 and 1907–1908. In the 1908–1909 Directory he was listed as a cabinetmaker for Peter Hall; in the 1913–1914 Directory and thereafter he was listed as a foreman for Crown City Manufacturing Company. *Sources:* Pasadena City Directories; 1910 Federal Population Census, volume 55, enumeration district 297, family 393; and *Pasadena Star News*, May 13, 1949.

William E. Coolbaugh (1879–?). Massachusetts-born Coolbaugh worked as a cabinetmaker for Ye Arts and Crafts Company in 1904, for Crown City Manufacturing in 1906, and for Peter Hall in 1911. In 1920 he was identified as a draftsman for an unspecified manufacturing company. *Sources:* Pasadena City Directories; and 1920 Federal Population Census, volume 37, enumeration district 116, sheet 8, line 36.

Anton Erikson. According to oral history, this Swedish-trained craftsman worked on the Gamble house furniture. He does not appear in Pasadena Directories until 1914–1915 when he worked as a cabinetmaker for Binderheim Studios with David Swanson. Two years later he is identified as a pattern maker, which suggests he had some carving skills. He worked as a cabinetmaker for W. H. Smith in 1919 and became a partner in Swanson, Erikson, and Company in 1920, later named Swanson and Peterson. *Sources:* Gamble House Craftsman file (Greene and Greene Library); Pasadena City Directories.

John Hall (1864–1940). Born in Stockholm, Hall and his parents had immigrated to Illinois by 1872. Less is known about John than about his brother, but he did work in Port Townsend, Oregon, between 1889 and 1892. He returned to Pasadena in 1892 and began to work at Pasadena Manufacturing Company, first as a carpenter, then as a foreman. He joined Peter Hall at the end of 1906 and ran the mill. In the census schedules he always was listed as a cabinetmaker. *Sources:* Randell Makinson, *Greene & Greene: Furniture and Related Designs* (Salt Lake City, Utah: Peregrine Smith, 1979); Makinson, *Greene & Greene: Architecture as Fine Art* (Salt Lake City, Utah: Peregrine Smith, 1977); Gamble House Craftsman file (Greene and Greene Library); Pasadena City Directories; 1910 Federal Population Census, volume 54, enumeration district 301, family 194; and 1920 Federal Population Census, volume 62, enumeration district 518, sheet 7, line 92.

Peter Hall (1867–1939). Like his brother John, Peter Hall was born in Sweden and had moved to Illinois by 1872. He worked as a carpenter and stair builder in Pasadena, Seattle, and Port Townsend before returning to Pasadena in 1892 to work on Thaddeus Lowe's mansion. He worked for Pasadena Manufacturing Company until 1900 when he started work on his own, of which he was president when the firm incorporated in 1911. He seems to have been involved more with the construction of the houses rather than with furniture. In the federal census records he is listed as a carpenter or contractor. *Sources:* Makinson, *Greene & Greene Furniture*; Makinson, *Greene & Greene Architecture*; Pasadena City Directories; 1910 Federal Population Census, volume 54, enumeration district 308, family 24; and 1920 Federal Population Census, volume 62, enumeration district 517, sheet 1, line 53.

Frank Holtz. Holtz was a benchhand for the Pasadena Manufacturing Company in 1906 and a cabinetmaker for Peter Hall in 1911. Whether Holtz is the same Frank Holtz from Wisconsin listed as a farmer in Pasadena in the 1910 census is unclear. *Sources:* Pasadena City Directories; 1910 Federal Population Census, volume 57, enumeration district 342, family 13.

George F. Jackson. Jackson was listed as cabinetmaker for Peter Hall in 1911. Little else is known about him. There was a George F. Jackson, age 45, listed in the 1910 census, but he was a farmer from an English colony in Africa. *Sources:* Pasadena City Directories; 1910 Federal Population Census, volume 54, enumeration district 308, family 175.

Horsen G. Kelsey. Horsen G. Kelsey was listed as a benchman for Peter Hall in the Directory of 1908–1909. One Horsen Briar Kelsey was listed as a cabinetmaker in the Directory of 1909–1910 and one Horace S. Kelsey as a carpenter in the Directory of 1911. They are probably all the same person, but nothing else is known about him. *Sources:* Pasadena City Directories.

Bror F. G. Krohn (1878–1963). A Swede who became a naturalized American citizen in 1900, Krohn reportedly worked on the Gamble house furniture. He was listed in the city directories starting in 1909–1910, but not with any firms. In 1929 he is finally identified as a foreman for Crown City Manufacturing Company. The records refer to him as Bror F. G. Krohn, but he was known to others in the shop as Fred Krohn. *Sources:* Pasadena City Directories; 1910 Federal Population Census, volume 55, enumeration district 297, family 384.

Gottlob Karl Lapple (1877–1948). Born in Wiltonburg, Germany, Lapple immigrated to Pasadena in 1908. He worked as a cabinetmaker right from the start. Oral history maintains that he worked on the Gamble house. He is listed as a cabinetmaker for Peter Hall in the Directory of 1911 and for Crown City Manufacturing beginning in 1920. Later he worked for Swanson and Peterson, for Serendipity Antique Shop, and for H. A.

Jesson. *Sources:* Pasadena City Directories; Gamble House Craftsman file (Greene and Greene Library); and 1920 Federal Population Census, volume 61, enumeration district 509, sheet 8, line 99.

John Lundquist (1870–?). Trained in Sweden, Lundquist arrived in America in 1891. He was listed as a benchman for Peter Hall in 1908–1909. *Sources:* Pasadena City Directories; 1910 Federal Population Census, volume 55, enumeration district 297, family 128.

George Nelson (1879–1959). Trained in Sweden, Nelson arrived in America in 1896. According to oral history he worked on the Gamble house and was regarded as the best chairmaker in the Hall shop. In the city directories, he was listed with no shop affiliation until the mid-1920s, at which point he was working with Swanson and Peterson. *Sources:* Gamble House Craftsman file (Greene and Greene Library); Pasadena City Directories; 1920 Federal Population Census, volume 61, enumeration district 499, sheet 2, line 38.

Erik Peterson (?–1970). Trained in Sweden, Peterson made some of the furniture for the Gamble house according to oral history. He was listed as cabinetmaker without a specific firm in the city directories beginning in 1913. *Sources:* Gamble House Craftsman file (Greene and Greene Library); Pasadena City Directories; *Pasadena Star News*, April 27, 1970.

David Swanson (1888–1969). After training in Sweden, Germany, and Denmark, Swanson emigrated in 1907 to escape military service. He was in Pasadena in 1908 and made furniture for the Gamble house according to oral history. He was proudest of his work on the furniture in the Gamble master bedroom and guest room on which he worked with Fred Krohn. He first appears in the city directory in 1913 as a cabinetmaker for Binderheim Studios. In 1920 he was a founding partner of Swanson, Erikson, and Company, which became Swanson and Peterson in 1922. *Sources:* Gamble House Craftsman file (Greene and Greene Library); conversations with Kathryn Swanson, daughter-in-law of David Swanson; 1920 Federal Population Census, volume 61, enumeration district 508, sheet 5, line 44; Pasadena City Directories; *Pasadena Star News*, August 30, 1970.

Henry Warne (1848–191?). Born in Ohio, Warne was listed as cabinetmaker for Peter Hall in the Directory of 1908–1909. His name appears in the 1910 census, but he is not listed in the directories after 1909. *Sources:* Pasadena City Directories; 1910 Federal Population Census, volume 55, enumeration district 310, family 30.

Nancy Goyne Evans

Design Transmission in Vernacular Seating Furniture: The Influence of Philadelphia and Baltimore Styles on Chairmaking from the Chesapeake Bay to the "West"

▼ THE MOVEMENT of individuals, products, and ideas from one region to another is a factor in studying vernacular furniture, particularly Windsor chairs made between the 1780s and 1860s. For example, the student of vernacular seating can observe Philadelphia influence on Windsor chairmaking in Boston, New York dominance of styles produced along the Long Island Sound, stylistic exchanges across the Connecticut–Rhode Island border, and New England and New York contributions to chair production in eastern Canada. The purpose of the present study is to explore the impact of Philadelphia and Baltimore vernacular design on chairmaking in still other regions: rural Pennsylvania and Maryland; Virginia, from the tidewater to the Shenandoah; and "the West," the vast territory beyond the Appalachians settled in the late eighteenth and early nineteenth centuries.

Following the American revolution, the coastal South became a lucrative market for products of the Philadelphia Windsor chairmaking community. A key area of distribution was the lower Chesapeake Bay where a vast network of waterways and a system of inland roads provided access to the interior. Several Philadelphia craftsmen eventually relocated to the bay area. Ephraim Evans moved to Alexandria in 1785, and Michael Murphy was a temporary resident of Norfolk in 1800 and 1804. Communication between Philadelphia and the interior parts of Pennsylvania was also substantial, despite roads that became quagmires in spring and dust bowls in summer. During a journey along the Great Wagon Road connecting Philadelphia with Lancaster and points beyond, Isaac Weld, a British traveler in America during the mid-1790s, commented, "It is scarcely possible to go one mile on this road without meeting numbers of waggons passing and repassing between the back parts of the state and Philadelphia." He noted further that Philadelphia traded "as far as Pittsburgh itself, which is on the Ohio, with the back of Virginia, and, strange to tell, with Kentucky, seven hundred miles distant." Weld, like other travelers before and after him, observed the prevalence of German settlers in rural Pennsylvania, especially in the vicinity of Lancaster and York. Their settlements continued southwest into Frederick County, Maryland, and to Winchester, Virginia, which served as the gateway for thousands of Germans to the fertile valley of the Shenandoah on the western side of the Blue Ridge Mountains.[1]

Germans and Scots-Irish occupied the valley of Virginia long before the Revolution, and new migrations of Germans took place after the war.

The Blue Ridge range virtually isolated the valley from eastern Virginia, but at the northern end trade with central Pennsylvania and Maryland was brisk. The southern outlet provided access to the Moravian settlements in central North Carolina and a route to the "western" lands for those who chose to move on to the new settlements in Kentucky and Tennessee.

Visiting Baltimore while a temporary resident in America during the 1790s, Englishman John Harriott observed that the community had experienced "the most rapid growth of any town in America." Depending upon the commentator, the flourishing city was denominated the third or fourth "commercial city" in the country by 1800, after Philadelphia, New York, and possibly Boston. In the decade between 1790 and 1800, the population of Baltimore almost doubled to more than 26,000. By 1810 the number had further risen by 87 percent. Baltimore already rivaled Philadelphia as a supplier of merchandise to the interior. Its merchants monopolized most trade within Maryland, realized a share of Virginia's commerce, competed with Philadelphia in filling the needs of the Pennsylvania back country, and furnished large amounts of goods for distribution in the western territories. In return, the business community received produce, primarily flour, for exportation.[2]

Before the Revolutionary War, the American frontier comprised all the lands beyond the Appalachian Mountains. Conditions changed rapidly in the postwar years. Kentucky and Tennessee were admitted to the Union in 1792 and 1796, respectively; Ohio followed in 1803, and Indiana in 1816. For purposes of the present study these four bodies politic constitute the "West." Preceding, accompanying, or following the settlers, whose principal focus was agriculture, were businessmen and administrators—land agents, merchants, government officials and military personnel, and lawyers. The Northwest Ordinance of 1787 established a government for the newly developing territory; the Treaty of Greenville (1795) helped to allay fears of Indian attacks. Whereas the West had a population of 150,000 by 1795, that figure exceeded 2.2 million by 1820.[3]

Settlers arrived in the West primarily by one of four principal routes: from southwestern Virginia overland through mountain passes and along rivers to Kentucky and Tennessee; across Pennsylvania on the Pennsylvania Road to Pittsburgh (on the Monongahela); through Maryland on the Cumberland Pike to Pittsburgh or to Wheeling (on the Ohio); and across upstate New York to the Great Lakes and on to northern Ohio. When traveling west by the Pennsylvania route in 1810, Connecticut native Margaret Van Horn Dwight, niece of the president of Yale College, believed that "the State of Ohio will be well fill'd before winter, Waggons without number every day go on." Morris Birkbeck, an English gentleman farmer who settled in Illinois, was more emphatic a few years later in 1817: "Old America seems to be breaking up, and moving westward." His contemporary, British traveler John Bristed, explained the phenomenon: "The Americans are unquestionably the most locomotive, migrating people in the world. Even when doing well in the northern, or middle, or southern states, they will break up their establishment, and move westward with an alacrity and vigor that nothing but the necessity of adverse circumstances could induce in any other population." The dangling carrot was, of course, the opportunity to acquire land at a low price.[4]

Both Birkbeck and Bristed assessed the magnitude of the eastern trade to the West, although their figures vary. The number of freight wagons traversing the 300 miles between Philadelphia or Baltimore in the East and Pittsburgh at the gateway to the West was between 12,000 and 20,000 annually. The average burden of a wagon was 35 to 40 hundred weight. Birkbeck noted the cost of carriage was about $7 per hundred weight. Bristed suggested that freight charges exceeded $2,000,000 annually, but the figure may well have reached $5,600,000, as calculated using the high figures. Business expanded as new modes of transportation were introduced and old land routes improved: turnpike roads were built; the Erie Canal, which opened in segments across New York state to Lake Erie (and beyond through connector canals), was completed in 1825; and steam transport was inaugurated on the eastern and western waters in the 1800s and 1810s.[5]

Figure 1 Bow-back Windsor side chair, William Cox, Philadelphia, 1788–1795. Yellow poplar (seat) with maple, oak, and hickory. H. 36⅞", W. (seat) 17⅜", D. (seat) 15⅞". (Courtesy, Winterthur Museum, acc. 69.232.6.)

Eighteenth-Century Design

The principal vernacular chair throughout America in the 1790s was the bow-back Windsor side chair (fig. 1). Philadelphia, where the pattern was introduced in the mid-1780s, was the leading producer. The new round back was accompanied by turnings simulating the appearance of bamboo. Appropriately, one of the popular finishes during the 1790s was "straw"-colored paint, frequently accompanied by "penciled" striping of contrasting color in the bamboo grooves. Other painted lines accented the beads of the convex bow face and the groove delineating the flat spindle platform at the back of the seat. During the 1790s bow-back Windsor side chairs were the first choice for dining furniture, as indicated by frequent references to "Dining Windsor chairs," or simply "dining chairs," in household inventories throughout the East. The popularity of Windsor side chairs for this purpose continued through successive patterns until the mid-nineteenth century.

William Cox, whose brand is stamped under the seat of figure 1, had arrived in Philadelphia in the 1760s, probably from neighboring Delaware, and likely trained or completed his training with a city craftsman. He had set up in business for himself by March 8, 1768, when he took on an apprentice—William Widdifield, a poor boy, who later had a successful chairmaking business of his own in the city. Throughout his long career (d. 1811), Cox enjoyed the patronage of a number of prominent individuals, including Gen. John Cadwalader, Gen. Henry Knox, and merchant Stephen Girard. Cox furnished dozens of Windsors for Girard's extensive export business along the coast and in the Caribbean. The chairmaker delivered one group of "24 straw colour'd chairs" priced at 10*s*. apiece to Girard in March 1791. Four months later he supplied the merchant with a dozen "Green Dineing Chairs" and six companion "armd Windsor Chairs," the charges per chair calculated at 9*s*. and 15*s*., respectively.

Figure 2 Bow-back Windsor side chair, northern Maryland, from the Susquehanna River to Frederick Co., 1800–1810. Yellow poplar (seat) with maple and oak. H. 35 1/16″, W. (seat) 15 15/16″, D. (seat) 16″. (Private collection; photo, courtesy, Winterthur Museum.)

Cox also shipped chairs independently to coastal destinations, including Fredericksburg and Petersburg, Virginia, communities accessible via the Chesapeake Bay and its tributaries.[6]

The bow-back side chair of figure 2, with its lightly waisted back, is a basic copy of Cox's chair. The embellishments are evidence it originated outside the city. The outstanding feature is the decorated bow with its deeply channeled wigglework, which appears to be contemporary with the chair. (An almost identical undulating border ornaments the seat of a bow-back rocking chair from Frederick County, Maryland. The maker of that chair gouged the wavy channel into the spindle platform and around the front posts, bow ends, and spindles.) The arrow-like ornament in the center spindle is comparable to motifs on fancy Baltimore seating, although the feature sometimes appears in documented early-nineteenth-

Figure 3 Bow-back Windsor side chair, Michael Stoner, probably Harrisburg, Pa., 1790–1795. Yellow poplar (seat) with maple. H. 37″, W. (seat) 19⅜″, D. (seat) 15½″. (Private collection; photo, courtesy, Winterthur Museum.)

century Philadelphia Windsors. Several other elements in figure 2 relate to Philadelphia work. The modeled seat is a slightly later version of the plank seat in Cox's chair: the front pommel has been eliminated and the front and side edges are rounded. The medial stretcher turnings are fuller. Aside from the decorative wigglework, only the full-swelled side braces indicate that the chair has a rural origin.

A different focus is manifest in the work of rural Pennsylvania craftsmen of German descent. Their highly mannered chairs would hardly be mistaken for metropolitan products (fig. 3). The backs are broad and flat, however the nipped waist is retained. Although the depth of the seat is no greater than that in the Philadelphia chair, an awkward profile results from the extreme breadth of the seat, which produces a modified back curve. The pinched configuration of the spindles at the seat platform accentuates the awkward curve. The support structure also sets Pennsylvania German Windsors apart from all others. A dual leg system—bulb-tipped front feet and tapered back supports—appears nowhere else in eighteenth-century work. The Pennsylvania German Windsor is basically a turner's chair. The craftsman lavished skill on the roundwork rather than on the unity or proportions of the design.

Figure 3 is one of only a few Pennsylvania German Windsors identified by a maker's brand. Michael Stoner (Steiner; d. 1810) was probably working in Harrisburg when he constructed the chair in the early 1790s. Within a few years he had removed to Lancaster and modified his design by adopting a more regular spindle placement, comparable to that in Philadelphia Windsors (see fig. 1). Stoner, like many chairmaker-turners of his day, was also a cabinetmaker.[7]

Figure 4 Bow-back Windsor side chair, Frederick Co., Md., 1800–1815. Woods and dimensions not recorded. (Photo, courtesy, H. L. Chalfant Antiques.)

Figure 4 is a chair of broad seat, the oval bottom a Pennsylvania German alternative to Stoner's shield-type seat. The oval plank is a full 1½″ wider and 1¼″ shallower than that in Stoner's Windsor. The proportions in the upper structure are even more exaggerated than those in the typical Pennsylvania German chair (see fig. 3). This rural craftsman's choice of an exceptionally wide, shallow seat led to sizable voids between the spindles and bow ends. Structural stability for the flat back required that the bow terminate near the forward edge of the plank. Another common Pennsylvania German feature is the elongated leg baluster with a necked base. The chairmaker rejected the dual leg system in favor of heavy cylindrical feet with sharply tapered toes. The overall clumsiness of the design and the presence of a medial stretcher turned with two sizable lumps suggests that the craftsman was working out of his element. The profile of the feet further links the chair directly to German chairs from west of the Susquehanna, principally in York, Adams, and Frederick counties on the Pennsylvania-Maryland border. The specific chair, which is one of two known, is related to two broad, oval-seated fan-back Windsors with comparable, though slimmer, turnings. Those chairs have family histories associating them with Frederick County. In summary, figures 2–4 clearly represent the variability of the design-transfer process. Structure, proportions, and ornament were all features of transmission, sometimes singly, often together.[8]

A number of Windsor chairs documented to the shops of William Pointer and of brothers (?) Andrew and Robert McKim in Richmond, Virginia, appear to relate to Windsor seating produced in the late eighteenth century in rural Pennsylvania and Maryland, although the nature of the association is unclear. The clustered spindle placement at the back of a chair labeled by the McKims (fig. 5) is too mannered to be accidental, particularly when other chairs made in the two shops are constructed to normal patterns. The McKims, who were partners between 1795 and Andrew's death in 1805, produced fan- and bow-back Windsors (and perhaps other undocumented patterns), along with a few square-back writing-arm chairs. Their earliest bow backs were framed with baluster-turned supports; chairs with simulated-bamboo turnings followed. The elongated

Figure 5 Bow-back Windsor side chair, Andrew and Robert McKim, Richmond, Va., 1795–1802. Yellow poplar (seat) with maple and hickory. H. 35¾″. (Private collection; photo, courtesy, Museum of Early Southern Decorative Arts.)

leg balusters in the McKims' chair, which are also present in the work of William Pointer, are distinctive. The profile of this element compares with that in figure 4, suggesting a relationship. The small spool and thin ring turnings between the balusters and feet of the McKims' chair link the Windsor to other Germanic work produced in the Pennsylvania-Maryland border region. Since the backgrounds of the McKims and Pointer are unknown, it is possible that one or the other had family connections in that area. Although the German community in late-eighteenth-century Richmond was small, it included a chairmaker by the name of Samuel Scheerer; perhaps there was a working relationship between the craftsmen.[9]

Nineteenth-Century Design before 1815

An early-nineteenth-century example of the westward transmission of design by a migrating craftsman is found in the career of Andrew McIn-

Figure 6 Square-back Windsor side chair, Andrew McIntire, Pittsburgh, Pa., 1800–1805. Yellow poplar (seat). H. 35", W. (seat) 16¼", D. (seat) 15½". The medial and right stretchers and left rear leg are replaced. (Carnegie Museum of Art, gift of Mr. and Mrs. James A. Drain.)

Figure 7 Square-back Windsor side chair, Philadelphia, 1798–1802. Yellow poplar (seat) with maple and hickory. H. 34½", W. (seat) 17¾", D. (seat) 16". (Courtesy, Winterthur Museum, acc. 56.571.)

tire. He was probably a young man in 1773 and 1775 when he was listed as a joiner in Lower Chichester township, Chester (now Delaware) County, Pennsylvania, tax and land records. He lived in neighboring Philadelphia by 1785 when the first city directory was published; he is further identified as a cabinetmaker in the city tax list of 1786 and the directory for 1793. Between the latter date and his death at Pittsburgh in 1805, McIntire's activity is unrecorded; however, insights may be gained from a lone documented chair (fig. 6). Square-back seating was introduced to the Windsor chairmaking trade at Philadelphia in the late 1790s (fig. 7). The earliest had a low-arch top, or bow (bowed in a lateral direction), which echoes the arclike curve of the seat front. The design was short-lived, superseded before 1800 by a square-back that had one or two turned top members (see fig. 8). McIntire appears to have remained in Philadelphia just long enough to become familiar with the low-arch pattern before making the westward trek.[10]

McIntire's adaptation of the Philadelphia low-arch Windsor (fig. 6), which is branded on the plank bottom with his name and place name, can be distinguished from the prototype by several subtle features. The flat, beaded back posts of McIntire's chair lack the flare of the Philadelphia style, but as in that chair, he carried the beading across the top piece. The seats also vary in shape. Even before the new square back was introduced, Philadelphia chairmakers had begun to flatten the rounded front and side edges of the plank. In this respect, McIntire's chair seat is more modeled than the prototypes. The medial and right stretchers of the Pittsburgh chair are replacements, although it is likely that both braces originally had swelled centers like the left one. This variation of the common bamboo medial profile in Philadelphia chairs is suggested by the use of plain spindles in the chair back. Although beaded square-back chairs are uncommon, the Yale University Art Gallery (New Haven, Connecticut) has a large settee in this pattern. A related, square-back writing-arm chair labeled by Andrew and Robert McKim of Richmond, dated "1802," and a comparable example with a tradition of descent in a Madison County, Virginia, family, introduce a further dimension to the diffusion of the design.[11]

Figure 8 Square-back Windsor side chair with double bows, Joseph Burden, Philadelphia, 1801–1812. Woods not recorded. H. 34½", W. (seat) 16¾", D. (seat) 16¼". (Independence National Historical Park; courtesy, the Winterthur Library: Decorative Arts Photographic Collection.)

During a tour of the West in 1803, Unitarian minister Thaddeus M. Harris was impressed, as were others before him, with the commanding location of Pittsburgh at the confluence of the Allegheny, Monongahela, and Ohio rivers, the last of which was dubbed "the key to the Western Territory." A few years later, John Melish, a British commentator on the manufactures and commerce of America, predicted that "Pittsburg will in all probability become one of the largest towns in America." When Andrew McIntire arrived to take up residence in the town, sometime between 1800 and 1805, he found a fast-growing community consisting of about 400 houses and 2,000 inhabitants. Forty or fifty retail stores supplied local needs and those of the hordes of western settlers that streamed through town. Warehouses stored vast quantities of goods conveyed from the East in wagons awaiting shipment by riverboat to Kentucky and Louisiana. The boat-building industry was flourishing. Two glasshouses, a manufactory for the production of cut nails, and various smith's shops had been erected, all benefitting from the close proximity of "inexhaustible mines of coal." Small businesses and craft shops supplied hats, leather, tobacco products, beer, earthenware, cordage, lumber, and cabinetware. By 1807 five manufactories produced Windsor chairs. William Davis, who constructed baluster- and bamboo-leg bow-back chairs in the Philadelphia style, may have been in business during McIntire's residence.[12]

The first commercially successful square-back Windsor had single (or double) turned cross pieces forming the crest. At the top of the line were chairs with small medallions, or tablets, centered in the crest to provide a flat surface for painted ornament (see fig. 8). Joseph Burden's side chair is typical of the quality of Philadelphia production during this period. The seat is shaped much as it had been at the introduction of the first square-back Windsors, except that front corners are rounded (see fig. 7). The stout, well-modeled bamboowork is divided into four segments separated by gouged creases, rather than the three divisions common earlier (see figs. 1, 7). The use of four box-style stretchers was another departure from previous design, replacing the H-plan brace. The updated construction was based on the bracing system in the fancy chair, a new type of painted seating with rush or cane bottoms. The fancy chair, a slightly more expensive product than the Windsor, had been introduced from England in the postwar years and became economically attractive in the furniture trade during the 1790s. Many chairmakers, Burden included, donned two hats and produced both types of seating with ease, since the tools and materials were the same. The move enabled many urban craftsmen to broaden their economic base while remaining specialists.

Crest medallions in the square-back chair were shaped to one of several patterns. Most common are the square and rectangle, both usually formed with hollow (incurved) or canted corners. The small oval was next in popularity. Special shapes, such as hearts and urns, were rare. Chairmakers sometimes produced fancy interpretations of the square-back chair by introducing a small medallion corresponding to that in the crest to one or more of the bamboo-turned spindles (fig. 9). A similar medallion sometimes embellished the front stretcher.

The Philadelphia square-back chair with double bows and a medallion in the crest became popular with craftsmen in towns and villages in the Delaware Valley and eastern Pennsylvania. Along the river, chairmakers in Trenton, New Jersey, and Wilmington, Delaware, made chairs in this pattern. Pennsylvania craftsmen from Bucks County on the Delaware to Franklin County beyond the Susquehanna frequently introduced somewhat mannered features that identify their chairs as rural products: rectangular medallions with square corners; arms with thick tips; and stout seat planks. The delicate ornamental pattern of figure 9 is identified as originating in the shop of a Pennsylvania German chairmaker by the shape and breadth of the seat (see fig. 3). Extensive modeling around the seat edges has lightened the bulk of the plank in keeping with the overall proportions of the chair. At least one mate is known. In a chair of related pattern, an oval medallion in the crest is paired with vertical rectangular tablets in the spindles, producing a less unified design.[13]

Business stalemates during the war years, from 1812 to 1814, wiped out the old Windsor patterns and ushered in new designs at Philadelphia. From then until the early 1830s, mortise-and-tenon framing with slat-style crests positioned between the back posts prevailed. Philadelphia lost its premier position as style setter in vernacular seating as Baltimore became a center of the painted furniture trade. New York chairmakers introduced arrow-shaped spindles ("flat sticks") at about this time, and Boston craftsmen developed the extraordinarily successful stepped-tablet crest (modern, "stepped-down" Windsor), patterned after formal seating furniture. Nevertheless, Philadelphia chairs still had considerable impact on vernacular design within and beyond the local trading region.[14]

Figure 9 Square-back Windsor side chair with double bows, Pennsylvania, west of the Susquehanna River at the Maryland border, 1810–1820. Yellow poplar (seat) with maple. H. 37 1/16", W. (seat) 16 5/8", D. (seat) 14". (Private collection; photo, courtesy, Winterthur Museum.)

Figure 10 Slat-back Windsor side chair with tablet, Thomas Ashton, Philadelphia, 1810–1815. Yellow poplar (seat). H. 33″. (Old Salem, Inc.; photo, courtesy, Museum of Early Southern Decorative Arts.)

An unusual design because of its rarity, even in Philadelphia where it originated, is the slat-back Windsor with a centered rectangular tablet projecting from the crest (fig. 10). Thomas Ashton's chair frame generally duplicates that of Burden's double-bow, square-back Windsor. The seat is one of several shapes in the market during the 1810s and 1820s; the front and back edges are curved in arcs, the sides are sawed in serpentine profiles. Ashton, like William Cox before him, supplied chairs to export merchant Stephen Girard. He also constructed a dozen armchairs, perhaps of this pattern, for the senate chamber of the statehouse at Dover, Delaware, in 1812.[15]

The influence of the Philadelphia tablet-centered crest extended beyond rural Pennsylvania to the Shenandoah Valley. On September 4, 1820, Samuel Fizer, probably a relative newcomer to the chairmaking business, advertised from Fincastle, Virginia, that he was "prepared to execute work in a style that will rival any of the Northern Cities."[16] The design of Fizer's labeled chair leaves little doubt as to the sources of inspiration (fig. 11). Back posts with shaved faces had been introduced to Philadelphia chairwork about 1815 or 1816, and by the 1820s the execution of bamboowork was often perfunctory, as is reflected in the present chair. Fizer's use of a squared seat plank with steep, rounded edges producing a cushioned effect illuminates the impact of Baltimore chairmaking on his work. Knowledge about the seat shape, a common one in the city from about 1805, could have been transmitted to the valley by either of two routes: through Frederick, Maryland, and Winchester, Virginia, or via south central Pennsylvania, where many Baltimore trained chairmakers plied their trade. An almost identical plank is on a square-back chair with double bows made ca. 1807–1815 by John McClintic at Chambersburg near the Maryland border. The community lay adjacent to a major southwesterly thoroughfare passing through Hagerstown to the Virginia back country.

A small group of early-nineteenth-century square-back chairs related through the stout profile of the bamboowork legs has family and recovery histories from rural locations in the Susquehanna Valley, western Pennsylvania, and the Shenandoah Valley (figs. 12, 13). Baltimore styles were the principal influence on these chairs, although a knowledge of Pennsylvania work is evident in some of them. The group consists of square-back Windsors fitted with single- or double-cross bows of Philadelphia inspiration and chairs of a new tablet-style crest developed in Baltimore. Production probably occurred between 1805 and 1820. The vigorously turned legs are frequently accompanied by robust stretchers. Both turnings are heavier versions of the bamboo supports found on some early-nineteenth-century Baltimore Windsors. The comparative features in the two chairs are the pointed feet and the pronounced reduction in leg diameter from the bottom crease, or groove, to the top segment. The back posts are slimmer versions of the same Baltimore turnings (figs. 12, 13).

The chair in figure 12 was found in the Quarryville area of southern Lancaster County, Pennsylvania, although it may have been made farther west or south. In contrast to the Baltimore influence in the turned work, the shape and detailing of the plank reflect developments in the Philadelphia chair market of the late 1790s when the shield seat was squared, the sides flattened, and grooved beading was added to define the edges (see figs. 7, 8). This plank is thicker than the prototypes, however, and an extra groove marks the side surfaces. The chair's overall mannered character identifies it as a rural product. Another chair in the group, having a single, turned cross piece at the top and a better modeled shield-shape seat, was recovered at Sheppardstown, West Virginia, early in the present century.[17]

Figure 11 Slat-back Windsor side chair with tablet, Samuel Fizer, Fincastle, Va., 1820–1825. Woods not recorded. H. 33″, W. (seat) 17½″. (Old Salem, Inc.; photo, courtesy, Museum of Early Southern Decorative Arts.)

Figure 12 Slat-back Windsor side chair with double bows, southeastern Pennsylvania in the greater Susquehanna Valley, or northeastern Maryland, 1810–1820. Yellow poplar (seat) with maple. H. 34¾″, W. (seat) 16¾″, D. (seat) 15¼″. (Private collection; photo, courtesy, Winterthur Museum.)

The most sophisticated chair with heavy bamboo legs is the one illustrated in figure 13. Every feature is a reflection of Baltimore design, from the turnings, to the oval medallion centered in the back, to the new patterns of the seat and crest. A squared shield-shape seat with a striking center-front projection appeared in the Baltimore chair market shortly after 1800 and continued in occasional use for a decade or more. The projection, as interpreted on figure 13, is narrow, giving it a rudimentary appearance. The distinctive crest was introduced to the Baltimore market probably between 1805 and 1807. The central feature of the winglike design varies: rounded lunette; flattened arch; rectangular tablet; or rectangular projection with hollow corners (see fig. 14). The wings vary in height and angularity; some are squared at the ends. One version even has blocked rectangular ends.[18]

Figure 13 Tablet-top Windsor side chair, south central Pennsylvania, Maryland, or the Shenandoah Valley, Va., 1810–1820. Woods not recorded. H. 33¾", W. 18¾". The front and right stretchers are replaced. (Private collection; photo, courtesy, Museum of Early Southern Decorative Arts.)

The small Baltimore settee in figure 14 is a classic among Windsors. The features, which are more delicate and better designed than those in the rural chair in figure 13, are typical of the best Baltimore vernacular seating of the early nineteenth century: pencil-slim legs and posts; medallion-accented spindles and stretchers; carefully modeled seat-front projections; and intricately sawed elements, such as the crest, that provide a design focus. The pattern is neither rare nor common. Several specialized forms were made, including longer settees, a writing-arm chair, and a child's highchair.[19]

The winged-crest pattern was also attractive to craftsmen working outside Baltimore, as indicated by the number of design variants. That, in turn, suggests that Baltimore chairs in this pattern were well distributed. Histories associated with many examples bear out the hypothesis. Figure 13 descended either in the Haupe or Miller families of Greenville, Augusta County, Virginia, in the Shenandoah Valley. Its maker may have been of German background, for the crest face is scored near the edges to form a broad bead, and similar scoring is found on the crests of fan-back Windsors made in the German regions of southeastern Pennsylvania in the late eighteenth century. Another chair with a beaded border, one centered with a tablet like those in the settee, has a piedmont Virginia history. A child's highchair descended in the Randolph family living in Boyce, Clarke County, a village near Winchester. A side chair with a flat-arch projection at the crest center came from the same homestead in Frederick County, Maryland, as the mate to figure 4, which has distinctive German characteristics. Chairs with variations of the blocked-wing crest are found in reasonable numbers in western Pennsylvania, south of Pittsburgh.[20]

A crude woodcut accompanying a Nashville, Tennessee, newspaper notice of March 1808 is the basis for dating the introduction of Baltimore winged-tablet chairs to the 1805–1807 period. The woodcut advertising John Priest's chairmaking and painting business contains an image of a side chair with a winged, Baltimore-style crest. Since the initials *I. P* appear on the chair seat, it seems likely that Priest made his own printing block. The chairmaker was working in Petersburg, Virginia, in 1806,

Figure 14 Tablet-top Windsor settee, Baltimore, 1807–1815. Yellow poplar (seat) with maple and hickory. H. 36⅛″, W. (seat) 39⅛″; D. (seat) 15⅛″. (Courtesy, Winterthur Museum, acc. 59.3627.)

which is of particular relevance since Virginia communities in the Chesapeake region were directly influenced by Baltimore furniture design. Other examples of the winged-crest chair found in the West include the only standard-size armchair known to date, which is in a Kentucky private collection. Another Kentucky armchair, one of extraordinary height, has a history of use in an unidentified Masonic lodge. Its enormous crest piece is a rectangular tablet, winged variant of a type often found in western Pennsylvania. The front stretcher and several spindles are also embellished with rectangular tablets.[21]

Figure 15 Slat-back Windsor side chair (one of two), eastern Pennsylvania, 1820–1835. Yellow poplar (seat) with maple. H. 34¼″, W. (seat) 15½″, D. (seat) 15½″. (Private collection; photo, courtesy, Winterthur Museum.)

Figure 16 Slat-back Windsor side chair, Adin G. Hibbs, Columbus, Ohio, 1833–1839. Woods and dimensions not recorded. (Private collection; photo, Jane Sikes Hageman.)

Post-1815 Slat-Back Designs

By the mid-1810s, large crests for painted, and later stenciled, ornament were increasingly popular features on vernacular seating furniture. Chair backs were framed with either slat-style crests secured by mortises and tenons between the posts or tablet-style tops fixed to round tenons at the post tips or rabbets on the post faces. The basic crest is rectangular; the more ornamental top pieces are arched, scalloped, or shouldered along the upper edge. By mid-century, cut-out shapes were added to the lower edge. Chairs of both styles were marketed simultaneously until the 1830s, when tablet-top designs generally prevailed. For the most part, Philadelphia was the source of the slat-framed styles and Baltimore the source for the tablet top.

The first slat-back Windsors had full-length spindles. Cylindrical sticks, usually five in number, were the plainest option. The introduction of a single smooth-shaved "flat stick," or arrow-shaped spindle, at center back provided another surface for ornamentation (fig. 15). The use of multiple flat sticks, generally four, added variety and provided a smooth surface to support the sitter's back (fig. 16).

The geographic range of Philadelphia-style slat-back chairs with long spindles was broad, covering central Pennsylvania, Virginia, and the West. Documented Philadelphia examples are rare. Unmarked chairs made in both the cylindrical and flat-stick patterns still comprise part of the furnishings at the Athenaeum of Philadelphia. The plain-spindle ones, which are framed with bamboo-turned legs and back posts, are likely part of the dozen Windsors the institution purchased from Philip Halzel in 1822. Chairs of identical pattern with seats of a variant shape were labeled by Robert Burchall and William Wickersham of West Chester in neighboring Chester County during their partnership between August 1822 and February 1824. The Athenaeum's flat-stick chairs may date from a few years later. New features are backs in the bent style and cylindrical legs turned with multiple rings, top and bottom, the two bands connected originally with a broad, vertical stripe of paint.[22]

Fancy painted, slat-back Windsors were popular in rural, eastern and central Pennsylvania (fig. 15). The style featuring a central flat stick flanked by cylindrical spindles was probably slightly less common than the types with all cylindrical or all flat sticks. Documented chairs and chairs with recovery histories link some production to Berks, Chester, Lancaster, and Lebanon counties, east of the Susquehanna, and Centre, Mifflin, and Union counties, west of the river. Seat planks include the range of shapes found in the postwar market: balloon, serpentine, and shovel profiles. The last, which has a blunt front, is the latest in date and the most common.[23]

Slat-style Windsors were popular with chairmakers and consumers throughout Virginia, and, as in the past, such chairs often mixed Philadelphia and Baltimore characteristics. In the case of a bamboo-turned, plain-spindle chair labeled by Seaton and Matthews of Petersburg about 1814 to 1818, the squared, shield-shape seat has a front projection in the Baltimore style (see fig. 14). Slat-back Windsors made at Lynchburg by George T. Johnson and the firm of Johnson and Hardy (Chesley) in the early 1820s were divided between straight-back (canted) and bent-back patterns. The chairmakers' cheapest Windsor had plain cylindrical spindles. The introduction of a central flat stick increased the price slightly. Across the southern Virginia border, Moravian craftsmen at (Old) Salem, North Carolina, made slat-back Windsors that are well proportioned and have shapely bamboowork, good leg splay, and seats that are a better-contoured version of the Baltimore "cushioned" planks Samuel Fizer of Fincastle, Virginia, used in his chairs during the 1820s (see fig. 11). The influence of Pennsylvania work on chairmaking at Salem may have been direct, since the community had frequent communication with the Moravian settlements in eastern Pennsylvania.[24]

The slat-back Windsor is among the earliest patterns documented to western production. The distribution of manufactured goods at Pittsburgh and Wheeling helped to keep westerners abreast of furniture trends in the East. In 1817 Pittsburgh had seven cabinet shops and three Windsor-chairmaking establishments, the latter employing a total of twenty-three workers and realizing gross sales of more than $42,000 annually. Many of the "country towns" along the waterways had become "miniature cities," some with their own resident chairmakers. Western growth was phenomenal. The population of Ohio, estimated at 45,000 in 1800, rose to more than half a million by 1820, Cincinnati becoming the most important business center between Pittsburgh and the lower Mississippi. It has been estimated that by the early 1820s as many as 3,000 flatboats floated down the Ohio annually, many destined for New Orleans, the great entrepôt on the lower Mississippi for the distribution of western produce. Other vessels carried manufactured goods and western migrants to any of hundreds of landing sites along the way. Some prosperous families carried their household possessions with them; others traveled with few personal belongings, buying what they needed or could afford when they resettled.[25]

Steamboats plying the western waters could travel the entire distance between Pittsburgh and New Orleans by 1811. In 1820 alone sixty-nine vessels were engaged in river commerce. Western trade was revolutionized. Before the advent of the steamboat, the upriver trip by flatboat from New Orleans or other points was tedious, consuming several weeks or months, depending upon the destination. Merchandise from the East could now be carried upriver or down to any navigable destination, with a short portage around the falls at Louisville. Although the cost was considerable, John Bristed reported that the charges were still less than half those for freighting the merchandise across the mountains. The Great Lakes region was served via the Erie Canal by the 1820s.[26]

Adin G. Hibbs, a chairmaker who migrated from Pennsylvania to Columbus, Ohio, in 1832, advertised his manufactory at the sign of The Golden Chair the following year. His products included Windsor and fancy chairs in "a large and handsome assortment" (fig 16). Hibbs's arrow-spindle, slat-back Windsor is basically an eastern Pennsylvania chair. The ring-turned front legs are slightly later in date than the bamboo-style legs (see fig. 15); the broadly interpreted shovel-shape seat is contemporary to the early 1820s. Knowledge of Pennsylvania design is also evident in the work of Nathaniel Sprague of Zanesville (1823) and, later, McConnelsville (1827–1830s). Sprague may have vended his flat-spindle, slat-back Windsors along the Ohio River by way of the navigable Muskingum. The sharply tapered legs in a chair owned by descendants indicates that the chairmaker was also influenced by Baltimore design. A shop inventory of Moses Hatfield, a Dayton resident in 1835, provides further evidence of the popularity of slat-back Windsors in Ohio with the items: "1097 chair backs" (slats); "33 slat-backs" (framed and finished chairs) valued at $44; "72 slat-backed primed" worth $48; and "30 slat-backs finished."[27]

Indiana furniture is almost unknown, at least in published sources. A long, slat-back Windsor rocking settee with slim, flat sticks in the back, slat-style stretchers (front and back), and heavy arms scrolling forward in the manner of a rocking chair is said to have descended in the Newman family of East Germantown (now Pershing), Wayne County. A contemporary, related slat-back settee, labeled by the Louisville, Kentucky, partners James Ward and John M. Stokes, demonstrates the possibilities for variation within the pattern. The long seat, which has similarities to the Newman family settee in the spindles and slat-type stretchers, a brace that first appeared in the 1830s, is framed with an extra post at midback. The flat arms are mounted horizontally and terminate in large rounded pads at the front; the legs are stouter than those on the chair in figure 17, with the addition of a ball turning near the top.[28]

Figure 17 Slat-back Windsor side chair, Alexander H. and William R. Wood, Nashville, Tenn., 1817–1820. Yellow poplar (seat) with maple and hickory. H. 33½″, W. (seat) 15⅝″, D. (seat) 15½″. (Travellers Rest Historic House Museum, Inc.)

The chair illustrated in figure 17 is a rare documented Tennessee example. It was made in the Nashville shop of Alexander H. and William R. Wood, who were in business together from 1817 to 1820 and possibly later. The rear view emphasizes the unusual feature of the chair, the acutely angled back. As young men, the Wood brothers had trained at Richmond, Virginia, with Robert McKim, whose Windsor seating was heavily influenced by Philadelphia and Pennsylvania German design (see fig. 5). In an advertisement of 1819 the Woods made special note of their auxiliary business of sign and ornamental painting.[29]

Generally speaking, the Wood brothers' chair is a Philadelphia Windsor. The most distinctive modification to it is the sharp back bend. Since bent backs were used for Windsor seating at New York some years earlier than at Philadelphia, where the style was introduced only about 1816 or 1817, the brothers may have become acquainted with the feature through importations of New York seating into Richmond during their training in the early 1810s. The choice of a bent back may also reflect influences present in Tennessee. For example, James Bridges of Knoxville advertised in 1819 that he had "spared no pains or expense in procuring . . . Workmen of the first description" from New York, Philadelphia, Baltimore, and Washington. Samuel Williams, a local competitor of the Woods, also employed New York journeymen along with workers from Philadelphia. Baltimore influences on the Wood brothers' chair are the sharply pointed feet and pronounced leg tapers. Chairs made at Pittsburgh, a community exposed to the cross currents of Philadelphia and Baltimore furniture design, probably also had some impact on the regional market long before 1830 when John Rudisill of Jackson, Tennessee, advertised that he had just received "a large assortment of WINDSOR CHAIRS, manufactured at Pittsburgh, of various patterns and colors."[30]

During the late 1820s Philadelphia chairmakers introduced a slat-back chair of a new style with short spindles in the lower back below a rectangular cross piece to the greater Delaware Valley furniture market. An

Figure 18 Slat-back Windsor side chair (one of six), Thomas Thompson Enos, Odessa, Del., 1845–1860. Yellow poplar (seat) with birch and beech. H. 32⅛", W. (seat) 15½", D. (seat) 13⅞". (Courtesy, Winterthur Museum, acc. 81.70.1.)

example used in a bank in nearby West Chester about 1837 has bold spindles centered with ball turnings. Judging by the rarity of surviving examples, the plain rectangular crest was quickly superseded by several variant designs. One pattern—a slat with a low top arch—was particularly popular in eastern Pennsylvania and the Delaware Valley (fig. 18). Sometimes sawed, scalloped decoration was added at the center top. All variants were available before 1838 when James C. Helme of Luzerne County compiled a manuscript "Book of Prices" for framing and finishing fancy and Windsor seating furniture. The "common straight back" and "bent back" chairs on his list are Windsors with full-length spindles. The chair in figure 18 is a "Ball Back Chair with 2 Bows." The expense of producing this chair was one third more than a long-spindle chair. The addition of a scalloped top to the crest raised the figure to 50 percent above the basic cost.[31]

The arched slat-back, short-spindle pattern had a long life. Thomas Thompson Enos, whose chair is illustrated in figure 18, did not attain his majority until 1838. He probably framed chairs of this pattern during his first years in Smyrna, Delaware, prior to moving to neighboring Odessa, which place name he penciled on the seat bottom. William F. Snyder, who made similar chairs at his Mifflintown Chair Works in Juniata County, Pennsylvania, northwest of Harrisburg, was born only in 1845. Another set of chairs bears the signature of H. L. Rhein (owner?) of Reading, Berks County, a community on the Schuylkill. The arched slat-back Pennsylvania chair appears to have been a popular export item, as well. Chairs of this pattern are encountered with some frequency in the coastal South, although none are documented to southern production. Several dozen were acquired by the Masonic Lodge of Suffolk, Virginia, near Norfolk, during the second quarter of the nineteenth century. Another example was found in Clarke County, Georgia, probably transported inland by river vessel and wagon from Savannah, the second largest, early-nineteenth-century, southern entrepôt for Philadelphia vernacular seating furniture after Charleston, South Carolina.[32]

Despite the success of the Philadelphia (and area) arched slat-back pattern in southern markets, the plain slat-back design was the one reproduced by southern and western chairmakers. At Lynchburg, Virginia, Chesley Hardy made a chair reasonably close in design to Enos's, except for the slat modification, during the 1830s or 1840s. The pattern more commonly constructed, however, is one with short, broad, flat sticks in the lower back. A particularly handsome example with two, instead of one, midback cross slats was made for the Single Sisters' House in the Moravian settlement at (Old) Salem, North Carolina. Single-cross slat chairs, some with broad spindles others with narrow ones, have descended in Tennessee families. An 1840s flat-spindle chair was made at Wheeling, West Virginia, by Jonas Thatcher (fig. 19), one of a number of chairmakers there between the late 1820s and the Civil War. Its spindle and front-leg patterns are based on Baltimore prototypes (see figs. 22, 23, later in this article). Plain, slim rear legs pinched together near the top are the usual

Figure 19 Slat-back Windsor side chair, Jonas Thatcher, Wheeling, W.Va., 1839–1850. Yellow poplar (seat). H. 36″, W. (seat) 16¼″, D. (seat) 15¼″. (Oglebay Institute Mansion Museum; photo, courtesy, Winterthur Museum.)

accompaniment when Baltimore styling is prominent. Front stretchers in the form of slats were common in the late 1830s and early 1840s when Thatcher worked.[33]

Visitors to Wheeling in the 1830s complained of the city's sooty air, as they did of Pittsburgh. The region's bituminous coal deposits, which were important stimulants to industry in both communities, were mined as a local energy source and an export product. In the mid-1830s the population of the city stood above 10,000, many residents drawn there by the flourishing river trade. Warehouses filled with merchandise for the West lined the Ohio River; boat builders and owners, and wagoners prospered. In 1836 the city wharfmaster logged 1,602 steamboat arrivals and departures; 222 keelboats and flatboats carried other freight down the river.[34]

Several pieces of Windsor slat-back furniture are attributed to Kentucky. One is a writing-arm chair with short, flat sticks in the lower back; the other is a settee with diamond-shaped sticks and a front stretcher of the same profile. The slat-back pattern was apparently also popular in Indiana. German-born Jacob Maentel, who moved from Pennsylvania to New Harmony, Indiana, in 1838, painted a number of area residents posed in domestic settings furnished with slat-back chairs that had flat sticks in

Figure 20 *William Ferguson Cooper*, attributed to Jacob Maentel, New Harmony, Ind., ca. 1842. Watercolor, pen, and pencil on paper. 15½″ × 10½″. (Historic New Harmony, New Harmony, Indiana.)

the lower back (fig. 20). In a review of Maentel's Pennsylvania paintings, slat-back chairs with single midback slats substituting for spindles and slat-back chairs with long cylindrical spindles are the patterns delineated, a circumstance that strongly suggests Maentel was depicting chairs common to each area.[35]

Post-1815 Tablet-Top Designs

Five years or more before slat-back patterns appeared on the Philadelphia market (see fig. 10), Baltimore's Windsor chairmakers were producing a tablet-top design adapted from fancy-painted, cane-seated furniture (fig. 21). These prototypes had been available locally for several years, proba-

Figure 21 Tablet-top Windsor side chair, Baltimore, 1805–1812. H. 35¾". Woods not recorded. (Private collection; photo, courtesy, Museum of Early Southern Decorative Arts.)

bly perfected by the Finlay brothers, Hugh and John, who commenced their chairmaking business in 1803 (fig. 22). The sawtooth borders on the Windsor crest of figure 21 were copied directly from that on fancy chairs, although such ornament was probably produced by more than one local artisan. In an advertisement of 1805, the Finlays offered customers a broad range of decoration, including "trophies of Music, War, Husbandry, Love, &c.," that may have closely resembled the centered crest ornament of the illustrated Windsor.[36]

The structural units in the tablet-top Baltimore Windsor (fig. 21) represent a basic vocabulary of vernacular seating design current in the city and surrounding regions during the early nineteenth century. The elevated crest, though plain in outline, is the focus, since it received the principal decoration. Rounded crest shapes were introduced with the late patterns (see figs. 29, 31, later in this article). Cylindrical back posts are a major characteristic of the Baltimore style. The turnings became progressively thicker with time (see fig. 25) and sometimes were augmented with bulging, rounded shapes. The seat-front projection, a special customer option, remained only through the 1810s (see fig. 14). The pronounced leg taper of figure 17 is already present here, above and below the inset ankles, and remained a staple of the Baltimore design vocabulary beyond midcentury (see fig. 34 later in this article). Small, varied-shape medallions centered in spindles and front stretchers are found only in the best work, since such embellishment required extra labor on the part of both the chairmaker and the ornamenter.

Figure 22 Tablet-top fancy side chair (one of three), attributed to John and Hugh Finlay, Baltimore, 1800–1810. Maple, yellow poplar, and mahogany. H. 33¼", W. (seat) 19", D. (seat) 15". (Courtesy, Winterthur Museum, acc. 57.1060.1.)

The early Baltimore tablet-top design migrated beyond the immediate environs of the city within a decade of its initial development. Representative of the transmission is a group of northeastern Tennessee side chairs of unusual hybrid design, combining a Baltimore rectangular tablet and a Philadelphia-style central crest projection like that in the Ashton and Fizer Windsors (see figs. 10, 11). Several chairs have heavily mannered bamboo leg turnings of the type found in figures 12 and 13. The most sophisticated example has a center-back spindle featuring a medallion and a projection at the seat front, both ornamental elements borrowed from the Baltimore design vocabulary.[37]

A sizable body of special-purpose tablet-top seating furniture consists of bamboo-turned, writing-arm chairs of Virginia origin, ranging in date from the early 1800s to the 1820s. Most tablets on them are moderately deep with squared corners. The backs are of medium height, and some are centered with medallion spindles. The earliest chair in the group has an eighteenth-century-type, H-plan stretcher system and a shallow crest rounded at the upper corners. It belonged to lawyer William Wirt, who probably purchased the chair in Richmond, his sometimes residence beginning in 1800. The chair has several features similar to those in a writing-arm chair labeled by the McKim brothers of Richmond and dated "1802." The Wirt chair probably dates slightly later. Another chair has a history in the Carr family of Port Royal, Virginia, a small community on the Rappahannock River, near Fredericksburg, which was accessible by water from Richmond. The latest chair in the group, which descended in the Stoner family of Botetourt County in the Shenandoah Valley, could well have originated in that area. The lower back posts are distinctively styled with a rounded taper identical to that in chairs made by George T. Johnson and Chesley Hardy at Lynchburg, due east in Campbell County.[38]

Greater impact occurred on the vernacular seating trade in the 1820s when a neoclassical-style Baltimore tablet-top fancy chair with heavy, sawed elements and bold turnings was successfully marketed (fig. 23). The outsize crest, finished with an applied, scrolled lip at the upper back, provided a broad surface for painted ornament. The distinctive baluster posts were supported on large, multiringed oval balls, frequently repeated at the leg tops. The same ringed balls occur in English furniture of the late George III period, examples of particular note found in the pedestals of dining tables. The single cross slat of the chair back provided

Figure 23 Tablet-top fancy side chair, John Hodgkinson, Baltimore, 1820–1830. Woods not recorded. H. 32″, W. (seat) 18″. (Private collection; photo, courtesy, Museum of Early Southern Decorative Arts.)

structural stability, comfort, and a surface for additional ornament. The unusual side pieces framing the seat are Grecian in concept, truncated to form platforms for socketing the back structure. The stout front legs are turned to a Roman pattern. The domed turning at the top was a popular alternative to a multiringed ball. The ring centered in the concave element below the dome was termed a "gothic moulding" in furniture circles.[39]

Neoclassical Baltimore tablet-top chairs were widely marketed in America and abroad. City chairmakers advertised chairs for export in units up to several hundred dozen. Regional newspapers at such locations as Easton, Maryland, neighboring Frederick County, and Norfolk and Petersburg, Virginia, repeated the urban advertisements. Family histories associate other Baltimore chairs with Raleigh, North Carolina, Annapolis, Maryland, and even Ontario, Canada. John Hodgkinson, who made the chair in figure 23, set up shop in Baltimore about 1820. His career spanned several decades.[40]

Figure 24 Tablet-top Windsor side chair, William Cunningham, Wheeling, W.Va., 1828–1840. Yellow poplar (seat) with maple. H. 31⅛", W. (seat) 16¾", D. (seat) 15". (Oglebay Institute Mansion Museum; photo, courtesy, Winterthur Museum.)

Few plank-seat chairs are as close copies of the Baltimore tablet-top fancy style of the 1820s as that illustrated in figure 24, aside from several known Windsors of Baltimore origin. The variations in the turnings are those normal even in Baltimore work. The chair bears the label of William Cunningham, who worked in Wheeling, West Virginia, from 1828 until his death in 1851. The label is also inscribed in ink with the name of the purchaser: "Dr James Wood/Fairview." Fairview, a private residence, was located just south of Wheeling overlooking the Ohio River. Without the label, there would be little question that this was a Baltimore chair.[41]

A simpler style inspired by the Baltimore tablet-top pattern was typically framed with plain, stout back posts accented with ring turnings (fig. 25). The posts were an updated version of the slim supports of the early tablet-top chairs (fig. 21). Shovel or balloon shapes were commonly chosen for the Windsor planks. Frequently, the front legs were turned to a pattern plainer than those on the more expensive fancy chairs. The crests were usually lipless. The medium blue-green paint and yellow banded and penciled decoration of this chair are original. The banding appears to have once been bronzed; the scene on the crest was painted in grisaille. The buildings have a decided European appearance and may be based on a print source or copied from a piece of pottery. The painter may also have been a German, since an old chalk inscription on the plank bottom points to an original or early location of the chair: "W Ebbeck/Elizabeth Town/Lancaster Co./Pa."[42]

Two sets of documented Windsors are known in the tablet-top, stout-post pattern. One set—six chairs en suite with a settee—has the multiringed-ball feature at the leg tops. The tablet tops are skillfully painted with landscape scenes. The chairs were made during the early 1830s in the Carlisle, Pennsylvania, shop of Cornelius E. R. Davis. Chairs framed by William Bullock either at Carlisle or Shippensburg were far simpler in design. He turned both front and back legs in a plain style, and the front stretcher lacks extra embellishment. A chair with a later rounded-end tablet top and turned work almost as plain was made in West Virginia by

Figure 25 Tablet-top Windsor side chair, Lancaster Co., Pa., possibly Elizabethtown, 1830–1840. Woods not recorded. H. 32⅝", W. (seat) 16⅛", D. (seat) 14⅞". (Philip H. Bradley Co.; photo, courtesy, Winterthur Museum.)

William Graham, who migrated from Carlisle to Wheeling. Occasionally, a chairmaker framed his Windsor seating with a fancy, sawed slat at mid-back in place of the plain rectangular one.[43]

Throughout the years, many Baltimore-style, tablet-top Windsors have turned up in the Susquehanna Valley and central Pennsylvania. Some are versions made by local craftsmen; others represent the work of Baltimore-trained craftsmen who migrated north. The Baltimore city directory of 1829 lists forty-four practicing master chairmakers and eleven turners, some of the latter probably jobbers who supplied parts. Many masters employed journeymen and trained apprentices. When times were

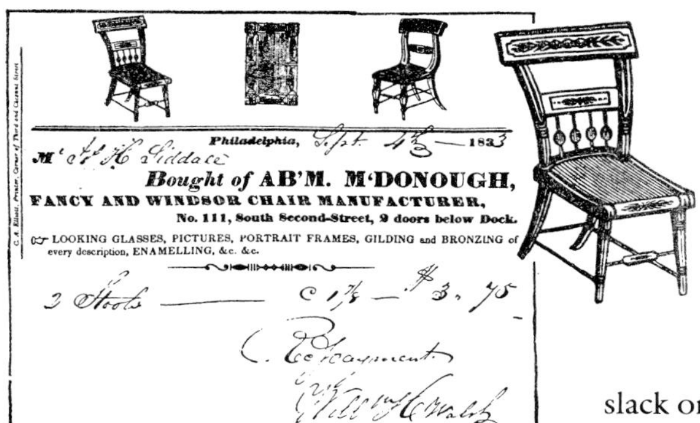

Philadelphia, 1833

Bought of AB'M. M'DONOUGH,

FANCY AND WINDSOR CHAIR MANUFACTURER,

No. 111, South Second-Street, 9 doors below Dock.

LOOKING GLASSES, PICTURES, PORTRAIT FRAMES, GILDING and BRONZING of every description, ENAMELLING, &c. &c.

Figure 26 Abraham McDonough billhead and bill to Joseph H. Liddall, Philadelphia, 1833 (inscribed). From Carl W. Drepperd, *Handbook of Antique Chairs* (Garden City, N.Y.: Doubleday, 1948), p. 160. (Photo, courtesy, Winterthur Museum.)

slack or indentures expired, some men traveled north in search of work. Baltimore is advantageously located south of the Susquehanna and Cumberland valleys, semirural regions where agriculture and light industry flourished. Baltimore-style tablet-top chairs were common everywhere in the region. Through drawings depicting community life, Lewis Miller, carpenter and chronicler of York, documented the presence of tablet-top seating in local households and businesses. The style reached Lafayette in west-central Indiana in 1839 when William Bullock migrated from Shippensburg, Pennsylvania.[44]

Tablet-top framing was also introduced to chairs fitted with short spindles in the lower back, similar to figure 18, before the close of the 1820s (fig. 26). The neoclassical-style Baltimore fancy chair that inspired the tablet-top Windsor of central Pennsylvania was also the vehicle for introducing similar framing to Philadelphia. The chair in figure 26, however, retains three important features of the Philadelphia style: front legs banded with rings linked by a vertical painted stripe, bent cylindrical back posts shaved to a flat surface at the front, and ball spindles in the lower back. By comparison, the absence of spindles in the Baltimore-style central Pennsylvania chair creates an awkward void in the lower back (fig. 25).

Abraham McDonough commenced in business in 1830. In the highly competitive chairmaking trade his products would have resembled those of other leading manufacturers; his success was dependent upon his business acumen and a measure of luck. McDonough supplied both the domestic and export markets, advertising that his merchandise was packed "in the most careful manner, either for land or water carriage, so as to avoid all risk of damage." He shipped six bundles of chairs to New Orleans in 1831. Eastern goods could be placed in almost any western market at this date via the water routes through the Erie Canal or the Mississippi at New Orleans and overland by wagon. Before his early death in 1852, McDonough had established business contacts in New York City; Burlington, New Jersey; Wilmington (Delaware or North Carolina); Fredericksburg and Petersburg; New Orleans; Missouri; and probably points in between.[45]

The Philadelphia rectangular tablet-top, short-spindle Windsor was about as popular across Pennsylvania as the spindleless variety (see fig. 25). The style was also known in the West, where chairs with short flat sticks in the lower back appear to have been somewhat more common than those with short ball-turned spindles. At Wheeling, Jonas Thatcher and a partner named Connelly chose flat sticks for a chair framed about the mid-1840s. Although the sticks lack the small beads of Thatcher's slat-back chair (fig. 19), the general profile is the same; the seats and front leg turnings are also comparable. The turned front stretcher is centered with a ball.[46]

Several Windsors in the Philadelphia tablet-top pattern are ascribed to Tennessee and Kentucky. A set of side chairs similar to the Wheeling example by Thatcher and Connelly descended in a Rutherford County, Tennessee, family. A Kentucky settee (fig. 27) has intricately designed short, flat spindles. The craftsman who made this piece of furniture in the Philadelphia style was also familiar with Baltimore vernacular design,

Figure 27 Tablet-top Windsor settee, Kentucky, 1835–1845. Yellow poplar (seat) with maple and hickory. H. 34½", W. (seat) 77", D. (seat) 20¾". (National Society of the Colonial Dames of America in the Commonwealth of Kentucky; photo, J. B. Speed Art Museum.)

either from first-hand experience several decades earlier or from having examples to study. The profile of his flat sticks is based on an urn shape found in Baltimore fancy seating from the beginning of the century (see fig. 22), with a short, flaring element added to the top. When inverted, the flaring shape is the small dome-on-a-shaft profile found in the backs of cane-seated furniture made in 1814 or 1815 by Thomas Renshaw and John Barnhart of Baltimore. The same domed shape appears in the leg tops of the Baltimore chair in figure 23. The ornamental spindles of the settee contrast effectively with the horizontal emphasis of the large, plain, framing members: tablet, slat, seat, and longitudinal stretchers. The front legs are a degenerate version of a Pennsylvania support (see fig. 19) and, with the posts, lack the sophistication of the short spindles. Just this kind of dichotomy is often encountered in nonurban chairmaking.[47]

Documented and attributable chairs of Ohio origin suggest the scope and nature of eastern influence in the late 1830s and 1840s. The character of the region's chairs derived principally from a fusion of Baltimore and Philadelphia design. One of the most ornamental and successful interpretations is a chair made by William Coles at Springfield, about forty miles west of Columbus on the National Road, a major east-west thoroughfare that stretched from Columbia, Maryland, to Vandalia, Illinois, by 1838 (fig. 28). For all practical purposes, Coles built a tablet-top Philadelphia Windsor from the seat up: the shaved posts and ball spindles are similar to those in figure 26; the seat is a vigorous interpretation of the Penn-

Figure 28 Tablet-top Windsor side chair, William Coles, Springfield, Ohio, 1840–1850. Yellow poplar (seat) with maple; H. 32″, W. (seat) 17″, D. (seat) 15″. (Private collection; photo, Columbus Museum of Art, Ohio.)

sylvania shovel-type (see fig. 15). Below the seat, the chair is a Baltimore design: the elements comprising the legs—ball turnings, flaring cones, and tapered columns—are adapted from those in figure 23.

The more common Philadelphia-style tablet-top, short-spindle Ohio-made chair was framed with flat sticks. Documented chairs constructed by John R. and William Wilson at Wooster and James Huey at Zanesville are supported on legs similar to those in Jonas Thatcher's Wheeling chair (see fig. 19). The front stretchers are similar to the forward brace in another West Virginia chair (see fig. 30). Rather than framed with a tablet-style crest, Huey's short-spindle chair has a roll top, an alternative treatment that is perhaps more indicative of New England or New York influence than Pennsylvanian. Another tablet-top chair may also have originated in the Zanesville area, for its ornamental midback slat is closely related to one painted with cornucopias and bunches of grapes in a Huey settee. Wooster and Zanesville were centers of county government: business was usually brisker than in the surrounding communities, offering particular encouragement to artisans, young and old. Zanesville had other advantages. It was located on the National Road, about seventy miles west of Wheeling. From its location on the Muskingum River, Zanesville had access via steamboat to the Ohio River through a system of dams, locks, and short canals. Sixteen miles north at the village of Dresden, the Muskingum joined the Ohio Canal, a commercial waterway extending from Cleveland on Lake Erie to Portsmouth on the Ohio. At Akron, along the canal route north to Cleveland, a connection with the Pennsylvania Canal gave access to Pittsburgh. Huey's trading potential was matched by few.[48]

Surprisingly, documented vernacular chairs of Cincinnati origin are almost unknown, despite the fact that Cincinnati was the most prominent commercial city in the West and dominated the Ohio River trade below Pittsburgh. Carl David Arfwedson, a Swedish traveler in America, reported seeing "some fifty to one hundred steamboats besides other craft" riding at anchor there in 1833. A few years earlier, Frances Trollope had described the quay as about a quarter of a mile in length with space for as many as thirty steamboats to unload at one time. From about 9,600 residents in 1820, the population had risen to almost 25,000 in 1830 and 47,000 in 1840. One commentator suggested 200 to 350 houses were erected each year from 1827 to 1840, despite a disastrous flood in 1832 and economic depressions. Gross sales in the furniture trades amounted to about $400,000 in 1836and $700,000 in 1840.[49]

William Smith Deming of Newington, Connecticut, who resided in Cincinnati in 1837 and 1838, commented on the cosmopolitan character of the western states, which he described as "composed of every nation on the globe." The Cincinnati directory for 1840, lists 88 chairmakers, turners, ornamental painters, and chair caners and identifies the birthplace of most: 37 individuals were born in Pennsylvania, Maryland, or New Jersey, 11 in Ohio, 10 in Germany or Austria, 9 in Great Britain, 7 in New York, 7 in New England, and 2 in the South. Community awareness of eastern chairmaking trends was high. Isaac M. Lee offered chairs in "the latest and most improved fashions, from the Eastward" in 1829, a statement Samuel Stibbs echoed. The Skinner brothers, Corson C. and Philip, war-

Figure 29 Tablet-top Windsor side chair (one of two), George Turner, Philadelphia, 1835–1842. Woods not recorded. H. 33¼″, W. 16″. (Private collection; courtesy, The Winterthur Library; Decorative Arts Photographic Collection.)

ranted their work "equal to any manufactured in the western country, or even in the eastern Cities." Still other eastern influences were at work in the furniture-making community at large. Philadelphia craftsmen published seven price books for cabinetworkers between 1786 and 1828, a practice Pittsburgh and Cincinnati cabinetmakers imitated in 1830; the Cincinnati interests also published another volume in 1836. The distance between East and West was diminishing.[50]

Philadelphia chairmakers introduced a rounded-end tablet to vernacular seating about the mid-1830s (fig. 29); it quickly replaced the rectangular crest. Impetus for the pattern derived from a new design in formal seating furniture dating to about 1830: a scroll-end crest sawed at the center top with a tablet and at the lower edges with small, shaped arches flanking a large, vertical, baluster-shaped back splat. Rounded-crest chairs had been current in Europe since the early part of the century but perhaps came to particular American notice only with the publication and circulation of George Smith's *Cabinetmaker and Upholsterer's Guide* (London) in 1826. The imported title was advertised by Baltimore booksellers in January 1830. A formal Baltimore chair with the new, rounded crest and the baluster splat bears the stencil of Anthony H. Jenkins and is dated 1832 to 1837 by the address and firm name.[51]

A rounded-end tablet-top crest may have been introduced to Philadelphia vernacular seating before it was used on painted furniture in Baltimore, where the rectangular tablet top was popular. A rounded tablet was still current in eastern Pennsylvania, with modifications, after the Civil War. George Turner's labeled chair is a straightforward Pennsylvania design (fig. 29), varying from the McDonough chair (fig. 26) only in

Figure 30 Child's tablet-top Windsor side chair, Jonas Thatcher, Wheeling, W.Va., 1845–1851. Yellow poplar (seat). H. 30⅞", W. (seat) 14½", D. (seat) 12⅝". (Oglebay Institute Mansion Museum; photo, courtesy, Winterthur Museum.)

tablet shape. Even the front stretcher ornament is similar. A subtle change soon occurred in the rounded-end tablet-top crest. John D. Johnson and John T. Sterrett, partners in Philadelphia from 1843 to 1848, made a chair with the new top piece: they sawed the ends in higher arches and flared the bottom corners outward. This shouldered tablet soon became the norm in local vernacular seating (see fig. 31).[52]

The tablet on a child's chair from Wheeling, West Virginia (fig. 30), falls somewhere between the two Philadelphia designs. Baltimore features, however, dominate the hybrid pattern. The swelled legs with ringed balls at the tops are elongated and inverted versions of the back supports of figure 23. The front stretcher, which is identical to the front brace in the James Huey roll-top chair made at Zanesville, is derivative of an earlier Baltimore fancy chair framed with a sawed, "Grecian," or scroll, back. That fancy chair also had a large medallion centered beneath the crest. Medallion shapes varied from an anthemion to pairs of cornucopias or swans to the present figure—a modified Baltimore lyre disguised with floral ornament. Below the cross slat, the flat sticks with small beads in the shafts are virtually the same as those in the lower back of figure 19, a chair also from the Wheeling, West Virginia, shop of Jonas Thatcher.[53]

Mid-Nineteenth-Century Styles

The successor to the rounded-end (fig. 29) and the shouldered-tablet chairs with midback slats and short spindles was the Pennsylvania (and Philadelphia) shouldered-tablet baluster-splat Windsor (fig. 31). Formal furniture provided the prototype. The basic Windsor design is the same as earlier, modified only by a ring-turned front stretcher in place of the medallion brace and a deeper shouldered crest. The substitution of a bold, vertical splat at the center back for the stick-and-slat structure is radical and dramatic. The sizable splat provides an additional flat surface for the lavish display of ornament. John Swint, whose small name brand appears on the plank, had a shop in Lancaster, Pennsylvania, from the mid-1840s. Judging by the number of chairs bearing his brand, his business flourished, and production was substantial. The craftsman's aggressive advertising likely contributed to his success: "Chairs! Chairs! Chairs! the subscriber has removed his Chair Manufactory . . . next door to Schofield's tavern . . . where he keeps on hand or will make to order Chairs and Settees of all kinds."[54]

The shouldered-tablet baluster-splat chair is marked by considerable variety. Some splats are narrow and considerably less curved in profile; a few have an angular bulge at the center (see fig. 32). More expensive versions are pierced by a large inverted keyhole or similar shape. Far more variation occurs in the crest. The Swint tablet, sawed with moderate shoulders, a low top projection, and a straight lower edge, is one option. Occasionally, the projection is higher. The latest examples have a scalloped, wavy, or flattened profile and simple rounded ends. Tablets sawed with small arches on the lower edge (see fig. 32) are stylistically later than those with a straight lower edge; the usual arch shapes are lunettes and cusps.

In rural Pennsylvania, shouldered-tablet, baluster-splat patterns continued in use long past the Civil War. Frequently, a single shop produced several styles simultaneously. Two cases in point are the shops of William F. Snyder (1845–1921) at Mifflintown, Juniata County, and of James Wilson (b. 1826) of Taylorstown, southwest of Pittsburgh. Snyder became proprietor of the Mifflintown Chair Works established by his father-in-

Figure 31 Tablet-top Windsor side chair (one of four), John Swint, Lancaster, Pa., 1845–1855. Yellow poplar (seat). H. 33, W. (seat) 15³⁄₈″, D. (seat) 14⁵⁄₈″. (Lancaster County Historical Society; photo, courtesy, Winterthur Museum.)

law, probably in the 1860s. He produced short-spindle, slat-back chairs and shouldered-tablet chairs (plain or arched on the lower edge) with solid or pierced splats. Wilson opened for business in 1852 in his native western Pennsylvania, having trained at Philadelphia, where he worked for several years as a journeyman. Wilson's one-and-a-half-story log structure with a rear shed survives, along with many of his chair templates, or patterns. He produced side chairs, armchairs, rocking chairs, and settees in curved-, angular-, and pierced-splat styles coordinated with crests having rounded, shouldered, or scrolled ends and either flat or lunette-arched lower edges.[55]

A few splat-back chairs have highly stylized crests. An excellent example is the chair in figure 32, one of five with a matching rocker that came from a Shenandoah Valley family living in Rockingham County. The low projection on the square-shouldered crest is scrolled backward, forming a heavy lip, but is otherwise reminiscent of the small center tablet in Samuel Fizer's slat-back chair (see fig. 11) made elsewhere in the valley several decades earlier. The angular splat is uncommon. That in the illustrated chair elicits further comment, having an unusually narrow frontal profile where the neck sweeps into the asymmetrical crest arches. Side pieces curving continuously from the seat to the crest are a Windsor rarity borrowed from the fancy chair (see fig. 23). (Plank-seat chairs with this feature also turn up occasionally in central Pennsylvania, and an unusual broad-seated example bears the stencil of William Coles of Springfield, Ohio.) The shape is loosely based on the *chaise gondole*, a chair of French origin, although the immediate prototype may be a design in the 1808 supplement to *The London Chair-Makers' and Carvers' Book of Prices*, which is termed a "Roman" chair. The front legs are a highly stylized form of Baltimore turning, adapted from designs such as those in figure 23. (Other stylized variations of Baltimore prototypes occur in figures 19 and 25.) Even the rear legs are different; the cylinders curve inward sharply above the rear stretcher. The red and black grained surface finished with yellow and salmon-colored banding and penciling is original.[56]

Figure 32 Tablet-top Windsor side chair (one of five with a rocking chair), Shenandoah Valley, Va., probably Rockingham Co., 1850–1870. Woods and dimensions not recorded. (Photo, Mint Spring Antiques.)

The last nineteenth-century design to fall within the basic tradition of Windsor chairmaking established in the mid-eighteenth century has a round top and what is today referred to as a balloon back (fig. 33). Production concentrated in Pennsylvania and Ohio. Few, if any, chairs predate 1855. The understructure of figure 33 bears a remarkable similarity to the Enos chair made in Delaware about mid-century (fig. 18), suggesting an eastern Pennsylvania origin and underscoring the adaptability of some designs and the importance of interchangeable parts to the trade. Angular splats such as this one appear to have been favored in late Pennsylvania work, and decoration, sometimes lavish, frequently combines delicate penciled ornament with bold fruit and floral motifs. A suite of seating furniture consisting of two rocking chairs and six side chairs has a large painted shell centered in the crest. An inscription on the base of one rocking chair reads: "Painted and decorated by Frederick Fox, Chair Maker, August 25, 1877." Fox was a longtime resident of Reading, Pennsylvania. His side chair is comparable to the one illustrated, with some loss of vigor in the leg turnings.[57]

Few Ohio balloon-back Windsors are documented. Some are indistinguishable from the eastern counterparts, although a distinctive Ohio style appears to have been produced as well (fig. 34). George Deckman stenciled both his name and Malvern location beneath the plank of the illustrated chair. The back is considerably lighter in his design than the Pennsylvania pattern. The serpentine profile and slot relieve the mass of the top. Frequently referred to as a handhold but more the size of a fingerhold, the opening probably was intended as an ornament. The points of the splat complement the peaks of the crest and unify the design. The seat is less modeled than the Pennsylvania plank, but the trim lines harmonize with the delicacy of the back. The front legs are characteris-

Figure 33 Balloon-back Windsor side chair, probably eastern Pennsylvania, 1855–1870. Woods not recorded. H. 33¼″, W. 18⅜″, D. 20½″. (The Museum of Fine Arts, Houston; The Bayou Bend Collection, gift of Miss Ima Hogg.)

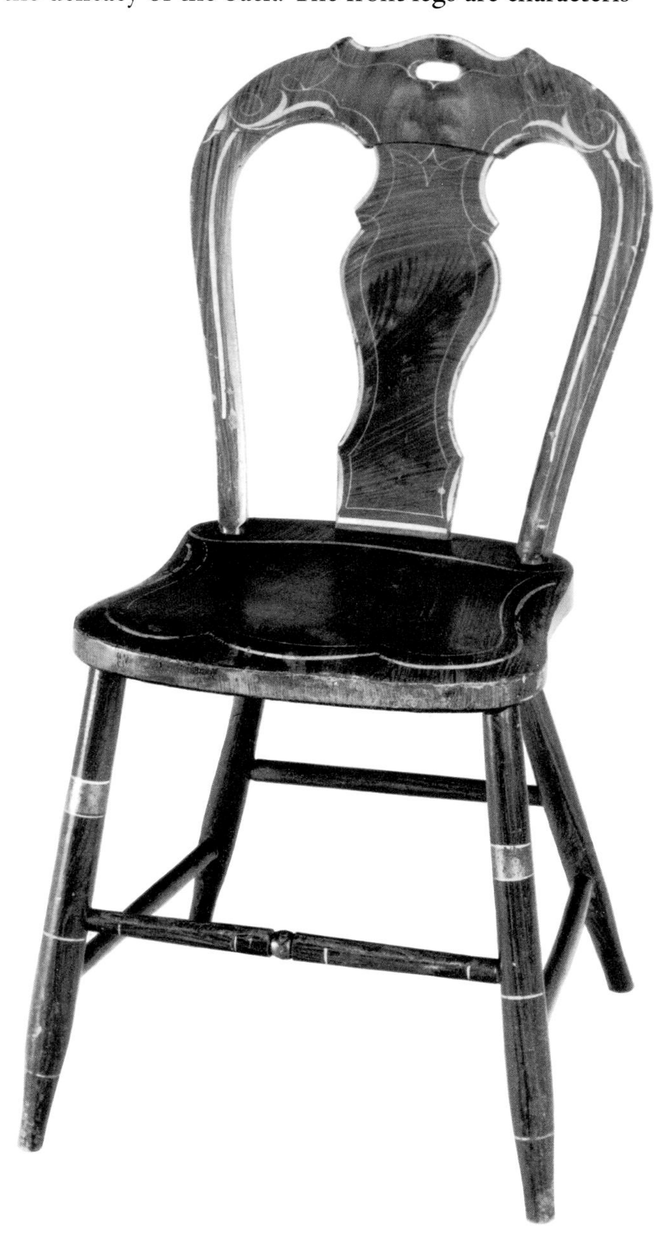

Figure 34 Balloon-back Windsor side chair (one of six), George Deckman, Malvern, Ohio, 1862–1880. Maple and other woods. H. 33⅞″, W. (seat) 16½″, D. (seat) 18½″. (Henry Ford Museum & Greenfield Village, Dearborn, Michigan, B18868.)

tic of late work: bands of contrasting paint simulate ball and ring turnings. Other Ohio-ascribed chairs have turned elements closer to those in figure 19.[58]

George Deckman, the maker of the Ohio chair, was of Prussian birth but grew up in Philadelphia, where he received his training. He followed his parents to Ohio in the late 1850s and by 1862 had established a furniture manufactory at Malvern, Carroll County, employing eleven men. Carroll County is hilly and in Deckman's day was well wooded. Sandy Creek may have been the power source for the manufactory. Deckman's enterprise also benefited from the routing of a spur of the Cleveland and Pittsburgh Railroad through Malvern. With power at his door, raw materials in the neighborhood, and substantial marketing potential, Deckman possessed the ingredients for success; indeed, his business flourished into the twentieth century. By then, the small craft shop had all but disappeared, and even regional marketing was being supplanted by national distribution.[59]

In summary, Eastern businessmen and chairmakers found profitable commercial contact in the South and West from the establishment of the new American republic through the mid-nineteenth century. The entrepreneurial spirit, common among Philadelphia's craftsmen, extended to the chairmaking community at Baltimore, an up-and-coming commercial center advantageously located on the Chesapeake Bay. Knowledge of furniture design was further disseminated as migrating families transferred household goods beyond the vicinity of both cities and kinsfolk maintained interregional ties. Of particular importance in promoting the transfer process were the transient chairmakers trained in Eastern centers who carried their craft expertise and knowledge of the latest patterns from region to region. Expediting and broadening the flow of ideas were advances in transportation technology. Even as early as the 1810s and 1820s, Philadelphia and Baltimore influence in vernacular seating furniture had pervaded most settled areas of the South and West.

1. Isaac Weld, *Travels through the States of North America*, 2 vols. (London: John Stockdale, 1800), 1: 59, 115.

2. Lieutenant John Harriott, *Struggles through Life*, 3 vols. (Philadelphia: James Humphreys, 1809), 2: 70; Henry Tudor, *Narrative of a Tour in North America*, 2 vols. (London: James Duncan, 1834), 1: 73; François Alexandre Frédéric La Rochefoucault Liancourt, *Travels through the United States of North America*, 2 vols. (London: R. Phillips, 1799), 2: 129; John Melish, *Travels through the United States of America*, 2 vols. (Philadelphia: author, 1815), 1: 185; Weld, *Travels* 1: 59–60.

3. James M. Miller, *The Genesis of Western Culture: The Upper Ohio Valley, 1800–1825* (Columbus: Ohio State Archaeological and Historical Society, 1938); Malcolm J. Rohrbough, *The Trans-Appalachian Frontier: People, Societies, and Institutions, 1775–1850* (New York: Oxford University Press, 1978). Farther west, Mississippi, Illinois, Alabama, and Missouri were admitted to the Union in 1817, 1818, 1819, and 1821, respectively.

4. Miller, *Genesis*, pp. 13–15; Max Farrand, ed., *A Journey to Ohio in 1810, as Recorded in the Journal of Margaret Van Horn Dwight* (New Haven: Yale University Press, 1913), p. 47; Morris Birkbeck, *Notes on a Journey in America* (Philadelphia, 1819), as quoted in John W. Harpster, ed., *Pen Pictures of Early Western Pennsylvania* (Pittsburgh: University of Pittsburgh Press, 1938), p. 274; John Bristed, *America and Her Resources* (1818; reprint ed., New York: Research Reprints, 1970), p. 427.

5. Birkbeck, *Notes*, in Harpster, *Pen Pictures*, p. 275; Bristed, *America*, p. 427.

6. William MacPherson Hornor, Jr., *Blue Book: Philadelphia Furniture* (1935; reprint ed., Washington: Highland House, 1977), p. 298. The William Widdifield indenture is listed in "Bonds of Indemnity & Memorandum of & Indentures of the Poor," 1751–97, Municipal Archives, Philadelphia, (microfilm, Joseph Downs Collection of Manuscripts and Printed Ephemera, Winterthur Library, Winterthur, Del., hereafter cited as Downs, WL). Cadwalader's patronage is noted in Nancy A. Goyne, "Francis Trumble of Philadelphia, Windsor Chair and Cabinetmaker," *Winterthur Portfolio 1*, (Winterthur, Del.: Winterthur Museum, 1964), p. 230. Henry Knox Papers, Maine Historical Society, Portland; Invoices, William Cox to Stephen Girard, March 12, July 7, 1791, Girard Papers, Girard College (microfilm, American Philosophical Society, Philadelphia, hereafter cited as APS); manifests of schooner *Fredericksburg Packet* (August 10, 1791), sloop *Nancy* (June 13, 1799), and sloop *Betsey* (October 3, 1799), Philadelphia Outward Entries, U.S. Custom House Records and French Spoliation Claims, National Archives, Washington, D.C. (hereafter cited as NA).

7. Stoner is listed as a Harrisburg resident in the 1790 federal census. On December 3, 1793, Stoner, identified as a chairmaker, and his wife sold a piece of land in Harrisburg; Registry of Deeds, Dauphin Co., Harrisburg, Pa. (reference, courtesy of Joe Kindig, Jr.). The craftsman's one-story, 15- by 19-foot frame shop is described in the U.S. Direct Tax of 1798, City of Lancaster, Federal Archives and Records Center, Philadelphia. Stoner had an apprentice of German background, who is identified as David Trissler in the *Lancaster Journal* of August 15, 1801.

8. The fan-back chairs are privately owned.

9. Giles Cromwell, "Andrew and Robert McKim Windsor Chair Makers," *Journal of Early Southern Decorative Arts* 6, no. 1 (May 1980): 1: 1–20; Klaus Wust, *The Virginia Germans* (Charlottesville: University Press of Virginia, 1969), p. 105.

10. Margaret Berwind Schiffer, *Furniture and Its Makers of Chester County, Pennsylvania* (Philadelphia: University of Pennsylvania Press, 1966), p. 151; Hornor, *Blue Book*, p. 324. Information on McIntire's death, courtesy of Mr. and Mrs. James A. Drain.

11. The McKim writing-arm chair is in the Museum of Early Southern Decorative Arts, Winston-Salem, N.C. (hereafter cited as MESDA). For a photograph of the Madison Co. chair, see research file S-7067, MESDA.

12. Thaddeus M. Harris, *The Journal of a Tour into the Territory Northwest of the Alleghany Mountains* (Boston, 1805), as quoted in Harpster, *Pen Pictures*, pp. 242–43; Thomas Ashe, *Travels in America, Performed in 1806* (Newburyport, Mass.: William Sawyer, 1808), pp. 25–26; Christian Schultz, Jr., *Travels on an Inland Voyage* (1810; reprint ed., Ridgewood, N.J.: Gregg Press, 1968), pp. 124–26; Melish, *Travels*, 2: 55; Dorothy Smith Coleman, "Pioneers of Pittsburgh: The Robinsons," *Western Pennsylvania Historical Magazine* 42, no. 1 (1959): 61, 70.

13. Craftsmen working outside Philadelphia who made the double-bow medallion chair include Ebenezer P. Rose (Trenton), Jared Chesnut (Wilmington), Storel Hutchinson (Bucks Co.), Samuel Lobach (Berks Co.), Frederick and Jacob Fetter (Lancaster Co.), and John McClintic (Franklin Co.). An armchair is associated with a Chester Co. family. The mate chair is illustrated in an advertisement of Brentwood Auction Gallery, *Antiques and the Arts Weekly* (Newtown, Conn.), January 28, 1977. The chair with rectangular tablets in the spindles is illustrated in an advertisement of Carl W. Stinson, *Antiques and the Arts Weekly*, September 22, 1978.

14. The New York and Boston patterns mentioned here are illustrated in Nancy Goyne Evans, "Design Sources for Windsor Furniture, Part II: The Early Nineteenth Century," *Antiques* 133, no. 5 (May 1988): 1134, fig. 6; 1133, pl. 4, fig. 5.

15. Invoice, Thomas Ashton to Stephen Girard, August 18, 1815, Girard Papers, Girard College (microfilm, APS); Delaware Legislative Accounts, Hall of Records, Dover.

16. Fizer advertisement, *Virginia Herald of the Valley* (Fincastle, Va.), September 4, 1820 (MESDA research files).

17. For a photograph of the chair recovered at Sheppardstown, see research file S-10,459, MESDA.

18. Joshua Johnson (attributed) painted the Hasson brothers of Baltimore seated in Windsor chairs with crests of this pattern when they posed for their portrait about 1815 to 1818. The portrait is in the Winterthur Museum collection.

19. For other settees, see Emma L. Middleton advertisement, *Antiquarian* 9 (April 1928): 20; *American Heritage Society*, November 16–18, 1972 (New York: Sotheby Parke Bernet, 1972), lot 734. For the writing-arm chair, see *American Antiques*, November 27, 1976 (Hy-

annis, Mass.: Richard A. Bourne, 1976), lot 104. For a photograph of the highchair, see research file S-10,692, MESDA.

20. The chairs associated with piedmont Virginia and Frederick Co., Md., are in private collections. For photographs of chairs found in western Pennsylvania, see Visual Resources Collection, Winterthur Library, 78.1941, 78.1942 (hereafter cited as VRC, WL).

21. Priest advertisement, *Imperial Review and Cumberland Repository* (Nashville, Tenn.), March 24, 1808. For the armchair owned in Kentucky, see Edna Talbott Whitley, *A Checklist of Kentucky Cabinetmakers from 1775–1859* (Paris, Ky.: author, 1970), fig. G (right). Snapshots of the Masonic Windsor are courtesy of Frank Tammaro.

22. The Athenaeum chair purchases are discussed in Robert C. Smith, "The Athenaeum's Furniture—1," *Athenaeum Annals* 4, no. 1 (January 1958): 1–2. The Burchall and Wickersham chair is in the Chester County Historical Society, West Chester, Pa.

23. The documented or attributed chairs referred to are in private collections, except as follows: a Joseph Jones (Chester Co.) arrow-spindle chair illustrated in Margaret Bleecker Blades, *Two Hundred Years of Chairs and Chairmaking*, exh. cat. (West Chester, Pa.: Chester County Historical Society, 1987), fig. 20; Mifflin Co. attributed chairs illustrated in Chuck Riser advertisement, *Maine Antique Digest* (Waldoboro, Me.), December 1990; chairs documented and attributed to Centre and Union Co.'s illustrated in Marie Purnell Musser, *Country Chairs of Central Pennsylvania* (Mifflinburg, Pa.: author, 1990), figs. 63, 66, 71, 84.

24. For photographs of the Seaton and Matthews, Johnson and Hardy, and Moravian chairs, see research files S-6569, S-6139, S-6805, MESDA. For the George T. Johnson chair, see Patricia A. Piorkowski, *Piedmont Virginia Furniture, Product of Provincial Cabinetmakers*, exh. cat. (Lynchburg, Va.: Lynchburg Museum System, 1982), cat. 17. A Wheeling example by Jonas Thatcher is in the Oglebay Institute Mansion Museum, Wheeling, W.Va.

25. Harris, *Journal*, as quoted in Harpster, *Pen Pictures*, pp. 243–44; Melish, *Travels*, 2: 57; Henry Bradshaw Fearon, *Sketches of America*, 2d ed. (London: Longman, Hurst, Rees, Orme, and Brown, 1818), pp. 203, 281; Miller, *Genesis*, p. 31; Rohrbough, *Trans-Appalachian Frontier*, pp. 163, 176; Samuel R. Brown, *The Western Gazetteer, or Emigrant's Directory* (Auburn, N.Y.: H. C. Southwick, 1817), p. 149.

26. Melish, *Travels*, pp. 60–61; Rohrbough, *Trans-Appalachian Frontier*, p. 173; Bristed, *America*, pp. 31, 66.

27. Jane Sikes Hageman, *Ohio Furniture Makers, 1790–1845*, 2 vols. (Cincinnati, Ohio: author, 1984), 1: 115–17, 120–21, 167–68; illustration, p. 61 (lower right).

28. For the Indiana-ascribed settee, see Jerard and Pat Jordan, *The Spirit of America* (Des Moines, Iowa: Wallace-Homestead, 1975), p. 52. For a photograph of the Ward and Stokes settee, see 70.584, VRC, WL.

29. A. H. and W. R. Wood advertisements, *Nashville Whig and Tennessee Advertiser*, January 31, 1818, May 1 and August 7, 1819 (MESDA research files). Notices concerning a land dispute and Alexander Wood's election as an officer of the Grand Masonic Lodge of Tennessee are in *Nashville Gazette*, June 3, 1820, and *Clarksville [Tenn] Gazette*, October 21, 1820 (MESDA research files).

30. Ellen Beasley, "Tennessee Cabinetmakers and Chairmakers through 1840," *Antiques* 100, no. 4 (October 1971): 613, 617–18, 620–21.

31. The West Chester bank chair is in the Chester County Historical Society. A scalloped-crest chair is illustrated in Evans, "Design Sources," p. 1139, pl. 13. James C. Helme, "Book of Prices for Making a Cabinet & chair furnature August 20th 18[38]," Downs, WL.

32. The Snyder chair is illustrated and discussed in Musser, *Country Chairs*, pp. 37–38, fig. 23. For the Rhein chairs, see Frank R. Gaglio advertisement, *Maine Antique Digest*, August 1979. A Henry Rhein is listed in Reading in the 1840 census, a Henry E. Rhein is listed in Berks Co. in 1850 and 1860, and a Henry R. Rhein is listed in Berks Co. in 1860. For photographs of the masonic chairs, see research files, MESDA. The example found in Clarke Co., Ga., is illustrated in *Neat Pieces: The Plain-Style Furniture of 19th Century Georgia*, exh. cat. (Atlanta: Atlanta Historical Society, 1983), fig. 32.

33. For the Hardy chair, see Piorkowski, *Piedmont Virginia Furniture*, cat. 18. The Moravian-owned chair is in Old Salem, Winston-Salem, N.C. For the Tennessee associated chairs, see Derita Coleman Williams and Nathan Harsh, *The Art and Mystery of Tennessee Furniture and Its Makers through 1850* (Nashville: Tennessee State Museum Foundation, 1988), p. 255. Robert E. and Cherry G. DiBartolomeo, "Wheeling's Chairs and Chairmakers, 1828–1865," *Spinning Wheel* 26, no. 4 (May 1970): 14–16, 50.

Graham Hood

American or English Furniture? Some Choices in the 1760s

▼ IN JULY 1768 in London, Norborne Berkeley, baron de Botetourt, learned that he was to become the next governor of Virginia, the first full governor to take up residence in the colony in almost sixty years. With a sense of haste brought on by the ministry's alarm at the colonists' fiery opposition to the Stamp Act of 1765 and the subsequent Declaratory and Townshend Acts, Botetourt prepared for his departure and actually embarked in August. He stepped onto American soil at Little England in Hampton Roads on October 26 and that same evening arrived by coach in Williamsburg. By the time of his sudden and much lamented death two years later, Lord Botetourt had endeared himself to a wide range of Virginians and had deeply impressed them with his sincerity, his wisdom, his industry, and his taste.

The remarkable documentation that has survived from this man's English and American careers enables us to gauge the level of his cultural experience in England and identify many of the preparations he undertook and the supplies he ordered for his American residence (about which he was evidently fully informed in London as soon as his appointment became known). It also explains the atmosphere and environment he created in Williamsburg, as the official representative of the king and, further, as a sensitive and sympathetic compatriot of the residents of the distant province. In particular, the evidence contained in hitherto unpublished accounts (reproduced in the appendix) reveals his dealings with a London cabinetmaker and his petty cash disbursements in Williamsburg and throws some light on what was considered appropriate for stylish and elegant rooms in a British colony in the third quarter of the eighteenth century.[1]

Born into a west country family of ancient lineage, Berkeley inherited a comfortable estate in 1736, which he proceeded to develop and expand with considerable acumen. He served as a Tory Member of Parliament for Gloucestershire for more than twenty years and maintained a secondary residence in London. In 1746 he had the good fortune to see his sister (and only sibling) become the fourth duchess of Beaufort, which created an important niche for him in one of the most powerful west country families. On the death of the fourth duke (1756), Botetourt became a guardian for his nephew, the fifth duke (then in his minority)—a most influential appointment. A significant presence in the burgeoning port city of Bristol, Berkeley also developed the coal fields on his estates and invested in local brass and copper industries to the point where he

Figure 1 Ballroom, Governor's Palace, Williamsburg, Virginia. (Photo, Colonial Williamsburg Foundation.) The Governor's Palace was reconstructed on its eighteenth-century foundations in the early 1930s. It was refurbished in 1981, based on extensive historical research conducted by the staff of Colonial Williamsburg into Lord Botetourt's inventory, account books, cash books, and other documents that he sent back to England.

became enormously successful, although a major investment collapsed in the period from 1766 to 1768. In 1760 he gained a position as Groom of the Bedchamber at the court of the young George III, the Whigs having finally lost their long ascendency. Four years later he petitioned for and assumed an ancient barony associated with his family, thus becoming a member of the House of Lords and a Lord of the Bedchamber at court.[2]

Although a man of business and a politician more than a connoisseur or collector, Botetourt was a longtime and active member of the Society of the Dilettanti and, through his sister's connections, was involved with levels of patronage that tapped such great figures as architects William Kent, James Gibbs, Robert Adam, and landscape architect Thomas Wright. Painters such as Antonio Canaletto, Joshua Reynolds, and the more pedestrian John Wootton, Thomas Hudson, and Joseph Highmore, as well as sculptors like John Michael Rysbrack received commissions to produce works for his family. Leading London silversmiths and even the incomparable Paris firm of Germain made elaborate wares for use at Badminton or the Beauforts' house in Grosvenor Square, London.

Botetourt's brother-in-law was a charter subscriber to Thomas Chippendale's *The Gentleman and Cabinet-Maker's Director* (1754) and commissioned furniture from the London cabinetmaking firm of William and John Linnell, most conspicuously for his lavish Chinese bedchamber at Badminton. Both Botetourt's nephew and a niece (who married Sir Watkin Williams Wynn) gave extensive patronage to Robert Adam in the 1760s. Through his position at court and his manifest interest in cultural matters, he became familiar with an even wider range of artistic endeavors than his ducal connections would normally have warranted.[3]

Given his rank, his wealth, his connections, and his experience, it was natural that in 1768 Botetourt had a network of accomplished and trustworthy tradesmen to call on whenever he needed additional furnishings and supplies. On learning that he was to depart promptly for Virginia and a new residence, it was perhaps inevitable for him to order items that he believed he would need for his new abode from established, reliable sources. On the other hand, diplomacy—at which he was most adept—might have suggested that he reserve some patronage for provincial tradesmen, a well-established practice for affluent patrons with both London houses and country seats. He was, moreover, given detailed information about his new habitat that surely included opinions on the availability and reliability of sources of household supplies (and furnishings) in the colonial capital. This information was sufficient for him, before he left London, to order at the cost of several hundred pounds cut-glass chandeliers, iron warming machines or stoves, and stylish wallpaper with gilt border (plus the necessary materials for installing it) for the Governor's Palace ballroom and supper room (fig. 1). He also directed that his replicas of the full-length state portraits of the monarch and his consort, which he had commissioned earlier from Allan Ramsay, be sent to Williamsburg on completion. Thus he had obviously determined, even before he embarked, that the primary social rooms in the Palace needed repapering, that they lacked heat, and that they were grand enough to accommodate chandeliers and royal portraits. Clearly he felt sure enough of this information that he decided against waiting until his arrival in Williamsburg before committing to this large expenditure.[4]

Such supplies as mentioned above were obtainable from colonial tradesmen only with the greatest difficulty at best, so it was most practical for Botetourt to order them in London. But much of the furniture that he ordered before his departure could have been procured in Williamsburg from one or more of several cabinetmakers in the colonial capital or in the largest city nearby, Norfolk. The long list of items in Botetourt's account with London cabinetmaker William Fenton in the summer of 1768 contains numerous pieces that Botetourt might have purchased in Williamsburg. For reasons that at this point can only be surmised, he chose not to.[5]

That someone acquainted with Williamsburg would have indicated what goods were available there to Englishmen about to depart for the colony is suggested by an account of comments made in London in 1765 by William Small, former professor of mathematics (and later of rhetoric and moral philosophy) at the College of William and Mary. Small had been a close friend of Francis Fauquier (lieutenant governor and resident in the Palace from 1758 to 1768), and of George Wythe, mentor of Thomas Jefferson during his Williamsburg years. His observations on the colonial capital were reported by Stephen Hawtrey to his brother Edward, who was investigating a post at the college in 1765. Hawtrey had sought out Small in London, through the Virginia Coffee House, and a few days later wrote to his brother what to expect. A professor's rooms in the college, Small noted, had a certain "homeliness of . . . appearance." He continued, "you may buy Furniture there, all except bedding and blankets, which you must carry over; chairs and tables rather cheaper than in England . . . you must [also] have one Suit of handsome full-dressed Silk cloaths to wear on the King's birthday at the Governor's. . . . As to the rest of your wearing apparel, you may dress as you please, for the fashions don't change, and you may wear the same coat 3 years. . . . Shoes and Stockings are very dear articles."[6]

Although the requirements and the level of sophistication expected of a governor would have been different from those of a young college professor, the situation described by Small presumably would have led any future resident of the colonial capital to think that all but the very smartest items for the most public spaces of a fashionable residence would be obtainable there. There would be savings involved in initial cost and in shipping, and there would be political advantages in the patronage of local tradesmen.

That Botetourt was given information about Williamsburg (probably similar to that described above) before he left London is confirmed by a long letter from George Mercer to his brother James in Williamsburg, dated August 16, 1768. George Mercer, Virginia agent for the Ohio Company was in London petitioning, among others, the Earl of Hillsborough, Secretary of State for the colonies, for a government post. In his letter (known only through a nineteenth-century transcript), Mercer confided that Botetourt had "employed [him] as his councillor as to the first arrangement of his family affairs in Virginia." Mercer claimed that he had given the governor-designate advice and information "such as indeed it is impossible any one about him could have given." Mention of a number of contemporary Williamsburg names and a long, careful assessment of Botetourt's character and qualities that corresponds remarkably closely to the many evaluations made by Virginians two years later, after the governor's demise, lend real credence to Mercer's claims, although caution in interpreting his remarks is necessary. He noted, for instance, "I wrote to your Landlord Mr. Nicolson to take the conduct, and direction of his Lordship's Household, till he arrives, and have told him his character—I wish he may be of use to him, however he will supply him genteelly for his trouble now, and will use him in his way of business for the future." The landlord was presumably Robert Nicolson, tailor, who advertised for lodgers as early as 1766, and who had a business connection with James Mercer. Botetourt certainly did use Nicolson in his way of business, but the surviving account (lengthy as it is) does not begin until November 1769, a year after the governor's arrival.[7]

It is also possible that Catherine Fauquier, widow of the late lieutenant governor, called upon her husband's successor before his departure from the city. She had returned to London in 1766 after an eight-year residence in the colony. Such a thoughtful and genteel gesture would have provided Botetourt with a singular insight into conditions in Williamsburg in general and in the Palace in particular. It is also possible that one of

Figure 2 Parlor, Governor's Palace. (Photo, Colonial Williamsburg Foundation.) The design of the reproduction couch conforms to one that George Washington ordered from Philip Bell in London.

her two adult sons, who had spent periods of time in the colony, paid visits of compliment and offered information and observations. Either visit would have been of particular interest to Botetourt since he had been approached by the executors of the late lieutenant governor's estate in Virginia to determine if he would purchase furnishings left in the Palace at the time of Fauquier's death. Botetourt had accepted the offer and acquired almost £500 worth of goods, in addition to the contents of the well-stocked cellars and one female slave. Though this seems an ample sum, and the list of goods is a lengthy one, these items (the furniture especially) constituted only a relatively small proportion of the more than 16,000 items listed in the sixty-one living and working spaces of the Palace at the time of Botetourt's death two years later.[8]

Botetourt's surviving account with London cabinetmaker William Fenton (see appendix), which includes items clearly destined for Williamsburg, begins with orders dated May 7 and May 20, 1768. These are problematical since it is unclear whether the furnishings were intended for Botetourt's London townhouse, or his country house near Bristol, and were later perhaps diverted to Williamsburg. Very probably Fenton had supplied his aristocratic patron with furnishings before his appointment as governor; he certainly continued to supply labor as well as goods for Botetourt's London townhouse while the latter was in Virginia.

No settee is listed in Botetourt's Williamsburg inventory, which is somewhat unusual for he had one stuffed and repaired by Fenton (possibly for his townhouse) and purchased another from Fauquier's estate for £6 (Virginia currency). He purchased a couch, too, from the same source for £2. Two couches are listed in the Botetourt inventory, one specified as mahogany in the parlor (fig. 2), the other as "ticken" in the butler's pantry. Both were equipped with check covers.

Botetourt kept a reading desk, along with a library table and a mahogany desk, in his dining room in the Palace. Possibly it was the same one that Fenton repaired in May 1768 with a new hinge. The large print frames complete with glass and packing case from Fenton could have been intended for the library in the Palace, along with the seventeen others that were "brass nailed" to the walls there by Joseph Kidd in November 1769 (fig. 3); or for the butler's pantry, among the fourteen there. To achieve the decorative effect in the library, Kidd needed some of the "16 Doz of

Figure 3 Study, Governor's Palace, showing prints "brass nailed" to the walls. (Photo, Colonial Williamsburg Foundation.)

brass headed Stoco nails of Differant Sorts" billed by Fenton on August 12. Though numerous maps, some of them framed perhaps, were listed as Botetourt's property, the only other prints listed in the residence were "standing furniture"—the property of the colony, left by or purchased from previous occupants. No prints were transferred from Fauquier to Botetourt, a surprising omission. Spring curtains were known at the Palace but, again, they were the property of the colony. No other curtains listed in the Botetourt inventory were specified thus. The bedside carpet, 6′ 9″ long, in Fenton's bill may well have been one of the two "bed carpets" or the more tersely noted "carpet" that were listed in the three principal bedchambers of the Palace (fig. 4).[9]

With Fenton's entry of August 7, the destination of the items becomes clearer. The "Large feild bedstead on Castors with Crimson Check furniture made up with lace proper" complete with two mattresses, bolster, two pillows, two blankets, and a quilt with linen backing was supplemented by six identical beds (three of which had quilts with woolen backs and lacked the pillows—for a slightly lower price), all for a total cost of £106.10.0. This not inconsiderable sum was laid out for the principal servants' bedchambers in the Palace. Two years later, Botetourt's Williamsburg inventory included seven field bedsteads—four of them specified as mahogany and six of them listed as complete with red check curtains (fig. 5). Two stood in the garret room probably occupied by the butler, William Marshman, and under butler, Thomas Fuller; one in the garret room of Silas Blandford, whose post was equivalent of land steward; one in the cook's bedchamber, occupied successively by Thomas Towne, John Cooke, William Sparrow, and Mrs. Wilson, a local woman; one in coachman Thomas Gale's room; one in groom Samuel King's room; and a small one with green and white cotton curtains in the room of gardener James Simpson and his successor James Wilson (son of the last cook).[10]

It is possible that the last bed listed above, distinguished by its different colored curtains and "small" size, was the one Botetourt bought from Fauquier's estate for £4—considerably less than the sum Fenton charged for each of his. If so, one of the new beds probably stayed in England. Even at that, the cost of supplying beds for the governor's principal servants amounted to approximately one year's salary for them all together. That Botetourt judged it appropriate to purchase the beds in England, that he did not defer the decision until after his arrival in Williamsburg where he might have acquired similar furniture, new or used, from cabinetmaker Benjamin Bucktrout, for example, who bought from Fauquier's estate "a parcel bedsteads" for £1.10.0, is a significant commentary on the status of his servants in Botetourt's mind, or perhaps of their expectations in signing up for service abroad with him.[11]

The remainder of Fenton's August 7, 1768, bill consisted of large quantities of Wilton carpet and green "bazse," only obtainable from England. The carpeting was probably chosen for the supper room, the library, perhaps the dining room, and the ballroom. Carpets for the first three

Figure 4 Bedchamber, Governor's Palace, showing a chintz bed and bed carpet. (Photo, Colonial Williamsburg Foundation.)

rooms listed above were itemized in the inventory (although several had been taken up for the summer and were thus in storage). Wilton strip-carpeting must have been destined for the ballroom also. Botetourt's "Groom of the Chambers," Joseph Kidd, after he had left the governor's service and had set up for himself in Williamsburg, charged his former employer 10s. "for Pressing and Nailing down a large Carpet for the Ball Room" in November 1769.[12]

Fenton's lengthy itemization of goods on August 12, 1768, includes certain items identified in the Governor's Palace later, although about the first object on the list some doubt remains. The couch bed, for which Fenton supplied mahogany posts and a folding tester, may have been the one that was specified in the inventory in the butler's pantry. It was noted that the couch there had a mattress and bolster, but no curtains were listed. The twelve mahogany chairs covered with hair seating and double brass nailed were very likely ordered for the dining room in Williamsburg, where Botetourt's sociability would have been at its most active,

Figure 5 Field bed with red check curtains, stable, Governor's Palace. (Photo, Colonial Williamsburg Foundation.)

though the governor also bought eighteen hair-bottom chairs for £18 (Virginia currency) from Fauquier's estate, comparable in value to those from Fenton (figs. 6, 7). Botetourt's inventory also included twelve such chairs in the ballroom and twelve in the "Passage up Stairs"—the anteroom to the most formal "Middle Room" on the second floor—in addition to those in the dining room.[13]

The "best Verdeter . . . prusian blew," whiting, leather specks, brushes, and "2 Ream of fine large Elephant paper" were all destined for the ballroom as, probably, were the 20,000 tacks (figs. 1, 8). Certainly the chandeliers and a stove from other London tradesmen as well as the Ramsay portraits were acquired for that handsome space. The "500 foot of Gooder oun Gilt moulding at 9p" for which Fenton charged the governor on October 6 was also part of the above scheme. That these supplies were intended for the grand ballroom is suggested by the quantity of the elephant folio-sized paper (about 1000 sheets) and the amount of border. That it was the ballroom is confirmed by Joseph Kidd's small charges in No-

Figure 6 Dining room, Governor's Palace. (Photo, Colonial Williamsburg Foundation.)

vember 1769 and June 1770 for "Mending Paper in the Ball Room." Since Kidd was groom of the chambers and later advertised (when in business for himself in Williamsburg) that one of his skills was paperhanging, the deduction is that he installed the paper soon after the governor's arrival and did some touch-up repairs to it about a year later. That the furnishing scheme was impressive is attested by the 1771 comment of Cambridge-educated, Virginia great planter, Robert Beverley, in a letter to a London merchant: "I observed that Ld B had hung a room with plain blue Paper and border'd it with a narrow stripe of gilt Leather, wch. I thought had a pretty Effect." Thomas Jefferson was also impressed—in 1769 he ordered identical supplies for a room in his new house. Robert Carter of Nomini Hall purchased plain blue paper in 1773. Col. George Washington began to plan the addition of a ballroom to his house in this period, too, which he intended to decorate with a plain colored paper.[14]

Though the cost of the border that Fenton supplied to Botetourt, £18.15.0, was almost as much as the rest of the wallpapering supplies combined, it was still, to judge by the cost per foot noted in Chippendale's accounts, a papier-mâché border rather than a carved one. The stiffness of this (requiring it to be shipped and stored in "a long box"), yet its apparent difference from carved and gilded wood, is probably what led Beverley to describe it as gilt leather. It, too, would have required some of the plentiful supply of tacks mentioned above for its installation.[15]

Fenton also charged on October 6 for twelve more chairs "the same as the others"—presumably a reference to the ones invoiced on August 12. Because they were new and smart, it is likely that they were destined for the public, highly social ballroom rather than another space in which the inventory lists hair-bottom chairs, such as the anteroom upstairs—a room of service for petitioners and servants to wait in attendance. In the ballroom the presence of monarchy was proclaimed and groups of prominent colonists were entertained at formal receptions and at dinner. The plain blue wallpaper that Botetourt had installed had been (not coincidentally) the personal choice of George III for his private rooms in Buckingham House in the 1760s. The Williamsburg ballroom bore the further, and powerful, imprint of monarchy with the full-length portraits of the king and his consort, Queen Charlotte. The most important occasion for the room's use throughout the year was the annual ball to celebrate the birthday of the king, which "all English Gentlemen" were expected to "attend and pay their respects." With such overtones, and with the dining function for important groups such as the colony's legislators (too numerous to accommodate in the dining room) further established in this space, it is highly likely that the smart, double brass-nailed chairs were intended to be part of the ballroom's accoutrements, just as they were of the dining room's.[16]

Figure 7 Side chair, England, 1760–1770. Mahogany with beech. H. 37½", W: 22½". (Colonial Williamsburg Foundation, acc. 1985-259.) According to tradition, this chair was purchased at the sale of Governor Dunmore's furnishings by a member of the Ambler family; however, identical chairs survive at Badminton, and they could be associated with Botetourt. It is conceivable that this chair was Botetourt's and that it was used by Dunmore after Botetourt died.

The following item on Fenton's list for October 6 shows Botetourt's interest in fashion: "12 Bamboo Chears Blew & gold with lutestring quishons," complete with check cases, were exceptionally stylish. Ten years later such items would have been less conspicuous. As it is, only one earlier reference, with the objects surviving to match the document, is known—a set of bamboo chairs supplied in May 1767 by William Linnell to William Drake for Shardeloes, a house for which Robert Adam had provided designs and advice on modernization in 1765. The Linnell chairs were intended for bedchambers and it was in that location that Botetourt placed his set in the Governor's Palace, eight in the larger room and four in the smaller (figs. 4, 9, 10). When they were inventoried in Williamsburg in October 1770, however, they were described as "Green bamboo chairs with check'd Cushions." Confusion between certain shades of the colors blue and green is not unusual today and probably was not then. (An eighteenth-century instance of this occurs in the well-documented furnishings for Harewood House, Yorkshire, made by Thomas Chippendale.) It is unlikely that Botetourt had his smart new chairs repainted in Williamsburg—there is no hint of it in the accounts—though it is, of course, possible. In placing this fashionable order, Botetourt may have been at least partially inspired by his late brother-in-law, who had commissioned extraordinary Chinese-inspired furniture for his sumptuous Chinese bedchamber at Badminton in 1752–1754.[17]

Figure 8 Ballroom, Governor's Palace, detail showing the wallpaper and border. (Photo, Colonial Williamsburg Foundation.)

Three "large mohogainy Cloaths presses with slideing shelves & drawers 2 of them lined with Green Bazse" for £45 represented heavy, bulky objects that surely would have been less expensive if purchased in Williamsburg. They were clearly of importance to Botetourt since he also purchased a clothespress for £10 (Virginia currency), a large chest of drawers for £12, and four further chests of drawers (presumably smaller) for £12.10.0 from Fauquier's estate. By the time of the governor's death the mahogany clothespresses stood in the two principal bedchambers on the east side of the Palace and in the more formal, ceremonial Middle Room. Botetourt's own bedchamber, however, contained the large walnut and the small chest of drawers, probably acquired from Fauquier, that housed his intimate clothing, whereas the newer presses in the other rooms held his suits and other formal garments. The mahogany basin stands were also intended for bedchambers and were inventoried on the second floor of the Palace (including the Middle Room) as well as in the bedchambers of the senior male servants, Marshman and Blandford (figs. 11, 12). Only three of Fenton's six dressing glasses seem to have been taken to Williamsburg; even then it appears that the item in the governor's bedchamber listed as "1 Wash bason & Mahog. stand compleat with a dressing glass" was a single piece of furniture, whereas the others were described as a "small lookg Glass Mahog. frame," and "1 Swing Looking Glass" (in the coachman's room).[18]

Figure 9 Opposite view of the bedchamber in fig. 4 showing the bamboo chairs. (Photo, Colonial Williamsburg Foundation.)

Figure 10 Arm chair (left), England, 1770–1780. Beech. H. 36⅝″, W. 19½″. (Colonial Williamsburg Foundation, acc. 1936-344.) A somewhat more robust version of the bamboo chair than the Linnell examples referred to above, this chair originally was painted yellow-white with a glazed overcoat of varnish in imitation of bamboo. The chairs to the right are from a set of twelve reproductions made for the Palace.

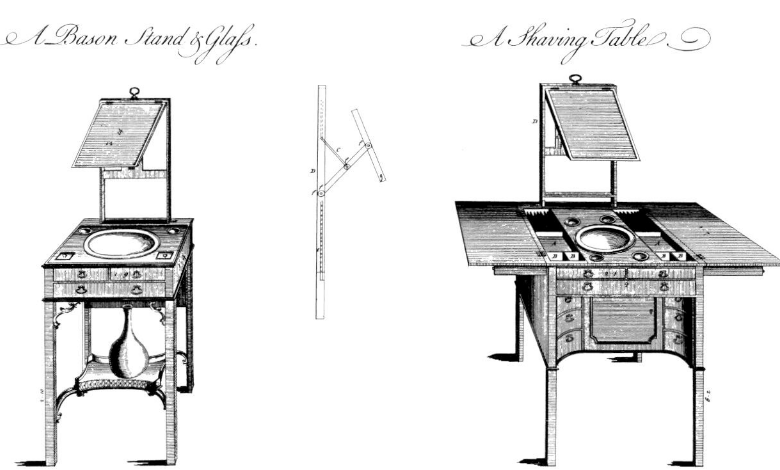

Figure 11 Plate 54 from Thomas Chippendale's *The Gentleman and Cabinet-Maker's Director* (3d. ed., 1762). (Photo, Colonial Williamsburg Foundation.)

Figure 12 Nightstand, eastern Virginia, probably Williamsburg, 1765–1775. Mahogany with yellow pine. H. 32¾″, W. 18¼″. (Colonial Williamsburg Foundation, acc. 1985-40.) This nightstand is typical of the sophisticated, London-style furniture made by Williamsburg cabinetmakers during Botetourt's residence.

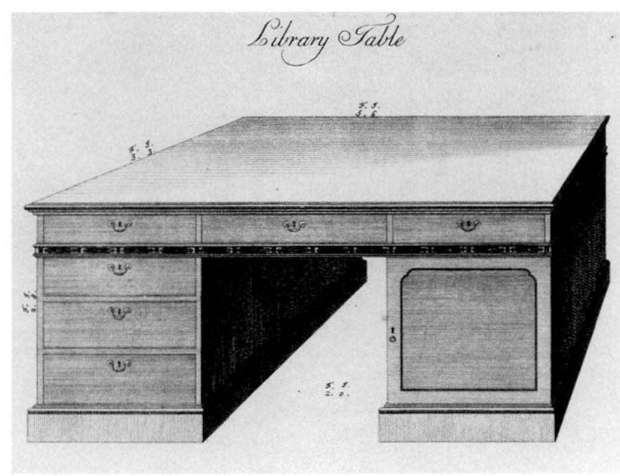

Figure 13 Plate 54 from Thomas Chippendale's *The Gentleman and Cabinet-Maker's Director* (1st. ed., 1754). (Photo, Colonial Williamsburg Foundation.)

Fenton's next entry for furniture and supplies was dated April 15, 1769. The original bill was endorsed (probably by Thomas Conway, the fifth duke's auditor on whom Botetourt relied for supervision of his accounts while he was abroad) "Goods for Virginia." The most expensive item in the bill became the centerpiece of the governor's workspace (fig. 13): "a large & very neat mohogainy lybery table of very fine wood Covered with leather the moulding Richly Carved on 8 3 wheel Castors." At a cost of £24 it was equivalent to a year's wages for a household servant. Clearly a piece of considerable presence, it was destined for the dining room, a large, handsome room that also served as the governor's office. It was inventoried in October 1770 as "1 mahogy library table containg papers public & private," a terse description that gives little insight to its inherent qualities and richness. It did not take kindly to the Virginia climate, for in June 1770 it was necessary to bring in a tradesman who charged 2s. 6d. for "Easeing Drawers and fixing on Moulding To My Lord's Library Table."

A further insight into Botetourt's perceptions of his furniture and the local trade is that, although it appears he had already patronized a Williamsburg artisan (the petty cash disbursements, for February 22, 1769, include "To the Cabinet Maker's bill . . . £3.0.2.3") he delegated the repair of his new and elegant library table to the former carpenter in his retinue, Joshua Kendall. This man could just as readily supply a grease box to the coachman, cut a tub for the gardener, or mend a sifter for the cook (all of which he did the same month). Either the governor had a high regard for his skills or he did not believe that the repair was otherwise likely to jeopardize his expensive new table.[19]

In the same order Fenton also supplied two "3 foot 6 Inch desks & one 3 foot." Perhaps one of these accompanied the library table in the dining room. In this space the inventory listed "1 mahogy Desk, containg sundry papers private & public, one embroidd pocket book a miniature drawing, 1 Diamd mourng ring & a pair of Gold Sleve buttons, pruning knife & a steel pencil." It is, however, possible that the desk Botetourt kept, and clearly used, in his dining room was rather the one (wood unspecified) that he had acquired from Fauquier's estate—"1 boreau and book case"—for £8. In the latter's inventory (somewhat jumbled and not divided by room) this piece was listed near the library table that Botetourt also purchased from the estate for £6. Yet Botetourt relegated this library table to the butler's pantry and for his own use imported something more to his taste. Only four other desks were listed in the entire compound, mahogany ones in the guest bedchamber on the second floor and in Blandford's garret room, and walnut ones in the cook's and coachman's bedchambers.[20]

The disparity between the number of desks Fenton supplied plus those that Botetourt bought used from Fauquier, and the number listed in the Botetourt inventory is repeated in the case of firescreens. Fenton charged £3.10.0 for "3 fire Screens with maps on both Sides." Only two were inventoried in October 1770, a mahogany one in the dining room and

Figure 14 Firescreen, probably Virginia, 1760–1770. Mahogany with oak and yellow pine. H. 42¾″, W. 74″. (Kenmore Association, on loan to Colonial Williamsburg; photo, Colonial Williamsburg Foundation.)

"1 claw fire screen" in Silas Blandford's bedchamber. Significantly, the only surviving piece of furniture in Virginia with a Botetourt history is a firescreen—not a claw type, but rather a folding kind, with three panels (fig. 14). In each panel is a stretcher on which is mounted an eighteenth-century print (the reverse side of each panel consists of plain paper). The stretchers are yellow pine and were probably early replacements. This screen would seem to match the Fenton reference quite closely, although where the others he supplied ended up is a mystery.[21]

The final piece of furniture that Fenton listed in his account was "a mohogainy Cellor lind with lead" at a cost of 4 guineas. This was presumably the "mahogy wine cooler" later inventoried in the dining room, the only such item in the entire inventory, yet the butler's accounts of the petty cash disbursements in Williamsburg include a charge for a "large wine cooler" on May 5, 1770, for a cost of only 10s. Another one for an identical sum was entered on June 29. The following September a payment of 1s. 3d. was recorded "to the cooper for mending a wine cooler," which makes it unlikely that these two locally acquired items were the "2 japann'd wine Cisterns" listed in the pantry when the inventory was taken. By the summer of 1770 a local cabinetmaker's name had appeared twice in the petty cash accounts—"To Mr. Bucktrout's bill" on November 1, 1769, and an identical reference on June 26, 1770, for £2.11.3. There is no evidence what these charges were for.[22]

On April 29, Fenton charged Botetourt for another 500 feet of gilt molding, an amount identical to that he had supplied in October 1768. It was not that 500 feet was insufficient for the ballroom. Rather, the governor had probably decided to refurbish the other main assembly room in the residence, the supper room. For reasons that are unclear today, this was never done. The "osnabrigs" (linen to paste on the plaster walls), the "common brown Paper" (to paste on the linen, probably to cover the seams and make a stronger layer), and about 175 sheets of the white or "cartridge" paper were still in storage in October 1770. According to the inventory takers, the osnabrigs were "intended to paste the Paper on in the Supper Room." Some pigment and a long box of gilt bordering also "intended for the Supper Room" were also recorded in storage.[23]

Smaller items that might be categorized by the word "sundries" among Fenton's accounts were just as important to the functioning of the household and to Botetourt's performance of his duties as many of the pieces listed above. Quilts and blankets, tammy for curtains, green baize and green sarsnet, large quantities of brass nails for upholstery, mahogany basin stands (bottle sliders or coasters), turned wooden trays for various aspects of the dinner ceremony, half cases for chairs (that is, covers for the seats only), inkstands with cut glasses (ubiquitous in the inventory), the iron chest or strong box for cash, thread, lead, oil, turpentine, almost 50,000 nails and tacks of different kinds, curtain line and rings, cloak pins, pulleys for curtains on windows and beds, a venetian blind—virtually all of these items the governor could have obtained in Williamsburg. That he did patronize one of the leading cabinetmakers locally, Benjamin Bucktrout, is shown by the petty cash disbursements—slightly more than £22 worth of goods between November 1769 and 1770. A vague tradition has it that Botetourt was also involved in what must have been Bucktrout's most demanding commission, the great masonic master's chair for an unidentified Virginia Lodge, the only known piece of furniture marked or labeled by this immigrant tradesman. If Botetourt ever saw this tour de force of the furnituremaker's art he would not have doubted Bucktrout's level of ability. Yet when Botetourt's executors and staff were hastily gathering supplies in the four days between the governor's death on October 15, 1770, and the funeral on October 19, they rejected japanned handles for the coffin that Bucktrout sent in favor of silver ones supplied by local silversmith and engraver William Waddill.[24]

Among the questions implicit in this study, one of the most challenging and tantalizing is that of perceived differences in quality between what was available in London from a tradesman who has no other claim in history than certain apparently routine work for a minor aristocrat (plus a small amount for the duke of Beaufort), and what was available in a colonial capital. Botetourt's preferences cannot simply be explained away by the fact that he was coming from England and that it was more expedient to use known, reliable sources. He was a thoughtful and most considerate man and surely realized that he would earn, by extensive local patronage, much goodwill that would be helpful in a period of unusual tension between the colonies and the mother country. Indeed, after his death there was a resounding endorsement from each social group in the colony—servant, merchant, great planter—of his extraordinary qualities, his empathy for his colonial compatriots, his sensitivity, his considerateness. That he did patronize certain local tradesmen is established by his petty cash disbursements. Yet payments to cabinetmakers are few and the amounts inconsiderable. It is undeniable that he thought it important to make, through his furnishings in the principal chambers of the residence, a statement of his own status. What is clear is that other men of affluence in the colony, whose accounts have survived in sufficient detail, followed similar patterns and had the same kinds of perceptions. For finer quality, they bought abroad. How true was this for the residents of the other colonies?

1. Botetourt's papers are preserved among the Badminton archives, both in the muniment room of the great house and at the County Record Office, Gloucester. Copies and microfilms of virtually all the relevant papers are at Colonial Williamsburg. The working copy of the 1770 Botetourt inventory of the Governor's Palace and the list of standing furniture in the building are in the Botetourt Papers, Virginia State Library Archives. See also Graham Hood, *The Governor's Palace in Williamsburg: A Cultural Study* (Williamsburg: Colonial Williamsburg Foundation, 1991). The inventory and the list of standing furniture are reprinted in Hood as app. 1; the Fauquier inventory referred to in this article is Hood's app. 2.

2. Botetourt's background is given in some detail in Bryan Little, "Norborne Berkeley, Gloucestershire Magnate," *Virginia Magazine of History and Biography* 63, no. 4 (October 1955): 379–409.

3. Hood, *Governor's Palace*, pp. 145–48.

4. Hood, *Governor's Palace*, pp. 182–84.

5. Wallace B. Gusler, *The Furniture of Williamsburg and Eastern Virginia, 1710–1790* (Richmond: Virginia Museum of Fine Arts, 1979). Ronald L. Hurst and Sumpter Priddy III, "The Neo-Classical Furniture of Norfolk, Virginia, 1770–1820," *Antiques* 137, no. 5 (May 1990): 1, 140–53.

6. Hood, *Governor's Palace*, pp. 141–43, 174–76.

7. Hood, *Governor's Palace*, p. 184. Vouchers for tradesmen's services and supplies to Botetourt, subsequently submitted to the trustees of the late governor's estate, were retained by Robert Carter Nicholas, treasurer of the colony, and are among his papers in the Library of Congress (microfilm M-22-3, Colonial Williamsburg Foundation). See also *Virginia Gazette*, Rind, ed., November 4, 1773, for the James Mercer/Robert Nicolson connection, and Purdie and Dixon, eds., July 23, 1772, for Nicolson's lodgers.

8. Hood, *Governor's Palace*, pp. 184, and apps. 1 and 2. William Nelson to Francis Fauquier, Jr., August 16, 1768. Letterbook of William Nelson, 1766–1775, p. 87, Colonial Williamsburg. York County Records, Wills and Inventories, no. 22, pp. 83–99, includes the list of goods purchased by Botetourt (and others in the community) from Fauquier's estate (recorded July 20, 1772).

9. See, Hood, *Governor's Palace*, app. 1, and Robert Carter Nicholas papers (the Kidd bill runs from November 28, 1769, to September 1, 1770). William Fenton may have been related to William Fenton, Great Suffolk Street, Haymarket, London, who advertised in 1744. He also worked for the duke of Beaufort between 1767 and 1773 (Geoffrey Beard and Christopher Gilbert, eds., *Dictionary of English Furniture Makers, 1660–1840* [Leeds: Furniture History Society and W. S. Money and Son, 1986], p. 296).

10. See Hood, *Governor's Palace*, pp. 236, 238–40, 244–54, for a discussion of the servants' living spaces. In 1766 Chippendale charged Sir Rowland Winn at Nostell Priory £1.8.0 for a "four post servants bedstead" (Christopher Gilbert, *The Life and Work of Thomas Chippendale*, 2 vols. [New York: Macmillan, 1978], 1: 184). This suggests that Fenton's charges for Botetourt's bed furniture are disproportionately high.

11. List of items sold from Fauquier's estate, York County Records, pp. 83–99.

12. Kidd bill, Robert Carter Nicholas papers.

13. List of items sold from Fauquier's estate, York County Records, pp. 83–99, and Hood, *Governor's Palace*, app. 1. In 1766 Chippendale charged Sir Rowland Winn at Nostell Priory the identical sum of £1.5.0 apiece for "Mahog parlour chairs coud w. horse hair and double brass nailed" (Gilbert, *Chippendale*, 1: 183).

14. Joseph Kidd's charges are recorded in the Robert Carter Nicholas papers. Hood, *Governor's Palace*, pp. 183–88, 244. Robert Beverley to Samuel Athawes, April 15, 1771, Robert Beverley Letterbook, 1761–1775, Library of Congress. The papers purchased by Jefferson, Carter, and Washington are discussed in Hood, *Governor's Palace*, pp. 187–88.

15. Gilbert, *Chippendale*, 1: 185, 189, 207, 229, 231. In 1767 for Mersham-Le-Hatch Chippendale charged for "Papie Mashie Border Painted blue and white" at £0.0.6 per foot. Gilt

border would have been a little more expensive. The least expensive carved, gilt border was 1s. per foot. The most expensive was £0.5.3.

16. Hood, *Governor's Palace*, pp. 174–76, 184–88.

17. Hood, *Governor's Palace*, pp. 214–15, 227. Helena Hayward and Pat Kirkham, *William and John Linnell: Eighteenth Century London Furniture Makers,* 2 vols. (London: Rizzoli, 1980), 1: 101, fig. 58 and 1: 106–108, 162. Linnell charged £2.5.0 apiece for his "Neat Bamboo chairs w. loose seats stuffed in canvas" in contrast to Fenton's £1.18.0. Conversation with Christopher Gilbert regarding some distinctive curved benches or settees at Harewood that were inventoried about fifty years apart, were variously described, and were never refinished. Some painted furniture from the eastern shore of Virginia has oxidized from blue to green, also.

18. Chippendale charged £9.9.0 and £12.0.0 for clothespresses in 1766 and 1767 and £1.0.0 for basin stands (Gilbert, *Chippendale*, 1: 184).

19. Badminton Papers. In 1766 Chippendale charged Sir Rowland Winn £12.0.0 for a very large library table covered with leather (Gilbert, *Chippendale*, 1: 183). Robert Carter Nicholas Papers. Kendall's accounts run from May 11, 1770, to October 20, 1770; see also Hood, *Governor's Palace*, pp. 156–59, 253. February 22, 1769, Marshman account book, petty cash disbursements, Badminton Papers.

20. Hood, *Governor's Palace*, app. 1. In 1767 Linnell charged William Drake £4.14.0 for a "mahog. writing table with 3 drawers" (Hayward and Kirkham, *Linnell*, 1: 162).

21. The screen, on long-term loan to Colonial Williamsburg, was given to Kenmore Association, Fredericksburg, Virginia, in the 1930s by James Young, a direct descendant of the king's attorney of the same name who lived in Norfolk and Williamsburg in the 1770s. On March 1, 1896, the screen was described by Francis Whittle Lewis as being in the possession of the Young family and as having been acquired at the Botetourt sale of 1771 (Diary 1844–1847 in Conway Whittle Papers, Swem Library Special Collections, College of William and Mary). It has the inscription "Botetourt 1768" deeply scratched into the top of the frame.

22. May 5, June 29, 1770, Nov. 1, 1769, June 26, 1770, Marshman account book, petty cash disbursements, Badminton Papers.

23. Hood, *Governor's Palace*, app. 1.

24. Nov. and Dec. 1769, Marshman account book, petty cash disbursements, Badminton Papers. Gusler, *Furniture of Williamsburg*, pp. 75–79. Robert Carter Nicholas papers, Library of Congress.

Appendix

Botetourt Account, Including Charges with William Fenton, Cabinetmaker

Botetourt Mss from Badminton (M–1395)
D 2700 I Shelf No. 15
ffr: 274–289 Account book including carriage and Fenton
1768 Sept. 30–1769 July

1768 Sep[r] 30	M[r] Catton To painting & gilding A State Coach The painells gilt with pale gold and painted with the Arms Supporter and mottos of the province of Virginia all within a rich Border of Ornamt. The framing gilt The Carriage and Wheels gilt	73	
	Car[d] Over		73. – . –
	Bro[t] Over		73. – . –
	M[r] Butler For a Second hand State Berlin that was the Late Duke of Cumberlands	35	
	For taking out the fore Glass Unhanging the Body washing Cleaning scraping & smoothing up the Joynts of the Body & Carriage repairing the Carv'd work of D[o] for painting & for Additional Carv'd Work to the Carriage	5	
	For a new Sett of very Handsome turn'd spoke Wheels & Iron work with Beaded felloes Clouting the Axletrees fitting on the Wheels & 4 nees Linspins	12	
	Carried forward ..	52	73

Mr Butler brot forward	52	73. – .
For Cutting the fore Standards Shorter fitting & letting in the seat Irons & straining on the Cradle a Coach Box Seat Covered with Canvas 2 new seat straps & tying it on a pair of Pole peices almost Equal to New a new pole Bolt a Brass buckle Chape & flap to the futchells a brass buckle & Chape to the pole hook & a new peice of leather to hold up the pole peices 4 new large Wrought Brass buckles to the Check braces & sewing them in	2. 14. –	
Carried over	54. 14. –	73. – . –

Butler brought over	54. 14. –	73. – . –
For Drawing the Brass within side & without & taking out the greatest part of the Lining & for 6 yards of very good Additional Velvet & 20 yards of very good silk Lace & 7 yards of very Good silk fringe to the Doors, Elbows, fore End & falls of the seats putting in the lining & garnishing it with new large Gold Varnishd brass Nails	10. 10	
For Covering the Roof Back & four sides with neats leather	6.	
For Black japaning & pollishing the Roof sides & Back & Black Japaning the Main & Check Braces	2. 10	
For a new very handsome carv'd Ornament all Bound the Roof & a Bead under it & fitting them on	8. 8.	
	82. 2. –	73.

Butler brought forward	82. 2. –	73. – . –
For 8 very large Wrought Brak tops (in Exchange for the Old One & Garnishing round the Vallene with 2 Rows of new large gold Varnish'd brass Nails taking of the locks of the Doors repair them & new making them up covering the steps with new neats leather japaning) & Garnishing them with 1000 new large Gold Varnishd Brass Nails Covering the tops of the Door frames with Crimson Velvet & fixing in the fore Glass	8. 10. –	
For a new Carpet to the bottom bound & putting it in with brass pins	– . 10. –	
Carried over . . .	91. 2. –	73. – . –

Butler brought over	91. 2. –	73
For a handsome Sett of flatt worsted footmans Holders and tassells & Sewing them on with 4 new Chapes	1. – . –	
For 6 yards of new Crimson flowerd Velvet for a Seat Cover For Cutting Out & making up the Seat Cover lining it with peu shalloon bound with silk lace & one Row of Handsome Silk fringe with a Gimp head & Button Hangers round the falls & up the Corner	25. – . –	
For a very Handsome pair of town Harness & Bridles all the brass Work new made up & Gold Varnishd new flat worsted Crimson Reins & new handsome Worsted Toppings to the Bridles & a new pair of Bitts with Wrought brass bossess	15. – . –	
	132. 2. –	73. – . –

	Butler brought Forward	132. 2. –	73. – . –
	For a new Bayes Cover & shings to Cover the Body & packing up the Body with tow & Canvas squabs to prevent the Case from rubbing it	3. – . –	
	For Casing up the fore Glass & for a remarkable strong Deal Case with a Number of Iron Clouts to strengthen it & packing up the Body	6. – . –	
	For packing up the Carriage & Wheels carefully in paper and Matts & sewing them up in Canvas Cartage Wharfage Attendance Expences & getting on board	6 . 15. –	
	Butlers Bill Total	147. 17	
	Card Over		220. 17. –

1768	Brot Over		220. 17. –
May 7th	Willm Fenton		
	For Iulire [entire] new Stuffing the Seat of a Sette mending the frame one new Castor	– . 12. –	
	For a new hinge to a reading desk	– . – . 6	
	For 3 Large print frames & glasses & packing Case	1. 10. –	
	For 6 Crimson Check Cases to 6 Stuffed back & Seat Chears	1. 13. –	
	For 9 brass hooks & Several Jobs done	– . 3. –	
	For new green Tammey to 2 Spring Curtons and mending them	1. 5	
20	For a bedside Carpet 2 yards & 1/4 long	– . 11. 6	
	For 2 11/4 linning quilts	4. 4. –	
	For 2 10/4 ditto	3. 16. –	
Janry 17	For Cleaning 24 Blankets	1. 18. –	
July 11	For 2 fine 10/4 Caleco quilts	6. 6. –	
August 7	For a Large feild bedstead on Castors with Crimson Check	21. 19	220. 17. –

			Totals
	Fenton brought forward	21. 19	220. 17
	furniture made up with lace proper 2 large thick matterases bolster & 2 pillows apair of $^{10}/_4$ blankets one $^8/_4$ ditto a $^{10}/_4$ quilt linning Back all very good	£15. 10. –	
	3 beds the Same	46. 10. –	
	3 Ditto but without pillows & the quilts Stuff backs	44. 10. –	
	For 234 yards of wilton Carpet at S5 p yds	58. 10. –	
	For 52 & ½ yards of green Bazse yard wide at 19^d p yds	4. 3. 1½	
	For a large packing Case	1. – . –	
	For 18 matts & Cord	1. 8.	
	Expences putting the goods on board	– . 12. –	
12	For 4 mohogainy posts to a Couch bed plates & Scrws & a mohogainy folding teaster	1. 10. –	
	For 19 yards of green sarsnet at 3S6^d p yd	3. 3. 6	
		183. 5. 7½	220. 17. –

		Totals
Fenton brought over	183. 5. 7½	220. 17. –
For 10 yards of Tammey	– . 15. –	
For Silk ferret &c and making a Counter payne bolster Case & Cover to the bead board of bed	– . 18. –	
For 12 mohogainy Chears Covered with hair Seating and Double Brass nailed at £1.5 p	15. – . –	
For 50 lb of the best Verdeter at 6^s p	15. – . –	
For 24 lb of prusian blew at 10^d p lb	1. – . –	
For 6 Brushes 30^{lb} of leather Specks 4 doz of Whiteing 2 firkins &c.	– . 15. –	
For 2 Ream of fine large Elephant paper	2. 10. –	
For 4 peices of boot tape 2 lb of Carpet thrid	– . 15. –	
For 10^m tacks 10^m white tacks	1. 1. 6	
For 16 Doz of brass headed Stoco nails of Differant Sorts	1. 8. –	
For 8 Doz of brass hooks	– . 9. –	
	222. 17. 1½	220. 17

			Totals
	Fenton brought forward	222. 17. 1½	220. 17. –
	For 2000 brass nails 64 yards Crimson lace	1. 6. 6	
	For 8 matts & packing goods at my lords house	– . 16. –	
	For a neat traveling box with Scrws & key to dite	1. 15. –	
October 6	For 500 foot of Gooder oun Gilt moulding at 9p	18. 15. –	
	For 12 mohogainy Chears the same as the others	15. – . –	
	For 12 Bamboo Chears Blew & gold with lutestring quishons at 1lb.18s p	22. 16. –	
	For Check Cases to Ditto	1. 10. –	
	For 3 large mohogainy Cloaths presses with slideing shelves & drawers 2 of them lined with Green Bazse	45. – . –	
	For 6 mohogainy Bason Stands	4. 16. –	
	For 4 Dinner trays 2 Butter trays	4. – . –	
	For 4 Knife trays	1. 10. –	
		340. 1. 7½	220. 17. –

		Totals
Fenton brought over	340. 1. 7½	220. 17. –
For 6 Dressing glasses	2. 7. –	
For 4 large Inkstands with Cut glasses	4. 4. –	
For 12 bottle boards & 6 waiters	1. 10. –	
For 18 matts & Cord	1. 5. –	
For 590 foot in 8 large packing Cases at 3d p	7. 7. 6	
For 6 half Cases for 12 Chears	2. 8. –	
For Cart load of goods from my lords house & 2 from my house	– . 17. –	
For Warfage & 2 large boats to take the goods to the Ship	1. 6. –	
Fentons First Bills Total	361. 6. 1½	
Card Over	582. 3. 1½	

	Bro^{t} Over		582. 3. 1½
1769	Coggs & Crump		
Feb. 28	To 60 Wax Candles	8. 10. –	
	Box & Cord	–. 2. 6	
		8. 12. 6	
1769	Late Basnetts		
Feb. 14	6 Broad richsilver Livery hat Laces . . . at 13/7	4. 1. 6	
	6 Buttons & Chain Loops at 15^{d}	–. 7. 6	
		4. 9. –	
	Charles Vere		
	a Compleat Sett of Fine nankeen Tea China	5. 5. –	
	6 Fine nankeen ½ Pint Basons & Plates	1. 7. –	
	Box	–. 1. 6	
		6. 13. 6	
	Charles Coles		
	1 Rm ff Cap broad	1. –. –	
	4 qrs best Demy	–. 8. –	
	2 qrs Roy^{l}	–. 6. –	
		1. 14. –	
			582. 3. 1½

Bro^{t} Over		582. 3.1½
John Steerces		
3 Scollop'd Shell Tureen Ladles at 12/–	1. 16. –	
Box	–. –. 6	
	1. 16. 6	
Coggs Wax Chandler	8. 12. 6	
Vere for China	6. 13. 6	
Barrel for Lace	4. 9. –	
Cole Stationer	1. 14. –	
Steers for Soup Ladles	1. 16. 6	
Two Red Tea pots	. 2. 4	
	23. 7. 10	
Total paid Mr Capper		25. 7.10
Car^{d} Over		607. 10.11½

1769	William Fenton		607. 10.11½
Apr 15	For 2 3 foot 6 Inch desks & one 3 foot	21. – . –	
	For a large & very neat mohogainy lybery table of very fine wood Covered with leather the moulding Richly Carved on 8 3 wheel Castors	24. – . –	
	For a small Iron Chest to be put in one of the Cuberts of the table	3. 8. –	
	For a mohogainy Cellor lind with lead	4. 4. –	
	For 3 fire Screens with maps on both Sides	3. 10. –	
	For large packing Cases & matts	2. 2. –	
	For Expences putting on board	– . 12. –	
	Fentons Bill Total		58. 16
	Car[d] Over		666. 6.11½

	bro[t] Over		666. 6.11½
1769	William Fenton		
March 4	For 2 peices of Blew moreen	5. 5.	
	For 2 pair of 12/4 Blankets	5. 18.	
	For a 13/4 Caleco quilt	5. 12	
	For 35 ½ yards of blew Bazse at 17[d] p yd	2. 10. 3½	
	For 10 peices of Broad quality at 2[s] 6[d] p P	1. 5.	
	For 6 pieces of narrow Ditto at 18 p P	– . 9.	
	For 4 pound of Coulered & white thrid	– . 16. –	
	For ¾ of a pound Differant Coulered Silk	1. 10. –	
	For 2 Hundred of white lead	3. 18	
	For 7 Gallons of linseed oyle	1. 4.	
	One Gallon of turpintine	– . 3. 6	
	For 2 Casks & a bottle	– . 8. –	
	For 4000 Brass nails	2. – . –	
	For 10 thousand tacks	– . 11. –	
	For 10 thousand white tacks	– . 12. –	
	Car[d] forward	32. 1.9½	666. 6.11½

Fenton brought forward	32. 1.9½	666. 6.11½
For 8 grose of Brass owes	– . 16. –	
For a grose of Curton rings	– . 5. –	
For a grose of polished D°	– . 9. –	
For 8 grose of Studs	– . 5. 6	
For 2 Doz. of Cloakpins	– . 8. –	
For 6 Doz of Brass Scrue hooks	– . 6. –	
For one grose of 2 Inch Scrues	– . 5. 6	
For 3 grose of Curton line	1. 19. –	
F 12 tossels	– . 13. –	
For 3 Peices of breed	– . 7. 6	
For 36 yards of Strong worsted line	2. 5. –	
For 36 yards of Silk ditto	4. 1. –	
For 2 grose of pullys	– . 13. –	
For half a grose of long pullys	– . 4. –	
For a Venetian blind	1. 9. –	
For a large packing Case & a small D°	– . 15. –	
Paid the freight & Expences putting on board	2. 5. –	
Fentons Bill Total		49. 8. 3½
Car[d] Over		715. 15.3

Bro[t] Over		715. 15. 3
Rob[t] Woodifield		
20 Doz Burgundy Bott[s] Corks & cement	60. – . –	
2 seven & 1 six dozen Chests & packing	1. 6. –	
Paid Wine porters putting up the Chests	– . 3. –	
Cart to the Key 5 J. Wharfage & Porters 3	– . 8. –	
Boat hire to the Ship	– . 3. –	
Custom house Fees	– . 17. 6	
Debenture & Receiver	1. 2. 1½	
	63. 19. 7½	
deduct for draw back	5. 2. 1½	58. 16. 6
Sanxay & Bradley		
A Chest Hyson Tea Ship[d] on board the Experiment Captain Hamtin, For Virginia		
N° 2379 . . . q[z] 66[lb] @ 12p	39. 12. –	
12 Six pound Cannisters @ 2/6	1. 10. –	
Two Chests, and Charges on board	– . 3. –	
	41. 5. –	41. 5.
		815. 16. 9

	Bro[t] forward		815. 16. 9
	Hannah Jones		
	140 white wax Lights at 2/–	14. – . –	
	Box	– . 4. –	
	100 wallnuts	– . 8. –	
	2 Jarrs	– . 2. –	
	1 Basket	– . – . 6	
	Charges	1. – . –	
		15. 14. 6	15. 14. 6
1769			
Ap[l] 29	W[m] Fenton		
	For 500 feet of Goodroon Gilt		
	Moulding at 9[d]	18. 15. 0	
	To 12 Ounces of Brass Nails	– . 6. –	
	To Packing Case	– . 10. –	
			19. 11. –
Ap[l]	W[m] Sparrow (Cook)		
	For Bedding for the Voyage	2. – . –	
	For Glass & Box	. 13. –	
			2. 13. –
	Car[d] Over		853. 15. 3

1769	Bro[t] Over		853. 15. 3
April	John Sewell		
	For Robertson His Cha[s] 5 & Box		3. 1
May	Phillip Hall		
	2 Jars of Raisons a 58[s] p lb	1. 9. 6	
	2 [?] 0. 7[lb] Currants a 54[s]	5. 11. 4	
	Bar[l] 2[s] Cart 18[d] Shiping Charges 5.8	9. 2	
			7. 10.
	John Shearwood		
	For 2 Hatts	2. 2. 0	
	Box	. 1. –	
			2. 3.
	M[r] Crofts		
	For minutes of H. Lords in Session		
	begining 10 May 1768	1. 1. –	
	For D[o] begining 8 Nov. 1768 End		
	9 May 1769	5. 5. 0	
			6. 6.
	Car[d] forward		872. 15. 3

1769		Bro^t forward		872. 15. 3
June	John Newman			
	For 3 [?] Nutmegs		1. 7. 0	
	Black Pepper	8^{lb}	. 14. 8	
	White D°	2	. 8.	
	Alspice	2	. 2.	
	Jordan Almonds	6	. 8.	
	Bitter D°	1	. 1.	
	Mace	1/4	. 5.	
	Cloves	1/2	. 6.	
	Bitter Alm: Powder	6	. 6.	
		Box & Sufferage	. 3. 8	
				4. 1. 4
	Sarah Lauder			
	To half a Hund. Powder		1. 3. 9	
	500 Toothpicks		. 1. 6	
				1. 5. 3
				878. 1. 10

1769		Bro^t Over		878. 1. 10
June	Gataker & C°			
	4 Bottles of Arquebusade		1. – . –	
	Q^t of Oppadeldock		. 16. –	
	2^{lb} Venice Soap		. 3.	
	2 Rochell Salts		. 16. –	
	8 O^z Ipocacuana		. 8.	
	2^{lb} purging Salts		. 2. 8	
	Packing Case &c.		. 8. 4	
	Tow to pack the things with		. 3.	
	Portorage		. 1. –	
	Broabers Introduction to Physick &c.		. 14.	
	Toothdrawing Instruments		. 9.	
				5. 1.
		Car^d forward		883. 2. 10

1769	Bro^{t} forward		883. 2. 10
July	Robt Douglas		
	Livery Button 12 Doz Coat 12 D^{z} britches	1.7.0	
	Making Coat & Waiscoat	. 13. 6	
	4y^{ds} Blue Cloth	4. – . –	
	5y^{ds} rattanet	. 14.	
	Coat sleeves lining Coat & Waiscoat pockets		. 3. –
	Treble Dimaty for body Linings	. 9.	
	Velvet for a Coller	. 1. 6	
	22 Coat & 15 Britches buttons	. 7. 4	
	Sewing Silk & Twist	. 3. 6	
	Buckram Canvas & Stays	. 3. –	
	Box & Cord	. 2. –	
	To making a full trimed Suit	1. 4. –	
	4 [?] Black Cloth	4. 10. 3	
	6½ Ratanet	. 18. 5	
	Coat Sleve lining & Coat & Waiscoat pockets		. 3. –
	Treble Dimaty for lining Body &c.	. 9.	
	Britches lining & pockets	. 5. –	
	Buckram &c.	. 4.	
	Car^{d} Over	15. 17. 8	883. 2. 10

1769			
June	Robt Douglas & bro^{t} Over	15. 17. 8	883. 2. 10
	Sewing Silk, Twist & 88 Buttons	. 12. 6	
	To making a Roqueleau	. 10. 6	
	4¼ y^{ds} Scarlet Cloth	4. 9. 3	
	Trimming Buttons & Neckloop	. 5. 6	
	Making Coat & Waiscoat	. 13. 6	
	4 y^{d} black Cloth	3. 16. –	
	6½ Ratanet	. 18. 5	
	Coat Sleve lining Coat & Waiscot Pockets	.3.	
	Dimaty for Body Lining	. 9.	
	Buttons	. 3. 4	
	Silk & Twist	. 3. 6	
	Buckram &c	. 3.	
	Box & Cord	. 4. –	
			28. 9. 2
	Car^{d} forward		911. 12. –

1769	Bro^{t} Over			911. 12. –
July	Messrs Sanxey & Co			
	60^{lb} best Turkey Coffee @ 3^{s}		9. – .	
	Box		. 4. 8	
	12^{lb} Chocolate	5/6	3. 6. –	
	6 Isinglass	7	2. 2. –	
	20 Hartshorn Shavings	20^{d}	1. 13. 4	
	12 Fr Lentals		. 12. –	
	6 Italian D^{o}		. 6.	
	a Chest		. 1. 6	
				17. 5. 6
				928. 17. 6

Transcribed by Jan K. Gilliam
8/26/91

Gregory Landrey

The Conservator as Curator: Combining Scientific Analysis and Traditional Connoisseurship

▼ DURING the last decade, the line separating the furniture conservator and the furniture curator has grown thin as members of both professions have combined information derived from documentary research, scientific analysis, and connoisseurship. Such was the case when the Winterthur Museum's furniture conservation staff examined an eighteenth-century Philadelphia chest-on-chest to determine the originality of its finish and carving (fig. 1). The "lamb-and-ewe chest," as it has come to be known, was purchased by Henry Francis du Pont from noted antiquarian Joe Kindig, Jr., in June 1940 and subsequently installed in the Port Royal Parlor at Winterthur.[1]

The chest-on-chest had been made between 1765 and 1775 in an as-yet-unidentified Philadelphia cabinet shop. The construction techniques used were typical of lower-echelon London cabinetmakers such as Samuel Bell. The ornament consists of floral rosettes, flame finials, an appliqué portraying a nursing lamb and ewe, and a central cartouche that is remarkably similar to a twentieth-century drawing of a reproduction ornament in Wallace Nutting's *Furniture Treasury*.[2] In typical Philadelphia fashion, the cabinetmaker attached the rosettes with hide glue and forged nails and made the finials in three parts—flame, urn, and ring—with round mortise-and-tenon joints.

The lamb-and-ewe appliqué sets this chest apart from contemporary Philadelphia case pieces (fig. 2). During the eighteenth century, many architectural and decorative engravings were available as sources for animal figures. James Stuart's *The Antiquities of Athens* (1762–1786) and Antoine Desgodets' *Les Edifices antiques de Rome* (1682) were highly regarded as references for classical detail. George Marshall, who republished Desgodets' work in 1771, noted that the author was "too well known to the professors of architecture, and too much reverenced by all lovers of the art, to require . . . either account or encomium." Stuart's *Antiquities* included details of the Parthenon, perhaps the most notable source of animal figures in an entablature, and Desgodets' work contained engravings of similar details on other buildings and monuments. The *Arch of Titus* in *Les Edifices* featured bulls in high relief, and the *Tomb of Bacchus* was shown with a sheep that strongly resembles the ewe on the chest-on-chest.[3]

Most eighteenth-century cabinetmakers and carvers had a working knowledge of classical architecture and of the rules of balance and proportion. In the preface to *The Gentleman and Cabinet-Maker's Director* (1754), Thomas Chippendale wrote, "of all the arts which are either im-

Figure 1 Pretreatment view of the lamb-and-ewe chest-on-chest showing the locations where finish samples were taken, Philadelphia, 1765–1775. Mahogany with white oak, white cedar, and yellow pine. H. 86", W. 42⅞", D. 22¾". (Courtesy, Winterthur Museum, acc. 60.1056.)

Figure 2 Pediment of the chest-on-chest showing the locations where finish samples were taken. (Photo, Winterthur Museum.)

proved or ornamented by Architecture, that of Cabinetmaking is . . . capable of receiving as great assistance from it as any whatever."[4] Although Chippendale's statement was true, there were strong classical overtones in all arts and literature. Even simple children's fables and pastorals had representational engravings depicting classical ruins and subjects.

Allegorical illustrations were also an important design source for eighteenth-century artisans. Francis Barlow's engravings of Aesop's Fables (1666, 1687) inspired several designs in London carver Thomas Johnson's *One Hundred and Fifty New Designs* (1761), one of the most influential English pattern books in Philadelphia. Numerous examples of eighteenth-century carving attest to the popularity of Johnson's designs, especially those based on Barlow's engravings. Moral fables depicted in Philadelphia interiors of the 1760s and 1770s include the "Dog and Piece of Meat" on a chimneypiece tablet from the Samuel Powel House and the "Dog in the Manger," "The Crow, the Deer, the Tortoise, and the Rat," and the "Young Gobbler" on the tablet and frieze panels of the parlor chimneypiece from the Blackwell House (Winterthur Museum). Although the carver of the Blackwell parlor is unknown, the Powel House carving is attributed to Hercules Courtenay who apprenticed with Thomas Johnson before immigrating to Philadelphia.[5] It is reasonable to presume that Courtenay was familiar with Barlow's illustrations, since they often were referred to by his master.

At least seven Philadelphia case pieces made between 1765 and 1775 have carved animal forms derived from moral fables. The "Fox and Grapes" high chest and dressing table (Philadelphia Museum of Art) and the "Pompadour" high chest, whose tableau drawer depicts Aesop's "Swan and Serpent" (Metropolitan Museum of Art), are among the most notable. The "Swan and Serpent" appliqué was copied from a design for a chimneypiece tablet on plate 5 of Johnson's *New Book of Ornament* (1762).[6]

Although the lamb-and-ewe appliqué is reminiscent of the abovementioned carving, the design appears to have been derived from illustrations in pastoral literature rather than a fable. Pastorals were particularly popular in England from about 1650 to 1800, and there were many examples that could have influenced this appliqué. One by Barlow in Edward Benlowe's *Theophilia* (1652) included a ewe and nursing lamb by a tree—quite similar to the carving on the chest-on-chest (figs. 2, 3), representing "The Sweetness of Retirement, or The Happiness of a Private Life."[7]

Figure 3 Francis Barlow, engraving for *Theophilia*, London, 1652. (Courtesy, Chapin Library, Williams College.)

It is reasonable to speculate that a pastoral such as *Theophilia* inspired the carver of the lamb-and-ewe chest since Barlow's illustrations were reinterpreted in design books and available to tradesmen and patrons on both sides of the Atlantic. Pastoral illustration was apparently the source for the carved tablet from a chimneypiece in Sanbeck Park—a house built for the Earl of Scarborough during the 1750s in Yorkshire, England. This tablet so closely resembles the lamb and ewe on the chest-on-chest that we wonder if the Philadelphia carver had any direct connection with the designers or carvers at Sanbeck Park (fig. 4).[8] In either case, it is clear that pastoral scenes were the source for the lamb-and-ewe motif.

Having established the general design source for the appliqué, conservators and curators used traditional connoisseurship skills to identify the extent of restoration to the appliqué, rosettes, finials, and cartouche. Discontinuous tool marks and variations in workmanship indicated that parts of the C scrolls were modern and raised the possibility that there were repairs that were unobvious to the naked eye (fig. 2). This was a major issue, given the significance and rarity of the lamb-and-ewe motif. Minor variations in the carving of the rosettes and apparent inconsistencies in the oxidation and finish of the individual sections of the finials also caused concern. The cartouche clearly was out of character with the rest of the carving, and records indicated that it was carved by Jesse Bair of Hanover, Pennsylvania, about 1940.[9]

To refine these gross observations, we examined the surface coating on several parts of the chest-on-chest. Eighteenth-century cabinetmakers used a variety of dyes, stains, and finishes to accentuate the figure and color of wood. The most common surface coatings were simple oil finishes (usually linseed), fixed oil varnishes (oil and solvent mixed with one or more resins), essential oil or spirit varnishes (solvent mixed with one or more resins), and beeswax.[10] Since there was no evidence that the chest was ever completely stripped, scraped, or sanded, we knew that the original finish would be in the cellular structure and on the surface of the wood and that subsequent finishes and/or polishes would form distinct,

Figure 4 Detail of a carved tablet on a chimneypiece, Sanbeck Park, Yorkshire, England, 1750–1760. (Photo, Bradley Brooks.)

successive layers—a unique stratigraphy that should be consistent on all of the original components of this piece.

Identifying the predictable surface layers and their components was the next step in determining the originality of carved and structural elements. We used established microscopic techniques to determine the order and nature of the surface stratigraphy: we removed minute surface samples (less than the size of a period on this page) from selected areas and embedded them in a polyester resin; ground each embedded sample at a right angle to the surface plane to expose the finish layers; and examined the cross-sections through a microscope. Using an ultraviolet light source with the microscope, we characterized the material composition of each layer by its fluorescence.[11]

We photographed the samples illustrated in figures 5–15 through a microscope at 200X magnification.[12] Natural resins, which appear amber colored under normal light, fluoresce orange, yellow, off-white, white, or blue-white, depending on the type and age of the finish. The luminescence of these coatings make them easily identifiable under a fluorescence microscope. Oils, waxes, pigments, and other particulates tend not to fluoresce and remain relatively dark under ultraviolet light. We gained additional information by applying dye to a sample. Reactive dyes can confirm the presence of certain materials, such as oils, by causing them to fluoresce a specific color. The objective, verifiable information provided by these techniques sheds light on the condition and original appearance of the object being studied.

We took finish samples from the scrollboard (or tympanum), the ewe, a rosette, a finial, a side board of the upper case, a drawer front, the cartouche, and areas of carving that appeared restored (figs. 2, 5–15). Our initial objective was to establish a "standard"—a sample with a complete surface history that could be used to evaluate the others. We chose the sample from the scrollboard to be the standard because of the board's status as a structural component and the high probability that its stratigraphy was the most complete (fig. 5). The first (or bottom) four layers of the scrollboard matched those of the ewe, confirming that the lamb and ewe were original components of the appliqué and were original to the piece (figs. 5, 6). These samples also were noticeably different from those taken from areas that had visually been identified as restored (figs. 9, 11). Although new finishes can be made to appear old to the eye, the surface layering that is visible under a microscope would be extremely difficult to simulate.

Comparisons of other samples to the scrollboard sample revealed that most of the carving on the scrollboard was original and that restoration had occurred on the terminals of some C scrolls. The rosettes and finials were more perplexing. A letter in Winterthur's files stated that the finials were contemporary with the circa 1940 cartouche.[13] Samples from the cartouche and parts of a finial established a standard for restored areas and confirmed the fluorescence microscope's capacity to reveal signature configurations of surface layers. Although the rings and plinths of the finials have surface stratifications that differ markedly from that of the scrollboard and matched that of the cartouche, the flames have an old multilayered surface with some similarities to the scrollboard standard (figs. 5, 10). This suggests that the flames are original or that they were added early on. Minor differences in the massing and articulation of the rosettes also caused speculation that they were by different carvers and that one was replaced. Although there was no history of their having been replaced, the vulnerability of such exposed elements warranted further investigation. Cross-sectional examination revealed that the layers on both rosettes matched those of the ewe and scrollboard, confirming their originality (figs. 5–7).

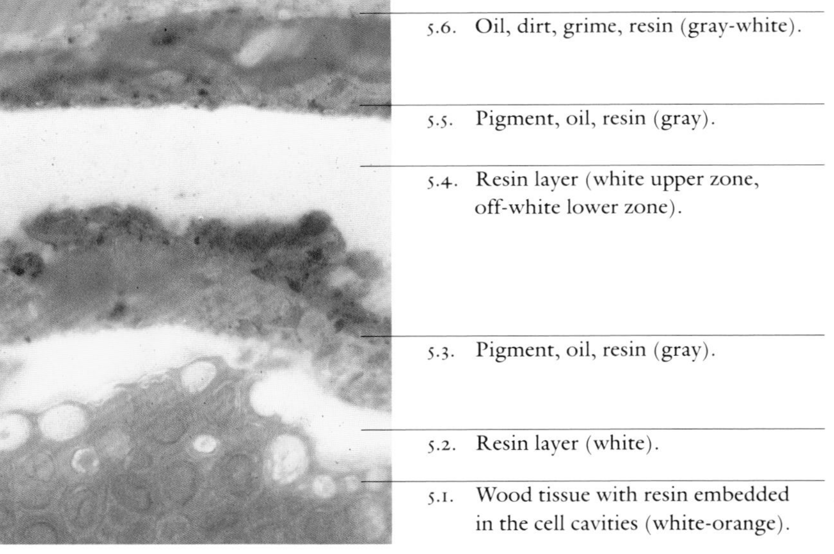

Figure 5 Sample from the scrollboard, average surface thickness 1.8 microns. (Photo, Winterthur Museum.) This sample was taken from a protected area of the scrollboard adjacent to the appliqué. Because the six layers represent an extensive finish history that might be complete, this sample was used as a standard for comparisons with other finish samples.

Figure 6 Sample from the rear leg of the ewe, average surface thickness 0.9 microns. (Photo, Winterthur Museum.) The layers in this sample compare favorably with four bottom layers of the standard (5.1–5.4). There is also a faint film on top of layer 6.4 that could be an oil polish corresponding to layer 5.6. The correlation between the layers on these samples supports the visual observation that the ewe is original.

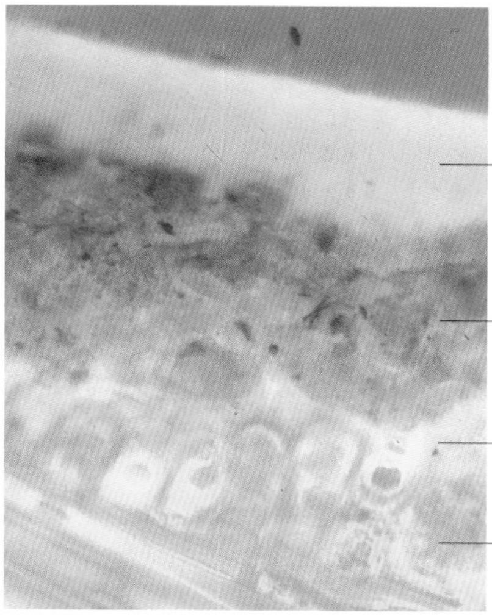

6.4. Resin layer (white upper zone, off-white lower zone).

6.3. Pigment, oil, resin (gray).

6.2. Resin layer (white).

6.1. Wood tissue with resin embedded in the cell cavities (white-orange).

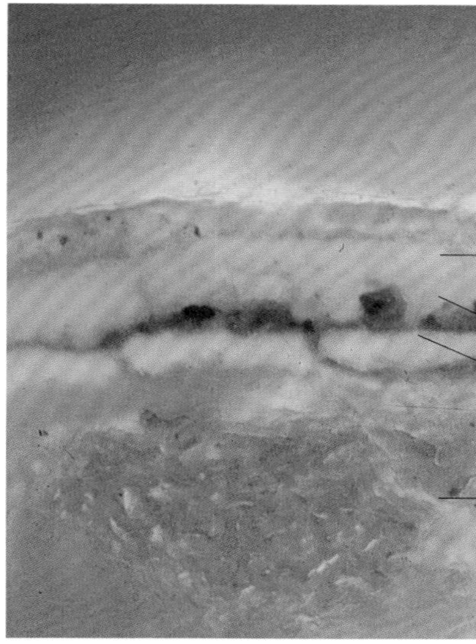

Figure 7 Sample from the right rosette, average surface thickness 0.75 microns. (Photo, Winterthur Museum.) The layers in this sample are consistent with the four bottom layers of the samples in figs. 5, 6. They also match cross-sections taken from the left rosette, indicating that both rosettes are original to the chest-on-chest.

7.4. Resin layer (white upper zone, off-white lower zone).

7.3. Pigment, oil, resin (gray).

7.2. Resin layer (white).

7.1. Wood tissue with resin embedded in the cell cavities (white-orange).

The second focus of our microscopic examination was to determine if any original finish was left on the chest-on-chest and to devise a method to treat its dark and sticky surface. A photograph taken in the early 1950s showed a relatively clear finish, suggesting that the surface had become more opaque over the last forty years. Samples revealed four finish layers on the flat surfaces of the chest. An oil and resin combination appears to have been used for the first (bottom) layer.[14] The cabinetmaker either applied the oil first or it settled out of a spirit varnish. Because these two materials were lodged permanently in the wood, they unquestionably were present in the original finish. This finish would have given the mahogany a highly saturated, glossy appearance.

A late-eighteenth-century finish recipe from the notebook of itinerant Connecticut tradesman Isaac Byington listed ingredients similar to those found in the cell cavities of the samples: "[For] A Varnish for all Colours

Take of the best L. [linseed] oil &. finest V. turpentine [Venice turpentine was a common natural resin]. Boyl them together add a little Brandy to it and boil it again. put less or more oil to make it thick or thin." Byington deemed gloss a worthy objective for a finish and described a particular resin varnish "which stands water and shines like glass." Late-eighteenth-century paintings show how such a finish probably appeared when new. Charles Willson Peale's portrait of the Cadwalader family painted in 1771 presents John and Elizabeth gathered around a card table on which their daughter Anne is seated. The glossy finished surface of the card table reflects the lace and other details of the child's dress.[15]

Evidence found on the lamb-and-ewe chest indicates that it had a comparable surface. Unfortunately, the remnants of that original layer proved to be discontinuous, largely undetectable to the naked eye, and irretrievable as a continuous presentation surface. The next layer constitutes the majority of the existing finish (see figs. 5.4, 6.4, 7.4, 8.4, 10.4). Because of its position in the surface stratification, its homogeneous nature, and its relatively good condition, we surmised that it was relatively recent but not later than 1940. The more recent outer layers, which tested positive for oil (probably linseed), were sticky, dark, and embedded with dirt, grime, and lint.

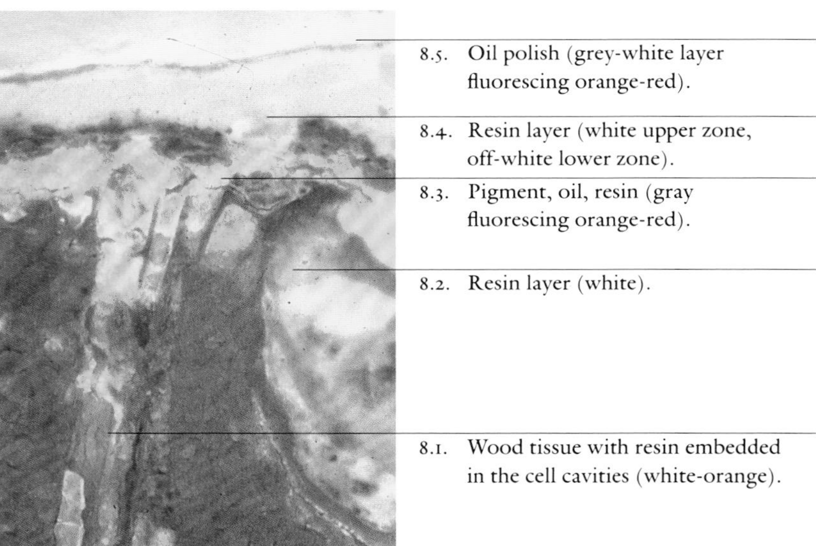

Figure 8 Sample from the left side of the upper case, average surface thickness 0.45 microns. (Photo, Winterthur Museum.) This sample was taken from a protected area on the back edge of the side. A reactive dye was added to this section to cause the oil layers to fluoresce orange-red. The surface stratification of samples in figs. 5–7 is repeated with the exception of the uppermost layer (8.5) that corresponds with 5.6 in the standard sample. It is clear from the deep, orange-red fluorescence of layers 8.2 and 8.3 that the original finish included oil mixed with a resin.

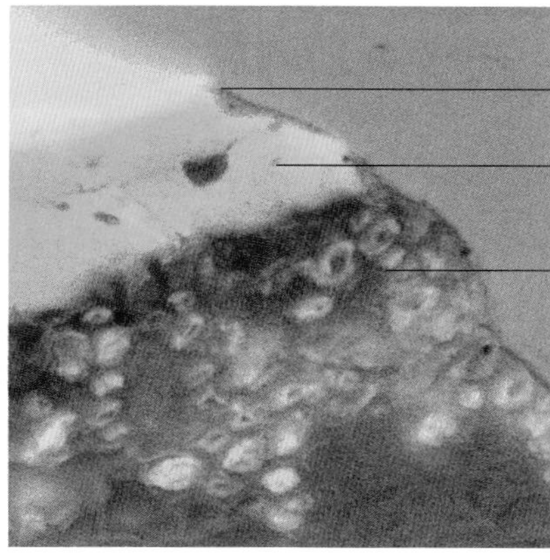

Figure 9 Sample from the cartouche, average surface thickness 0.7 microns. (Photo, Winterthur Museum.) This sample was taken from deep within the carving where it would have been extremely difficult to reach if the cartouche had been refinished. The surface stratification differs dramatically from that of the samples in figs. 5–8, lending support to the statement that the cartouche was added later.

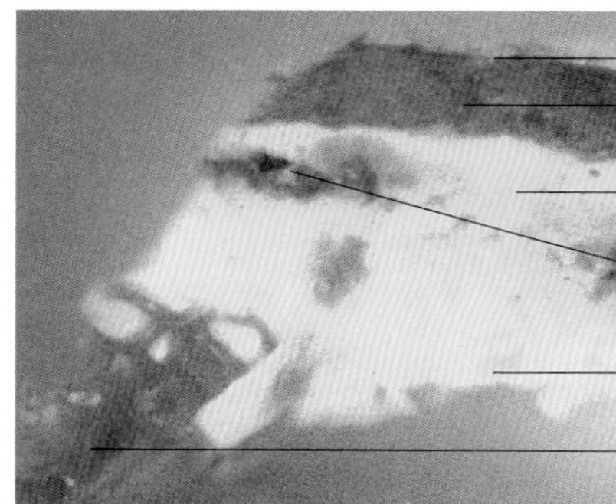

Figure 10 Sample from the flame section of the finial, average surface thickness 1 micron. (Photo, Winterthur Museum.) Although a note in the accession file states that the flames are new, they have a substantial finish history. The stratigraphy is very similar to that of the standard and suggests that the finials are old and probably original (compare with fig. 5). Philadelphia flame finials typically were made in three or four sections. Because individual sections could be lost or broken, a substantial number of period examples survive in a similarly restored condition.

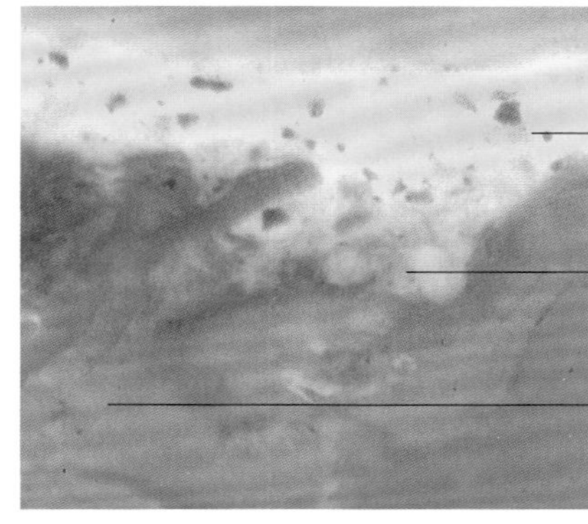

Figure 11 Sample from the turned section of the finial, average surface thickness 0.3 microns. (Photo, Winterthur Museum.) The surface history of this component contrasts with the flame but is similar to that of the replaced cartouche (figs. 9, 10). It may have been added at the same time as the cartouche.

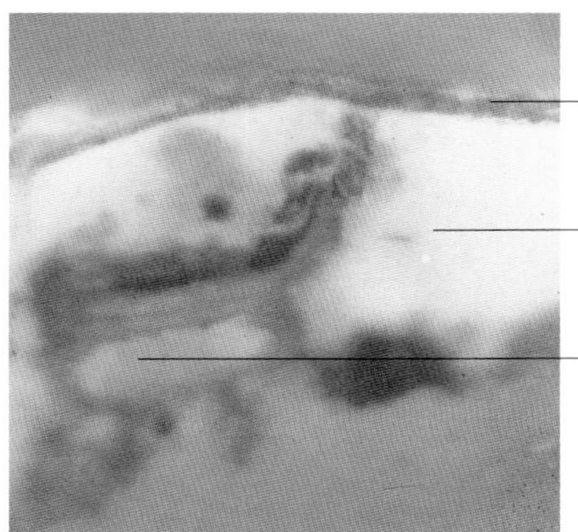

Figure 12 Finial plinth, average surface thickness 0.6 microns. (Photo, Winterthur Museum.) Although this section has a stratification that relates to part of the standard (5.4, 5.6), it is not possible to prove that the plinths are original. They probably are either original and have been refinished, or they are old replacements.

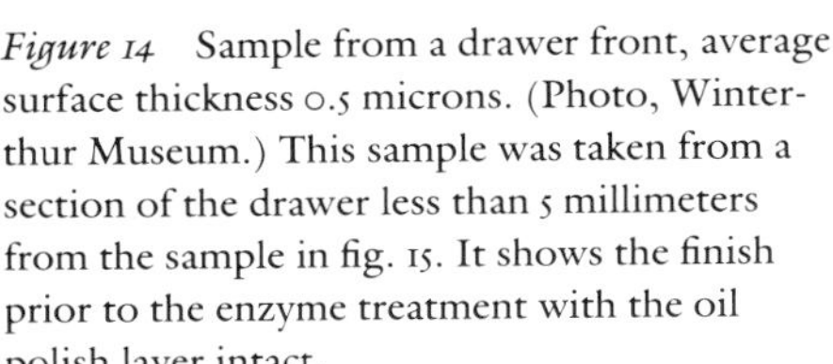

Figure 13 Sample from a scroll volute of the appliqué, average surface thickness 0.2 microns. (Photo, Winterthur Museum.) Samples were taken from areas of the carving which were thought to have been restored. This sample, taken from a scroll volute, has a stratigraphy that corresponds to the first two layers on the replaced cartouche (9.1, 9.2).

Figure 14 Sample from a drawer front, average surface thickness 0.5 microns. (Photo, Winterthur Museum.) This sample was taken from a section of the drawer less than 5 millimeters from the sample in fig. 15. It shows the finish prior to the enzyme treatment with the oil polish layer intact.

Figure 15 Sample from a drawer front, average surface thickness 0.5 microns. (Photo, Winterthur Museum.) This sample was taken from a section of the drawer less than 5 millimeters from the sample in fig. 14 after the application of the enzyme gel. The oil polish layer evident in fig. 14 has been removed and the underlying coatings left intact.

Figure 16 After-treatment view of the chest-on-chest illustrated in fig. 1. (Photo, Winterthur Museum.)

This information proved useful for treating the piece. Most of the surface was deemed worth retaining because of the condition and composition of the pre-1940 layers and the remnants of the original surface preserved beneath them. In addition, microscopy had revealed a thin oil layer on the surface that was problematic and of a different composition than the finish layer immediately under it. Based on this stratification, we devised a cleaning system that would remove the disfiguring outer layers without disturbing the underlying zones. Drawing on the technology pioneered by painting conservator Richard Wolbers, we applied an enzyme gel to remove the oil and dirt film on all of the flat surfaces.[16] Figures 14 and 15 graphically illustrate the results of this procedure at the microscopic level.

With the oil film successfully removed, the decision had to be reached as to what additional treatment was necessary. According to Thomas Sheraton, furniture could be kept in good order with nothing more than "a ball of wax and a brush." Astute cabinetmakers like Sheraton realized that wax would help protect a finish and enhance its appearance. Following historical precedent, we applied a mixture of beeswax and carnuba wax, completing the treatment (fig. 16).[17]

The successful study and conservation of this important chest-on-chest was the result of thorough historical research, traditional connoisseurship, scientific analysis, and methodical treatment. It is essential for conservators and curators to combine their expertise. To act as responsible custodians of these objects, we must explore every available avenue of research to ensure that they are properly understood and interpreted and survive intact for others to study.

1. Kindig felt that it was one of the most important pieces that he had ever owned (H. F. du Pont's secretary [probably J. F. Otwell] to David Stockwell, October 21, 1946, Winterthur, Delaware, Registrar's Office, Winterthur Museum).

2. These include oak drawer sides, veneered drawer fronts, full dustboards, and vertical foot blocks. Philip Bell made furniture for the British middle class and for export, and George Washington was one of his American customers (Helen Maggs Fede, *Washington Furniture at Mount Vernon* [Mount Vernon, Virginia: Mount Vernon Ladies Association of the Union, 1966], pp. 17, 18). Wallace Nutting, *Furniture Treasury*, 2 vols. (Framingham, Mass.: Old American Company, 1933), 1: 78.

3. George Marshall, *The Ancient Buildings of Rome by Anthony Desgodetez*, 2 vols. (London, 1771), 1: iv. James Stuart and Nicholas Revett, *The Antiquities of Athens*, 3 vols. (London: John Nichols, 1762–1786; reprint, New York: Benjamin Bloom, 1968), 1: pl. 3. Antoine Desgodets, *Les Edifices antiques de Rome* (Paris: Jean Baptiste Coignard, 1682), pl. 5.

4. Thomas Chippendale, *The Gentleman and Cabinet-Maker's Director* (London, 1754), p. iii.

5. Helena Hayward, *Thomas Johnson and English Rococo* (London: Alec Tiranti, 1964), pp. 11, 15. Luke Beckerdite, "Philadelphia Carving Shops, Part III: Hercules Courtenay and His School," *Antiques* 131, no. 5, (May 1987): 1044, 1046, 1048, 1051, 1058–59. Matthias Lock and Thomas Chippendale also incorporated Aesop's fables in their designs.

6. For more on fables as design sources for Philadelphia furniture carving, see David Stockwell, "Aesop's Fables on Philadelphia Furniture," *Antiques* 62, no. 6 (December 1952): 522–25. Stockwell incorrectly identified the figures on the Metropolitan Museum's high chest as pigeons. This piece is illustrated and discussed in Morrison H. Heckscher, *American Furniture in the Metropolitan Museum of Art, II, Late Colonial Period: The Queen Anne and Chippendale Styles* (New York: Random House, 1985), pp. 258–60. The high chest in the Philadelphia Museum of Art is illustrated and discussed in *Philadelphia: Three Centuries of American Art* (Philadelphia: by the museum, 1976), pp. 132–35. For other Johnson designs that have artistic compositions similar to the lamb and ewe, see Thomas Johnson, *Twelve Girandoles* (London: R. Sayer, 1761), frontispiece, Thomas Johnson, *One Hundred Fifty*

New Designs, pls. 14, 40, and Thomas Johnson, *New Book of Ornament* (London: R. Sayer, 1762), pl. 5.

7. Edward Benlowe, *Theophilia* (London: Roger Norton, 1652). Although the appliqué can not be tied directly to a fable, there are striking similarities in composition to some of the fable illustrations. See Francis Barlow, *Aesop's Fables with His Life in English, French, and Latin* (London: M. Mills, 1687), pls. 31, 61. Edward Hodnett, *Francis Barlow: First Master of English Book Illustration* (Berkeley: University of California Press, 1978), p. 132.

8. Sanbeck Park was designed ca. 1750 by architect James Paine, whose engravings of interior details demonstrate an appreciation for pastoral subject matter. Paine hired sculptor William Collins (1721–1793) to fabricate the interior details and described Collins as "ingenious" in his *Plans, Elevations, Sections of Nobleman's and Gentleman's Houses* (London, 1767). Collins was a student of prominent London sculptor and designer Sir Henry Cheere (1703–1781). The Victoria and Albert Museum has a design by Cheere for a chimneypiece, supposedly for Sanbeck Park. Either Cheere or Collins probably designed the tablet illustrated in fig. 4. For more on Cheere and Sanbeck Park, see Mark Girouard, "Sanbeck Park, Yorkshire," *Country Life* 138, no. 3580 (October 1965): 968–69. The author thanks Michael Podmaniczky for the information and references in this footnote. Podmaniczky's research and that of the present Earl of Scarborough eventually may establish a direct link between the carver (or carvers) at Sanbeck Park and the carver of the lamb-and-ewe chest.

9. Richard J. Bair to Charles F. Hummel, December 26, 1978, Registrar's Office, Winterthur Museum. Research for fabricating an appropriate ornament is underway.

10. Studies of traditional finishing practices can be found in Robert D. Mussey, "Old Finishes," *Fine Woodworking* 33, (March/April 1982): 7 and Robert D. Mussey, "Early Varnishes," *Fine Woodworking* 35, (July/August 1982): 54–57. Resins such as colophony, copal, mastic, sandarac, and shellac were the most common.

11. Fluorescence microscopy is used to make visible the stratigraphy and character of surface coatings that could not otherwise be seen. See Richard Wolbers and Gregory Landrey, "The Use of Reactive Fluorescent Dyes for the Characterization of Binding Media in Cross Sectional Examinations," *AIC Preprints* (Washington: American Institute for Conservation of Historic and Artistic Works, 1987), pp. 168–202 and Gregory Landrey, "The Use of Fluorescence Microscopy in Furniture Conservation," *ICOM Preprints*, ICOM Committee for Conservation, Ninth Triennial Meeting, Dresden, GDR (Los Angeles: ICOM, 1990), pp. 835–39. This preprint includes citations of other publications on microscopy.

12. The microscope was a Nikon Labophot with an episcopic-fluorescence attachment EF-D and a filter cube V2B.

13. Bair to Hummel.

14. The flurochrome Rhodamine B for Lipids was applied to this sample, and the stratigraphy was studied under the fluorescence microscope. For more on this procedure, see Woblers and Landrey, "Use of Reactive Fluorescent Dyes."

15. Isaac Byington Manuscript, Diaries, and Recipes, Joseph Downs Collection of Manuscripts and Printed Ephemera, Library, Winterthur Museum. The painting is in the collection of the Philadelphia Museum of Art (acc. 1983-90-3). It is illustrated in Morrison H. Heckscher and Leslie Greene Bowman, *American Rococo, 1750–1775: Elegance in Ornament* (New York: Abrams, 1992), p. 187.

16. The enzyme gel was Lipase type VII from *Candida cylindracea* available from Sigma Chemical Company. Conservation technicians Scott Friedgen-Vietch and Nancy Rienhold applied the gel.

17. Thomas Sheraton, *The Cabinet Dictionary* (London, 1803), annotated reprint, Wilford P. Cole and Charles F. Montgomery, eds. (New York: Praeger Publishers, 1970), p. 290. The soft wax recommended by Sheraton (p. 289) was a mixture of beeswax and turpentine. The wax used in this treatment was Behlen's Blue Label Paste Wax, Brown B800-12455. Technicians Friedgen-Vietch and Rienhold applied the wax.

Figure 1 Desk-and-bookcase, Boston, 1735–1740. Courbaril, red cedar, and cherry with white pine, cherry, and oak. H. 97″, W. 40$\frac{5}{16}$″, D. 24$\frac{1}{8}$″. (Milwaukee Art Museum purchase through bequest of Mary Jane Rayniak in memory of Mr. and Mrs. Joseph Rayniak, acc. M1983.378; photo, Richard Cheek.) The scrollboard appliqué, finials, brass, and glass door plates are restored.

Alan Miller

Roman Gusto in New England: An Eighteenth-Century Boston Furniture Designer and His Shop

▼ IN 1767, German economist Justus Moser meticulously described the responsibilities of the master cabinetmaker in a large London shop:

> The master himself no longer touches a tool. Instead he oversees the work of his forty journeymen, evaluates what they have produced, corrects their mistakes, and shows them ways and methods by which they can better their work or improve their technique. He . . . will observe what is going on in the development of fashion. He keeps in touch with people of taste and visits artists who might be of assistance to him.

Although few colonial cabinet shops were as large as that described by Moser, many were hierarchical organizations in which the master, journeymen, and contractors had clearly defined roles. Design and construction details that identify a large group of furniture from a now anonymous Boston cabinet shop (fl. 1735–1755) provide compelling evidence of a differentiated designer/tradesman relationship and a level of specialization that was comparable with urban British practice.[1]

The furniture from this shop represents the collaborative efforts of several talented artisans—a designer, joiners, and at least one japanner, one turner, and one carver—and is the most advanced work from eighteenth-century Boston. What most distinguishes this furniture is its complex, varied design. As a group, these pieces reflect an intimate understanding of late-seventeenth-century baroque style, Palladian classicism, and the furniture traditions of eighteenth-century Boston. This is not urban British furniture made in the colonies; it is Boston furniture informed and transformed by the grandeur of European styles. Two explanations for this remarkable diversity can be proposed: either a British-trained designer assimilated Boston styles, or a Boston native moved to England during the first quarter of the eighteenth century, absorbed the intentions and details of then-current furniture and architectural design, and returned to design at home.[2]

If the designer was a Boston native he probably went to England during the 1720s or early 1730s when British architects and cabinetmakers began to abandon the baroque style and embrace the new classical interpretations, or Roman "gusto," of Lord Burlington and his protégés. If he was an immigrant, like Boston cabinetmaker William Price (1684–1771), he remained acutely sensitive to changes in British fashion. Price emigrated from London in 1714 and enjoyed a long and prosperous career as a merchant, picture seller, and cabinetmaker. As an importer of maps and prints he maintained close ties with England and reportedly made "recurring visits to the land of his youth." Commercial contacts and associations with other tradesmen helped keep colonial artisans informed of the latest styles. Price, for example, apparently employed at least one London-trained cabinetmaker. In 1726, he advertised "All Sorts of Looking-Glasses of the newest Fashion, & Japan Work, viz. Chests of Drawers, Corner Cupboards, Large and Small Tea Tables & c. done after the best manner by one late from London. . . ."[3]

Social contacts were nearly as important as skill for an eighteenth-century artisan, especially if he was designing or making expensive goods that were attainable only by the very affluent. The designer of this group of Boston furniture probably occupied a social position comparable to Price, who was an accomplished organist and influential figure in the design and furnishing of Anglican churches in Boston. Price's ability to supervise workmen and his knowledge of classical architecture prompted the trustees of Trinity Church to hire him in 1738–1739 to "Treat with a Carver about the Corinthian Capitals."[4]

Although there is no documentary evidence that Price was the designer of the furniture under discussion, his background, his commercial and social connections, and his career as a cabinetmaker and architectural designer fit the profile almost perfectly. He maintained a long association with Boston japanner, engraver, and organ builder, Thomas Johnston, and had business dealings with wealthy Boston merchants Peter Faneuil, James Bowdoin, and Thomas Hancock. More importantly, Price apparently had the financial resources to support a large cabinetmaking enterprise.[5]

Colonial artisans were essentially pieceworkers in a labor system where habit and repetition increased speed and generated profit. Although most American furniture was the result of rote practice rather than innovative design, the pieces attributed to this Boston shop are novel and reminiscent of the playful architectural fantasies of seventeenth- and eighteenth-century gentleman architects. Almost every foot design and ornamental detail is different from others in the group and from anything else produced in eighteenth-century Boston. Creating new designs and working them out on the shop floor was expensive, but this creator was interested in intellectual rather than habitual design. His shop also used expensive imported materials: exotic woods, fine brass hardware, silver and gold leaf, and Vauxhall plate glass—beveled, shaped, and silvered for door mirrors.[6]

The tradesmen who made these pieces were among the most skilled in eighteenth-century Boston, yet evidence suggests that they were only peripherally involved in the design. Joiners, for example, evidently misunderstood certain details and constantly improvised and invented new construction methods to execute them. On most desks-and-bookcases, the plinths of the scrollboard appliqués are awkwardly fitted around the door arches (figs. 9, 22, 23, later in this article). If the designer was one of the artisans in the shop, he clearly was orchestrating most of the work, rather than doing it himself. If not a cabinetmaker, then he may have been involved in a related trade such as architecture.[7]

Boston furniture makers formed a relatively closed, interrelated trade group by the second decade of the eighteenth century. Because immigration was negligible after the mid-1720s, most tradesmen were from families that had been in New England for several generations. The enclaved craft system and general conservatism of the furniture-buying clientele led to standardized furniture designs and construction techniques. In the use of urban British construction details—thin oak and red cedar backboards and drawer frames, ¾-depth dustboards, and composite foot blocks—ornate carving and japanning, and rigorous architectural design, the furniture attributed to this shop represents a significant departure from mainstream Boston work. Wealthy, cosmopolitan merchants, such as Col. Henry Bromfield and Gilbert Deblois, provided the initial market for these new furniture designs, which gradually inspired shop-tradition manufacturers who catered to Boston's middle class.[8]

An early desk-and-bookcase from this group (fig. 1) and a contemporary example from another Boston cabinet shop (fig. 5) graphically illustrate this point. Figure 5 is signed by Job Coit and Job Coit, Jr., dated 1738, and is the earliest documented piece of Boston (or American) blockfront furniture. Except for the blockfront and shaped desk interior, it is a standard Boston form made of walnut and white pine. The Coits obviously struggled to execute the blocked design (fig. 4). Although they cut the back edge of the base molding to the same shape as the front edge and attempted to cope the molding to the bottom board, patches on the board indicate that it was either cut initially for a different block facade or that the Coits made a layout mistake. They did not have a template or standard layout system for blocked base moldings, and they were unfamiliar with blockfront construction techniques.[9]

They also were unaccustomed to making drawers with receding fronts for the writing compartment of the desk. The sides of the drawers do not meet the fronts in right angles because of the curved interior design. The shoulders of the dovetails of these drawer sides should conform to the angles of the fronts to which they are attached. As the Coits executed them they do not; some of the drawers with asymmetrical plans have their side's front shoulders cut as though the plan were symmetrical. Different drawers are handled in different ways, and they did not settle on a systematic accurate way to make them during the manufacture of this desk-and-bookcase despite their experimentation.[10]

The Coits were attempting to produce a simplified version of the 1735–1740 desk-and-bookcase (fig. 1), which is part of the group of furniture upon which this article focuses. Unlike the Coit piece, the desk-and-bookcase in figure 1 represents the efforts of a designer, a British-trained joiner who was capable of executing exacting inlay work, a turner, a japanner, and a carver. It is the product of either a large organized shop or a carefully orchestrated network of subcontractors working with a cabinet shop.

Figure 2 Interior of the desk-and-bookcase illustrated in fig. 1. (Photo, Richard Cheek.) The door panels and large scrolled vertical dividers of the bookcase and the prospect door of the desk interior are restored.

The case is made of three primary woods, two of which are expensive exotics. The facade, feet, and moldings are made of *Hymenea courbaril* (guapinol, locust or rode lokus, algarrobo and Jatoba), a tropical hardwood whose growth range extends from southern Mexico and the West Indies to northern Brazil. A very heavy wood with tightly interlocked grain, courbaril is extremely difficult to work with edge tools. Because its red color is very fugitive and its pores are sparse and large, courbaril offers few advantages over mahogany and is rarely encountered in eighteenth-century furniture. Its use in this piece probably stems from its temporary availability in the mahogany trade and reflects the experimental inclinations of this designer/shop. Red cedar is the primary wood of the interior, and its selection may have resulted from exasperation over working with courbaril (figs. 2, 3). When freshly cut the woods are almost the same color. The cedar came from large trees and is *Juniperus* species, likely either *bermudiana* or *silicosa*, which are Caribbean and southeastern North American woods respectively. In Boston, red cedar was an expensive, exotic wood valued as highly as mahogany. Its smooth working qualities, color, aroma, and insect deterrence undoubtedly contributed to its popularity. Red cherry, a local hardwood that also is nearly the same color as courbaril when cut, was used for the case sides.[11]

Where the Coits' construction was either rote or uncertain, the structure of this desk-and-bookcase is exceptional. The desk has large drawers with thin frames and fine dovetails, ¾-depth dustboards, and embryonic composite feet—details that indicate that at least one of the shop joiners was British trained. The attachment of the base molding involved coping the ovolo element to the bottom board and gluing it to a shaped plate below, a construction technique that the Coits unsuccessfully attempted to emulate (fig. 4). The designer and joiners also devised a complex method to keep the fallboard supports from intruding on the top drawer. To raise the bookcase doors above the arc of the fallboard, the joiners made a horizontally configured box and attached it to the base of the bookcase. This box also houses the candle slides, which have molded recesses produced by turning them on the faceplate of a lathe.

The interior of the bookcase follows London designs of the 1720s and earlier and is one of the most elaborate produced in the colonies (fig. 2). The fascia, or valence, over the prospect door has a relieved ground and a beaded edge worked from the solid. Flanking the door are interlocking, three-part document drawers that separate at the junction of flame, Doric column, and plinth (fig. 3). The desk interior also has a central prospect with a beaded fascia, engaged Doric columns, and tiers of small blocked drawers surmounted by pigeonholes with shaped dividers and valences. The door, columns, and flanking convex drawers are encased in a removable cedar box that is held in place with two wooden spring locks. Document drawers behind the engaged columns are accessible only from the back. An elaborate secret compartment was behind the removable box, but all that remains are shallow mortises for two leather hinges for a false back that was lowered like a drawbridge.

Figure 3 Detail of the interlocking drawers and prospect box of the desk-and-bookcase illustrated in fig. 2 (Photo, Milwaukee Art Museum.) The lock on the prospect door of the bookcase controls access to eight smaller drawers. When this door is open, a wooden spring lock releases the fascia drawer above and sliding wooden bolts let into the underside of the shelf release the two Doric column document drawers. These interlock with drawers above and below. The prospect section of the desk is held with two wooden spring locks. It houses two secret document drawers and originally concealed a secret compartment faced by a hinged false backboard.

An accomplished japanner and carver contributed to the grandeur of this piece. The bookcase interior has silver gilt moldings and flames, and trompe l'oeil shells and moldings (figs. 2, 3). The japanner used several techniques to produce the trompe l'oeil effect: he probably tarnished the silvered shells with liver of sulfur, shaded selected areas with dilute asphaltum, and made bright accent lines using sgraffito techniques. Although any competent japanner should have been able to perform this work, silver gilding of this quality is rare in colonial furniture. The carved scrollboard appliqué and finials of the desk-and-bookcase are lost; however, they probably resembled those currently on the piece. The flames of the finials probably matched those on the columns in the bookcase, which have quadruple bine twists with beads worked in the valleys. Despite its losses, the bookcase is more elaborately and extensively carved than most Boston examples of the 1730s.

In its materials, joinery, and ornament, this desk-and-bookcase represents the pinnacle of its era in Boston; yet, its most remarkable feature is its design. It successfully combines late baroque features (such as the elevated returns of the cornice) with classical architectural details (such as Doric columns). Four engaged pilasters on the bookcase facade and

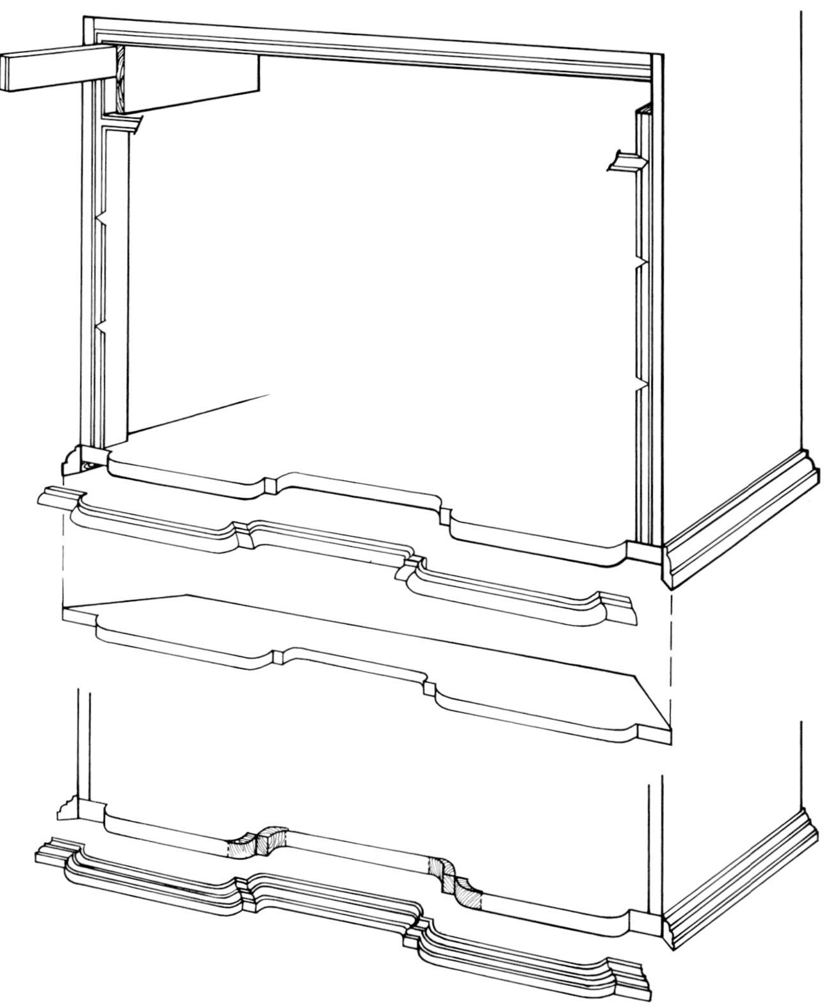

Figure 4 Diagram of (*a*) base-molding and fallboard support construction of the desk-and-bookcase illustrated in fig. 1; (*b*) base-molding construction of the desk-and-bookcase illustrated in fig. 5. The shaded areas on the front of the bottom board in *b* represent the patches resulting from layout or construction error. (Drawing by Alan Miller; artwork, Bradley K. Szollose, K2 Design.)

two pairs of engaged columns in the interiors make it one of the most architectonic pieces surviving from the colonies. The designer's meticulous attention to detail is reflected in the integration of the outer pilasters into the cornice molding to create a full classical entablature. When this piece was made (1735–1740), the blockfront style was just emerging in Boston, and if this designer did not actually introduce that style, his shop certainly gave it enough credence to ensure its survival. It would be difficult to overstate this influence on eighteenth-century Boston furniture. This designer's experiments became the standard, almost habitual, formats of later cabinetmaking traditions.

Figure 5 Desk-and-bookcase, signed by Job Coit and Job Coit, Jr., Boston, dated 1738. Black walnut with white pine. H. 99½", W. 39⅝", D. 24⅜". (Courtesy, Winterthur Museum, acc. 62.87.)

A blockfront desk, formerly in the collection of Jacob Paxon Temple, supports the 1735–1755 date range assigned to this designer's work (fig. 6). Although its present location is unknown, the 1922 auction catalogue stated that the desk in Temple's collection was made of walnut with line inlay and floral marquetry, fitted with "small drawers and pigeonholes on either side of [a] central arched and locked compartment, with four small drawers and a secret compartment," and dated 1739. Except for the inlay on the lid, slightly different brasses, and walnut (which may have been incorrectly identified), the desk is virtually identical to the desk section of the preceding piece.[12] The authenticity of the date and age of the inlay on the fallboard cannot be verified, but they probably are genuine, for early-twentieth-century furniture historians would have considered 1739 much too early for a blockfront, making it unlikely that the date was added to increase the piece's value. Moreover, the date fits perfectly with the chronology posed for this group. The joiner who inlaid the preceding desk-and-bookcase (figs. 1–3) undoubtedly was capable of executing compass-generated vine and flower inlay. Such inlay was common throughout the western world during the late seventeenth and early eighteenth centuries.

The remarkable desk-and-bookcase illustrated in figures 7 and 8 is the earliest known piece by this designer/shop and could be the earliest piece of American blockfront furniture. Although currently fitted with blocked bracket feet, it probably had turned ball feet similar to those of a later desk-and-bookcase from this shop (fig. 20). A photograph taken in the late 1940s shows the piece with late neoclassical turned feet that may have been tenoned into the sockets of the originals (fig. 7). The blocked desk interior likely predates the half-amphitheater format of the courbaril desk-and-bookcase (fig. 2) and the full amphitheater format of later desks from this shop (figs. 16, 22, later in this article).

Although most of the patterns, molding planes, and scratch stock cutters used to make the desks-and-bookcases in figures 1 and 7 are the same,

Figure 6 Desk, Boston, dated 1739. Possibly walnut, secondary wood undetermined. H. 41½", W. 37½", D. 21½". (Lot 1349, *The Jacob Paxon Temple Collection of Early American Furniture*, Anderson Galleries, 1922.)

Figure 7 Desk-and-bookcase with carving possibly by John Welch, Boston, 1733–1738. Mahogany with oak and white pine. H. 94", W. 41¼", D. 24". (Photo, Joe Kindig, III.) The left finial is original, and the original center finial is shown on the right corner. The finial in the center is incorrect. The top central portion of the scrollboard and a small piece of carving at the top of the appliqué are missing. The mirrors and backing panels, hardware, and feet are replaced. The bottom of the desk section had no evidence of bracket feet.

Figure 8 Desk-and-bookcase illustrated in fig. 7. (Art Institute of Chicago, major acquisitions Centennial Fund, acc. 1986.414; photo, © 1991, The Art Institute of Chicago. All rights reserved.)

Figure 9 Detail of the scrollboard appliqué and center finial of the desk-and-bookcase illustrated in figs. 7, 8. (Courtesy, Israel Sack, Inc., N.Y.C.)

Figure 10 Desk-and-bookcase with carving attributed to John Welch, Boston, 1740–1760. Woods and dimensions not recorded. (Courtesy, Bernard & S. Dean Levy, Inc., N.Y.C.)

the appearances of these pieces are remarkably distinct. The earlier example has more carving—large urn-and-flame finials and a scrollboard appliqué with clusters of grapes, flowers, and leaves—than other contemporary Boston furniture (figs. 7, 9). In stylistic intent, the appliqué recalls the work of London carver Grinling Gibbons (1648–1721). It is as naturalistic as its maker's technique will allow. The long-petaled flowers on the right side are carved in full relief and their front petals project 1½″. This seventeenth-century style carving could be considered old-fashioned when compared to the case design, but its bold declaratory quality is consistent with Palladian designs, which frequently include large-scale naturalistic carving. In design and ornament, this desk-and-bookcase has only one contemporary parallel from Boston—the courbaril example (fig. 1).

Although not examined by the author, a desk-and-bookcase illustrated in *Antiques* in December 1947 has an upper case with details consistent with several pieces by this Boston designer/shop and appears to date 1740–55 (fig. 10). It has four engaged Ionic pilasters that interrupt the cornice molding like the Doric pilasters of the earlier desks-and-bookcases (figs. 1, 7). The designer may have moved from the simpler to the more complex orders as he gained confidence in the carver he employed.[13]

The carved appliqué on the scrollboard of the desk-and-bookcase in

Figure 11 Detail of the appliqué and painted gilt shells of the bookcase illustrated in fig. 10.

Figure 12 Detail of the applied shell and upper rail of a picture frame carved by John Welch for John Singleton Copley's portrait of Nicholas Boylston, Boston, ca. 1767. White pine, gilded. 66¾" × 47⅜". (The Harvard University Portrait Collection, bequest of Ward Nicholas Boylston, acc. 1828 H 90.)

figures 10 and 11 is virtually identical to the shell on a picture frame made by Boston carver John Welch (1711–1789) for John Singleton Copley's portrait of Nicholas Boylston (fig. 12). A successful artisan with a long, distinguished career (fl. 1732–1780), Welch was one of the most important tradesmen contracted by the Boston designer. He did all of the carving on the pieces illustrated in figures 10–25, 27–30, 40–47, and 51–53 and possibly on the two early desks-and-bookcases (figs. 1, 7). Although there are minor differences between the carving on figures 1 and 7 and the later examples, a tradesman with a career as long as Welch's was bound to have an evolving style.[14]

Welch may have apprenticed with Boston carver George Robinson (1680–1737), whose granddaughter he married in 1735. In addition to carving numerous picture frames for Copley, Welch received several important public commissions including work for Brattle Street Church (demolished). In 1750 he received £377 for architectural carving on the rebuilt Massachusetts State House. His work included a carved lion and unicorn for the gable end of the east facade and Corinthian capitals for the pilasters flanking the balcony door (figs. 13, 14).[15]

Welch's long-term association with the Boston furniture designer is confirmed by the carving on an extraordinary desk-and-bookcase (fig. 15) probably originally owned by Boston goldsmith John Allen (1671–1760). An incised inscription on the top board of the desk—"*John Allen his desk . . . made for*"—nearly matches the signature on Allen's will drafted in 1736.

Figure 13 Detail of Paul Revere's *The Bloody Massacre Perpetuated in King Street Boston on March 5th 1770*. Colored engraving on paper. 9⅝" × 8⅝". (Chipstone Foundation, acc. 1969.1; photo, Gavin Ashworth.) This engraving shows the lion and the unicorn carved by Welch.

Figure 14 Detail of a Corinthian capital carved by John Welch for the State House illustrated in fig. 13. (Photo, Luke Beckerdite.)

John was the son of wealthy Boston landowner James Allen and partner of gold- and silversmith John Edwards.[16]

Comparison of the Corinthian capitals on the bookcase with those Welch carved for the State House leaves little doubt that they are by the same hand (figs. 14, 17). The Allen desk-and-bookcase is the most extensively carved piece attributed to this shop (figs. 15–19). The shells of the bookcase interior are carved rather than painted, and the facade is ornamented with urn-and-flame finials, festooned rosettes, and a scrollboard appliqué with flowers and acanthus leaves similar to those on the Boylston frame (figs. 12, 18). The flat surface of the prospect door echoes the shape of the bookcase mirrors, and the fascia over the door has an edge bead cut from solid wood and two relief carved cherubs on a punched ground. The winged cherubs probably were inspired by cast clock spandrels.

The carving on the feet suggests that Welch and the joiners had difficulty converting the designer's plans into three-dimensional forms (figs. 15, 19). To be architecturally and visually correct, the ring and bellflowers should be centered beneath the columns of the desk; however, that would have required large feet whose profile would have been difficult to integrate into the blocked facade. Instead, the carver shifted the bellflowers toward the outer edge of the feet and inserted a partial leaf (which is discontinuous with the blocking and other carved elements) to occupy part of the space. The joiners and carver appear to have worked from an

Figure 15 Desk-and-bookcase with carving attributed to John Welch, Boston, 1743–1748. Mahogany with sabicu, red cedar, and white pine. H. 97¼", W 42⅞", D. 23¼". (Courtesy, Winterthur Museum, acc. 60.1134.) One Corinthian capital, part of one rosette, and the extreme side elements of the scrollboard appliqué are restored. A hand drawn cartouche, illegible writing, and what may be the date 1746 is on a backboard of the prospect section of the desk. The desk also has a nineteenth-century inscription, "This desk was purchased by Josiah Quincy Braintree 1778."

Figure 16 Open view of the desk-and-bookcase illustrated in fig. 15. (Photo, Winterthur Museum.)

Figure 17 Detail of Corinthian capital from the desk-and-bookcase illustrated in fig. 15. (Photo, Winterthur Museum.)

elevation drawing. The joiners had to reconcile the design with the engaged columns and blocking, and the carver had to accommodate both the designer and joiners. The edges of the feet have convex strapwork similar to the beads on the prospect door fasciae of desks in this group, whereas the ring-and-bellflower drops and central shell pendant, unique in this designer's work, are Kentian in conception.

Like the desk-and-bookcase in figure 1, the Allen example has expensive brass, large shaped mirrors, and is made of exotic woods. The backboards and dividers of the bookcase are sabicu, a tropical hardwood referred to as "horseflesh" in the eighteenth century. The drawer sides and backs are red cedar. In true baroque fashion, the facade is interrupted in several areas: feet, base molding, drawers, ¾-engaged columns of the desk, and

Figure 18 Detail of the appliqué on the desk-and-bookcase illustrated in fig. 15. (Photo, Winterthur Museum.)

Figure 19 Detail of the left front foot of the desk-and-bookcase illustrated in fig. 15. (Photo, Winterthur Museum.)

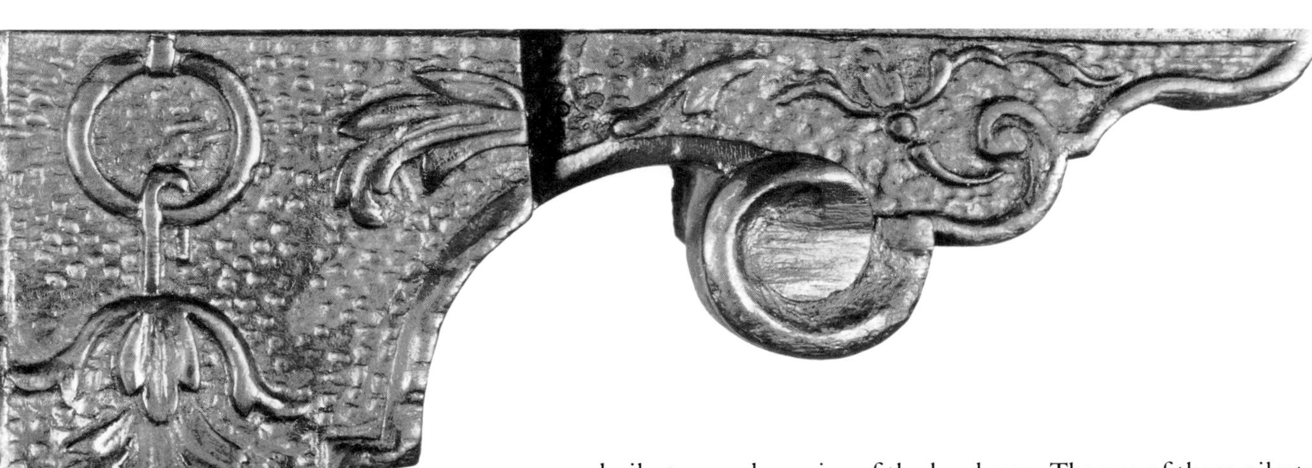

engaged pilasters and cornice of the bookcase. The use of three pilasters is an improvement over the four-pilaster plan. Although the outer pilasters are architecturally integrated into the cornice, the earlier use of two center pilasters was redundant, because only one is required as a spring post for the door arches and as a visual support for the appliqué. To make the change, the joiner reduced the width of the inner stile of the left door and positioned the pilaster of the right door to lap over it. This became the accepted format from the mid-1740s on. The seven examples of the Corinthian order make this desk-and-bookcase one of the most Palladian case pieces from colonial America.[17]

The desk-and-bookcase illustrated in figure 20 represents a simplification and clarification of several design and ornamental details introduced in the Allen example (fig. 15) and demonstrates this designer's and the shop's ability to produce thoroughly composed, distinctive furniture forms. Wood rather than mirrored doors freed the dimensions of the bookcase and allowed the designer to make the piece more vertical. Most Vauxhall plates exported to the colonies were premanufactured and sold by merchants and looking glass makers rather than being custom-ordered by cabinetmakers. On bookcases with mirrored doors, the dimensions of the plates, which generally came in standard sizes, dictated the approximate height and width of the upper case and thus, the width of the desk.

Figure 20 Desk-and-bookcase with carving attributed to John Welch, Boston, ca. 1751. Mahogany with white pine. H. 97″, W. 40½″ (38″ case), D. 23″ (21¼″ case). (Chipstone Foundation, acc. 1991.6; photo, Gavin Ashworth.) The brasses and molded faces of the fallboard supports are restored.

Figure 21 Detail of the right pilaster and gadrooned ball foot of the desk-and-bookcase illustrated in fig. 20. (Photo, Gavin Ashworth.)

Because writing heights of desks were relatively standardized, the overall dimensions of a desk-and-bookcase with mirrors was determined largely by the plate dimensions. The maker could vary its proportions only by adjusting the widths of the door stiles and the height of the scrollboard. Without glass, a bookcase could be narrower and proportionally taller. The designer further emphasized the verticality of the bookcase by reducing the width of the engaged pilasters (specifying five flutes rather than seven as on figure 15) and by centering the carving on the vertical axis.

Like Kent and Batty Langley, this Boston-based designer occasionally employed late-baroque details to solve problems he faced in applying classical architectural conventions to furniture design. The two inherent problems of blockfront design in desks-and-bookcases—the transition from the bottom of the blocking to the floor and from the top of the blocking to the pediment—may never have been resolved with more success than on the desk-and-bookcase in figure 20. Gadrooned ball feet, like those of figure 20, are baroque details used by early-eighteenth-century designers such as Daniel Marot (fig. 31) and by Palladian designer-architects during the 1740s. They completely resolve the problems encountered with the blocked bracket feet of the Allen desk and make a bold transition from the engaged pilasters to the floor (fig. 21). The designer called for Doric pilasters on the corners of the desk and Corinthian pilasters on the bookcase, a use consistent with the superimposed orders of classical architecture (figs. 20, 21). Coped and molded sections of the pilaster capitals originally formed the faces of the lid supports.[18]

The design of the bookcase interior is typical of later pieces from the shop (fig. 22). The arches have gilt trompe l'oeil shells with acanthus leaves and small lion heads at the bottom (fig. 23). A document drawer from the desk interior (figs. 24, 25) has a list of sums in pounds and shillings and the inscription, "Long [?] (L) 42–10 up to March 25th 51." Under this inscription is a profile sketch of a male head with a Roman nose, curly hair, and almond-shaped eyes. This facile drawing, which resembles a head from antiquity, may have been executed by the japanner or by the designer if he provided drawings of the shells for the japanner. In execution, it is closely related to the lion heads on the shells (figs. 23, 25). If the same artist was responsible for both, as seems likely, then the "51" in the inscription is the date of the desk's construction—1751. The shells inside the bookcase are virtually identical to those in figure 11 and similar to the shell on the drawer of a Boston high chest from another cabinet shop (fig. 26), indicating that the japanner worked as a contractor. This anonymous japanner worked for the designer from at least 1750 to 1755 and possibly as much as fifteen years earlier (figs. 1, 7).

The designer of this group of furniture also maintained a long-term association with a turner, although it is not known whether the latter was a contractor or a member of the shop. This man apparently made all of the turned finials and feet for every piece from this shop. His vocabulary of forms and handling of small torus moldings (which are somewhat pointed in profile) are distinctive. The inverted cup-shaped finials of the

Figure 22 Open view of the desk-and-bookcase illustrated in fig. 20. (Photo, Gavin Ashworth.) The carved appliqués on the fascia above the prospect door are restorations based on the spandrel appliqués of the clock case illustrated in figs. 27, 30.

Figure 23 Detail of the finials, rosette, appliqué, painted gilt shell, and Corinthian capital of the bookcase illustrated in figure 20. (Photo, Gavin Ashworth.)

Figure 24 Detail of the back of the prospect box of the desk-and-bookcase illustrated in fig. 20. (Photo, Gavin Ashworth.)

Figure 25 Detail of the inscription and drawing on the side of a document drawer from the prospect box illustrated in fig. 24. (Photo, Gavin Ashworth.)

bookcase in figures 20 and 23, for example, are related to the foot turnings of the desk section (fig. 21) and the cup-shaped urns of other finials in the group (figs. 15, 27). Similar comparisons can be drawn between the columns in later desk interiors and finials.

A clock case originally owned by wealthy Boston merchant Col. Henry Bromfield is almost exactly contemporary with the preceding piece (fig. 27). The case houses a movement by London clockmaker Thomas Hughes and is labeled, "This case made by George Glinn 1750 . . . it cost £10 lawf. money." Although the inscription clearly is genuine, research has failed to find a Boston cabinetmaker named George Glinn. Possibly the most remarkable achievement of this designer/shop and Welch, the case is a mid-eighteenth-century Boston form elevated by the conventions of classical architecture. The base and waist are like a building facade with corner plinths and pilasters, and the hood is reminiscent of eighteenth-century temples and garden follies.[19]

Figure 26 Detail of a trompe l'oeil shell on the drawer of a high chest, Boston, 1740–1750. (Courtesy, Israel Sack, Inc., N.Y.C.)

The cove and ovolo base molding and pilaster base moldings of the clock case match those of the preceding piece (figs. 21, 29). The pilasters of these pieces also have corners molded with the same ovolo scratch stock cutter. On the clock case, the pilasters have four flutes on the front and four on the side, whereas those of the desk have five on the front and three on the sides. The joiners who made the desk may have had a front elevation only and incorrectly executed the side elevations. On the clock the base molding, plinths, and pilasters rise from bilaterally symmetrical feet, so they had to be equal on the sides and front of the case. Although the capitals of the clock pilasters are missing, the dimensions of the space the originals occupied suggests that they were Corinthian. To make the transition to the hood (which does not have projecting corners like the cove molding beneath it), the joiners glued strips of wood to the upper edges of the cove recesses and returns to make the edges even with those of the corners (fig. 28).

The joiners used many other techniques that diverge from normal Boston practice. After working down the interior surface of the waist door, they cut the molded edge from the solid wood by reversing the scratch stock cutter they used for the arch above the dial. Then they attached the door with finialed butt hinges similar to those used for bookcase doors rather than conventional clock-door hinges. They made the sarcophagus top in three sections: large cove, large ovolo, and small cove beneath the ovolo (fig. 28). The top board is molded on the front and side edges and nailed. Marks of the original center plinth on the top board indicate that the plinth was flanked by scrolled brackets (probably carved). To allow the bell to ring clearly, the joiners cut through the scrollboard behind the arch fret and spandrel appliqués and covered the openings with crimson silk. The original paper pattern is still glued to the back of the fret.[20] They hinged the hood door to an applied beveled strip (slightly thicker than the door) that extends behind the colonette on the right. The corresponding strip on the left houses the door and has a mortise to accept the bolt from the lock. Instead of coping the molding

Figure 27 Tall case clock labeled by George Glinn, with carving attributed to John Welch, Boston, 1750. H. 100″. (The Art Institute of Chicago, Alyce and Edwin DeCosta and Walter E. Heller Foundation and Harold Stuart endowments, acc. 1990.395; photo, Sotheby's.) The case houses a movement by London clockmaker Thomas Hughes. The capitals of the waist pilasters and the center finial and plinth are missing.

on the inside of this door frame, they mitered it at the corners. They rabbeted the dial skirt to receive the clock dial, and made most of the skirt and the front base rail of the hood of a hardwood that appears to be courbaril. Possibly relegated to a secondary position because of its difficult woodworking properties, this wood may represent stock remaining from the courbaril desk-and-bookcase (fig. 1). This clock case is the only other piece of Boston furniture known with courbaril as a primary or secondary wood.

The winged paw feet are remarkable in design and execution and unprecedented in the history of American furniture (fig. 29). The joiners or carver (if fabricated in his shop) constructed them like bracket feet: the grain runs horizontally, and they are mitered at the corners (between the front toes). The feet are laminated for thickness where the toes of the paw and ball emerge from the ankle.[21] The case has only front feet; the backboard extends to the floor to support the case in the rear.

Welch must have felt comfortable with the design of the carving for the clock case, as his carving for it is so confident and fluid. Although he reverted to a rapid ground-covering style on the feathers, the muscular shoulders and tops of the wings, complex shape of the ankles, and powerful acanthus scrolls of the feet make them the most distinguished examples from mid-eighteenth-century Boston. The spandrel appliqués (fig. 30) have a playful elastic quality that differs from the bold naturalistic appliqués of figures 9 and 18. The leaves have delicate cabochons on their spines and are propelled by the strapwork intertwinings of the appliqués.

Although the exact working relationship between the Boston designer and Welch will probably never be known, it can be reconstructed partially by interpreting what is written in wood in the context of seventeenth- and eighteenth-century furniture design. The feet of the clock are derived from late-seventeenth- and early-eighteenth-century examples like those drawn by Marot (figs. 29, 31). An apostle of the baroque court style in France, Marot also drew clock cases with complex interrupted facades, engaged fluted pilasters, and carved ball feet, details frequently used by this Boston designer. The designer probably furnished Welch with a sketch of the clock case and a full-size profile drawing of the feet. As a carver of large animals for ships (i.e., two sea horses, 7½′ long for a ship) and public buildings (fig. 13), Welch was capable of producing anatomically accurate three-dimensional forms.[22]

The varying design of the finials on furniture in this group suggests that the designer drew them as well (fig. 28). The tradesmen who made the clock finials—Welch, the turner, and possibly a japanner or gilder—collaborated to make what became the prototype of most later Boston urn-and-flame finials. The larger flames, shorter spires, and flaring urn cap (made of white pine for gilding) make the clock finials an improved restatement of those on the Allen desk-and-bookcase (fig. 15). They reflect the designer's and the shop's efforts to refine and perfect their work. The earlier flames have deep recesses, whereas those of the clock finials are comprised of three graceful twisted elements and are open at the top and

Figure 28 Detail of the hood of the clock case illustrated in fig. 27. (Photo, © 1991, The Art Institute of Chicago. All rights reserved.)

Figure 29 Detail of the right foot of the clock case illustrated in fig. 27. (Photo, © 1991, The Art Institute of Chicago. All rights reserved.)

Figure 30 Detail of the right spandrel appliqué of the clock case illustrated in fig. 27. (Photo, © 1991, The Art Institute of Chicago. All rights reserved.)

pierced. The gadrooning and acanthus on the clock finials relate to the gadrooning on the feet of figure 21 and the acanthus on the finials of the Allen desk-and-bookcase (fig. 15) and figure 9.

A clock case reportedly made for loyalist Gilbert Deblois dates about 1751–1754 and has several subtle design improvements (figs. 27, 32). On the Bromfield case the plinths are wider than the space between them, which architecturally represents the wall on which they bear. To make the Deblois case more classically correct, the designer reduced the width of the plinths and left more space between the waist door and pilasters (figs. 32, 33). Because the plinths (and their base moldings) were too narrow to align with the wing feet, the designer enlarged the wings so they nearly meet in the center and increased the height of the base molding (compare figs. 27, 29, 32, 33). On the Deblois case, the molding above the dial arch is considerably larger than that of the Bromfield case and it is capped by a small bevel that surrounds the outer plinths (fig. 34). Had the sarcophagus survived, the large ovolo molding would have been on approximately the same vertical plane as the frieze—another subtle architectural refinement. The arch fret and spandrels of the Deblois case also are missing (fig. 34), but they probably resembled those of the Bromfield case (figs. 28, 30).[23]

Figure 31 Plate 21 in Daniel Marot's *Nouveau Livre d'Ornements* (ca. 1703). (Dumbarton Oaks, Trustees for Harvard University.)

The molding changes on the Deblois case required retooling planes and scratch stock cutters. It is almost inconceivable that the joiners would have made these subtle but troublesome alterations unless they were specified by the designer. No matter what changes the designer made, they invariably met with translation problems in the shop. The pilasters, for example, have five flutes on the front faces and four on the sides and their Corinthian capitals are noticeably off-center (figs. 32, 35)—architectural flaws that would have exasperated anyone with this artist's drive for classical perfection.

The Corinthian capitals show Welch in a very literal mode, employing small tools to produce exact, minute detail (fig. 35). These capitals are miniature versions of those Welch carved for the Massachusetts State House in 1750 (fig. 14). The colonettes of the hood also have exquisite Corinthian capitals and inlet brass stop fluting.

Both the Bromfield and Deblois cases were made to house expensive London movements, whereas simpler cases by this designer/shop have Boston movements. Typical of these restrained, architectural pieces are the clock cases illustrated in figures 36–38. With its horizontally configured base section, figure 36 is stylistically the earliest and probably dates around 1740. Its design, construction, and hardware details are related to those of the Bromfield and Deblois cases (figs. 27, 32) and another with a movement by Samuel Bagnall (fig. 37). The latter is the Boston model that provided the basic framework for the architectural details and carving that distinguish the Bromfield and Deblois cases. With the exception of the base molding and one small element of the hood, every molding section on the Bromfield case and figure 37 is the same. The joiners also repeated most of the construction and hardware details on the two cases

Figure 32 Tall case clock with carving attributed to John Welch, Boston, 1751–1754. Mahogany with mahogany and white pine. H. 96″, W. 21¾″, D. 11″. (Chipstone Foundation, acc. 1992.12; photo, Gavin Ashworth.) The case houses a movement by London clockmaker Marmaduke Storr. The sarcophagus top and finials are missing, and the original arch fret and spandrels are replaced with burl veneer.

Figure 33 Detail of the base of the tall case clock illustrated in fig. 32. (Photo, Gavin Ashworth.)

Figure 34 Detail of the hood of the tall case clock illustrated in fig. 32. (Photo, Gavin Ashworth.)

Figure 35 Detail of the left Corinthian capital of the tall case clock illustrated in fig. 32. (Photo, Gavin Ashworth.)

Figure 36 Tall case clock with movement by Samuel Bagnall, Boston, 1740–1745. Mahogany. H. 93″, W. 18½″. (Courtesy, Israel Sack, Inc., N.Y.C.) The sarcophagus top is restored.

(figs. 27, 37), but minor structural inconsistencies help establish a chronology. On figure 37, the joiners sawed openings in the scrollboard behind the frieze and spandrels *after* joining the supporting stage of the hood with dovetails. They abandoned this technique on the Bromfield and Deblois cases, omitting the dovetails, which would have to be cut away.[24]

A japanned clock case (fig. 39), probably made for a movement by James Atkinson (fl. 1744–1756), shares several details with the preceding examples (figs. 27, 32, 36, 37), although it cannot be attributed to this Boston designer/shop with the same degree of certainty.[25] The top board of the japanned case has clear witness for an original center plinth with flank-

Figure 37 Tall case clock with movement by Samuel Bagnall, Boston, 1740–1745. Mahogany with white pine. H. 100½″, W. 21⅞″, D. 11″. (Private collection; photo, LeVan Design.)

Figure 38 Detail of the hood and face of the movement of the tall case clock illustrated in fig. 37. (Photo, LeVan Design.) The finials, outer plinths, and upper concave element of the sarcophagus top are restored. The arch fret is a restoration based on surviving sections of the original frieze fret.

Figure 39 Tall case clock, Boston, 1745–1755. White pine. H. 94½″, W. 22¼″, D. 10¾″. (Courtesy, Winterthur Museum, acc. 55.96.3.) The Gawen Brown movement, finials, and arch fret of the hood are replaced. The original center plinth, scrolled brackets, and finial of the top are missing.

Figure 40 Desk-and-bookcase with carving attributed to John Welch, Boston, 1750–1754. Mahogany with white pine and red cedar. H. 94½″, W. 41¾″, D. 22¾″. (Photo of p. 118 in the 1902 ed. of Francis Clary Morse's *Furniture of the Olden Time*.)

ing brackets, as on the Bromfield case (fig. 27). The lower stage of the sarcophagus top has a chamfered element like that of figures 28 and 34 and the hood door has mitered joints and small butt hinges. The door is hinged to a beveled strip that extends behind the front colonettes like all of the clock cases in the group. The corners of the dial skirt also have carved mason's miters like those of the case with the Bagnall movement (figs. 37, 38).

The joiners used different planes and scratch stock cutters to cut the base moldings of the japanned case and the cases in figures 27–37; however, the basic shapes of the moldings are similar. The simplification of the moldings on the japanned case is logical considering that it is made of white pine, a soft wood less receptive to intricate, sharp detail. Many labor-intensive details, such as directly molded door edges, were unnecessary on cases with an elaborate (and semiopaque) decorative finish, so the joiners applied the molding on the waist door rather than cutting it from the solid as on figures 27, 36, and 37 or nailing it into a rabbet as on the door of the Deblois case (fig. 32).

A japanned case in the Henry Ford Museum and one advertised in *Antiques* appear from photographs to be nearly identical to figure 39, although their hoods lost all of the structure above their arched cornices. The basic design of these cases undoubtedly derives from figures 36 and

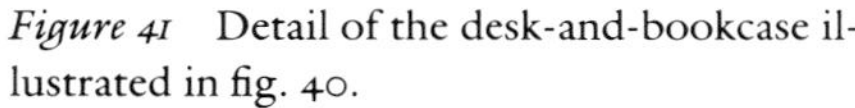

Figure 41 Detail of the desk-and-bookcase illustrated in fig. 40.

37, and the structural interrelationships suggest that at least some of the same tradesmen were involved in all of them.[26]

Unlike the preceding pieces, which have distinctly baroque details (blocked facades, elevated cornices, ball- and winged-paw feet), a desk-and-bookcase illustrated in Francis Clary Morse's *Furniture of the Olden Time* is almost entirely within the Palladian design mode (figs. 40–41). On this piece, the designer added engaged Corinthian pilasters to the rear corners of the bookcase to integrate the front and sides and provide an appropriate theater for the figural ornaments of the pediment. According to its former owner, Reverend William Reed Huntington of Grace

Church, New York, the side ornaments were "figures . . . carved from wood, of men at work at their trade of cabinet-maker." These figures and a central ornament were missing when Morse first published the piece in 1902. Assuming that the ornaments were original, which is very likely, the carving on this desk-and-bookcase may have surpassed the Allen example (fig. 15). Sketchy descriptions of Welch's sculptural carving for ships and

Figure 42 Detail of the right front foot of the desk-and-bookcase illustrated in fig. 40. (Private collection; photo, Brock Jobe.)

public buildings (fig. 13), the feet of the Bromfield and Deblois clock cases (figs. 29, 33), and the knees of figure 53 offer the only context for imagining the figural carving on this remarkable desk-and-bookcase.[27]

The reverse ogee feet of the Huntington desk-and-bookcase have exquisitely modeled acanthus leaves and scrolls with bold convex volutes that literally quote elements on the picture frame by Welch (figs. 12, 42). The ground of the foot is punched but with more regimentation than that of figure 19. Although the leaves on the scroll feet have almost no interior detailing or shading (like those on Welch's frames), the design is very clear and easily comprehended (figs. 12, 42). Scroll feet would have been extremely difficult to reconcile with a blocked facade, which probably explains why the piece has a straight front.

The desk-and-bookcase illustrated in figure 43 probably is the latest of the blockfronts in this group. Several construction details and minor aspects of its design differ from earlier blockfront desks-and-bookcases: the joiners made conventional blocked bracket feet, rounded the top corners of the blocking, and used fallboard supports that intrude on the top drawer. Although the stock preparation for the interior drawers of the desk-and-bookcase interiors is essentially the same, the construction varies from section to section, suggesting that at least two joiners were involved. The desk has a straight interior with a relatively simple prospect

Figure 43 Desk-and-bookcase with carving attributed to John Welch, Boston, 1751–1756. Mahogany with white pine. H. 95½″, W. 40″, D. 22″. (The Saint Louis Art Museum, Museum Shop Fund, acc. 84:1989; photo, Christie's.) The scrollboard is cut, and the roof and back boards of the head are missing. The original upper portion of the scroll moldings and scrollboard were reattached except for the center portion. The lower portions of the feet are restored and wood panels replace the original mirrors.

Figure 44 Detail of center finial, scrollboard appliqué, center capital, and carved molding of the desk-and-bookcase illustrated in fig. 43. (Photo, Christie's.)

section. The door is flat rather than being blocked, but, like others in the group, it has an arched fascia with a beaded edge worked from the solid. The interior of the bookcase also has an arched fascia and fluted pilaster document drawers, echoing the design of the prospect section.

Welch carved the Corinthian capitals (including those in the desk interior), the scrollboard appliqué, and the flame finials, in the same basic style as the capitals and appliqués on the Bromfield and Deblois clock cases (figs. 27–29, 32–35). For the appliqués he used broad scrollwork to propel small sprays of acanthus leaves (compare figs. 30, 44). Both sets of leaves have small cabochons on their spines and flutes applied in a similar manner. He also carved the upper elements of the turner's elegant finials—restatements of those made for figure 15—with pierced flames, almost the mirror image of those on the Bromfield clock (figs. 28, 43). Given the nature of the designer's and Welch's work, it is surprising that carved moldings, like the small ogee of the bookcase doors, were not used on the earlier pieces (fig. 44).

The preceding desk-and-bookcase and at least one other from the mid-1750s (fig. 45) suggest that this designer's attention to detail and his supervision of his workforce began to diminish during the mid-1750s. By 1755, some artisans associated with his shop were at least twenty years older than when their association began. Several journeymen must have come and gone between 1735 and 1755, eventually setting up their own shops or working for other cabinetmakers. Because these men continued to use many of the same designs and structural details they learned as journeymen, their work is difficult to separate from the original shop's as the following bombé desks-and-bookcases illustrate.

One of the earliest bombé desks-and-bookcases from Boston is by the designer and his shop (fig. 45). With the exception of the prospect door and its solid, beaded fascia, the interior of the desk is more consistent

Figure 45 Desk-and-bookcase with carving attributed to John Welch, Boston, 1751–1756. Mahogany with white pine. H. 97½", W. 45", D. 23". (The Museum of Fine Arts, Houston, Bayou Bend Collection, gift of Miss Ima Hogg, acc. B.69.363.) The feet, base molding, finial, drawers, and possibly the appliqué are restored.

Figure 46 Detail of the desk interior of the desk-and-bookcase illustrated in fig. 45.

with mainstream Boston work than with the preceding examples (fig. 46). The designer's shop either began to accept mainstream Boston styles or augmented its workforce with joiners who previously worked with more traditional cabinetmakers. The joiners who made the desk hollowed out the bombé sides by chopping them as though working curved house or ship timbers. The bookcase interior is similar to the Allen example (figs. 16, 47), but on the facade the designer added pulvinated or "swelled" friezes above the corner capitals—an architectural improvement over those of figure 43 and the trusses of the Huntington bookcase (compare figs. 41, 43, 47). Although Welch obviously carved the shells inside the bookcases of the Allen example and this bombé piece (figs. 16, 45), the leaves below the shells of the latter are completely undercut (fig. 47).[28]

Figure 47 Detail of the pediment and carved shells of the desk-and-bookcase illustrated in fig. 45.

A bombé desk-and-bookcase signed by Benjamin Frothingham, dated 1753, shares several details with the Welch-carved bombé piece and other examples from the designer's shop (fig. 48). Nothing is known of Frothingham's early career except that he was born in 1734 and that his father, Benjamin, was a joiner. Since the younger Frothingham was only 18 or 19 when he signed the desk-and-bookcase, it is unlikely that he had the capital, skills, or patronage to make such an imposing piece, which raises the possibility that Frothingham was an apprentice or journeyman in the aforementioned designer's shop.[29]

The Corinthian pilasters and mahogany, red cedar, and cedrela interior fittings (similar to the preceding piece but without carved or gilt shells) readily suggest the bookcase as a product of this designer's shop. The construction of the desk interior is also similar to several of the preceding pieces (fig. 49). The interior drawers have thin red cedar frames and bottoms that are rabbeted to the front, sides, and back; the engaged col-

Figure 48 Desk-and-bookcase signed Benjamin Frothingham, Boston, 1753. Mahogany with red cedar, cedrela, and white pine. H. 98¼″, W. 44½″, D. 24¾″. (Diplomatic Reception Rooms, U.S. Department of State, acc. 70.94; photo, Will Brown.) The mid-molding and finials are restored.

umns are similar to those in the prospect section of the Huntington desk-and-bookcase (fig. 40); and the prospect door is concave, although it lacks the beaded arched fascia. The joiners of the Frothingham-signed desk hollowed out its inner side surfaces more carefully than those of the preceding bombé desk-and-bookcase (fig. 45) but in the same method. They *inlet* the beads flanking the ends of the three bottom drawers of the desk into the front edges of the sides, which they left at full thickness. Then, they cut the rear edge of the beads and the corresponding edges of the case to match the outward swell of the facade. This is reminiscent of the exacting mentality of the joiners who developed the coped-base construction decades earlier. The element of the signed desk that most suggests involvement by the Boston designer is its molded plinth feet (figs. 48, 49). Although they occasionally occur on urban British pieces of the mid-eighteenth century, no other piece of furniture associated with Frothingham (and there are many) has plinth feet. The tall base molding, which provides a strong architectural resolution to the bombé sides, is also not typical of Frothingham's work. A bombé desk-and-bookcase illustrated in Morse's *Furniture of the Olden Time* has a similar base molding and feet (fig. 50). Whereas the construction of the latter departs more from the practices of the designer's shop, it too is very much in his style.[30]

Figure 49 Interior of the desk-and-bookcase illustrated in fig. 48.

It is almost inconceivable that the Boston designer and his shop only made case furniture. Although it is difficult to associate tables and chairs with case pieces because of inherent structural differences, an unusual concertina-action gaming table is probably by this shop (fig. 51). The front legs were sawn like the center leg of a sofa rather than like the legs in standard cabriole construction. This resulted in small feet, the toes having to be configured within the square side dimensions instead of extending to the diagonal extremes of the stock. The lower rail of the table is dovetailed to white pine corner blocks that appear to be butt- or bridle-joined to the side rails. Because of the unusual frame construction, the top of the leg is outside the frame and relies on the cheeks of the turrets and top for support. The drawer is constructed like the blocked interior drawers of desks from this shop and the front rail beads are worked from the solid like the prospect door fasciae of nearly every desk-and-bookcase in the group. Although these structural relationships are not conclusive, they are sufficient for a tentative attribution to the Boston designer and his shop.

Welch was a mature carver when this table was made (1745–1755). The delicate convex strapwork (or bead) on the knee blocks (fig. 52) is similar to that on the feet of the 1738–1748 Allen desk-and-bookcase (fig. 19); however, the leaves on the knees and pendant are more closely related to those on the feet and spandrels of the Bromfield clock (figs. 29, 30) and on other pieces that he carved during the late 1740s and 1750s.

Welch carved the center leg of a pier table to almost the same pattern, but used a human face or mask as the central element (fig. 53). Kent and Langley frequently used human and animal heads on the knees of pier tables and other architectonic forms in England during the 1730s and

Figure 50 Desk-and-bookcase with carving possibly by John Welch, Boston, 1750–1756. Mahogany with white pine and oak. Dimensions not recorded. (Photo of an illustration on page 135 of the 1917 ed. of Francis Clary Morse's *Furniture of the Olden Time*.)

1740s. Considering the Boston designer's penchant for Palladian detail, it is reasonable to speculate that it was he who hired Welch to do the carving on this table.[31]

The aforementioned designer had a profound influence on Boston furniture styles from the mid-1730s to the 1780s. Two desks-and-bookcases from the late 1730s or 1740s demonstrate his influence on competing cabinet shops. The first (fig. 54) has four Corinthian pilasters, line inlay, shaped beveled mirrors, and an amphitheater desk interior with a concave blocked prospect door—details that occur in different forms on several of the desks-and-bookcases. The construction and techniques used, however, differ significantly from those of the designer's shop: the desk has thumb-nail molded drawers; on the top drawer the blocking is rounded; the fallboard supports intrude on the top drawer; the case is not cockbeaded; and the interior arches of the bookcase are decorated with inlaid fans rather than trompe l'oeil or carved shells. The second desk-and-bookcase is probably from the same shop (fig. 55). The base molding is attached to the bottom board with a large dovetail, a standard practice in Boston

Figure 51 Card table with carving attributed to John Welch, Boston, 1745–1755. (Private collection; photo, courtesy, John Walton Antiques.)

Figure 52 Detail of the knee of the card table illustrated in fig. 51. (Photo, John Walton Antiques.)

Figure 53 Detail of the mask knee of a pier table, carving attributed to John Welch, Boston, 1745–1760. Mahogany, H. 29″, W. 28½″, D. 17⅛″. (Museum of Fine Arts, Boston, The M. and M. Karolick Collection, acc. 41.586.)

Figure 54 Desk-and-bookcase, Boston, 1738–1748. Black walnut with white pine. H. 98″, W. 41½″. (Parke-Bernet Galleries, Inc., *Important XVIII Century American Furniture From the Collection of Maurice Rubin, Brookline, Mass.*, October 9, 1954, lot. no. 174.) The gilt Corinthian capitals, festooned rosettes, and finials are above a cut line about four inches from the top of the scroll moldings.

around 1745–1780. In the production of sophisticated architectural forms, the cabinet shop that made figures 54 and 55 was the designer's most important rival; yet, the designs are almost completely derivative.

When Josiah Quincy purchased the Allen desk-and-bookcase (fig. 15) in 1778, the piece was over thirty years old, but it was stylish enough to satisfy one of Boston's wealthiest and most cosmopolitan citizens. In fact, most blockfront and bombé desks-and-bookcases made in Boston during the 1760–1780 period owe much to this designer. He and his workforce were responsible for the most varied, innovative furniture from eighteenth-century Boston. That city's cabinetmakers certainly made great furniture in the eras that followed, but this designer's spirit of exploration and adventure were unsurpassed.

Figure 55 Desk-and-bookcase, Boston, 1738–1748. Mahogany with white pine. H. 94", W. 40½", D. 22". (Courtesy, Bernard & S. Dean Levy, Inc., N.Y.C.) The feet and everything above the bookcase doors are restored.

ACKNOWLEDGMENTS For assistance with this article, the author thanks Gavin Ashworth, Luke Beckerdite, Michael Brown, Ned Cooke, Robert Fileti, Bill Finch, Elizabeth Gombosi, Anne Haley, John Hays, Brock Jobe, Leslie Keno, Joe Kindig, III, Gregory Landrey, Deanne Levinson, Frank Levy, Margaret Lichter, Joe Lionetti, Linda Lott, Anndora Morginson, Milo Naeve, Clark Pierce, John Pine, Michael Podmaniczky, Albert Sack, Harold Sack, Gail Serfaty, Laura Sprague, Laurie Stein, Jayne Stokes, Barbara Ward, Gerald Ward, and Philip Zimmerman.

1. As quoted in Christopher Gilbert, *The Life and Work of Thomas Chippendale*, 2 vols. (New York: Macmillan, 1978), 1: 22. Joe Kindig, III, was the first furniture historian to recognize the products of this designer and shop (Joe Kindig, III, The Renaissance Influence in Boston, unpublished, undated ms., copy in possession of the author). For additional discussions of this furniture, see Brock W. Jobe, "A Boston Desk-and-Bookcase at the Milwaukee Art Museum," *Antiques* 140, no. 3 (Sept. 1991): 412–19 and Jobe's catalogue entry for a desk-and-bookcase illustrated in Gerald W. R. Ward, ed., *American Furniture with Related Decorative Arts, 1660–1830: The Milwaukee Art Museum and the Layton Art Collection* (New York: Hudson Hills Press, 1992), pp. 122–26.

2. It is unlikely that a talented Boston native could have developed such virtuosity without having lived in England. The sophisticated baroque details used by his shop are difficult to explain by known examples of imported furniture or pattern books. Most British design books date later than the seminal pieces in this group, whose architectural detail resembles Palladian usage rather than published designs.

3. The most committed of the British Palladians were critical of the baroque style. They stood for a return to the "purity" of Roman classicism and against the European court styles epitomized by the designs of Jean Le Pautre (1618–1682) and Daniel Marot (c. 1663–1752). While traveling in Italy in 1715, British architect William Kent wrote Richard Boyle, third Earl of Burlington, "Since I have left Rome and Florence [I] cannot bear to see anything, except two fine palaces of Vitruvio and Genova that my Ld. carry'd me to see which he had order'd to be drawn. I hope by his Lordship's encouragement and other gentlemen who may have a better gusto than that dam'd gusto that's been for this sixty years past." According to Kent, the English gusto was "still in the little Dutch way" (Michael I. Wilson, *William Kent Architect, Designer, Painter, Gardner, 1685–1748* [London: Routledge & Kegan Paul, 1984)], p. 37). The stylistic framework of the designer of this group of Boston furniture was Palladian, but his aim was to be fashionable, not polemic. He seems to have been content to use almost any style that was sufficiently grand for his purpose. Mary Kent Davey Babcock, *The Versatile Mr. Price—Christ Church Salem Street, Boston* (Boston: Thomas Todd Company, 1947), p. 60. *Boston Gazette*, April 4–11, 1726 (the author thanks Brock Jobe for this reference). Although Price could have been referring to himself as the "one late from London," it is unlikely; he had been a twelve-year resident of Boston in 1726.

4. Two years later the vestry sought his advice on building a gallery around the church (Sinclair Hitchings, "The Musical Pursuits of William Price and Thomas Johnston," *Music*

in Colonial Massachusetts, Vol. II—Music in Homes and in Churches [Boston: Colonial Society of Massachusetts, 1985], p. 650). Price also is credited with the design and supervision of work on Christ Church (Babcock, *The Versatile Mr. Price*, p. 60). On April 1, 1737, he submitted a bill to the Wardens:

To projecting and drawing a draft of ye Organ	1.10.0
to directing ye workmen in making it	5.0.0
to drawing 6 large pannels of Cut Work	2.0.0
to ditto 6 smaller	1.0.0

Nine years later he submitted a bill for designing the steeple of Christ Church. He probably also designed the pulpit and interior furnishings (Hitchings, "Musical Pursuits," p. 650).

5. A British japanned desk-and-bookcase signed "W. Price: maker: 1713" is illustrated and discussed in Benno M. Forman, "The Chest of Drawers in America, 1635–1730: The Origins of the Joiner Chest of Drawers," *Winterthur Portfolio* 20, no. 1 (Spring 1985): 23. The bookcase has three engaged Corinthian pilasters, shaped, beveled mirrors, a double-dome cornice with arched returns, and three figural ornaments. The "W" is formed differently from the "W" in signatures by Bostonian William Price; however, the florid "P" and other letters of the last name are similar. The author examined this piece and discovered that its makers employed standard British construction practices. This neither proves or refutes the possibility that Price designed the Boston group. Price and Johnston were involved in the estate settlement of Boston japanner, Robert Davis (Esther Stevens Brazier, "The Early Boston Japanners," *Antiques* 43, no. 5 [May 1943]: 210). Price sold land to Peter Faneuil in 1738 and mortgaged a house and land to James Bowdoin in 1736 (Suffolk County Deeds, vol. 57, Dec. 6, 1738, and vol. 54, Sept. 7, 1736). On April 29, 1749, he received £55.15 from Thomas Hancock, although the subject of this transaction is unknown (Thomas Hancock Receipt Book, Massachusetts Historical Society, Boston).

6. Cash was rare in eighteenth-century Boston, and many transactions took place by barter. A desk-and-bookcase that cost its makers twice the standard time to make could be a dangerous item for stock.

7. Eighteenth-century architects, such as William Kent and William Buckland, frequently designed furniture, and the great European designers were usually enthusiastic about designing objects for almost any trade (Wilson, *William Kent Architect*. Luke Beckerdite, "William Buckland and William Bernard Sears: The Designer and the Carver" and "William Buckland Reconsidered: Architectural Carving in Chesapeake Maryland, 1771–1774," *Journal of Early Southern Decorative Arts* 8, no. 2 [Nov. 1982]: 1–88).

8. For more on the artisan community in eighteenth-century Boston, see Brock Jobe, "The Boston Furniture Industry 1720–1740," in Walter Muir Whitehill, Brock Jobe, and Jonathan Fairbanks, eds., *Boston Furniture of the Eighteenth Century* (Boston: Colonial Society of Massachusetts, 1974), pp. 9–12, and Brock Jobe and Myrna Kaye, *New England Furniture: The Colonial Era, Selections from the Society for the Preservation of New England Antiquities* (Boston: Houghton Mifflin, 1984), pp. 3, 4, 16–18.

9. The discrepancy between the shape of the back edge of the molding and the initial coped front edge of the bottom is about the same size as the flat area between the convex and concave portions of the blocking. The outside of this straight passage was probably confused with its inner corner when the base board was first cut.

10. For more on the Coits, see Margaretta Markle Lovell, "Boston Blockfront Furniture," in *Boston Furniture*, pp. 90–95.

11. Courbaril is from the huge *Leguminosae* family. This family includes the exotics bubinga, rosewood, purpleheart, and sabicu. Although courbaril is an excellent turning wood, the joiners and carver undoubtedly found it difficult to work. Its interlocked grain resists planing from any direction, and it is extremely difficult to carve. The author broke three carving tools while replicating the appliqué on this desk-and-bookcase. *Juniperus bermudiana* and *Juniperus silicosa* cannot be distinguished by microanalysis, nor can they be separated from *Juniperus virginiana*, which has a more northerly range. However, most northern *Juniperus virginiana* is afflicted with sap and bark intrusions and pin knots. Wood Information Sheets, Forest Products Laboratory, U.S. Department of Agriculture, Madison, Wisconsin. Microanalysis by Harry Alden and J. Thomas Quirk.

12. The location of the date is not given. Judging from the catalogue description, the interior was very similar, if not identical, to that of the courbaril desk-and-bookcase: "slope front enclosing pigeonholed interior of fine cabinet work of small drawers and pigeonholes

on either side of central arched compartment, with four small drawers and secret compartment" (*The Jacob Paxon Temple Collection of Early Antique Furniture*, Anderson Galleries, January 1922, p. 179).

13. *Antiques* 52, no. 6 (Dec. 1947): 445. I have not examined this desk-and-bookcase; however, elements described in this and ensuing paragraphs make it clear that the bookcase was made by at least two of the tradesmen who worked for the Boston designer and his shop. The foot pattern, base molding profile, blocking, lid supports, fallboard, and prospect door of the desk are different from others in the group.

14. Welch received £8.8 for carving the Boylston frame (Morrison H. Heckscher and Leslie Greene Bowman, *American Rococo, 1750–1775: Elegance in Ornament* [New York: Metropolitan Museum of Art, 1992], p. 138). The layout and execution of the flame sections of the finials on fig. 9 resembles that of later finials with very strong ties to Welch (figs. 15, 28) The scrollboard appliqués of figs. 9 and 18 also are closely related. If Welch executed all of this carving, he moved from a totally naturalistic phase to one that occasionally hints at rococo. If Robinson (1680–1737) was Welch's master, and figs. 1 and 7 date before 1737, Robinson also could have been the carver. A master-apprentice relationship would explain the affinity with the later work.

15. Mabel M. Swan, "Boston's Carvers and Joiners, Part I," *Antiques* 53, no. 3 (March 1948): 199. Robinson's granddaughter was Sarah Barrington (Myrna Kaye "Eighteenth-Century Boston Furniture Craftsmen," in *Boston Furniture*, p. 301). For more on Welch and carving attributed to him, see Barbara M. Ward and Gerald W. R. Ward, "The Makers of Copley's Picture Frames: A Clue," *Old-Time New England* 67 (Summer–Fall 1976): 16–20; Luke Beckerdite, "Carving Practices in Eighteenth-Century Boston," in Brock Jobe, ed., *New England Furniture: Essays in Memory of Benno Forman* (Boston: Society for the Preservation of New England Antiquities, 1987), pp. 123–62; Morrison H. Heckscher, *American Furniture in the Metropolitan Museum of Art, Vol. II—the Late Colonial Period: Queen Anne and Chippendale Styles* (New York: Metropolitan Museum of Art and Random House, 1985), p. 331; and Heckscher and Bowman, *American Rococo*, p. 138. The author thanks Robert Mussey and Anne Haley for information on Welch's carving for Brattle Street Church. Beckerdite, "Carving Practices," pp. 143–47.

16. Although Allen's will is dated 1736, he was declared non compus in 1756 and lived until 1760. The administrators of his estate were grandsons Hezekiah Welch and Hezekiah Blanchard (Allen Will, Dec. 8, 1736, Suffolk County Probate 12211). The author thanks Barbara McLean Ward for the information on Allen and his partnership with Edwards. More information will be included in Ward's catalogue entries in *A Biographical Dictionary of Massachusetts Silversmiths Working before the Revolution* (New Haven: Yale University Art Gallery, forthcoming). John Allen's daughter Susana married Boston mariner Ebenezer Welch. When their son Hezikiah was orphaned in 1753, John Welch was named guardian: "I Hezikiah Welch a Minor . . . constitute My kinsman Mr. John Welch of Boston Carver to be my Guardian" (Welch Guardianship Paper, Dec. 28, 1753, Suffolk County Probate 10625). The author thanks Anne Haley for research on Allen and Welch.

17. Microanalysis by Harry Alden. For more on sabicu and its use in the colonies, see Eleanor H. Gustafson, "Collector's Notes," *Antiques* 135, no. 5 (May 1989): 1002, 1006.

18. For ball feet used in a similar context, see the bracket and tall case clocks in pls. 13–21 in Daniel Marot, *Nouveau Livre d'Ornements* (1703 and 1713) and the chest of drawers in plate 158 in Batty Langley, *City and Country Builder's and Workman's Treasury of Designs* (1740) reproduced in Elizabeth White, *Pictorial Dictionary of British 18th Century Furniture Design: The Printed Sources* (Suffolk, Eng.: Antique Collector's Club, 1990), pp. 190, 438, 443.

19. The absence of evidence suggests that George Glinn was a journeyman in this shop, rather than the master. A tailor named George Glenn resided in Boston in 1737 and 1741 and a shopkeeper named George Glenn (Glen) was involved in two court cases there in 1754. A George Glen married Elizabeth Price in 1752 and a man of the same name married Elizabeth Tingley in 1760 (Jobe, "A Boston Desk-and-Bookcase," p. 419, note 16). A George Glenn lost his house to fire in 1769 (*The Post-Boy and Advertiser*, March 24, 1760, reprinted in the *New England Historical Register*, vol. 34 [Boston: David Clapp &. Son, 1880], p. 290). Irish-born cabinetmaker Robert Glen married Margaret Rankin in 1736 and made a cedar desk and a mahogany desk for Boston tailor William Waine in 1750 (Jobe, "A Boston Desk-and-Bookcase," p. 419, note 17). It is unknown whether Robert Glen and George Glinn were kinsmen.

20. The original silk, darkened and torn, was intact when Sotheby's sold the clock in 1990

(Sotheby's, *Fine American Furniture, Folk Art, Folk Paintings and Silver*, New York, June 27–28, 1990, lot 369). Robert Fileti of Israel Sack Conservation discovered the pattern for the fret. The author thanks Mr. Fileti for his insights and for photographs of the case.

21. These feet are unlike conventional cabriole ball-and-claw feet, which are made from one piece of wood, are vertically configured, and have separate applied knee blocks.

22. For related feet in Marot's work, see White, *Pictorial History*, pp. 438, 443, and Reinier Baarsen, Gervase Jackson-Stops, Phillip M. Johnston, and Elaine Evans Dee, *Courts and Colonies: The William and Mary Style in Holland, England, and America* (New York: Cooper Hewitt Museum, 1988), pls. 4, 41. Beckerdite, "Carving Practices," pp. 143–44.

23. The clock reportedly descended in the Wesson family of Boston. The author thanks Leslie Keno of Sotheby's for this information. The inventory of Gilbert Deblois' estate includes a clock valued at £9. Along with an equally valued desk-and-bookcase, the clock was the most expensive item inventoried (Suffolk County Probate 19898) The author thanks Anne Haley for research on Deblois.

24. The author has not examined the case with the horizontally configured base; however, its relationship to the Bromfield clock and the other example with the Bagnall movement is obvious. The hood of the latter was intended to have fret; its scrollboard is white pine. The shop also made simpler desks-and-bookcases. One dating 1745–1752 has a bookcase with arched doors with finialed hinges, shaped mirrors, and trompe l'oeil shells like those of figs. 11, 23, and 40 and a desk section with a straight interior and drawers with thin red cedar frames and fine dovetails. The original design of the bookcase (which had a broken-scroll rather than double-dome pediment) was a simplified version of the John Allen example. For an illustration of this piece, see Jobe, "A Boston Desk-and-Bookcase," pp. 416–17.

25. The name "Atkinson" was painted on the inner surface of the front board of the step before the joiner assembled the hood. This probably refers to Boston clockmaker James Atkinson. The author thanks Philip Zimmerman for the information on Atkinson.

26. The Ford Museum clock is illustrated in Helen Comstock, *American Furniture: Seventeenth, Eighteenth, and Nineteenth Century Styles* (New York: Viking Press, 1962), p. 187. For a discussion of the japanning on this case and the Atkinson case, see Dean A. Fales, Jr., "Boston Japanned Furniture," in *Boston Furniture*, pp. 51, 54. G.K.S. Bush advertisement, *Antiques* 135, no. 5 (May 1989): 1002–3. This clock has a replaced superstructure above the cornice arch.

27. Francis Clary Morse, *Furniture of the Olden Time* (1902; reprinted with additional illustrations, New York: Macmillan, 1917), p. 80. Morse also quoted a reference to this piece in "The Professor at the Breakfast Table" by Oliver Wendell Holmes: "A boy of twelve was looking at it . . . and . . . saw that all the space was not accounted for by the smaller drawers in the space behind the lid . . . he at length came upon a spring, on pressing which, a secret drawer flew from its hiding place."

28. Although the scrollboard appliqué appears to be poorly restored or replaced, elements of the design are consistent with the appliqués of other desks-and-bookcases by this designer/shop.

29. For more on Frothingham and this piece, see Robert Mussey's catalogue entry in Alexandra W. Rollins, ed., *Treasures of State: Fine and Decorative Arts in the Diplomatic Reception Rooms of the U.S. Department of State* (New York: Abrams, 1991), p. 94.

30. For an excellent overview of Frothingham's career and work, see Richard H. Randall, Jr., "Benjamin Frothingham," in *Boston Furniture*, pp. 223–49. Morse, *Furniture of the Olden Time*, pp. 134–36. The bombé desk-and-bookcase was first illustrated in the 1917 edition. It is shown in its currently altered form in Marshall B. Davidson, *The American Heritage History of Colonial Antiques* (New York: American Heritage Publishing Co., 1967), p. 220.

31. Welch carved a shortened version of this knee for the legs of a desk that is now in a private collection. The structure of the desk differs from those attributed to the Boston designer's shop.

Robert F. Trent

Mid-Atlantic Easy Chairs, 1770–1820: Old Questions and New Evidence

▼ AMERICAN easy chairs have enjoyed renewed attention over the last twenty years because of the emergence of previously unknown examples with original upholstery and the need of museums and private collectors to correctly reupholster stripped frames. Interpretive questions surrounding these objects will be examined in the following essay and in the accompanying catalogue that describes and illustrates the upholstery evidence on fifteen easy chairs. Controversy, such as it is, centers on three questions about the intended use of easy chairs. What is the significance of the close stools found in many of them? Were easy chairs intended for the aged? Or were they "sick chairs" of one sort or another? Strictly speaking, each of these questions constitutes a separate issue, and the issues need not be interrelated. A chair with a close stool need not have been intended for an old or ill person. Ill people were not necessarily aged, and aged people often were astonishingly vigorous.

Early furniture historians Charles Woolsey Lyon, Luke Vincent Lockwood, and Esther Singleton paid little attention to easy chairs, other than noting their existence and citing references to them in probate records. The first author to advance a strong interpretation of easy chairs was William Macpherson Hornor, Jr., who in 1931 argued that easy chairs always were used in second-story bedrooms or sleeping chambers and never in parlors or other public rooms on the ground story *because* most were fitted with close stools.[1]

Morrison H. Heckscher's 1971–1972 exhibition and catalogue on easy chairs endorsed some of what Hornor had claimed, but it added many subtle points about usage, most particularly that easy chairs were used by the aged and the ill. He specifically noted one of two Copley portraits (National Portrait Gallery and Los Angeles County Museum of Art) depicting aged women seated in easy chairs and cited "The Chair in which the late Duke of York died" from Peter and Michel Angelo Nicholson's *The Practical Cabinet Maker* (1826–1827). The latter illustrated a fairly standard square-back easy chair with saddle cheeks and an adjustable footrest.[2]

Recent scholarship suggests that easy chairs had a variety of functions in eighteenth- and nineteenth-century households. In *At Home: The American Family 1750–1870*, Elisabeth Donaghy Garrett cited numerous period references that indicate that easy chairs served as refuges for women before and after childbirth. She also emphasized that owners used slipcovers on easy chairs for the purposes of washability and to achieve unified decorative treatments in bedchambers.[3]

The only scholar to severely criticize these ideas is Myrna Kaye, who, in a 1984 catalogue entry, wrote:

> In recent years, scholars have stressed that easy chairs were chamber furniture for the elderly. They cite the origin of the form as an invalid's seat, the portraits of elderly sitters in such chairs, and the usual placement of eighteenth-century easy chairs in bedchambers. They even claim that easy chairs commonly were fitted with chamber pots. In their attempt to correct the impressions created by the modern use of easy chairs as parlor furnishings, they overstate their case. None of the easy chairs described . . . has a chamber pot fitting because there was no such practice with cabriole easy chairs. . . . Nor were they solely chairs for the elderly. . . . Easy chairs may have been favorites of the elderly, but the chairs were prestigious items purchased by men of means long before they retired to dozing while seated.[4]

Figure 1 Easy chair, Charleston, South Carolina, 1760–1770. Mahogany with cypress and tulip poplar. H. 48½", W. 36¾", D. 24⅛". (Courtesy, Winterthur Museum, acc. 60.1058.)

Kaye's claim regarding the absence of close stools in cabriole-leg easy chairs is refuted by a Charleston, South Carolina, easy chair in the Winterthur collection (fig. 1), that has mortises in the front and rear seat rails, indicating that it originally was fitted with parallel supports of the sort needed for a board with a pothole.[5] Other mid-eighteenth-century American easy chairs with potholes have survived, but the practice of fitting them with close stools does not appear to have become widespread until after 1790. In short, Kaye may be factually incorrect but conceptually on target; easy chairs may not have been fitted with close stools all that often before 1790.

As for Kaye's assertion that easy chairs were not strictly for use by the elderly, one might note that younger people were subject to many debilitating illnesses, health problems, and conditions. Among these were frequent pregnancies for younger women and gout or arthritis for middle-aged men. Although people commonly slept in a semirecumbant position (achieved through the use of bolsters), many may have been forced to sleep or doze sitting upright because of chronic pulmonary disorders, which were widespread before antibiotics or antihistamines were available to combat the common cold, bronchitis, pneumonia, tuberculosis, asthma, or allergies.

The intended use of easy chairs can be determined by examining the prescriptive literature, including design books, price books, medical literature, and prints; probate inventories (which reveal a great deal about placement and usage); and the physical evidence of surviving examples. Because most of the chairs in the interpretive catalogue that follows were made in Philadelphia, the remainder of this essay contains references drawn from Philadelphia probate inventories in the period 1780 to 1810.[6]

The evidence about easy chairs that can be derived from design books and price books is not that profound. In fact, little can be gleaned from them that cannot be inferred from surviving objects. *The Journeymen Cabinet and Chair-Makers Philadelphia Book of Prices* (1795) listed what was probably a standard form there during the late eighteenth century: A chair with "plain feet" (straight legs with no reeding or term feet), "no low rails" (no stretchers), and a straight front seat rail. The close-stool options were a simple plank with a hole and either a "frame'd seat" or a

loose seat. Cleats or battens to reinforce either seat also were optional. *The Journeymen Cabinet and Chair Makers' Pennsylvania Book of Prices* (1811) listed a few other choices, including a "slider under the frame, to draw out behind, with the pan," an ingenious feature that made it possible to empty the vessel without disturbing the chair's occupant. To avoid having the pan hit a rear stretcher when the slider was withdrawn, such chairs were made with "no lower back rail."[7]

Another option for easy chairs found in many provincial English price books was a hinged back that could be set at various angles. This feature is described in the second edition of *The Cabinet & Chair Makers' Norwich Book of Prices* (1801): "the back part is made to fall back with racks, and hinged to the back feet, the wings fast to the back, and work in the elbows." The "fall back" could be supplemented with a "foot board, hinged to the front rail, to raise with one rack." This was obviously a fully developed invalid's chair, specifically identified with nursing the ill and women immediately after childbirth.[8]

Thomas Sheraton was the first British designer to comment on how easy chairs were used. In his description of a "tub" easy chair in *The Cabinet Dictionary* (1803) he noted that "a tub easy chair, stuffed all over, and is intended for sick persons, being both easy and warm; for the side wings coming quite forward keep out the cold air, which may be totally excluded from the person asleep, by laying some kind of covering over the whole chair." This chair was not quite what we think of as an easy chair, because it had a lower back. However, its D-shaped form was similar to that of a circular easy chair. Sheraton also illustrated a "hunter's chair," which was an easy chair with streamlined wings, or cheeks lacking scrolls or rolls, and a pull-out leg rest. The leg rest probably was for propping up the feet of those stricken with gout.[9]

Sheraton was the only designer to describe specifically how easy chairs functioned; however, their use was implicit in the writing of others. On plate 15 in *The Cabinet-Maker and Upholsterer's Guide* (1794), George Hepplewhite illustrated what he called "a design for a Saddle Check [i.e., cheek], or easy chair; the construction and use of which is very apparent," as well as a design for a "Gouty Stool," which could be raised or lowered at both ends. His recommendation that such chairs "be covered with leather, horsehair; or have a linen case to fit over the canvas stuffing as is most usual and convenient" implies that they were to be covered with washable textiles. During the eighteenth and early nineteenth centuries, leather and haircloth often were used for covering dining chairs because of their washability.[10]

Philadelphia probate inventories of the 1780–1810 period reveal other aspects of easy chair ownership, form, and use that have a direct impact on the interpretation of surviving frames with original upholstery foundations. Easy chairs were expensive and relatively rare, and other seating forms were preferred for lounging outside the confines of a bedroom. Rush-bottomed couches with comfortable, hair-stuffed mattresses were used in Pennsylvania throughout the eighteenth century. In 1790 merchant Philip Boehm had "1 Couch & Bed & Furniture" worth 40s. in the second-story back room of his house. Six years later Deborah Cordry had "One Couch and Couch Bed and Bolster" worth 10s.[11] Another alternative to the easy chair may have been the Windsor settee or sofa with a hair-stuffed mattress. Distinguishing among inventory references to a Windsor settee and an upholstered settee or sofa can be difficult, unless significant qualifiers are present in the citation. A Windsor settee could be valued as much as a set of six Windsor chairs if the settee had a stitched hair mattress. The inventory of the wealthy merchant Peter LeMaigre, taken in 1794, included:

1 Large Settee covered with blue moreen	£4.10.0
1 Chintz Settee cover	£0.15.0
1 Large Mahogany easy chair	£3.00.0
1 Settee Mattress & Quallico covers	£2.05.0
1 green easy chair	£0.05.0
1 green settee	£2.05.0

The mahogany easy chair and settee covered with blue moreen may have been standard forms with fixed upholstery and the chintz cover was probably for that settee. But the other two settees may well have been Windsors, even the one with the mattress and cover valued at £2.05.0. The green easy chair almost certainly was a Windsor, perhaps with a high raked back that permitted lounging. More clearly described were the "Green Windsor Sophia With Cushin" valued at £2.5.0 in the estate of Mary Brown in 1799 and the "Windsor easy Chair" valued at $2.50 in the 1806 inventory of Samuel Tatem.[12]

Upholstered sofas were the most expensive seating form. Almost invariably, they were placed in parlors on the ground floor, whereas easy chairs were confined to bedchambers. The probate inventories surveyed for this study revealed only one indisputable reference to an easy chair in a ground-floor room. James Bringhurst, who died in 1810, had one easy chair in his south front parlor and "Covers for Easy Chairs & others" stored in the third-story south back room.[13]

Philadelphia inventories of the 1770s frequently list old easy chairs with pans, reinforcing the idea that many examples originally were fitted with close stools. A number of euphemisms existed for indicating the presence of this fixture in a chair, including "close stool," "chamber chair," "night chair," and "stool chair," and almost any form of seating furniture could be adapted for a close stool by inserting a board with a hole to accommodate a pewter pan or ceramic pot. Among the most common were joined armchairs and corner chairs. Far rarer were slat-back armchairs made with a joined box frame to hold the pot and stools with hinged lids. Perhaps scarcest of all were Windsor chairs originally made with a pothole. The inventory of John Roberts, taken in 1802, listed a "Close-Stool windsor Chair &. Aparatus" appraised at 15s.; however, most Windsors were altered to accommodate close stools.[14]

Considering the wide range of seating furniture that could have accommodated a close stool, there must have been compelling reasons for fitting easy chairs with them. After all, why put a close stool in an expensive upholstered chair that might easily be soiled as the close stool is used? The most plausible answer is that these chairs were used by those who required a padded, warm environment, and that the occupants of these chairs were often too sick or too feeble to walk to a close stool in another chair. It was easier to lift them out of the chair momentarily, remove the cushion or the slip seat over the pan or pot, assist them in rearranging their outer garments, and sit them down again. The pans were deep and could be tightly stoppered with turned wooden lids, allowing the contents to be emptied when convenient. Slider mechanisms, like the one described in *The Pennsylvania Book of Prices* (1811), simplified matters by making it possible to empty the pan without disturbing the person seated in the chair.

In those cases where easy chairs were virtually lived in, one may assume that the loose covers would have been made of washable materials like plain linen. In a letter regarding a case for an easy chair, the head of the Gillow cabinetmaking firm of Lancaster and London wrote, "We presume [the chair] will require some sort of washing cover which requires a good deal of nicety to make them fit well to such sort of chairs." Such covers were laboriously tailored and sewn by hand on the stuffed frame, hence the term "nicety" in the Gillow letter. Occasionally an inventory indicates that an easy chair or a sofa had two covers, a provision that may have had to do with seasonal changes but also allowed covers to be rotated for laundering.[15]

Many Philadelphia inventories of the 1780–1820 period mention covers or cases for easy chairs, but few specify the textiles. Among fabrics mentioned were canvas, a coarse utilitarian linen; calico, an all-cotton cloth that usually was printed; and chintz, another variety of printed cotton. Calicoes and chintzes were sometimes glazed to seal in the colors; however, neither was as readily laundered as might be imagined. Their reputation for washability was more a polite fiction than a reality, because the glazes and printed inks did not hold up well after repeated washings. Their genuine attraction to consumers was as a fashionable furnishing textile. Most often an easy chair cover was made of a printed cotton because it was covered en suite with bed fixtures, window curtains, and other chair covers in a bedroom. In 1793, for example, Jonathan Dickinson Sergeant's bedroom had "1 mahogany bedstead £7.10.0," "Chintz Bed Curtains, Window Curtains, Chair Bottoms, & easy Chair Cover £25.0.0," "9 Cross backed Mahogany Chairs £11.5.0," "1 Easy Chair & Wash Stand £3.0.0," and "1 Mahogany Bureau £2.5.0."[16]

Furniture historian Peter Thornton has argued persuasively that easy chairs evolved from sick chairs and aristocratic sleeping chairs during the sixteenth and seventeenth centuries. Surviving sick chairs, treatises on the arts and sciences, and medical literature of the 1770–1820 period reveal that easy chairs continued to be used as invalid's seats. A leather-covered sick chair with a hinged back and footrest that was raised and lowered by arc-shaped ratchets was made for the Moravian Single Brothers House in Salem, North Carolina, during the late eighteenth century. It originally had loose covers that were attached to brass knobs on the sides. In its overall form and especially in its small wings, this chair strongly resembles leather-covered easy chairs (many fitted with close stools) made in Bethlehem and other German settlements in Pennsylvania. Although occasionally interpreted as clumsy copies of Philadelphia chairs, they actually were based upon more refined continental designs. This style of upholstered chair with small wings or *oreilles* (ears) was almost certainly Germanic in origin. Two such chairs with ears were illustrated in a French design print of the 1620s: one was fitted with casters; the other had a hand crank that drove two wheels via gears under the seat, making the chair essentially a hand-powered wheelchair.[17] As a seating form, the typical Louis XV sleeping chair with a hinged back and a seat that folded forward to become a footrest probably was introduced by German artisans working at the Louvre about 1720. It may be the immediate ancestor of the duchesse, a low lounge chair constructed in two or three parts.

Several similar "inventions" were popular in England during the Napoleonic Wars and probably were designed for officers who had been wounded. Rudolph Ackermann's *The Repository of Arts, Literature, Commerce, Manufactures, Fashions, and Politics* (1809–1828) included three: the "Royal Patent Invalid Chair" (1810), "Merlin's Mechanical Chair" (1811), and "Pocock's Reclining Patent Chair" (1813). All were for "aged persons or invalids." "Merlin's" chair, named after the fashionable London cabinetmaker Merlin von Luttich, had two hand cranks, gears, and wheels, as well as an adjustable back and footrest. American examples were made; however, not all had wings.[18]

Many mechanical chairs were fitted with separate rests for the right and left leg. Although this feature may have answered the needs of wounded officers, it far more likely reflected that scourge of British upper-class males, "the gout." Doctors recognized that attacks were common among "people that live plentifully, have a good stomach, and drink strong liquors, if they don't use a proportionate degree of labor or exercise," a discreet way of indicating the aristocracy and the gentry. Attacks were widely feared, because "the fits, especially when they begin to return frequently, so incapacitate our limbs for action and necessary exercise, that the health and habit of the body and constitution suffer extremely." To counteract the shooting pains in the joints, the common practice was "to sweat the part" by "wrapping the part up in flannels." British satirical prints frequently depicted gouty aristocrats seated in easy chairs with a swaddled limb resting on a gout stool that could be adjusted to the position least painful to the sitter.[19]

A final source that is extremely revealing is Charles White's *A Treatise on the Management of Pregnant and Lying-In Women*. White was an important medical theorist who recommended a number of advanced practices for the care of women during and after childbirth. Among those was elevating women lying in bed. White illustrated "an Iron Bedstead made at Birmingham, the invention of Doctor Vaughan, an ingenious Physician at Leicester. It serves every purpose of a bed-chair or dozer." The head of the bedstead was raised and lowered with a crank, gear, and toothed ratchet. White added: "Mr. Alexander Brodie, Whitesmith near Temple Bar [in London], has obtained a patent for a contrivance something similar to this, which he calls his new invented Bedscrew-Lever calculated for the ease of sick and gouty people, or child-bed women; which raises them from a lying to a sitting posture, and lowers them again so gently as hardly to be felt." White also noted that "a few hours after delivery, as soon as the patient has had a little rest, she should sit up in bed. . . . The patient should lie very high with her head and shoulders, and should sit up in bed when she takes her food, or as often as she suckles her child."[20]

Philadelphia probate inventories frequently mention bed chairs. This was a small version of the upper half of an easy chair, mounted on a base frame with curved rails, and usually fitted with a hinged flap and toothed rack on the back. Such chairs were listed in the Philadelphia price books for 1796 and 1828.[21] In the past scholars interpreted this as signifying props for reading in bed or perhaps for feeding invalids; however, White's treatise suggests that they may have been associated specifically with women who had recently given birth.

White also illustrated an easy chair with an adjustable back and footrest, "useful for lying-in women, and sick persons." In the days immediately after delivery,

> the patient should not only sit up often, but should every day get out of bed, staying up as long as she can without fatigue, and continuing it a little longer every day than she had done the day before. A very convenient easy chair has been invented, to which a foot-board is adapted, not only preserving the legs and feet from cold, but by the means of two straps, so contrived that the back of the chair may be depressed, and the footboard raised at pleasure. By means of this contrivance, if the patient is faint or fatigued with sitting up, she may be greatly relieved, and her posture made as easy as possible. As the chair runs upon castors, it may be readily moved, and by its assistance the patient may be enabled to continue a long time out of bed without inconvenience.

As his accompanying illustration revealed, this easy chair was not that different from a standard one. It had wings, enclosed scroll arms, and a tray footrest. Although White maintained that the strap-activated mechanisms were "not generally known," they had been standard features in aristocratic sleeping chairs and invalid chairs since the 1590s. This type of easy chair may have been mentioned in the diary of Philadelphia Quaker Elizabeth Drinker in 1799, "Sally [her pregnant daughter Sarah Downing] was all night in great distress, ye pain never quite off, sometimes on the bed, but most of the night in the Easy Chair as it is called." This chair may have been the more utilitarian model that had a U-shaped void in the seat, handgrips, and stirrups. Such "midwives' chairs" or "birthing stools" survive in Europe in some numbers, and they often have padded wings and arms.[22]

One may summarize all these scattered references by suggesting a fairly specific role for the easy chair in eighteenth- and early nineteenth-century households. Kaye's suggestion that they were being used as lounge chairs by healthy younger people is difficult, if not impossible, to accept. In Philadelphia, at least, the public entertaining spaces were the front and back parlors on the ground floor, and the seating forms there almost universally consisted of side chairs, armchairs, settees, and sofas. Easy chairs were largely relegated to bedchambers, and there were strong motivations for fitting these expensive forms with close stools and placing them in secluded rooms. The inevitable conclusion is that easy chairs with or without close stools were intended for nursing those in poor health. This idea is buttressed by the prescriptive literature as well as by the strong identity between standard easy chairs and those with special equipment for the care of invalids. The loose covers or secondary covers that most easy chairs had may have related to fashionable suits of textile furnishings, but the practical concerns for washing and cleaning them were well recognized during the period too.

Why then were easy chairs used in bedchambers? Because they formed part of a complex for nursing, one that also included beds augmented with bed chairs, couches or daybeds, close stools, gout stools, and perhaps bed warmers and bedpans, or urinals. Such a complex was of obvious utility in caring for the aged; lying-in women and gouty men also would have made use of it on a regular basis. The eventual disappearance of this complex in the later nineteenth century probably reflected the increased safety and reliability of public hospitals and clinics. Such furniture may have persisted in rural America until much later.

1. Irving W. Lyon, *The Colonial Furniture of New England: A Study of Domestic Furniture in Use in the Seventeenth and Eighteenth Centuries* (Boston and New York: Houghton, Mifflin, 1891), pp. 166–68. Luke Vincent Lockwood, *Colonial Furniture in America* (New York: Charles Scribner's Sons, 1901), pp. 162–63, 188; 2d. ed., 2 vols. (1913, 1921), 2: 64–69; 3d ed., 2 vols. (1926), 2: 64–69. Esther Singleton, *The Furniture of Our Forefathers* (New York: Doubleday, Page, 1900–1901), p. 620. Singleton quoted the second edition of *The Journeymen Cabinet and Chair-Makers Philadelphia Book of Prices* (Philadelphia: Ormrod and Conrad, 1795), which included specifications for adding a close stool and a loose "fram'd seat" to cover the pothole, but she made nothing of these options. William Macpherson Hornor, Jr., "A Survey of American 'Wing Chairs,'" *International Studio* 99, no. 410 (July 1931): 28–30, 71–73.

2. Morrison H. Heckscher, *In Quest of Comfort: The Easy Chair in America* (New York: Metropolitan Museum of Art, 1971); also Morrison H. Heckscher, "Form and Frame: New Thoughts on the American Easy Chair," *Antiques* 100, no. 6 (December 1971): 886–93. Christian Gullager's portrait of Mrs. Nicholas Salisbury in the Worcester Art Museum in Worcester, Massachusetts, also shows an aged woman seated in an easy chair; Peter and Michel Angelo Nicholson, *The Practical Cabinet Maker, Upholsterer, and Complete Decorator* (London: H. Fisher, Son & Co., 1826–1834).

3. Elisabeth Donaghy Garrett, *At Home: The American Family 1750–1870* (New York: Abrams, 1990), pp. 124, 135–36.

4. Brock Jobe and Myrna Kaye, *New England Furniture, the Colonial Era: Selections from the Society for the Preservation of New England Antiquities* (Boston: Houghton Mifflin, 1984), p. 366.

5. Steven L. Pine, "Construction Traits of the Eighteenth-Century American Easy Chair," paper presented in 1986 at the University of Delaware Course EAC 602, pp. 10–11. See also Pine's comments appended to photocopies of record photography of Winterthur's Charles-

ton easy chair, acc. 60.1058, Registrar's Office, Winterthur Museum. Charleston chairs at the Museum of Early Southern Decorative Arts (acc. 2788.2) and at the Metropolitan Museum of Art (acc. 18.110.25) do not display evidence for a pan-support board.

6. These inventories provide information for a specific time and place; some regional and chronological differences may have existed.

7. A serpentine front rail or "Commode front" was the principal option for changing the form in 1795. Stretchers, various forms of ornamentation on the legs, and brass casters also were optional, but they were not specific to easy chairs (*The Journeymen Cabinet and Chair-Makers Philadelphia Book of Prices*, pp. 80–81). *The Journeymen Cabinet and Chairmakers' Pennsylvania Book of Prices* (1811) introduced the circular easy chair or "barrel-back" in modern collectors' parlance. This design was more labor intensive for the cabinetmaker and the upholsterer. London price books add little to these options, other than "saddle tree cheeks," "hollow back[s]" (available since the 1760s), and hinged upper-seat covers.

8. *The Cabinet & Chair Makers' Norwich Book of Prices* (Norwich: J. Payne for the Company of Cabinet and Chair Makers, 1801). The 1801 Norwich price book is beautifully analyzed in Gerry Cotton, "'Common' Chairs from the Norwich Chair Makers' Price Book of 1801," *Regional Furniture* 2 (1988): 68–92; the quote for easy chair options is on p. 59 of the price book. An original copy is available in the Winterthur Library. Several other quotes from English price books, including Preston (1802), Nottingham (1791), and Leeds (1791), were kindly made available to me by Christopher Gilbert of Temple Newsam House, Leeds, Yorkshire.

9. Thomas Sheraton, *The Cabinet Dictionary* (London: W. Smith, 1803), p. 20, pl. 8, no. 1 and p. 19, pl. 8, no. 3. "Hunter's chair" was a silly but fashionable term.

10. George Hepplewhite, *The Cabinet-Maker's and Upholsterer's Guide*, 3d ed. (London: I. and J. Taylor, 1794), p. 3, pl. 15.

11. Boehm Inventory 1790: 6; Cordy Inventory 1796: 249, Philadelphia Wills and Inventories, microfilm, Winterthur Library.

12. LeMaigre Inventory 1794: 88; Brown Inventory 1799: 124; Tatem Inventory 1806: 85, Philadelphia Wills and Inventories.

13. Bringhurst Inventory 1810: 60, Philadelphia Wills and Inventories. Another possible exception is found in the 1807 inventory of John Keble, who had in his front parlor "1 Easy Arm Chair" worth $4 and "1 Round Back Easy Chair" valued at only $1 (Philadelphia Wills and Inventories, 1807: 101). However, these references are not ironclad proof of the use of an easy chair in a parlor, because an "Easy Arm Chair" probably indicated a lolling chair. The cheap "Round Back" version may have been an old high-back Windsor armchair from the 1770s or 1780s.

14. See John Mark Bacon, "Delaware Valley Slatback Chairs: A Formal and Analytical Survey," Master's thesis, University of Delaware, 1991, fig. 11. Roberts Inventory 1802, 77, Philadelphia Wills and Inventories.

15. For the Gillow letter, see Florence M. Montgomery, *Printed Textiles: English and American Cottons and Linens, 1700–1850* (New York: Viking, 1970), p. 79. In some instances, cases protected valuable fixed covers. A series of bills from 1743–1745 for furnishing an aristocratic country house in County Durham specifies the materials used to make an easy chair for one of the bedrooms:

> For an Easy Chair to match Do [the bedstead] on Brass Leather [-wheeled] Castors, stuft with curled Hair in Canvas, & cover'd with green glazed Linen, the Cushion made of Ticking filled with the best Goose Feathers, cover'd with green glazed Linen and making tight Cases to Do of the beforementioned Cotton [chintz], corded and laced and 8 yds ½ of fine white Linen to line the Cases and other Materials used . . .
>
> For 20 yds ¾ of fine Cheque Cotton to make loose Cases, to the 6 Chairs, Easy-Chair Cushion and Stools at ls 6d per yd.

The green, glazed-linen cover probably helped prevent the horsehair from poking through the canvas. The tight formal cover was made of chintz and the loose cover was made of "Cheque Cotton," a fashionable textile at a time when most checks were still made of linen. For more on this suite, see Sarah Medlam, "William Greer at Gibside," *Furniture History* 26 (1990): 142–56. Inventories taken in other eighteenth-century aristocratic English houses confirm that easy chairs were associated with bedchambers and almost always fitted with cases that were en suite with the other textile fixtures in the rooms. The most popular textile for covers during the eighteenth century was checked linen, although striped linen or cotton gained popularity after 1770. For more on covers, see L.O.J. Boynton, "Sir Richard Worsley's Furniture at Appuldurcombe Park," *Furniture History* 1 (1965): 46–47; Christopher Gilbert, "The Temple Newsam Furniture Bills," *Furniture History*, 3 (1967): 23; Jill Low, "Newby Hall: Two Late Eighteenth-Century Inventories," *Furniture History* 22 (1986): 149–58; and Jane Geddes, "The Prince of Wales at the Grange, Northington: An Inventory of 1795," *Furniture History* 22 (1986): 187.

16. Sergeant Inventory 1793: 324, Philadelphia Wills and Inventories.

17. Peter Thornton, *Seventeenth-Century Interior Decoration in England, France & Holland* (New Haven: Yale University Press, 1978), p. 195–98. The Moravian sick chair is illustrated in Charles F. Montgomery, "A Word about the Arts & Crafts of Old Salem," *Walpole Society Notebook* (1964), p. 17, where it is erroneously identified with a second such chair purchased in 1796. It is also illustrated in John Bivins, Jr., and Paula Welshimer, *Moravian Decorative Arts in North Carolina: An Introduction to the Old Salem Collection* (Winston-Salem: Old Salem, 1981), p. 20. I thank Frank Horton for clearing up my misunderstandings regarding the correct dating of this object. For more on Germanic influences, see Benno M. Forman, "German Influences in Pennsylvania Furniture," in Scott T. Swank et al., *Arts of the Pennsylvania Germans* (New York: Norton, 1983), p. 119–22. Thornton, *Seventeenth-Century Interior Decoration*, p. 198, pl. 174.

18. Rudolph Ackermann, *The Repository of Arts, Literature, Commerce, Manufactures, Fashions, and Politics* (London: R. Ackermann, 1809–1828). See also Frances Collard, *Regency Furniture* (Woodbridge, Suffolk: Antique Collectors' Club, 1985), p. 22; Brian Austen, "Morgan & Sanders and the Patent Furniture Makers of Catherine Street," *Connoisseur* 187, no. 753 (November 1974): 180–91; Edward T. Joy, "Pocock's: The Ingenious Inventors," *Connoisseur* 173, no. 696 (February 1970): 88–92.

19. See William Stukeley, *Of the Gout*, 2d. ed. (London, 1736), pp. 11, 13, 17 for the quotations.

20. Charles White, *A Treatise on the Management of Pregnant and Lying-In Women* (London: Printed for Edward and Charles Dilly, 1773; reprint Worcester, Massachusetts: Isaiah Thomas, 1793), pp. 49, 74, 75, pl. 2.

21. *The Philadelphia Cabinet and Chair Makers' Book of Prices* (Philadelphia: Richard Folwell, 1796), p. 22, describes the bed chair as having a "frame to raise and fall." *The Philadelphia Cabinet and Chair Makers Union Book of Prices* (Philadelphia: William Stavely, 1828), n.p. The bed chair is described as having "round [i.e., arched] rails [to fit over the bolster at the head of the bed], two [side-to-side] stretchers, back and wings stuffed."

22. White, *Treatise*, pp. 59–61, pl. 1. Cecil K. Drinker, *Not So Long Ago: A Chronicle of Medicine and Doctors in Colonial Philadelphia* (New York: Oxford University Press, 1937), p. 60. I am grateful to Amanda Carson Banks, a doctoral candidate in the Department of Folklore and Folklife at the University of Pennsylvania, for bringing White's treatise to my attention and for sending me photographs of two German birthing chairs in the Deutsches Medizin Historisches Museum in Ingolstadt. One of these chairs has wings, and both are made to fold up for ease in carrying. I am also grateful to Robert Blair St. George who obtained the 1987 reprint of White's treatise for me.

Figure 1 Easy chair, Philadelphia, 1765–1780. Mahogany with white oak, white pine, and tulip poplar. H. 45½", W. 37", D. 35¼". (Dietrich American Foundation, on loan to the Philadelphia Museum of Art; photo, Philadelphia Museum of Art.) The tightly fitted silk damask cover with silk galloon or binding was fabricated in 1989.

Mark Anderson and Robert F. Trent

A Catalogue of American Easy Chairs

▼ THIS CATALOGUE illustrates and discusses fifteen easy chairs, with original upholstery foundations or other significant upholstery evidence, most of which are from the mid-Atlantic region. Although we recognize that this is a restricted sample, we believe that these chairs answer questions that are of more than regional or antiquarian interest. We have arranged the chairs in chronological order, but no developmental sequence is implied, except as noted.

An easy chair made for David Deshler of Germantown, Pennsylvania, exemplifies the framing, stuffing, and tailoring of the double-scroll design that was the commonest type produced in Philadelphia from the 1730s to the 1760s (figs. 1–5).[1] No exact English prototypes are known; however, robust English frames with single vertical arm scrolls may have provided some of the profiles (figs. 6, 7). For example, English chairs frequently have a strong compass-seat plan with a distinct break behind the vertical arm scrolls similar to that on some Philadelphia frames. They also show a preference for oak as a secondary wood and a seat frame construction in which the rails are laid with their broad dimension flat and the front legs are tenoned up into the rails—elements that Philadelphia chairs share. Variations of these techniques, however, are common in all compass-seat easy chair frames.

Most certainly present in the robust English frames, but not in Philadelphia examples, are dramatic profiles. The curving outline of the wings proceeds directly from the tops of the posts without an intervening straight ramp. Many English chairs also have curved rear posts that are spliced on the bias atop the cabriole rear legs, whereas Philadelphia chairs typically have straight or nearly straight back frames that are almost totally frontal (or at most ¾ frontal) in their impact.

Because of their overall heaviness and their bold curvilinear forms, English easy chairs repel the same American collectors that applaud Philadelphia ones; yet, research in areas of design transmission strongly suggests that the frames and the stuffing of Philadelphia chairs had English prototypes. If we try to see Philadelphia easy chairs as embodying a tradition where the first frames were designed by splicing the double-scroll arms of baroque examples onto early Georgian frames, then we find informative parallels between English chairs and the Deshler chair. Both frames have thin board upper wings, or cheeks, normally associated with the use of edge rolls (edge rolls require that the wings be tailored with panels rather than with simple rounded edges that fall away towards the

Figure 2 Easy chair illustrated in fig. 1 with the original curled horsehair stuffing removed to expose the sackcloth and edge rolls. (Photo, Winterthur Museum.)

Figure 3 Easy chair illustrated in fig. 1 with the original stuffing in place. (Photo, Winterthur Museum.)

frame), and both required a substantial edge roll on the front seat rail to retain a heavy cushion with fairly deep boxing. The back of the English chair may have had stuffing as thick as that of the Deshler chair, which is heavily stuffed by the standards of contemporary New England chairs.[2]

The surviving stuffing and top linen of the Deshler chair contain important clues of the development of Philadelphia upholstery. The seat stuffing, edge roll of the front seat rail, and cushion are lost. Our reconstructions were based on surviving English chairs with original upholstery and cushions and were designed to correct the modern misconception that these chairs had down cushions with low (approx. 2″) boxings. Eighteenth-century English cushions frequently have 4″ boxings, and Louis XV cushions are often huge, with 5- or 6″ boxings. Furthermore, tailoring the cushion so that its upper edges are even with the lower scrolls of the arms pulls the composition together in a way that makes a great deal of sense.

Figure 4 Side view of fig. 1 after conservation and addition of the missing outside covers. Note the line of the seam running down the wing and along the upper arm scroll. (Photo, Winterthur Museum.)

Figure 5 Rear view of fig. 1 after conservation and lining of the original outer back. (Photo, Winterthur Museum.)

Figure 6 Easy chair, England or Ireland, 1730–1760. Walnut with oak. H. 46″, W. 36″, D. 27″ (at seat). (Private collection; photo, John Bly.)

Perhaps the most important insight the Deshler chair offers is in the tailoring of the long seams running from the tops of the wings down to and along the sides of the upper arm scrolls. These seams prove that the linen and show covers of the outside wings and arms were not modeled to emphasize the upper arm scrolls as they often are today. The practice among modern historic upholsterers is to make the inside wing and the inside arm out of two separate pieces, so that the arm fabric can wrap completely around the upper (horizontal) arm cone. This technique allows the outer wing and arm fabric to run in one plane directly under the upper arm cone and butt against the back of the lower arm cone.

On the Deshler chair the inner wing-and-arm cover was made of one piece. The rounded forms required very tricky compass cuts on this one piece of textile at the turn of the wing into the upper arm cone. These cuts left only enough fabric for the textile to reach partially over the upper arm cone. Philadelphia upholsterers hid the compass cuts with a panel that covered the wing and wing edge roll and flared outward at the bottom just behind the upper arm cone. Although this technique was fairly straightforward, they developed a clever solution to the problem of how to shape the outside cover when the inner cover did not completely encircle the upper arm cone: they pinned the outer cover along the outer edge of the wing as far down as the upper arm cone, then pinned it across the side of the arm cone where the inner cover ended. Finally, they worked the cover around and under the cone (although they could never get the fabric to go completely beneath it).

This tailoring method varied slightly from frame to frame. Some upholsterers made sharp turns at the juncture of the upper cones and the panels, whereas others finessed this transitional point with an odd, applied quarter-round bracket. Sharp turns deemphasize the wavering lines of the outside arm panels, whereas quarter-round brackets (which are more revealing of the lines) soften the transition from the upper arm cones to the outside panels underneath them. Period tacking evidence (square shanked tacks with forged heads or holes made by them) varies considerably from frame to frame, but no chair examined by the authors has indisputably original tacking evidence all the way along the innermost areas of the upper arm scrolls.

Figure 7 Side view of fig. 6. (Private collection; photo, John Bly.)

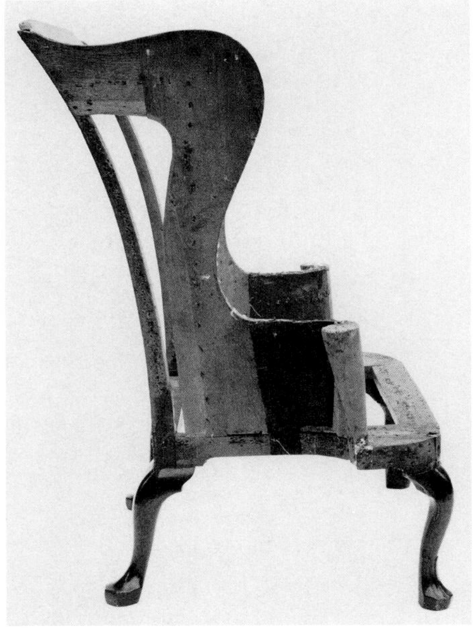

The upholstery techniques used on the upper arm scrolls of the Deshler chair remained standard practice in Philadelphia and New York from about 1730 to 1830. Modern upholsterers, who are used to rationalized workmanship that conforms tightly to the frame, and collectors, who see Philadelphia frames as lightly padded wood sculptures that should be crisp, neat, and clean, are often puzzled and annoyed by this rediscovered treatment of upholstery; however, this was a period practice, and modern treatments of period frames should seek to recapture this effect.

Another characteristic of late-eighteenth- and early-nineteenth-century Philadelphia frames was the extensive use of tacking struts. These struts facilitated stuffing the chair and created clean straight lines at the tuckaways (the junctions of different panels where fabric is drawn

Figure 8 Easy chair made by Thomas Affleck with carving attributed to Nicholas Bernard and Martin Jugiez, Philadelphia, 1770. Mahogany with white oak, yellow pine, and tulip poplar. H. 45″, W. 36½″, D. 34″. (H. Richard Dietrich, Jr., on loan to the Philadelphia Museum of Art; photo, Metropolitan Museum of Art.)

through and tacked in place). On the Deshler chair, the junctions are between the back and the wings and between the wing-and-arm panel and the seat deck.[3] Although loose covers might be held in the tuckaways with several loose stitches, on the Deshler example the stuffing was so deep that loose covers could simply be pushed into the tuckaways and held by the pressure of the stuffing alone.

A final point about this frame is the design of the outward-flaring arms. Philadelphia easy chairs dating from the 1730s to the 1790s are framed in a specific way. Each of three successive vertical members—rear posts, wing-and-arm posts, and upper arm scroll posts—tilts a bit more to the outside, contributing to a gradual splay. Although making the arms seem more "inviting," these splayed supports mean that the outer wing-and-arm panels are concave, not flat (the elimination of heavy splay in neoclassical frames flattened the outside wing-and-arm panels).[4]

Figure 9 Frame of the easy chair illustrated in fig. 8. (Photo, Winterthur Museum.)

Figure 10 Nonintrusive upholstery foundation fabricated for fig. 8. (Photo, Winterthur Museum.)

The interdependence of traditional techniques and stylistic change in the eighteenth century is demonstrated by the tacking evidence left by the lost upholstery foundation of an easy chair made in 1770 for John Cadwalader (1742–1786) of Philadelphia (figs. 8–11). This is the earliest datable easy chair with single-scroll arms and a trapezoidal seat. When the problem of how to develop a nonintrusive (tackless) system for this frame arose, we assumed that the chair was an experimental design, a transitional form, a special order, and a rushed job. Documents associated with building and furnishing Cadwalader's house suggest that he ordered a quantity of furniture from the city's leading cabinetmakers and carvers and that it was produced over an astonishingly short period of time; however, similarities of form and proportion suggest that the joiners who made the Cadwalader frame consulted an English prototype such as that in figures 12 and 13. Although this English chair has a double-scroll frame, the lower scrolls are attenuated, and it is easy to imagine the frame without them and with the lower panels straightened into simple ramps as on the Cadwalader chair. Other parallels include the serpentine crest rail; low stay rail or lower back rail; flat rear back rails; wings with straight ramps leading off from the rear posts; tacking struts; size and moderate splay of the upper arm scrolls; open diagonal braces in the seat frame; and relatively squarish trapezoidal seat plan. Of course, significant differences remain. The English easy chair has upper arm scrolls framed with flat upper boards, long triangular blocks, and skimpy outer rolls that are completely unlike those of Cadwalader's chair or other Philadelphia chairs, and it has applied secondary-wood brackets under the seat rails that support knee brackets made of the primary wood.

What the English frame provides no precedent for are the carved rails on the Cadwalader frame. Carved rails suggest that the Cadwalader chair is not, in strict conceptual terms, an easy chair. The Cadwalader chair is a hybrid of single-scroll easy chairs and "French chairs" (several French chairs with carved skirts, trapezoidal seats, and serpentine fronts were illustrated in plates 17–20 of Thomas Chippendale's *The Gentleman and Cabinet-Maker's Director*).

Cadwalader's extraordinary carved frame cost £4.10.0. The upholstery cost £2.3.5 *exclusive of the covers*, for the frame was finished "in canvas" only. Surviving bills suggest that the chair had a blue check cover and a blue silk damask cover with fringe and silk binding on the seams. It was made en suite with the three sofas that were used in the principal parlors of Cadwalader's house and may represent the rare instance of an easy chair being used in a parlor rather than a bedroom. Cadwalader's wife was of child-bearing age, and this chair may have been intended for her use.[5]

The evidence left by tacks suggests that the chair did not require radically new stuffing or tailoring methods. The wings have chamfered edges that made edge rolls inappropriate and eliminated tailoring the wings with panels. Because we could not infer the appropriate shape of the curled horsehair stuffing from the frame alone, we used another Philadelphia chair with original stuffing as a model for the conservation (figs. 14, 15).[6] On this chair, the stuffing is fairly light at the edges of the chamfered wings but extremely heavy at the tuckaways. Comparable shaping and bulk appear on the arms. The stuffing was intended to soften the interior

Figure 11 Rear view of fig. 8 showing the jog in the upholstery line at the bottom of the outside back. (Photo, Winterthur Museum.)

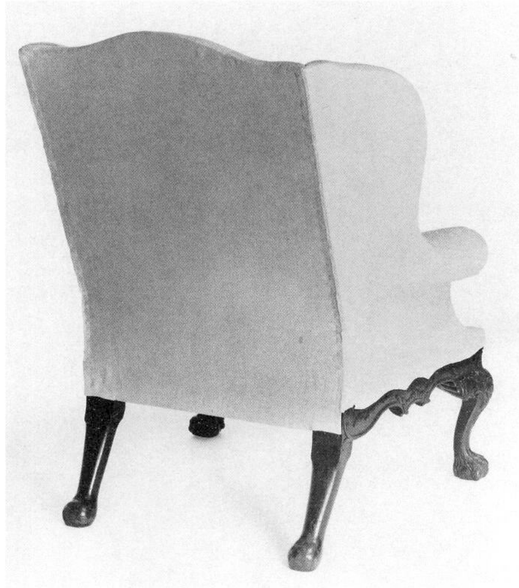

Figure 12 Easy chair, England, 1750–1770. Mahogany with Scots pine and ash. H. 41", W. 30", D. 33". (Private collection; photo by owner.)

Figure 13 Side view of fig. 12 showing the arm and scroll construction. (Private collection; photo by owner.)

Figure 14 Easy chair, Philadelphia, 1770–1790. Mahogany with walnut, tulip poplar, red gum, yellow pine, oak, and possibly white pine and maple. H. 46⅜", W. 36¼", D. 29½". (Courtesy, Winterthur Museum, acc. 92.31.)

Figure 15 Side view of fig. 14. (Photo, Winterthur Museum.)

of the chair for the occupant; however, it had the additional effect of exaggerating the apparent splay of the frame.

The nonintrusive upholstery system developed for the Cadwalader chair left one important question unanswered: how were the seats of both Philadelphia chairs treated? On figure 14, the collapsed seat deck indicates a complete loss of stuffing, but the original bulk can be inferred from the tacking for the top linen of the seat. The front seat rail has tacking evidence that suggests that it had an edge roll but inevitably raises the question of how anyone sat on this chair. If the seat was a tight seat (a seat with no cushion), it would have been substantially padded, but if it supported a down cushion, it needed a heavy edge roll on the front seat rail to contain the cushion. A third possibility is that the chair had a

Figure 16 Easy chair, Philadelphia, 1795–1805. Mahogany with tulip poplar and pine. H. 43¾″, W. 30¾″, D. 31″. (Courtesy, Winterthur Museum, acc. 91.37.)

Figure 17 Rear view of fig. 16. (Photo, Winterthur Museum.)

stitched or tufted hair mattress of the same sort mentioned in inventories and seen on the chair in figures 28 and 29.[7]

Unfortunately, the upholstery evidence on this chair did not resolve the question of what the original treatment of the Cadwalader seat was. Because the front of the arm ramps of the Cadwalader chair are only 1″ above the top of the front seat rail, the ramps and roll are level when the rail is upholstered with an edge roll. Therefore, we concluded that the seat is not likely to have had a hair mattress. A 1764 portrait by Johan Zoffany shows a sofa with a tight seat that is level with the arm ramps.[8]

A stylish Philadelphia-made neoclassical frame of the 1795–1805 period (figs. 16, 17) appears far more rigid and squarish than the earlier rococo examples. This is not a consequence of the individual panels of the frame, for they are practically identical to those of the chair in figure 14 but of the manner in which they are assembled. The following measurements demonstrate that the rococo frame is lower, wider, and deeper than its neoclassical counterpart and that its arms splay much farther out to either side.

	Fig. 14	Fig. 16
Width at rear seat rail	24″	22⅝″
Width at crest rail	27½″	25½″
Width across arms	36¼″	30¾″
Width at front seat rail	27½″	26¾″
Overall height	46″	48″
Seat depth	23⅜″	24¾″

On the tight, beautifully stuffed neoclassical chair an entirely new effect was achieved using the same patterns. All the framing of the side panels is on a single plane, which makes the chair quite boxy and prevents the scrolls from extending out any great distance. Most remarkable are the original board linings for the wings, arms, and back. Although some scholars might interpret these foundations as a rural deviation, or at the very least as an economy measure, the sophisticated design of the frame proves that it is an urban product. Moreover, the savings in fitting and nailing the board linings would have had little impact on the cost because the utilitarian heavy linen of which the sackcloth in the frame usually was made was not very expensive. Board linings probably were intended to block strong drafts that easily penetrate the stuffing of a chair.

Despite the use of board linings on the neoclassical chair, no holes are present that indicate that the upholsterer used twines to anchor the horsehair stuffing of the back in place. Two holes in each arm lining mark the location of original twines for the arm stuffing. Settling of horsehair stuffing in frames is a common failure, quite apart from the displacement of stuffing because of restless heads, backs, and elbows. This was a critical problem when curled horsehair was laid over wood, which, unlike a textile, offers little to cling to. The presence or absence of twining to secure stuffing is a key factor in understanding upholstery practices of the late eighteenth and early nineteenth centuries. Although American upholsterers were using twines to secure stuffing by the mid-1770s, fully stitched upholstery foundations were first executed in New York and Philadelphia during the 1790s.[9]

Although the serpentine (or "commode") front seat rail makes the chair in figures 16 and 17 appear deeper than it actually is, the frame is relatively high, narrow, and shallow. The heavy bulk at the tuckaways guaranteed that the occupants were squeezed in between the wings and arms. Although the original stuffing of the seat is lost and it is not clear how it was treated, the ramps at the bottoms of the arm panels are relatively low. As in the previously discussed frame, this suggests that the chair may have had a hair mattress rather than a down cushion.

The foundation upholstery of the neoclassical chair reveals two other important features. First, the tailoring of the outside of the frame, with

Figure 18 Easy chair, eastern Pennsylvania or Winchester, Virginia, 1790–1800. Mahogany with tulip poplar, maple, and white pine. H. 43⅝", W. 33", D. 30⅞". (Courtesy, Winterthur Museum, acc. 91.44.)

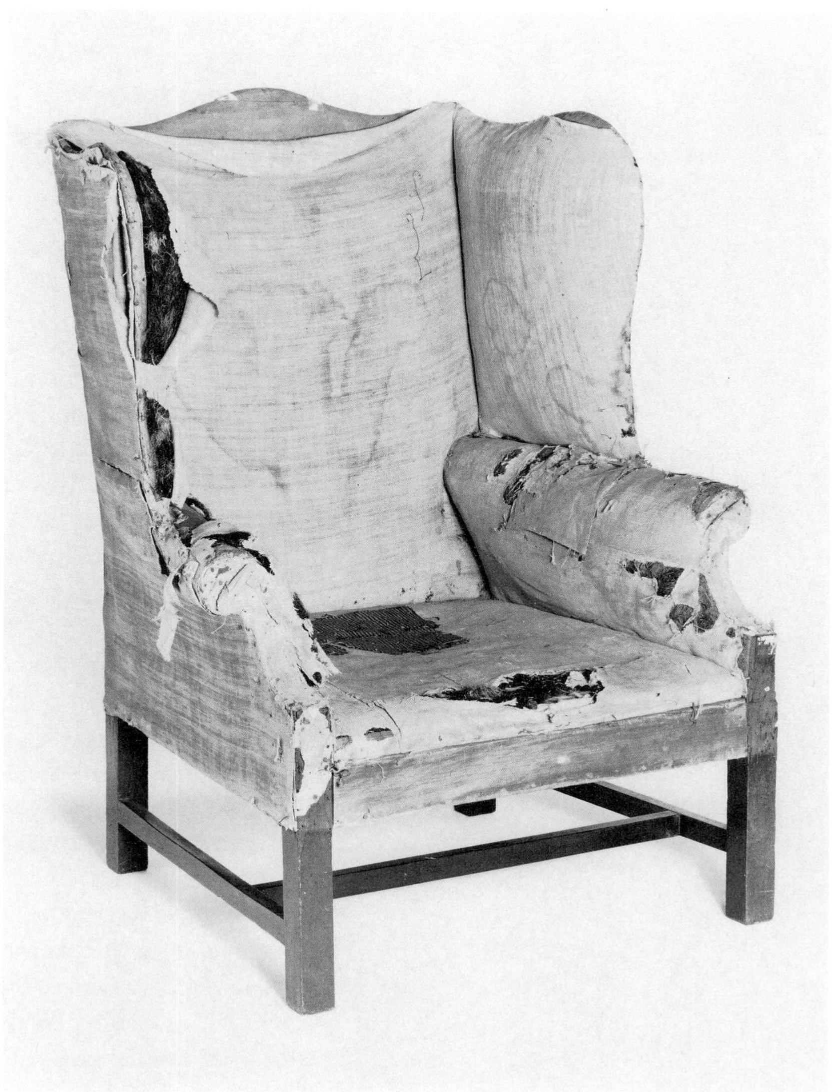

Figure 19 Rear view of fig. 18. (Photo, Winterthur Museum.)

long seams that run from the crest along the edges of the wings and onto the sides of the arm scrolls, is similar to that of the Deshler easy chair. Second, this frame did not have fixed covers until the late nineteenth century when chintz covers (fragments survived) were amateurishly tacked to the frame. The original tacking sites indicate that the chair had a loose cover and support documentary evidence that loose covers were not limited to chairs with close stools.

The chair in figures 18 and 19 illustrates several options and stylistic details that were available during the late rococo and the early neoclassical periods and that were described in *The Journeyman Cabinet and Chair-Makers Philadelphia Book of Prices* (1795) and *The Journeyman Cabinet and Chair Makers' Pennsylvania Book of Prices* (1811). The heavy, low proportions of this late rococo frame are common among mid-eighteenth-century English chairs but rare in the United States. The seat is deep and consists of a loose (or slip) seat that must be pulled straight forward to be removed, given the bulk of the arm stuffing. This loose seat covers a simple arrangement: four large vertical corner blocks, two side tracks with rabbeted upper edges, and a board with a hole that rests in the rabbets. No provisions were made for an upper seat board to separate the user and the rim of the pewter pan.

The plain legs divert attention from two unusual features of the undercarriage: the rear legs are absolutely vertical, and no rear stretcher connects them. The first feature has a straightforward explanation: because the frame contained a close stool, the chair probably had a loose cover with shirred bases (dust ruffles) to conceal the pan, and straight rear legs would have allowed the bases to fall straight to the floor. The absence of a rear stretcher was an option cited in some price lists. Normally it was combined with tracks nailed under the seat rails to support a pan rack that slid out the rear of the chair, but racks are absent on this chair. Perhaps the owner preferred to place a ceramic chamber pot on the floor below the opening as an alternative to hanging a pewter pan.

At 13¼″ high including the slip seat, the seat seems remarkably low. The undersides of the feet have marks from two successive sets of casters, one of which may have been original. The casters would have brought the seat to about 14½″ in height, still a bit low but acceptable for a small, elderly person. As the frame sits without casters, the stretchers are 3″ from the floor, whereas on most eighteenth-century chairs stretchers are about 4″ to 4½″ from the floor. The frame has curled horsehair stuffing heavily applied over the entire surface of each panel. The outside wing-and-arm panels have continuous seams running down the wings and onto the sides of the arm cones, as with the Deshler example. The chair has experienced heavy use; its linen foundation covers have been patched repeatedly and restless elbows have dented the arms on both sides.

Although this chair conforms to Philadelphia designs, the slip seat is inscribed "Sitting/Chair/and/pot/Winchester/Virginia." Although it is possible that the chair was taken to the Valley of Virginia from eastern Pennsylvania, it could as easily be a Winchester product, because many artisans from the Delaware Valley resettled in the Shenandoah Valley during the eighteenth and nineteenth centuries.

A very similar easy chair could have been made in either Philadelphia or New York City (fig. 20). It is approximately the same size as that in figure 18, although the seat is about 1″ higher (if an inch is added to the previous chair's seat height to compensate for lost casters). It has a more elaborate close-stool arrangement with a lift-out panel that separates the user from the rim of the pewter pan. On it, too, long seams run down the wings and the sides of the arms.

Almost unquestionably from New York City, the easy chair in figures 21–23 is later in date. It has a heavy frame and lyre arms that extend (in their scroll shape) to the rear of the frame. Such arms are extremely rare on American examples, and the chairmaker carried the shape of these mahogany faced arms to the rear of the frame by applying haunch blocks to the sides and the back of the rear posts. Another unusual feature is

Figure 20 Easy chair, probably Pennsylvania, but possibly New York, 1795–1805. Mahogany with oak and pine. H. 45⅞", W. 32⅝", D. 32⅝". (Courtesy, Bernard & S. Dean Levy; photo, Helga Studio.)

the high arched crest, possibly a holdover from earlier New York chairs. The heavy, turned legs have carved beads and socket casters, the latter of which were introduced about 1810. The close-stool board, which has a hole for a pan, was secured with glue blocks and was covered originally by a slip seat (here restored).

The framing of this New York chair has other unusual features besides the peculiar haunch blocks. The wings are solid boards, and the crest rail is extraordinarily deep. These details and the overall heavy framing make the chair exceptionally stable (its closest parallel is an equally massive New York settee made for Daniel Wadsworth of Hartford about 1825). Its strong, exquisitely made frame is similar to those made in Regency London.

The restored loose cover suggests what the chair might have looked like when in use.[10] The shirred bases stop above the floor to avoid snagging in the caster wheels. In the eighteenth and nineteenth centuries, loose covers often were fabricated around the arm panels and generally

Figure 21 Easy chair, New York, New York, 1810–1825. Mahogany with ash and pine. H. 48½″, W. 31½″, D. 30″. (Courtesy, Winterthur Museum, acc. 88.37.)

Figure 22 Front view of fig. 21 showing the original top linen. (Photo, Winterthur Museum.)

Figure 23 Rear view of fig. 21 showing the outside back top linen. (Photo, Winterthur Museum.)

were fairly snug. Because the original outside wing-and-arm panels of the top linen were not basted to follow the front-to-rear curve of the arms precisely, the slipcover was loosely tailored in those areas. As with other easy chairs, the long seams run from the wings onto the sides of the arm scrolls. A traditional indifference to the tailoring of the outside arms may explain the original upholsterer's failure to fit the fabric to the lyre scrolls more closely. The tape ties of the rear corners are one of several systems for closing eighteenth- and nineteenth-century loose covers, others being hooks and eyes and light tacking.

Scholars frequently have associated chairs of a lean, somewhat pinched design with New York. One such example is that in figures 24 and 25, although it lacks the ogee turning above the casters that is typical of early-nineteenth-century New York turning. On this chair, each side panel is built around a large plank to which modest half-rolls are applied.[11] The extremely thick padding of the wings and arms minimized the skimpy

Figure 24 Easy chair, New York, New York, 1795–1810. Mahogany with maple, tulip poplar, and pine. H. 46¼", W. 31", D. 22½". (Courtesy, Bernard & S. Dean Levy; photo, Helga Studio.)

lines of the frame. Slots cut in the plank panels to thread the webbing through demonstrate that this was a standard frame that someone simply adapted for a close stool since no webbing is needed over a plank supporting a slip seat. The chair retains its original turned lid, or stopper, for the seat hole. The track nailed under the seat indicates that it was intended to have a ceramic chamber pot, for the tracks held a box or rack in which the pot rested and the rack could be pulled out to empty the vessel after use. Similar tracks sometimes supported frames or boxes that slid out from the front accommodating rests for gouty legs and feet.

A provincial version of the same style of chair has an elliptic front rail, serpentine crest, and open diagonal struts in the seat frame (figs. 26, 27). Holes in the side panels suggest they were intended for twines to secure the stuffing, which in the original back foundation is a deep layer of tow (crushed flax stems). Tow was used frequently during the early nineteenth century, despite its tendency to crumble and compress with use. The

Figure 25 Easy chair illustrated in fig. 24 with the slip seat and stopper visible. (Courtesy, Bernard & S. Dean Levy; photo, Helga Studio.)

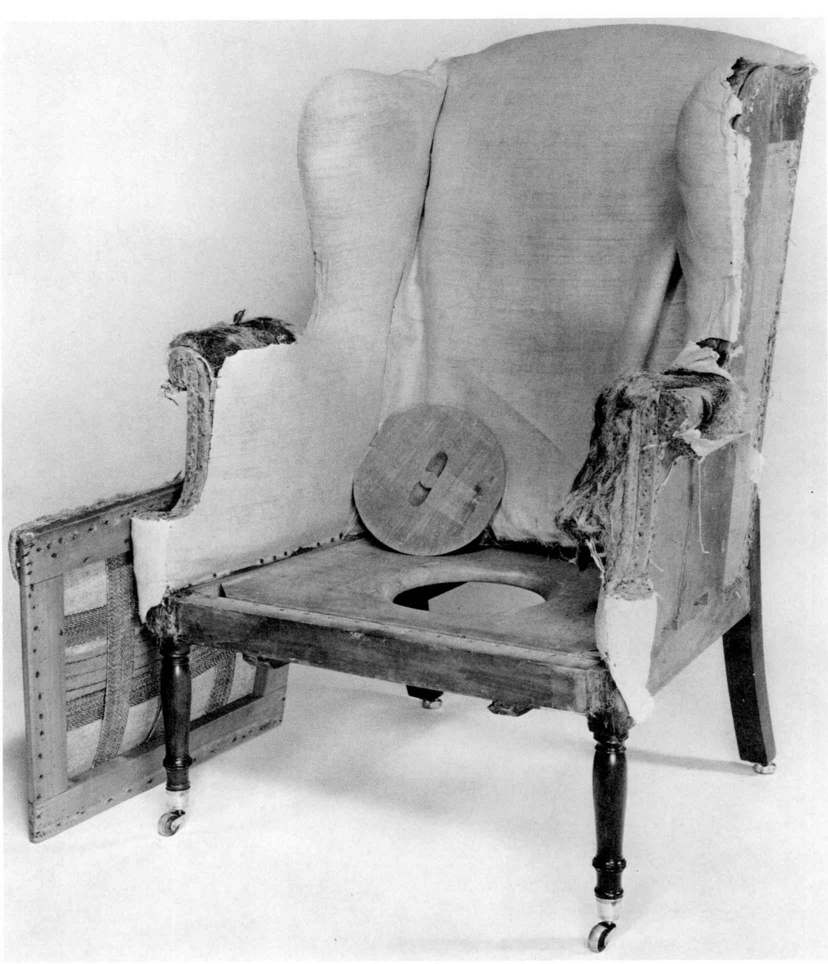

Figure 26 Easy chair, New York or New Jersey, 1810–1830. Walnut with cherry and maple. H. 45½″, W. 33¼″, D. 38½″. (Private collection; photo, Winterthur Museum.)

Figure 27 Rear view of fig. 26. (Photo, Winterthur Museum.)

front rail is padded by a substantial roll stuffed with reeds. The difference in the height of the roll and small vertical arm cones suggests that the chair had a cushion seat.

The Philadelphia chair illustrated in figures 28 and 29 is a highly inventive variant of the standard circular chair produced from about 1805 to 1820. These chairs were framed on a D-shaped plan and required that the seat rails and crest rails be laminated (brick-built). On this example, the seat rails are three laminations high and the crest is five. What distinguishes this frame is the structure of the back. On most circular easy chairs, the crest is mounted on extensions of the rear legs, that results in frames having practically no rake or layback.

By adapting the framing system then generally used on cabriole sofas, the chairmaker overcame the limitations of traditional circular chair design. He mounted the crest on three struts, toeing the center strut on the rear seat rail and toeing the two outer struts in front of the rear leg tusks. He set the struts at so radical an angle that the rear edge of the crest is 12¾″

Figure 28 Circular easy chair, Philadelphia, 1805–1815. Mahogany with maple, cherry, and pine. H. 46″, W. 34″, D. 34″. (Courtesy, Winterthur Museum, acc. 91.36.)

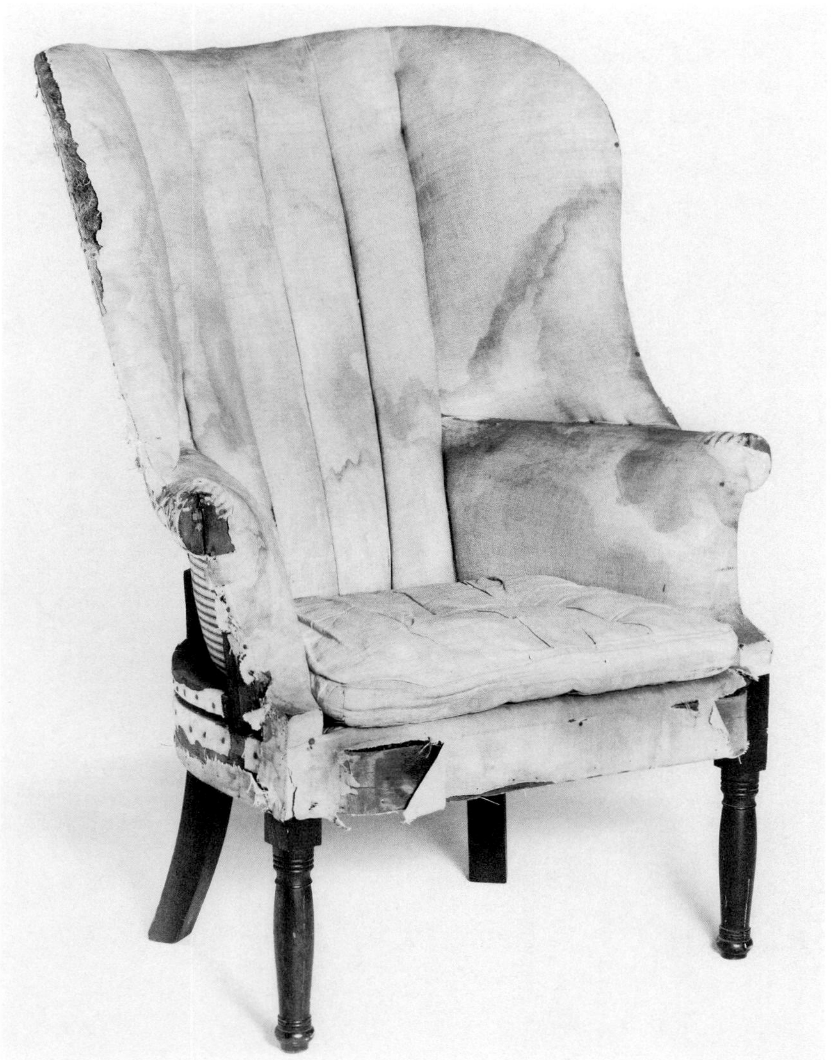

Figure 29 Rear view of fig. 28. (Photo, Winterthur Museum.)

behind the rear seat rail. Because the rear legs extend only a few inches above the seat rails, he could not frame the arms into them, and they extend from the outer back struts to the front struts. He framed the wings into the crest rail and the arms. All this unusual framing resulted in a narrower back and wings that met the arms much farther back than on most circular chairs. Most chairmakers extended the wings so far forward that practically none of the arm scroll was available for an armrest.

The narrow back of figure 28 has four flutes rather than the usual five. These are sharply tapered (from an average width of 5″ at the top to 3¼″ at the bottom) to compensate for the severe rake of the back. As the rear view shows, the central crease between the two inner flutes was tacked to the front face of the central strut, whereas the others were twined and either tied off on the sackcloth or tacked to the outer struts. Striped ticking was used as the sackcloth. The front edge roll was stuffed with chopped wool, known as "flocks" or "dust" during the period. The roll contained the tufted and stitched hair "mattress," which has a 2″ boxing.

Figure 30 Easy chair, eastern Massachusetts or coastal New Hampshire, 1820–1840. Mahogany with maple, cherry, tulip poplar, pine, and ash. H. 49¼″, W. 33″, D. 28″. (Private collection; photo, Alexander Studio.)

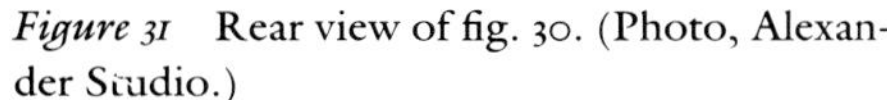

Figure 31 Rear view of fig. 30. (Photo, Alexander Studio.)

The mattress covers a loose pan-hole cover and a square panel that can be lifted out to empty the pewter pan. The deck is lined with linen and the one-piece deck board is held in place by several small glue blocks. The legs on the frame may have lost small conical turnings under the surviving ring turnings. The seat rail height is now 14½″. With the 2″ cushion, the original seat height would have been about 17″. It is difficult to imagine a chair of this height being used without a footstool.

A New England easy chair with a close stool and four heavy vertical turned legs provides an interesting contemporary comparison with the later mid-Atlantic examples (figs. 30, 31). The heavy frame is beautifully constructed, and the chair retains its original Spanish moss stuffing. Spanish moss was used frequently by northern urban upholsterers after 1790 and was especially favored for mattresses. The springing in the slip seat is a later addition that distorts its shape, and the seat board with pan hole is missing. The back slats are original and have holes drilled for

Figure 32 Easy chair, New York, 1800–1825. Mahogany with ash and white pine. H. 49″, W. 32½″, D. 26½″. (Private collection; photo, Winterthur Museum.)

Figure 33 Rear view of fig. 32. (Photo, Winterthur Museum.)

twines that secured a bed of grass that supplements the Spanish moss laid over it. The slats are thin enough to flex under the occupant's weight, yet thick enough to block drafts. The loss of the outer linen has not obliterated the evidence of the standard long seams running down the edges of the wings and along the sides of the arm rolls. As on the chair illustrated in figures 18 and 19, the four straight legs permitted the shirred bases to hang straight to the tops of the casters.

The New York chair illustrated in figures 32–34 had a pot rack that slid out from the rear, and the frame was constructed without a rear stretcher. What distinguishes this chair is the extremely thick stuffing of the wings with lamb's wool and a skimmer of hair. The stuffing is thick right up to the lead edges of the wings; it was secured with twine that passed through a series of holes drilled along the edges of the wings. The bulk and composition of the stuffing identifies the chair as a rural product that may have been upholstered by a saddler.

Figure 34 Detail of fig. 32, showing drilled holes and twines along the outer lead edge of the wing. (Photo, Winterthur Museum.)

Figure 35 Easy chair, New Jersey, 1820–1840. Curly birch with maple, basswood, pine, and black ash (later oak stretchers). H. 48⅞", W. 32", D. 29⅜". (Private collection; photo, Winterthur Museum.)

Another rural example is a New Jersey chair with eccentric construction and stuffing techniques (fig. 35). The frame was made without back posts; the wing-and-arm panels and the back frame are pegged together with long wooden pins. The arm framing was laid on top of the seat planks, which in turn were nailed atop the seat rails. Although the seat planks have been sawn out, originally they probably contained a pot hole. The most unsophisticated details are the black ash splint webbing with textile tacking strips and the corn-husk edge rolls on the arms. The original stuffing is lost, but, according to the previous owner, it consisted of grass with a skimmer layer of tow.

Our joint examination of easy chairs during the last five years has allowed us to expand our understanding of the use of easy chairs in the eighteenth and early nineteenth centuries and has provided us with benchmarks to assist curators and conservators interested in stuffing and tailoring frames in museums and private collections. Our goal now is to encourage museums to aggressively collect frames with original upholstery and to remind even well-meaning collectors that irrevocable damage occurs when they seek to reinforce original foundations enough to be sat upon. Use of these objects is dangerous, for often the textile components are so weak that they cannot take the stress. Loose covers provide curators an excellent solution to the problem of preserving fragile foundations and making an object presentable for display. The tailoring of such covers is not that difficult, and the covers can range from being closely to loosely fitted. A looser fit is best if the covers are to be removed with any frequency, as a great deal of damage can be inflicted on the original textiles by abrasion alone.

ACKNOWLEDGMENTS The authors thank the following for their help at many stages of compiling the essay and catalogue: John Bly, Frances Bretter, Harold Chalfant, Anthony Collins, Stephen Corrigan, Richard Dietrich, George Fistrovich, Christopher Gilbert, Morrison Heckscher, Barbara Hencheck, John Hencheck, Frank Horton, Douglas Jackman, Leigh Keno, Joe Kindig III, Frank Levy, Jack Lindsey, Robert Luck, Alan Miller, Steven Pine, Deborah Rebuck, Robert St. George, George Sansoucy, Elizabeth Schaefer, Darien Sergeant, Gary Sergeant, Bruce Sikora, Frederica Struss, Susan Swan, Ronald Vukelich, and Manfred Woerner. We extend special thanks to Luke Beckerdite for his help throughout the editing process.

1. This chair is part of a large suite of furniture probably owned by David Deshler of Germantown. The knee carving matches carving on eight side chairs, several of which have slip seats with an eighteenth-century ink inscription "Deshler." One of the marked side chairs was illustrated in "Exhibition of Furniture of the Chippendale Style," *Bulletin of the Philadelphia Museum of Art* 19, no. 86 (May 1924): 164, pls. 4, 9, with a Fisher family chair, but the captions were switched. The easy chair descended in the same line as the side chairs, and the mixup in captions led scholars to associate the easy chair with the Fisher rather than Deshler families. The authors are grateful to Alan Miller for clarifying the history of the easy chair. Mark Anderson, Robert Trent, Dora Shotzberger, Ruth Lee, and Terry Anderson conserved the foundation upholstery and fabricated the cover in 1989. Alan Miller of Quakerstown, Pennsylvania, conserved the frame.

2. See Andrew Passeri and Robert F. Trent, "Two New England Queen Anne Easy Chairs with Original Upholstery," *Maine Antique Digest* 11, no. 4 (April 1983): 26A–28A; and Edward S. Cooke, Jr., "The Nathan Low Easy Chair: High Quality Upholstery in Pre-Revolutionary Boston," *Maine Antique Digest* 15, no. 11 (November 1987): 1C–3C.

3. In many other schools of upholstery (e.g., Boston), struts were not used.

4. The authors thank Alan Miller for the information on arm construction.

5. The bills for the easy chair frame, foundation upholstery, covers, and fabrics are reproduced in Nicholas B. Wainwright, *Colonial Grandeur in Philadelphia* (Philadelphia: Historical Society of Pennsylvania, 1964), pp. 40–41, 44, 51, 69.

6. This chair recently entered the collection of the Winterthur Museum.

7. Mark Anderson designed the nonintrusive upholstery foundation and Anderson and Robert Trent fabricated it. Anderson, Trent, Dora Shotzberger, Ruth Lee, and Susan Heald fabricated the blue silk damask loose cover with silk binding and fringe. Alan Miller conserved the frame. The nonintrusive upholstery is illustrated and discussed in Mark Anderson, "More on Non-Damaging Upholstery," American Institute for Conservation/Wood Artifacts Group Preprints, Annual Meeting (Cincinnati, 1989), n.p. For a 1784 print depicting an enclosed armchair in the background with a slipcover over what appears to be a hair mattress on the seat, see Florence M. Montgomery, *Printed Textiles* (New York: Viking, 1970), p. 75, fig. 48. Note that the mattress is level with the ramps coming down from the arm scrolls.

8. Gervase Jackson-Stops, "Johan Zoffany and the Eighteenth-Century Interior," *Antiques* 131, no. 6 (June 1987): 1265, pl. 2.

9. The chair illustrated in figs. 14 and 15 has a twine running down from the front face of the crest rail. This may have been used to confine stuffing in that location. An eighteenth-century Charleston easy chair in the Museum of Early Southern Decorative Arts has twines attached to the stiles with wrought nails. These apparently were threaded through the back to hold the stuffing in place. See Kathleen Catalano and Richard C. Nylander, "New Attributions to Adam Hains, Philadelphia Furniture Maker," *Antiques* 117, no. 5 (May 1980): 1112–16.

10. Dora Shotzberger and Ruth Lee fabricated the loose cover. Susan Heald conserved the top linen.

11. It is unclear why these makers reverted to a double-scroll arm nearly half a century after it passed out of fashion in most other American cities (Philadelphia excepted). Charles Montgomery noted that some of these chairs have an arched or elliptic crest, whereas others have serpentine ones. Although he believed that the arched crests were earlier, they actually may have been made later (Charles F. Montgomery, *American Furniture: The Federal Period* [New York: Viking, 1966], pp. 170–72).

Gerald W. R. Ward and Karin E. Cullity

The Wendell Family Furniture at Strawbery Banke Museum

▼ THE DWELLING on Pleasant Street in Portsmouth, New Hampshire, that became known as the Jacob Wendell house was built by Jeremiah Hill in 1789 (fig. 1). It is a substantial home, somewhat conservative in plan and ornament, with a wide front hall (fig. 2) and a Georgian floor plan with two generously sized parlors, a dining room, a kitchen, and five bedchambers. The house was purchased by Jacob Wendell (1788–1865) in 1815 and was home (and later summer home) to succeeding family members until 1988: Caroline Quincy Wendell (1820–1890), James Rindge Stanwood (1847–1910), Barrett (1855–1921) and Edith (1859–1938) Wendell, and William G. (1888–1968) and Evelyn (1909–1988) Wendell.[1]

By 1988, when the estate was broken up, the Wendell house had gained a nearly legendary reputation as an "untouched" family collection of antiques. Several series of photographs, including sets taken in 1887, 1902, 1912 (with detailed annotations by William G. Wendell), 1940 (again with notations by William G. Wendell), 1966 (by Samuel Chamberlain), and, finally, Strawbery Banke's record shots taken in 1988, show a remarkable continuity of furnishings. Inventories, lists, and appraisals taken in the first half of the nineteenth century and in 1890, 1912, 1968, 1977 and 1988 also document an amazing continuity over time. Adding to the mystique of the house was the successive owners' penchant for preserving family records and for annotating their own history. Particularly important for the purposes of this paper are the business ledgers and invoices preserved in Jacob's papers that document his acquisitions in 1815 and the succeeding years and the later notations of James Rindge Stanwood. As a result, the Wendell collection is exceedingly well documented in collections of papers at Houghton Library and Baker Library at Harvard University, the Portsmouth Athenaeum, and Strawbery Banke Museum's Cumings Library and Archives.

These same pictures and inventories, however, also reveal a good deal of change, both in the arrangement of objects and in the handling of surfaces, including carpets, wallpapers, and paint. Although the family sideboard seems to have had a place of honor in the room used as a dining room, for example, a series of photographs of that room from 1887 (fig. 3), ca. 1900 (fig. 4), 1902 (fig. 5), and 1940 (fig. 6) reveals changes in the chairs, prints, wallpapers, painted woodwork, looking glasses, and other details. A comparison of the family parlor shows similar alterations from 1902 (figs. 7, 8) to 1940 (fig. 9), although one can again trace the presence of major objects, such as the Portsmouth china table (fig. 14) from

Figure 1 Jacob Wendell house, Pleasant Street, Portsmouth, New Hampshire, built 1789. Photograph by Lafayette Newell and Co., ca. 1902. (Wendell Collection, Strawbery Banke Museum.)

Figure 2 Front hallway, Wendell house. Photograph by Lafayette Newell and Co., ca. 1902. (Wendell Collection, Strawbery Banke Museum.)

Figure 3 Dining room, Wendell house. Photograph by Arthur T. Greenwood, August 1887. (Courtesy, Ronald Bourgeault.)

image to image. Pictures of the large bedchambers (figs. 10, 34) also reflect considerable change and updating of decoration over time. Many of the objects illustrated in this essay can be seen in these earlier pictures.

These images, the various inventories, and other documents also reveal that some objects left the family collection prior to the final breakup in 1988. The Newport oval table with claw-and-ball feet that held such a prominent place in the dining room (see figs. 3–5) is one such major object. Many others were sold in the late 1970s and early 1980s and have

Figure 4 Dining room, Wendell house. Photograph, ca. 1900. (Wendell Collection, Strawbery Banke Museum.)

Figure 5 Dining room, Wendell house. Photograph by Lafayette Newell and Co., ca. 1902. (Wendell Collection, Strawbery Banke Museum.)

Figure 6 Dining room, Wendell house. Photograph by Douglas Armsden, ca. 1940. (Wendell Collection, Strawbery Banke Museum.)

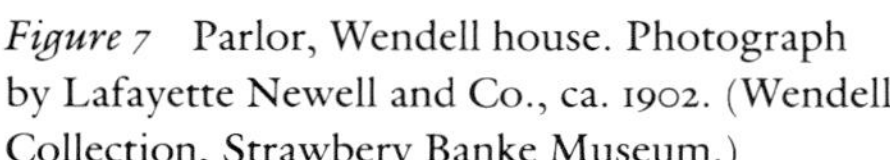

Figure 7 Parlor, Wendell house. Photograph by Lafayette Newell and Co., ca. 1902. (Wendell Collection, Strawbery Banke Museum.)

entered private collections. Thus the Wendell house was not intact in 1988, but a high percentage of key objects had been there for a century and a half.

When the house was sold and its contents dispersed in 1988 and 1989, Strawbery Banke Museum was fortunate to receive a large and important collection of furnishings from the house. The vast majority of these were the generous gift of Penelope and Gerrit van der Woude of Eastry, Sandwich, in Kent, England, both family descendants. The van der Woude

Figure 8 Parlor, Wendell house. Photograph by Lafayette Newell and Co., ca. 1902. (Wendell Collection, Strawbery Banke Museum.)

Figure 9 Parlor, Wendell house. Photograph by Douglas Armsden, ca. 1940. (Wendell Collection, Strawbery Banke Museum.)

Figure 10 Parlor chamber, Wendell house. Photograph by Lafayette Newell and Co., ca. 1902. (Wendell Collection, Strawbery Banke Museum.)

gift, which includes ceramics, glass, silver and base-metal objects, paintings, and prints as well as the furniture discussed here, represents the single most important gift of objects to come to Strawbery Banke since its incorporation in 1958.

Other Wendell family materials were given to the museum by Ronald Bourgeault, who recently purchased the house; Bourgeault also loaned several major Wendell family pieces that he acquired. A small number of Wendell family objects were purchased by the museum, and a few with Wendell family associations were already in the Strawbery Banke collection. Those that did not come to Strawbery Banke were sold at auction by Sotheby's in New York in January 1989 at several sales, principally the *Important Americana* sale, January 26–28 (sale 5810).

Our purpose here is to provide an overview of the Wendell family furniture in the collection of Strawbery Banke Museum. This constellation of objects provides a unique look at the possessions of one New England family. The pivotal figure in the story is Jacob Wendell. As was true for many other New Englanders of his station, Jacob inherited or acquired through marriage many outstanding pieces of colonial furniture. Jacob, like so many in Portsmouth, prospered financially during the federal period and, using his newfound wealth, furnished his home in the mid-1810s with elaborate and fashionable neoclassical furniture, much of it acquired from Portsmouth's leading cabinetmakers. Jacob's financial losses in the late 1820s, although not so severe that he was forced to lose his house, kept him from updating his furnishings during the later part of his life. As was perhaps true in other Portsmouth families, a growing fondness or nostalgia for Portsmouth's heyday of colonial and federal prosperity made Jacob and his heirs look back fondly on the material manifestations of that era, especially the stylish furniture produced in a town dominated by the woodworking trades. Later members of the family, particularly James Rindge Stanwood and Barrett Wendell, were interested in preserving and rehabilitating the relics of the family's earlier glories. By the 1980s, this combination of circumstances and attitudes turned the Wendell house into a form of time capsule.[2]

The Wendell family furniture at Strawbery Banke can be divided into two groups: a small group of objects from the colonial era, many in the rococo style, and a much larger body of furniture from the federal period.

Figure 11 John Wendell (1737–1820). Taken from a modern photograph of a drawing (current location unknown) dated 1791. (Strawbery Banke Museum, gift of Gerrit van der Woude; photo, Bruce Alexander Photography.)

Eighteenth-Century Furniture

The early objects are associated with the time of John Wendell (1731–1808), Jacob's father. John (fig. 11), the son of Major John and Elizabeth (Quincy) Wendell, was born in Boston. After graduating from Harvard College in 1750, he moved to Portsmouth where he developed an active real-estate business. John's two marriages connected him to several of the most prominent families in Portsmouth and suggest a variety of avenues in which the baroque and rococo furniture in the Wendell collection entered the family. John was married first to Sarah, daughter of Captain Daniel and Elizabeth (Frost) Wentworth of Portsmouth. After her death in 1772, he married Dorothy Sherburne in 1778, a much younger woman who was the daughter of the Honorable Henry and Sarah (Warner) Sherburne, also of Portsmouth. The associations through marriage with the Wentworth, Frost, Warner, and Sherburne families connected John Wendell to many of Portsmouth's oldest and most socially prominent families.[3]

This early part of the Wendell collection includes a New England high chest of drawers of circa 1720 (fig. 12). The drawer arrangement and leg turnings suggest that it was made in Massachusetts; however, little is known about Portsmouth furniture of this period. The drawer fronts are veneered with herringbone edge banding and flitches of crotch walnut, whereas the sides of the upper and lower case are solid walnut. The complex cornice moldings disguise a "secret" or document drawer. The high chest was repaired in Portsmouth in the 1880s by John H. Stickney, a local craftsman who repaired many antiques in the Portsmouth area and had a penchant for signing his work. He inscribed the high chest in pencil: "John H. Stickney/Sept 25 1886/Ports N.H." It was probably Stick-

Figure 12 High chest of drawers, New England, probably Massachusetts, 1700–1730. Walnut, walnut veneer, and maple with pine. H. 65½", W. 39¾", D. 22¼". (Strawbery Banke Museum, gift of Gerrit van der Woude; photo, Bruce Alexander Photography.)

Figure 13 Stretcher-base table, probably Portsmouth, 1740–1780. Maple and pine. H. 27", W. 54", D. 36". (Strawbery Banke Museum, gift of Richard L. Mills; photo, Bruce Alexander Photography.)

ney who added the current reproduction brasses, replaced the stretchers, and made other repairs.[4]

A mid-eighteenth-century stretcher table with turned legs (fig. 13) was given to the museum by Richard L. Mills of Exeter, New Hampshire, in 1972. According to the donor, this table was found in the Wendell house shed in a bad state of disrepair. Mills felt it was worthy of preservation, and he had a new pine top, drawer, and drawer runners made to fit the surviving maple base. The base has traces of red paint over an earlier coat of black. Similar vase-and-ring leg turnings are found on other tables from the region, including an example branded "J. HAVEN" in the Aldrich Memorial at Strawbery Banke.[5]

Figure 14 China table attributed to Robert Harrold, Portsmouth, 1760–1775. Mahogany with soft maple and eastern white pine. H. 27¼″, W. 35⁹⁄₁₆″, D. 23⅜″. (Strawbery Banke Museum, gift of Gerrit van der Woude; photo, Bruce Alexander Photography.)

Figure 15 Side table, Portsmouth, 1760–1775. Mahogany with birch. H. 37″, W. 60¾″, D. 27¼″. (Strawbery Banke Museum, lent by Ronald Bourgeault; photo, Bruce Alexander Photography.)

A rectangular china table dating 1765–1775 is one of the Portsmouth masterpieces in the Wendell collection and probably the most familiar (fig. 14). Six other tables by the same cabinetmaker, probably the English immigrant Robert Harrold (fl. 1765–1792), are known, and nearly all have strong Portsmouth histories. The construction, woods, and decorative details—carved saltire stretchers, pierced finial, brackets, and rail moldings—of this table are characteristic of this group. Like nearly all of these tables, the Wendell example has lost its original pierced gallery.[6]

The Wendell china table descended en suite with a kettle stand that is now in the collection of the Warner House Association in Portsmouth. According to family tradition, both pieces, along with a large sideboard table (fig. 15), were acquired by John Wendell at the sale of the effects of Sir John Wentworth (1737–1820), New Hampshire's last royal governor, when he fled the colony in 1775. Wentworth lived in a large mansion on Pleasant Street, just south of the Wendell house, and served as governor of New Hampshire between 1766 and 1775. He was a graduate of Harvard College (class of 1755) and took his master's degree there in 1758. After working with his father, he went to England in the early 1760s and was living there when he received his appointment as governor. He returned to America and reached Portsmouth by June 1767. With his aristocratic position, English experience, and significant wealth, Wentworth would have been a likely candidate to acquire locally made furniture in the British taste. This tradition of Wentworth ownership, however plausible, is unconfirmed. The objects could have entered the Wendell family through one of any number of channels. However, it is tempting to speculate that the kettle stand, the china table, and the sideboard table are the same as

Figure 16 Pair of armchairs, Portsmouth, 1760–1775. Mahogany with birch. H. 40½″, W. 27″, D. 23″. (Strawbery Banke Museum, gift of Gerrit van der Woude; photo, Bruce Alexander Photography.)

the "1 Mahogany stand $2 [and] 1 Mahogany large Table $6 [and] 1 Mahogany Sideboard $10" listed in John Wendell's estate inventory.[7]

Based on English and Irish designs, the Wendell table is a fine example of sophisticated rococo design in late colonial New Hampshire. It is particularly important for Strawbery Banke's collection because another china table in the group, now at the Carnegie Museum in Pittsburgh, Pennsylvania, was owned originally by Stephen Chase (1742–1805), a Portsmouth merchant and owner of Strawbery Banke's Chase House (built in 1762) from 1799 until his death. Chase's china table probably was the object listed in his inventory as a 3′ mahogany table valued at $4.50 and located in his parlor; it appears in the inventory just before an itemization of tea wares.[8]

The pair of upholstered armchairs illustrated in figure 16 probably were made in Portsmouth in the 1760s or 1770s, also in a very English style, having low proportions, broad seats, and curved or swelled front seat rails. Although these have their original upholstery foundations, they were recovered in 1912–1913 in a "handsome red brocade." Slipcovers (made of a Schumacher reproduction of a 1775–1785 English plate-printed textile and fashioned after a design depicted in John Hamilton Mortimer's *Sergeant-at-Arms Bonfoy, His Son, and John Clementson, Sr.*, ca. 1770) recently were made to cover the soiled brocade. The use of birch as a secondary wood confirms the American origin of these armchairs, and they are related to a relatively large group of chairs with Portsmouth histories. Like the china table, they reflect the sophisticated English-dominated taste in Portsmouth in the 1760s.[9]

Figure 17 Card table (one of a pair), Portsmouth, 1760–1775. Mahogany with eastern white pine, red pine, and birch. H. 27⅝″, W. 35⁵⁄₁₆″, D. 17¹³⁄₁₆″. (Strawbery Banke Museum, gift of Gerrit van der Woude; photo, Bruce Alexander Photography.)

Dating to about the same time, and again probably made in Portsmouth, are a pair of rococo card tables (fig. 17) with Marlborough legs strongly related to those on the china table and sideboard table and with a somewhat unusual wide drawer. William G. Wendell's notes of 1912 indicate that "these tables were in different parts of the house, one being used as a washstand, the other as a tool chest," which may well account for the legs of each having been shortened. The family reclaimed them from their "degradation" (as they put it), had them repaired, and placed them in a parlor.[10]

The rococo side chair illustrated in figure 18 dates 1760–1790. Its legs also have been cut down (about 1"), its side stretchers have been replaced, and its slip seat has modern upholstery over the original frame; however, this chair is significant as a representation of a simple pierced splat and a "Chinese" crest rail that are common Portsmouth patterns.[11]

Six fan-back Windsor side chairs (fig. 19) also are among the early Wendell objects in the collection. Four bear the brand of Joseph Henzey, a

Figure 18 Side chair, Portsmouth, 1760–1790. Birch and maple. H. 35½", W. 21⅝", D. 16⅜". (Strawbery Banke Museum, gift of Gerrit van der Woude; photo, Bruce Alexander Photography.)

Figure 19 Fan-back Windsor side chair (one of a set of six), branded by Joseph Henzey (b. 1743), Philadelphia, Pennsylvania, 1775–1790. Hickory, white oak, yellow poplar, and soft maple. H. 36⅝", W. 22¾", D. 16". (Strawbery Banke Museum, gift of Kenneth E. and Evelyn S. Barrett; photo, Bruce Alexander Photography.)

Figure 20 Box with three drawers, probably Portsmouth, ca. 1770. Walnut with eastern white pine. H. 14⅝", W. 11¹⁵⁄₁₆", D. 17¼". (Strawbery Banke Museum, gift of Gerrit van der Woude; photo, Bruce Alexander Photography.)

noted Windsor chairmaker of Philadelphia; one is unmarked; and the sixth, in poor condition, is branded by James C. Tuttle (ca. 1772–1849) of Salem, Massachusetts. Originally painted green, the chairs are now painted black with gold striping. All seem to have been together since the date of this repainting, probably in the late nineteenth century, and all have a history in the Tibbetts house, just north of the Wendell house on Pleasant Street. It is likely that they came to Portsmouth in the eighteenth century as part of Henzey's large export trade. William G. Wendell probably acquired them as antiques; he gave them as a wedding present in 1953 to his stepdaughter Evelyn and her husband, Kenneth E. Barrett.[12]

A small box with three drawers (fig. 20) represents a type of common, utilitarian furniture made in Portsmouth that rarely survives. It has three dovetailed drawers with rosehead nails securing the bottoms to the backs, suggesting that it was made before 1790. When it was found in the Wendell barn, the box still contained papers and documents.

In addition to the above-mentioned objects that came to Strawbery Banke, the Wendell household included many other important pieces of eighteenth-century Portsmouth and New England furniture that subsequently entered public and private collections. Perhaps most notable among these is a large upholstered rococo couch with scrolled ends and an open back. Other significant early objects are a mahogany dressing table and looking glass in the late baroque style, a Portsmouth blockfront chest of drawers branded "I. SALTER," probably for its original owner, a set of Portsmouth side chairs with pierced splats, and a basin stand with Marlborough legs.[13]

It is presumed that many of these eighteenth-century objects eventually descended from John Wendell to his son, Jacob, although how this transaction took place remains unclear. John's will, written in 1808, the year of his death, left nearly all his estate, including all his real and personal property, to his much-younger wife Dorothy, who continued to live in the Wendell house as a widow. At her death in 1838, Dorothy left only modest amounts to her sons in her will, since they were in difficult financial straits and she wished to avoid having her legacy attached by creditors. Instead, she divided her estate among her daughters-in-law, including Jacob's wife Mehitable. Most of Dorothy's personal goods sold at auction in 1838. The items in her inventory and in the auction list do not closely correspond to the objects later in the Wendell house, although one or two parallels might be drawn. Thus exactly how this cluster of furniture entered into and descended through the family remains somewhat unclear.[14]

Nineteenth-Century Furniture

Understanding the acquisition of the nineteenth-century furniture in the Wendell collection is much more straightforward, although not without its pitfalls in the slippery business of linking surviving objects with terse descriptions in inventories or invoices. The records of Jacob Wendell provide numerous opportunities for identifying the date, source, and original cost of many pieces of family furniture.

Jacob (fig. 21) was the sixth child born to John and Dorothy Wendell. At the time of his birth in 1788, the family fortunes were diminished. Although John intended to send his sons to Harvard, this proved financially impossible, and Jacob was educated in Portsmouth. After completing his education Jacob entered business life and shortly became a merchant and importer of Russian and West Indies goods. His first successes came during the War of 1812, when he profited through privateering and various shipping ventures. He turned from shipping to manufacturing and, in 1815 at the age of twenty-seven, he entered into business with his brother Isaac and others to establish cotton mills on several of the rivers that feed Great Bay. The first structures were built in Dover, and operations began in 1821. Two years later, another mill, the Great Falls Corporation, was built on the Salmon Falls River. For several years these enterprises flourished and brought Jacob handsome profits.[15]

Figure 21 Jacob Wendell (1788–1865). Taken from a modern photograph of a crayon portrait by Seth Wells Cheney (1810–1856) of Boston, ca. 1854. (Strawbery Banke Museum, gift of Gerrit van der Woude; photo, Bruce Alexander Photography.)

In the 1820s Jacob also ran a ship chandlery and hardware store in partnership with his brother Abraham at the corner of State and Water streets in Portsmouth. The commercial panic of 1827–1828 had devastating effects, however, crippling the Wendell brothers financially. The remaining years of Jacob's life were spent in a variety of clerical positions as he attempted to pay off his debts and reestablish the family fortunes.[16]

During the early stages of Jacob's career, he was in the process of purchasing a home and setting up house. On June 21, 1815, Jacob bought the house on Pleasant Street which remained in his family for the next 173 years. About six months later, he began acquiring goods to furnish this large dwelling. A ledger dated 1814–1827 includes a section related to Jacob's household accounts. It is headed "Account of cash pd for sundries for furnishg my house Jan 7, 1816," and includes an itemized list of household goods purchased and services paid for during the 1816–1827 period, such as furnishings, food, clothing, and labor. Many of the nineteenth-century objects in the house can be related to entries in this ledger and, occasionally, to separate itemized bills. Jacob bought directly from Portsmouth cabinetmakers, but he also purchased a significant amount of furniture, some of it presumably used, at auction from Samuel Larkin and others. Jacob also occasionally went outside Portsmouth for his purchases.[17]

On August 16, 1816, just about a year after he bought the house, Jacob married Mehitable Rindge Rogers (d. 1859), the only child of Mark and Sarah (Rindge) Rogers of Portsmouth. (Her father was a first cousin, on his mother's side, of Sir John Wentworth, the purported original owner of the china table [fig. 14] and other rococo objects, suggesting another way in which they entered the family.) Jacob and Mehitable lived the remainder of their lives together in their Pleasant Street home.[18]

The nineteenth-century furniture from the Wendell family is rich in its associations with local makers and diverse in its variety of forms and materials. One of the earlier examples is a mahogany chest of drawers

Figure 22 Chest of drawers, attributed to Langley Boardman (1774–1833), Portsmouth, 1795–1810. Mahogany with eastern white pine. H. 35¾″, W. 43″, D. 22⅞″. (Strawbery Banke Museum, gift of Gerrit van der Woude; photo, Bruce Alexander Photography.)

with a serpentine front and canted front corners (fig. 22). This characteristic Portsmouth example is part of a group that includes a chest at the Society for the Preservation of New England Antiquities's Rundlet-May House thought to have been purchased in 1802 by James Rundlet from the cabinetmaker Langley Boardman (1774–1833). Boardman was a well-known local craftsman, and this chest of drawers joins a significant group of work from his shop already at Strawbery Banke, including a massive sideboard, a secretary, and a group of chairs. The Wendell chest lacks the string inlay and quarter-fans found on some examples, but otherwise conforms to the norm for these large, bold chests. The mid-eighteenth-century plate brasses are replacements, probably added at the instigation of James Stanwood or Barrett Wendell in the late nineteenth or early twentieth century with the thought that the chest was made a generation earlier than is actually the case.[19]

Figuring prominently in this body of furnishings is a subgroup of furniture acquired by Jacob from the Portsmouth cabinetmaking firm of Jonathan Judkins (1780–1844) and William Senter (1783–1827), active at a variety of locations on State Street from 1808 to 1826. These include a pair of mahogany card tables (fig. 23) and a mahogany sofa (fig. 24) sold to Jacob on June 7, 1816, for a total of $70, and paid for by him on July 31. The card tables are square with an elliptic front, half-elliptic ends, and ovolo corners, a design often used in Portsmouth card tables and dressing tables and echoed in the configuration of the sideboard discussed below. The tables are distinguished by the use of rosewood veneer and by their pointed, ebonized feet. The sofa (covered with twentieth-century horse-

Figure 23 Card table (one of a pair), by Judkins and Senter (fl. 1808–1826), Portsmouth, 1816. Mahogany, mahogany veneer, and rosewood veneer with eastern white pine, birch, and white oak. H. 30″, W. 37″, D. 18″. (Strawbery Banke Museum, gift of Gerrit van der Woude; photo, Bruce Alexander Photography.)

Figure 24 Sofa, by Judkins and Senter, Portsmouth, 1816. Mahogany with beech, birch, eastern white pine, and ash. H. 35⅝″, W. 73¾″, D. 24¼″. (Strawbery Banke Museum, gift of Gerrit van der Woude; photo, Bruce Alexander Photography.)

Figure 25 Detail of sofa illustrated in fig. 24. (Photo, New Hampshire Historical Society.)

Figure 26 Sideboard, by Judkins and Senter (fl. 1808–1826), Portsmouth, 1815. Mahogany, mahogany veneer, birch veneer, bird's-eye maple veneer, *Casuarina* spp. veneer, and light- and dark-wood inlays, with eastern white pine, basswood, yellow birch, and unidentified tropical hardwood. H. 43″, W. 70½″, D. 22⅛″. (Strawbery Banke Museum, gift of Gerrit van der Woude; photo, Bruce Alexander Photography.)

hair upholstery) has multiple horizontal reeds along the crest rail and is related to the card tables through the use of multiple ring turnings and incised rings on the legs (fig. 25).[20]

The Judkins and Senter sideboard illustrated in figure 26 is documented in several ways. It is signed "Made/& [?]/January 22/1815/by J & Senter" and bears the brand "J. HAVEN," possibly for Joshua Haven, who lived in the Pleasant Street home when it was purchased by Jacob Wendell in June 1815, or for Joseph Haven, a wealthy merchant who lived across the street from the Wendell house from 1780 to 1820. Judkins and Senter had reacquired the chest by December 20, 1815, when they sold it for $70 to Jacob. (One wonders if the sideboard was merely left behind in the house by Joshua Haven.) Jacob's ledger notes "Cash pd. Side Board—$70—" on January 1, 1816. A drawer in the sideboard also bears later inscriptions, difficult to decipher, but that include the name "George Wendell" and the date of "July 18, 1838," each written twice. The handwriting of these is a somewhat childish scrawl, and the inscriptions may represent the doodling of Jacob's son, George Blunt Wendell, who was age seven in 1838.[21]

Figure 27 Lolling chair, Portsmouth, 1815–1825. Mahogany with soft maple and eastern white pine. H. 44″, W. 26⅜″. D. 21⅜″. (Strawbery Banke Museum, gift of Gerrit van der Woude; photo, Bruce Alexander Photography.)

Figure 28 Lolling chair, Portsmouth, 1810–1820. Mahogany and birch veneer with soft maple, beech, and eastern white pine. H. 44″, W. 22½″, D. 18¼″. (Strawbery Banke Museum, gift of Gerrit van der Woude; photo, Bruce Alexander Photography.)

The sideboard, like the high chest (fig. 12) and other Wendell furniture, was repaired by a local craftsman in the late nineteenth century, probably at the urging of family descendant James R. Stanwood (1847–1910), who lived in the house nearly his whole life. A penciled inscription on the underside of the top reads: "Repaired by John H. Stickney May 25, 1887, in the Old Custom House Penhallow St. Portsmouth, N.H." A century later, the sideboard was treated by the Boston conservation firm of Robert Mussey, whose work brought back to light the magnificent color contrasts that had been obscured by years of dirt and discoloration.[22]

Jacob's other purchases from Judkins and Senter included, along with repair work and a variety of tasks, a secretary valued at $36 (private collection) on September 6, 1813, a bedstead priced at $19 (private collection), a set of chairs ($28), a table and stand ($11.50), a work table ($10), a second table and stand ($14.50), "pieces round hearth" ($1.50), a bed cornice ($13), a window cornice ($7.50), and a bed top ($2) documented in the bill of May 10, 1816, that includes the sideboard, sofa, and card tables now at Strawbery Banke.[23]

Figure 29 Desk, Portsmouth, 1810–1820. Mahogany, mahogany veneer, birch veneer, and rosewood veneer with eastern white pine. H. 34¼", W. 30", D. 17⅞". (Strawbery Banke Museum, gift of Gerrit van der Woude; photo, Bruce Alexander Photography.)

Figure 30 Desk illustrated in fig. 29 in open position. (Photo, Bruce Alexander Photography.)

Figure 31 Card table, Portsmouth, 1820–1825. Mahogany with eastern white pine, basswood, and birch. H. 31", W. 36½", D. 18½". (Strawbery Banke Museum, gift of Gerrit van der Woude; photo, Bruce Alexander Photography.)

Two Portsmouth lolling chairs probably were acquired by Jacob during the 1810s–1820s. One (fig. 27) is still covered in its original black horsehair upholstery secured by cast-brass nails and has mahogany arms and legs with ring turnings and carving. It closely resembles an example at the Rundlet-May house that shares the same curved arms and style of carving and was owned originally by Samuel Lord of Portsmouth. The second (fig. 28) has been reupholstered (in a modern yellow brocade given to

Figure 32 Dressing table and dressing glass, Portsmouth (table) and England or Portsmouth (glass), 1815–1825. Mahogany and mahogany veneer with pine. (Table), H. 37¾″, W. 39¼″, D. 18¼″; (glass), H. 21¼″, W. 15¼″, D. 7⅞″. (Strawbery Banke Museum, gift of Gerrit van der Woude; photo, Bruce Alexander Photography.)

Edith Wendell by Henry Francis du Pont) and has mahogany arms and legs embellished with a band of inlaid figured birch at the juncture of the front and side seat rails. This chair bears an ink inscription reading $12 on the inside of the rear seat rail, perhaps an indication of the original price of the chair or the chair frame.[24]

Figured birch also distinguishes a small desk (fig. 29) that exhibits the strong color contrasts so typical of Portsmouth furniture, created by playing dark mahogany and rosewood veneer against light, figured birch veneer. The desk, which is made as one piece, opens to reveal a slanted writing surface originally covered with broadcloth and a row of small drawers for writing implements; the upper writing flap conceals a row of pigeonholes in the compartment underneath (fig. 30).[25]

Two objects in the collection may date from the 1820s. One, a mahogany card table (fig. 31), might well be the "Grecean card table" Jacob pur-

Figure 33 High-post bedstead, Massachusetts, probably Boston or Salem, 1800–1810, with later cornice, ca. 1830. Mahogany, mahogany veneer, and light- and dark-wood inlay with pine. H. 88¾″, W. 56¹¹⁄₁₆″, D. 79″. (Strawbery Banke Museum, gift of Gerrit van der Woude; photo, Bruce Alexander Photography.)

Figure 34 Bedchamber, Wendell house. Photograph by Lafayette Newell and Co., ca. 1902. (Wendell Collection, Strawbery Banke Museum.)

chased from an unspecified source for $17.50 in September 1821. The four arched legs terminating in volutes and twin acanthus-carved pedestals suggest that this table would have been considered Grecian in the 1820s. Its shape and basswood secondary wood points toward a New Hampshire origin. The leaves of the top, when opened, swivel to lie flat for gaming. The second, a dressing table (fig. 32), is also of mahogany and has elaborate turned legs. It is distinguished by having its original dressing box, which is fitted to the top of the table. On September 29, 1825, Jacob Wendell bought at auction a "mahogany dressing table" for $12.25, which conceivably could be this object, especially since the heavy ring and twist turnings of the legs suggest this date. For many years the dressing table has been associated with a small dressing glass, possibly from Portsmouth or England.[26]

Although Jacob patronized Portsmouth firms frequently, he occasionally purchased objects produced in other areas. A case in point is a mahogany bed (fig. 33), probably made in Massachusetts. Although Jacob purchased some beds locally, from Judkins and Senter and others, the carving, inlay, and other details of this bed point to an origin in Boston or

Figure 35 Double settee, Portsmouth, ca. 1815. Sweet gum, soft maple, birch, and hickory. H. 35″, W. 45¾″, D. 18″. (Strawbery Banke Museum, gift of Gerrit van der Woude; photo, Bruce Alexander Photography.)

Salem. Whereas the carved and inlaid footposts are fashioned in a delicate manner typical of the 1800–1810 period, the thick cornice rods and bulbous gilt terminals clearly are later additions. William G. Wendell described this cornice as consisting of "heavy bars of wood, round, painted white and terminating in fluted bulbs, gilded. These bars matched the curtain bars over the windows [also now at Strawbery Banke], and were used to support heavy curtains in winter." These early bed hangings and the window curtain bars can be seen in a 1902 picture of a bedchamber (fig. 34).[27]

The collection is enhanced by the presence of two large sets of fancy painted seating furniture. One set, known in the family for obvious reasons as the "red set," includes eight side chairs, two armchairs, and two double settees that probably are of Portsmouth manufacture (fig. 35). They resemble a set of six chairs acquired by James Rundlet in 1806 from James Folsom of Portsmouth at a cost of $4 each. The red set has a curious history. In 1912, William G. Wendell noted that "this set was formerly in the best parlor (sitting room) and was painted white and gold. It had gotten into rather shabby condition, as regards the paint but the frame and seats were in good order. Many of the chairs, however, had been relegated to the attic. In 1912 one of the chairs was sent to a local furniture painter, to be repainted, with a view of retouching the entire set. In scraping off the white and gold paint the man came upon an entirely different pattern underneath, showing the chairs originally to have been painted red and gold. The design on the back of the chairs is that of three ostrich plumes with ends curving." The entire set was repainted red and gold in 1913, following the original design.[28]

The second set of chairs, however, has survived in pristine condition.

It includes two armchairs, twelve side chairs, and a triple-back settee (figs. 36, 37). They are painted in gold and black, with eagles on the crest rail (fig. 38) and a row of floral decoration along the seat rails. Although the basic formula for the decoration on each crest rail is consistent—an eagle, two leaves and tendrils, and a cluster of berries—the execution varies considerably from chair to chair, with minor differences evident, for example, in the number and composition of the berries. (It is possible that the leaves and stylized berries depicted are strawberries, since they resemble the ones depicted on polychrome painted pearlware of the period.) This set was purchased by Jacob in January 1816 from Bailey and Willis, retail merchants at 109 Front Street in New York City. He paid $30 for the settee, $5.25 apiece for the fourteen chairs, and $2.50 for packing (described as "bandages" in Jacob's ledger) to have the chairs shipped from New York City on board the schooner *Friendship*. Jacob's order also included dry white lead and pork, suggesting that Bailey and Willis were retail merchants rather than furniture makers.[29]

Because of the large number of chairs, the unusual triple settee, and the distinctive decoration of the set, the "gilt" or "eagle gilt" suite can be traced easily in various house inventories and lists. Caroline Quincy Wendell's inventory, taken in 1890, listed these pieces in the south parlor and described them as "a rush-bottomed set in buff, with gilt ornamentation, each piece bearing a design upon the back representing an Eagle grasping his prey, specified as follows: 1 Settee, triple design, 2 Armchairs, 12 chairs."[30]

Figure 36 Triple settee, New York City, 1816. Hickory, yellow poplar, soft maple, and ash. H. 34", W. 71⅝", D. 19¾". (Strawbery Banke Museum, gift of Gerrit van der Woude; photo, Bruce Alexander Photography.)

Figure 37 Armchair, New York City, 1816. Hickory, yellow poplar, soft maple, and ash. H. 33⅞″, W. 19¾″, D. 16⅛″. (Strawbery Banke Museum, gift of Gerrit van der Woude; photo, Bruce Alexander Photography.)

Figure 38 Side chair (detail), New York City, 1816. Hickory, yellow poplar, soft maple, and ash. H. 33⅝″, W. 18″, D. 16⅛″. (Strawbery Banke Museum, gift of Gerrit van der Woude; photo, Bruce Alexander Photography.)

Figure 39 Windsor side chair, Portsmouth, 1815–1820. Later painted decoration by George N. Porter (fl. 1856–1867), Portsmouth, 1856–1860. Birch, eastern white pine, and soft maple. H. 34¾″, W. 15¾″, D. 15¼″. (Strawbery Banke Museum, gift of Gerrit van der Woude; photo, Bruce Alexander Photography.)

Figure 41 Canterbury, by James C. Brown, Portsmouth, 1846 (before restoration). Mahogany and mahogany veneer with eastern white pine. H. 21″, W. 20″, D. 17″. (Strawbery Banke Museum, gift of Gerrit van der Woude; photo, Bruce Alexander Photography.)

Figure 40 Stenciled label of George N. Porter on bottom of chair illustrated in fig. 39. (Photo, Bruce Alexander Photography.)

Three Windsor side chairs and one armchair, fitted with rockers, from another group of chairs also came to Strawbery Banke (fig. 39). A stenciled label (fig. 40) on the underside of the seat of several of them reads "G. N. PORTER/FURNITURE/PAINTER/NO 4 LADD ST./PORTSMOUTH, N.H." Porter was active in the mid-nineteenth century and was responsible for one of the four coats of paint these chairs have had. Whether or not he did the current coat (green with yellow striping and lyres flanked by flowers at the center of the crest rail) is unclear. Porter is listed in the Portsmouth city directories at the 4 Ladd Street address in 1856–1857 but had moved to 7 Ladd Street by the time of the 1860–1861 directory. He is listed in the directories in 1867, but not in 1873.[31]

One unusual later object in the house is a canterbury (fig. 41), a form uncommon in American furniture, named (according to tradition) for one of the archbishops of Canterbury and used to hold sheet music. It has a penciled signature on the underside of the drawer that reads "J. C. Brown/Maker/March 21st 1846." In the 1850s, James C. Brown lived on Court Street and worked as a cabinetmaker for the firm of E. M. Brown and Company on Market Street. He may have made the canterbury while working on his own in the 1840s, although information about his career remains sparse.[32]

Although the Wendell furnishings that did not come to Strawbery Banke were scattered widely in 1988 and 1989, an important group was acquired by Ronald Bourgeault, who also purchased the house from the family's estate. Bourgeault generously loaned five pieces of furniture to Strawbery Banke, including a timepiece with a gilt case and eglomise panels (fig. 42), one of which is inscribed "S. WILLARD'S PATENT." The clock is additionally documented on the back of the throat panel, "Painted by John R. Penniman, Boston, May 1st, 1811" and on the back of the eglomise panel on the door "Enamelled by John R. Penniman, Boston, May 1, 1811." According to Penniman scholar Carol Damon Andrews, these are the "only such panels [Penniman] is known to have signed and dated." The clock seems to have been in the parlor since at least the 1830s, and it hangs in the same position against the south wall in all photographs. It may have been purchased at auction by Jacob.[33]

The Bourgeault loan also includes a mahogany chest of drawers (fig. 43) with an elliptic front and ovolo corners, reeded columns, and turned feet

Figure 42 Patent timepiece, by Simon Willard (1753–1848), with painting by John R. Penniman (1782–1841), Boston, Massachusetts, 1811. Mahogany, gilded wood, and glass. H. 43″, W. 10½″, D. 4″. (Strawbery Banke Museum, lent by Ronald Bourgeault; photo, Bruce Alexander Photography.)

characteristic of Portsmouth work. The chest is distinguished by having backboards that are dovetailed to the sides (fig. 44) rather than nailed into a rabbet. A large dining table (fig. 45), also loaned by Bourgeault, has six legs and deep hinged leaves supported on each side by two fly legs. The legs are decorated with simple ring turnings.[34]

A mahogany cradle (fig. 46) may be by Judkins and Senter. (Jacob and Mehitable had eight children born between 1817 and 1831.) On June 10, 1817, Judkins and Senter billed Jacob $10 for a "Cradle (Mahogany)" but noted on the bill that he would receive a $1 "discount on cradle." Jacob was cutting it close; his first son, Mark Rogers, was born on June 18. A "Mahogany Cradle" valued at $9 was subsequently entered on Jacob's ledger for August 16, 1817.[35]

The Wendells were not alone in Portsmouth, of course, in preserving their family homestead and treasuring their family possessions. The Wendell "experience" in this regard forms a remarkable parallel, in many respects, to that of the house built by James Rundlet on Middle Street in

Figure 43 Chest of drawers, Portsmouth, 1815–1820. Mahogany and mahogany veneer with eastern white pine. H. 39″, W. 45″, D. 20″. (Strawbery Banke Museum, lent by Ronald Bourgeault; photo, Bruce Alexander Photography.)

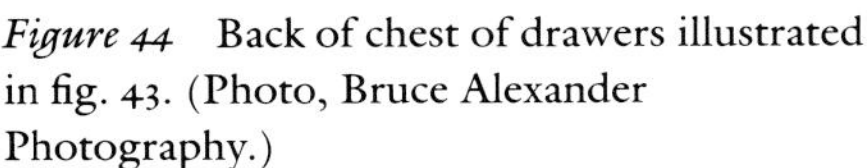

Figure 44 Back of chest of drawers illustrated in fig. 43. (Photo, Bruce Alexander Photography.)

Figure 45 Dining table, Portsmouth, 1810–1820. Mahogany with birch. H. 29¼″, W. (open) 67½″, W. (closed) 17½″, D. 56″. (Strawbery Banke Museum, lent by Ronald Bourgeault; photo, Bruce Alexander Photography.)

1807–1808 and now owned by the Society for the Preservation of New England Antiquities.[36] Fortunately, the Rundlet-May house has survived with its furnishings more or less intact, and they, too, are documented in the business papers of their original owner. But such instances are indeed rare and therefore the more to be treasured. The Wendell collection presents a challenging opportunity for ongoing research, as the process of matching bills, receipts, and inventories with surviving objects continues and as our understanding of Portsmouth cabinetmaking and taste increases in depth.

Figure 46 Cradle, Portsmouth, 1810–1820. Mahogany with pine. H. 26½", W. 38", D. 23½". (Strawbery Banke Museum, lent by Ronald Bourgeault; photo, Bruce Alexander Photography.)

ACKNOWLEDGMENTS The authors are deeply grateful to Brock Jobe and staff of the Society for the Preservation of New England Antiquities (SPNEA) for generously sharing their research on Portsmouth furniture. Jobe's catalogue contains more detailed information on the ornamental and construction characteristics of Portsmouth furniture than is possible to give here and will place the Wendell objects into a deeper context. We are also grateful to SPNEA for sharing the results of R. Bruce Hoadley's wood analysis on many of the objects illustrated here. Any mistakes in identification or attribution made here are the sole responsibility of the authors. We are also indebted to Jane C. Nylander, Carolyn Parsons Roy, Rodney Rowland, and Greg Colati at Strawbery Banke Museum; to the librarians at the Baker Library, Harvard Business School, and the Portsmouth Athenaeum; to Ronald Bourgeault; and to Mr. and Mrs. K. E. Barrett for their assistance.

1. The Wendell house, family, and furnishings are the subject of research by Strawbery Banke Museum on a wide variety of fronts. For a capsule history of the house and its owners, see the entry by Jane C. Nylander in Sarah L. Giffen and Kevin D. Murphy, eds., *"A Noble and Dignified Stream": The Piscataqua Region in the Colonial Revival, 1860–1930* (York, Me.: Old York Historical Society, 1992), cat. 4; an entry by Anne Masury (cat. 24) on the Wendell gardens is in the same volume. The Wendell house is discussed in James Leo Garvin, "Academic Architecture and the Building Trades in the Piscataqua Region of New Hampshire and Maine, 1715–1815" (Ph.D. dissertation, Boston University, 1983), pp. 304–6.

2. The Wendell collection formed a significant part of the study of Portsmouth furniture by Brock W. Jobe, formerly of the Society for the Preservation of New England Antiquities, and several of them were included in the exhibition catalogue that resulted from that project, where they are treated at greater length and more contextually than is possible here. See Brock W. Jobe, ed., *Portsmouth Furniture: Masterworks from the New Hampshire Seacoast* (Boston: SPNEA, 1993).

3. For John Wendell, see his biography in Clifford K. Shipton, *Biographical Sketches of Those Who Attended Harvard College in the Classes 1746–1750 with Bibliographical and Other Notes*, Sibley's Harvard Graduates, vol. 12 (1746–1750) (Boston: Massachusetts Historical Society, 1962), pp. 592–97. For society in colonial Portsmouth, see James L. Garvin, "Portsmouth and the Piscataqua: Social History and Material Culture," *Historical New Hampshire* 26, no. 2 (Summer 1971): 3–48, and Charles E. Clark, *The Eastern Frontier: The Settlement of Northern New England, 1610–1763* (New York: Knopf, 1970).

4. Stickney is listed as a cabinetmaker and furniture repairer in the Portsmouth city directories from 1860–1861 until 1901.

5. The table is accession number 1980.606.

6. The form is discussed in Brock W. Jobe's entry in Alexandra W. Rollins, ed., *Treasures of State: Fine and Decorative Art in the Diplomatic Reception Rooms of the U.S. Department of State* (New York: Abrams, 1991), cat. 61.

7. The kettle stand is illustrated in *Important Americana*, sale 5810 (New York: Sotheby's, January 26–28, 1989), lot 1455. In his annotation to the picture of the parlor in 1912, William G. Wendell noted: "These tables are supposed to have belonged to the last Colonial Governor, Sir John Wentworth, and are thought to have been bought in on the confiscation of his property and ensuing auction by John Wendell." See William G. Wendell, "The Jacob

Wendell House" (typescript, Strawbery Banke Museum, October 1912), p. 8. The sideboard table, first published by Luke Vincent Lockwood in 1913 along with several other Wendell family things, has been repaired and refinished. For Wentworth, see John Wentworth, *The Wentworth Genealogy* (Chicago 1870), 1: 313–20. See also David R. Starbuck, ed., "America's First Summer Resort: John Wentworth's Eighteenth-Century Plantation in Wolfeboro, New Hampshire," a special issue of *New Hampshire Archeologist* 30, no. 1 (1989), for a discussion of Wentworth's sophisticated taste. Rockingham County Probate Records, Exeter, New Hampshire, docket 7985.

8. The Chase china table is illustrated in Morrison H. Heckscher and Leslie Greene Bowman, *American Rococo, 1750–1775: Elegance in Ornament* (New York and Los Angeles: The Metropolitan Museum of Art and the Los Angeles County Museum of Art, 1992), cat. 102. Chase's inventory is in Rockingham County Probate Records, Exeter, New Hampshire, docket 7381.

9. The authors are grateful to Brock W. Jobe for sharing information about this important group of Portsmouth upholstered chairs. The Wendell family also owned a related chair; see *Important Americana*, lot 1451. The Mortimer painting is in the collection of the Yale Center for British Art, New Haven, Conn. The SPNEA owns a very similar English chair.

10. See William G. Wendell, "The Jacob Wendell House," p. 8.

11. See Brock W. Jobe and Myrna Kaye, *New England Furniture: The Colonial Era, Selections from the Society for the Preservation of New England Antiquities* (Boston: Houghton Mifflin, 1984), cat. 126.

12. For Henzey and Tuttle, see Charles Santore, *The Windsor Style in America*, 2 vols. (Philadelphia: Running Press, 1987), 2: 254, 267. See also *Philadelphia: Three Centuries of American Art* (Philadelphia: Philadelphia Museum of Art, 1976), pp. 156–58.

13. For more on the couch now in the Winterthur Museum, see Robert F. Trent, "The Wendell Couch," *Maine Antique Digest* 19, no. 2 (February 1991): 34D–37D. The dressing table (lot 1453) and chest of drawers (lot 1454) are illustrated in *Important Americana*; see also lot 1449 (basin table). The rococo side chairs are in a private collection.

14. Estate papers of John Wendell (docket 7985) and Dorothy Wendell (docket 13503), Rockingham County Probate Records, Exeter, New Hampshire. A handwritten "List of Articles Remaining on Hand," based on John Wendell's inventory, bears pencil notations, probably in Jacob Wendell's hand, as to the disposition of individual items, which were distributed among members of the family and others, or marked as "gone." The list indicates that, although some items were dispersed, much of John's furniture remained in the family. See the folder titled "Inventories, 1827–29," in case 14 of the Wendell Papers, Baker Library. We are grateful to Brock Jobe for bringing this document to our attention.

15. Alexander Du Bin, *Wendell Family* (Philadelphia: Historical Publication Society, n.d.), p. 5. For John's later career, see his biography in *Sibley's Harvard Graduates* noted above. Jacob's life is amply documented in the family papers at the Portsmouth Athenaeum and the Baker Library at the Harvard Business School. Capsule information is given in James Rindge Stanwood, *Direct Ancestry of the Late Jacob Wendell of Portsmouth, New Hampshire* (Boston: David Clapp & Son, 1882), pp. 28–31.

16. Stanwood, *Direct Ancestry of the Late Jacob Wendell*, pp. 29–30.

17. Wendell purchased the house from John Dean of Newburyport, merchant, for $5,910. Rockingham County Registry of Deeds, Exeter, New Hampshire, 207: 170. The ledger is catalogued in the Baker Library at the Harvard Business School as part of the Jacob Wendell papers and as Ledger 2, 1814–27 (number IB–6) (hereafter referred to as Ledger 2).

18. Stanwood, *Direct Ancestry of the Late Jacob Wendell*, pp. 30–31. For the Wentworth connection, see M. A. DeWolfe Howe, *Barrett Wendell and His Letters* (Boston: Atlantic Monthly Press, 1924), p. 8.

19. The Rundlet chest is illustrated in Penny J. Sander, ed., *Elegant Embellishments: Furnishings from New England Homes, 1660–1860* (Boston: Society for the Preservation of New England Antiquities, 1982), cat. 59. See also Brock W. Jobe's entry on the form in Rollins, *Treasures of State*, cat. 115. For Boardman, see *Plain and Elegant, Rich and Common: Documented New Hampshire Furniture* (Concord: New Hampshire Historical Society, 1979), pp. 141–42. Furniture associated with Boardman in the Strawbery Banke collection includes a set of chairs (1974.43-44), a sideboard (1974.653), and a secretary (1983.6) inscribed by Ebenezer Lord as having been made in Boardman's shop.

20. *Documented New Hampshire Furniture*, cats. 9–10; see also pp. 147–48, 151 for information on Judkins and Senter. Portsmouth examples largely were overlooked in Benjamin A.

Hewitt, Patricia E. Kane, and Gerald W. R. Ward, *The Work of Many Hands: Card Tables in Federal America, 1790–1820* (New Haven, Conn.: Yale University Art Gallery, 1982).

21. *Documented New Hampshire Furniture*, cat. 7. A closely related example is in the collection of the New Hampshire Historical Society. The deed that recorded when Jacob bought the house mentions that it is "now in the occupation of Joshua Haven"; see Rockingham County Registry of Deeds, Exeter, New Hampshire, 207: 170. Joseph Haven lived across the street from the Wendell house; see Charles Caleb Gurney, *Portsmouth Historic and Picturesque* (1902; reprint, Portsmouth, N.H.: Strawbery Banke, Inc., 1981), p. 80. The various possibilities concerning the J. Haven brand are discussed in Myrna Kaye, "Marked Portsmouth Furniture," *Antiques* 113, no. 5 (May 1978): 1101–2.

22. Conservation report, Robert Mussey, Inc., April 20, 1990, in object file 1988.228.

23. These bills are in case 13, folder 4, Wendell papers, Baker Library.

24. This chair apparently was a favorite of Edith Wendell's, who was photographed in it ca. 1930 holding her pet dog. Among the many related examples are chairs at the Metropolitan Museum of Art, Bayou Bend, the Anglo-American Art Museum in Baton Rouge, and ones illustrated in *American Antiques from Israel Sack Collection*, 9 vols. (Washington, D.C.: Highland House Publishers, 1976), 5: 4210, and Oscar P. Fitzgerald, *Three Centuries of American Furniture* (New York: Gramercy Publishing Company, 1985), fig. V–7, p. 90.

25. It has not been possible to pinpoint the acquisition of this object in Jacob's papers. He purchased "1 Gentleman's writing desk" at auction for $9.25 on July 31, 1813 (Jacob Wendell papers, Baker Library, IB-6, folder 4), but this form is usually called a lady's writing desk (see Charles F. Montgomery, *American Furniture: The Federal Period in the Henry Francis du Pont Winterthur Museum* [New York: Viking, 1966], cat. 193). For other related examples, see *American Antiques from Israel Sack Collection*, 1: 470, 2: 801, 7: 5,315; and Edwin J. Hipkiss, *Eighteenth-Century American Arts: The M. and M. Karolik Collection* (Cambridge, Mass.: Harvard University Press for the Museum of Fine Arts, Boston, 1941), cat. 31.

26. Ledger 2, p. 62. The bill is in the Wendell papers at the Baker Library. The shape of the card table (square with an elliptic front and half-elliptic ends) was found only rarely by Benjamin A. Hewitt on earlier tables with turned and straight legs, and then only on tables from Salem, Massachusetts, and northward (Hewitt, Kane, and Ward, *The Work of Many Hands*, pp. 69, 188). A painted table and washstand originally owned by Jacob are illustrated in *Antiques* 128, no. 3 (September 1985): 347. A painted dressing table, originally owned by Abraham Wendell, was acquired by the Abby Aldrich Rockefeller Folk Art Center in 1974; it is discussed in a letter from Richard Miller, Associate Curator, December 19, 1989, Strawbery Banke curatorial files.

27. The bed is described in William G. Wendell, "The Jacob Wendell House," p. 35. For a remarkably similar example attributed to Boston or Salem, see Montgomery, *American Furniture*, cat. 1. It is not clear that the cornice rods have always been associated with the bed now at Strawbery Banke, although such was the case in 1988.

28. For the Folsom chairs, see *Documented New Hampshire Furniture*, cat. 5. William G. Wendell, "The Jacob Wendell House," p. 31. For a view of a settee prior to repainting, see Luke Vincent Lockwood, *Colonial Furniture in America*, 2nd ed. (New York: Charles Scribner's Sons, 1913), fig. 635; a side chair after repainting is illustrated in fig. 604. An 1890 inventory described them as being "white, with foliated ornamentation in gilt and black"; see a photocopy of a manuscript copy of the "Inventory of Furniture, Etc., Belonging to the Personal Estate of Caroline Quincy Wendell," in the handwriting of James Stanwood, in the Strawbery Banke curatorial files. In May of 1992 Strawbery Banke purchased a pair of red Portsmouth fancy painted side chairs with rush seats with a history in the family of Mr. and Mrs. Barrett ("Bud") Wendell of Beverly Farms, Massachusetts.

29. Benjamin Bailey and Walter Willis are listed as partners in New York City directories at 109 Front Street in the 1810s. We are grateful to Deborah Dependahl Waters for providing information on Bailey and Willis; see her letter of May 23, 1991, in the object file 1980.230. Bailey and Willis's bill is in the Jacob Wendell papers at Baker Library; the purchase also is recorded in Ledger 2, p. 63. Related chairs have been published in many works, including Roderic H. Blackburn, *Cherry Hill: The History and Collections of a Van Rensselaer Family* (1976), p. 86 (including a triple settee); *Fine American Furniture*, sale 5883 (New York: Sotheby's, June 21, 1989), lot 346 (very similar side chairs); Zilla Rider Lea, ed., *The Ornamented Chair: Its Development in America (1700–1890)* (Rutland, Vt.: Tuttle, 1960), figs. 25, 33, 34.

30. "Inventory of Furniture . . . Belonging to . . . Caroline Quincy Wendell."

31. Portsmouth city directories. Porter's ad in the 1867 directory refers to him as a "Furni-

ture & House Painter, and Grainer." Strawbery Banke's collection also includes a pair of chairs with a history in the Goodwin family; one with Porter's stencil and the other branded by J. and G. Brown.

32. Information on James C. Brown is derived from the Portsmouth city directories. For Edmund Brown, see Jane C. Giffen, "New Hampshire Cabinetmakers and Allied Craftsmen, 1790–1850: A Check List," *Antiques* 94, no. 1 (July 1968): 79.

33. See Carol Damon Andrews, "John Ritto Penniman (1782–1841): An Ingenious New England Artist," *Antiques* 120, no. 1 (July 1981): 149 (quotation), 166 (checklist). The clock was in the Sotheby's sale (sale 5810) containing most of the Wendell things (lot 1382), but did not sell. It was subsequently acquired from the Wendell estate by the current owner.

34. The chest was auctioned at Sotheby's Arcade Auction (New York: Sotheby's, January 26, 1989), sale 1269, lot 534. The table was also auctioned at Sotheby's Arcade Auction on January 26, 1989 (lot 482).

35. The bill for the cradle is in the Jacob Wendell papers at Baker Library; the corresponding ledger entry is in Ledger 2, p. 61. Jacob's children are listed in Stanwood, *The Direct Ancestry of the Late Jacob Wendell*, p. 31. The cradle was acquired by the current owner directly from the Wendell estate. In 1988, it was located in a storage area on the second floor of the barn at the rear of the house.

36. See Robert D. Mussey, Jr., "Rundlet-May House, Portsmouth, New Hampshire," *Antiques* 129, no. 3 (March 1986): 642–44.

Book Reviews

Clement E. Conger and Mary K. Itsell; Alexandra W. Rollins, editor, Will Brown, photographer. *Treasures of State: Fine and Decorative Arts in the Diplomatic Reception Rooms of the U.S. Department of State*. New York: Abrams, 1991. 497 pp.; 422 color and 8 bw illus., bibliography, index. $95.00.

Clement E. Conger has assembled for the State Department's diplomatic reception rooms one of the country's premier collections of Americana. *Treasures of State* is a handsome production that makes this collection available to scholars and collectors. Distinguished decorative arts scholars have catalogued 316 important objects (furnishings made in America or pertinent to our democratic heritage), approximately half of it furniture, the rest ceramics, silver, paintings, sculpture, prints, and maps. With the exceptions of a few early maps and some late-nineteenth-century paintings and sculpture, the decorative arts collection dates from the formative years in United States history: the decades just prior to the Revolution, and the era of the new republic. The furniture was almost all made in the mid-Atlantic and New England areas. Will Brown's fine color photographs of the objects and elegant period-room settings enhance the detailed catalogue discussions.

Conger's inspired vision of transforming the State Department's sterile post-war architectural spaces with their "airport decor" into a celebration of the best of American architectural and decorative arts style has been a noble task. The transformation that he has effected in once-dreary institutional offices is truly remarkable. Before and after views of the various rooms offer a particularly interesting aside to the catalogue. Conger and his formidable team of architects—Edward Vason Jones, Walter Macomber, John Blatteau, and Allan Greenberg—have given the nation's ceremonial functions of state an appropriately dignified setting. They worked Herculean wonders creating spectacular settings to showcase the collection and to provide an appropriately impressive background for conducting affairs of state. The settings alone would charm and impress any diplomat.

Introductory essays explain the origins and significance of the collection. Wendell Garrett, in "A National Collection: Treasures of State," calls the Diplomatic Reception Rooms at the Department of State "one of the nation's least-known cultural treasures." He writes that the icons of our national heritage displayed here reveal "high American culture" to students and the visiting public: "These pieces of craftsmanship are used to elucidate an important aspect of the early republic—the fact that America shared in the elegance and grandeur of the age of Enlightenment."

Robert C. Williams and James H. Lide discuss the purpose of such a setting for United States diplomacy in "Diplomatic Reception in America: Private Interiors in Public Service." The last part of their essay addresses diplomatic reception in a contemporary democratic society; they cite the creation of the rooms as the State Department's reaction to the turmoil of the Vietnam War and the civil rights movement. The collection would allow Americans to look proudly to their cultural heritage and to see the products of a "simpler America before industrialization, urbanization, immigration, and expansion had created a more complex and diverse nation."

The catalogue's fulsome entries include the usual information regarding date, origin, materials, dimensions, and provenance; writers offer detailed discussions about objects from both art historical and material cultural perspectives. Curators have been refreshingly candid about the condition of objects, making every effort to note replaced or conjectural components. This is a delicate diplomatic issue for museums, particularly so for this collection, which is composed entirely of gifts. A new approach, and one that should become standard in such publications, involves the footnoting of conservation files and the acknowledgment of conservators and upholsterers who worked on pieces.

One of the great strengths of the catalogue is the diversity of its contributing scholars. Thirty of this country's leading authorities in fine and decorative arts wrote in their areas of expertise. No single curator could have comparable knowledge of all the media represented in the collection. Such an approach requires strong supervision, which this project had in editor and project director Alexandra W. Rollins. She deserves kudos for organizing such a large and disparate group of authors and for the overall high quality of the catalogue's scholarship and appearance.

Editorial policy might have been stronger regarding standardization of terms for decorative arts styles, such as consistently using *baroque* and *rococo* versus *Queen Anne* and *Chippendale*. Although Jonathan L. Fairbanks writes (p. 71) that the early Georgian style has been misnamed "Queen Anne," some scholars (for instance, Gib Vincent in catalogue entry no. 4, a New York settee) still use the old misleading terminology. Brock Jobe is one scholar who has embraced the newer art historical stylistic terms—his description of the Portsmouth high chest of drawers (entry no. 5) as "bravura baroque" is appropriately alliterative for an object that uses visual repetition of theme so successfully. Admirably, writers and editors have used period terms to define forms: "looking glass," "high chest," or "china table" rather than the modern terms "mirror," "highboy," or "silver table."

Individual entries exhibit first-rate decorative arts scholarship. Authors have considered the historical perspective of the objects, putting them into a period frame of reference. Several authors refer to various Philadelphia price books in calculating how much a maker would have charged for a piece of furniture. Alan Miller relates a Philadelphia marble slab table (entry no. 28) with applied carving on the skirt to the most expensive sofa frame, such as that of the Chew family sofa at Cliveden. Brock Jobe includes the inventory of the back parlor of Robert Hooper's house in Marblehead, Massachusetts, because a desk-and-bookcase (entry no. 48) was included in the room. David Barquist points out, in discussing a Philadelphia high chest (entry no. 85), that these lavishly carved pieces were intended to rival the fully draped bed as the showpiece of the bedchamber.

Barquist diligently considers upholstery, especially original components. His discussion (entry no. 55) of a pair of Philadelphia armchairs notes that evidence from remaining nail shanks reveals that the original nails were gilded. He does not say whether spectro-analysis was done; it could reveal that the nails were pseudogilded, a treatment more common on period upholstery nails than gilding. He might also have considered whether the Philadelphia armchairs (entries no. 55 and no. 56) and sofa (entry no. 69) originally had "French edge" upholstery, which was typical on such forms.[1]

A curatorial decision regarding upholstery reveals a colonial revival tendency in the presentation of the State Department's collection. When the original upholstery fabric of the pair of armchairs (entry no. 55) was revealed to be red silk damask, a comparable reproduction fabric was used in reupholstery. But when an important set of rococo chairs (entry no. 17) that descended in the Loockerman family of Dover, Delaware, appeared to match an inventory reference to "leather bottomed Walnut chairs," they nevertheless were reupholstered in yellow silk damask rather than the documented leather.

Vincent analyzes the New York chest-on-chest (entry no. 16) made for John Stevens and cites that Steven's mother-in-law's will has been reprinted several times to indicate the opulence of midcentury New York interiors. He does not, however, give her name or say where her will has been transcribed. Students of period interiors would be interested to read it. In discussing a New York side chair (entry no. 11) he cites Joshua Delaplaine's 1740 bill to Judah Hayse for a "Large Claw table" as the first documentation of the use of the ball-and-claw foot in New York. However, the London Society of Upholsterers' and Cabinetmakers' *Genteel Household Furniture in the Present Taste* (ca. 1763) illustrates three tripod-base tables with scroll feet and calls them "claw tables," indicating that "claw" referred to the three-legged form, rather than to ball-and-claw feet.[2]

Candor regarding replacement parts is admirable. It is disconcerting, however, that Robert Mussey, in his entry on a Boston bombé desk-and-bookcase (entry no. 82), discusses related pitched pediment pieces in detail before stating that the pediment on the State Department example is a conjectural replacement. He might have mentioned the replacement up front and then discussed related examples with surviving pediments for possible relationships to the missing original pediment on this piece.

Several notes from my southern perspective: the book (p. 31) names Westover plantation on the James River in Virginia as a source for Edward Vason Jones's design for the entrance hall and gives bracket dates for Westover as 1674–1744, the birth and death dates of owner William Byrd II. According to architectural historian Mark R. Wenger, however, the house was built in the mid-eighteenth century by Byrd II or his son William Byrd III.[3]

Gregory Weidman, in cataloguing the two pieces in the collection made south of Maryland—a Charleston clothespress (entry no. 107) and a Williamsburg china table (entry no. 75) — cites in both entries that Virginians and South Carolinians imported a great deal of English furniture. This was equally true of colonists in the North, but it is seldom mentioned because more scholarship has been published on products from the New England and mid-Atlantic states. Perhaps the relatively recent arrival of research on southern furniture prompted Weidman to name (in footnote 2 to the entry on the Williamsburg china table) leading scholars who have worked on southern material. She credits most effort to Sumpter Priddy and Luke Beckerdite, who have both published excellent research on southern furniture. Weidman ignores, however, pioneers in the field, including Frank Horton (who founded the Museum of Early Southern Decorative Arts in Winston-Salem, North Carolina), John Bivins, Bradford Rauschenburg, J. Roderick Moore, and Wallace Gusler.

Although the book is handsomely presented and the pieces skillfully catalogued, its organization is frustratingly vague. Media are grouped together, but within those categories they are arranged neither by form nor by date or region of production. I searched the preface and the "notes to the use of the catalogue" fruitlessly for clues to the designers' intent. Most scholars and collectors use a book like this as a reference when acquiring or researching a particular piece of furniture; they want to compare all examples of a similar form, or all pieces by the same maker or from the same area of production. A catalogue, therefore, is most useful when it groups entries by form and subdivides those categories by date and place of production. Tea tables might have been grouped, for instance, then arranged in approximate order of production; pieces from the same region could be clustered within the chronology.

The index does little to speed the finding of specific objects. As an example, it lists fifteen chests of drawers, giving the catalogue number, but does not differentiate them by region of production, by maker, or by date. Index entries for production cities and makers are not categorized by form.

The catalogue also has a few editorial or design quirks. The first part of the catalogue entries — listing form, dates, origin, materials, dimensions, inscriptions, provenance, and donors — was difficult to read due to small text and lack of periods. Captions to the room views would have been more legible if hard copy were separated from accession numbers and photograph credits and if a space were left between each caption. The capitalization in Garrett's introductory essay of "the Rooms," the "Collection," "the Curator" seems unnecessary aggrandizement. The bibliography alphabetizes a book on Chatsworth by the Duchess of Devonshire under *Duchess* rather than *Devonshire*.

The book's sheer scale, although impressive, is a drawback: 497 pages on heavy stock weigh six-and-one-half pounds, making the book cumbersome. In the course of doing the review, the spine of my copy has cracked. A two-volume edition, although more expensive, would have been more manageable. Volume one could have contained the furniture, whereas a second volume could have included silver, ceramics, maps, sculpture, and paintings.

In critiquing this book and taking a tour of the Diplomatic Reception Rooms I was saddened that such a rich collection of America's history and material culture is secreted on the top floors of the State Department building rather than shared with a large audience. The book reports that over one hundred thousand people per year see the collection at diplomatic receptions. But fewer than one hundred and fifty people receive interpreted tours of this important collection on any weekday and then only by appointments made weeks in advance.

There is no permanent exhibition celebrating the arts of early America in either the National Gallery of Art or the National Museum of American History. It is unfortunate that some of this rich trove of Americana is not available for the edification and enjoyment of the American public. Much is made of the First Ladies' gowns in the National Museum of American History; an exhibition of fine and decorative arts made in the colonial and early republican periods would teach as much about the talents and aspirations of our forebears.

Putting some of these historically important decorative arts objects on view at a national museum would serve the additional preservation purposes of making them less vulnerable to damage suffered during tours and receptions. Although the curatorial staff has taken precautions (such as putting glass on the tops of case pieces), priceless antiques are inevitably subject to damage when more than a hundred thousand people per year attend receptions in the rooms. Antique carpets will be destroyed with such traffic. Even well-meaning visitors can inadvertently damage the collection: several members of the group with which I toured leaned on chairs, and children curiously fingered brasses. This invariably happens when pieces are incorporated into inviting room settings rather than displayed on protective platforms or behind barriers.

Personal concerns about limited public access to the State Department collection in no way diminish my praise for the catalogue. A very strong curatorial effort, its only serious drawback is ineffective organization. *Treasures of State*, with excellent scholarly essays and color photography of over three hundred important pieces of Americana, makes an important contribution to scholarship in the decorative and fine arts and brings this seldom-seen collection into prominence. At $95, it offers very good value. I recommend it for the libraries of serious students or collectors of American decorative arts.

Elizabeth Pitzer Gusler
Colonial Williamsburg Foundation

1. Wallace Gusler, Mark Anderson, and Leroy Graves, "The Technique of 18th-Century Over-the-rail Upholstery" in Edward S. Cooke, Jr., ed., *Upholstery in America and Europe from the Seventeenth Century to World War I* (New York and London: Norton, 1987), pp. 90–96.

2. Wallace B. Gusler, *Furniture of Williamsburg and Eastern Virginia, 1710–1790* (Richmond: Virginia Museum of Fine Arts, 1979), p. 57.

3. Mark R. Wenger, *Westover, William Byrd's Mansion Reconsidered* (master's thesis, University of Virginia, 1981).

Morrison H. Heckscher and Leslie Greene Bowman. *American Rococo, 1750–1775: Elegance in Ornament.* New York: Metropolitan Museum of Art and Los Angeles County Museum of Art, 1992. Distributed by Abrams. xv + 288 pp.; 250 bw and color illus., bibliography, exhibition checklist, index. $60.00.

During the third quarter of the eighteenth century, American artisans produced some of the most richly ornamented furniture, silver, textiles, and other household furnishings that many colonists had ever seen. Even today, these artifacts—now termed rococo in style—capture our imagination as much for the technological achievements they represent as for their artistry. Despite decades of scholarship in the field of American decorative arts, a serious and inclusive treatment of this important material had never been attempted until Morrison H. Heckscher and Leslie Greene Bowman wrote *American Rococo, 1750–1775: Elegance in Ornament.* Essentially a catalogue, the book was produced as a companion to an exhibition of the same name organized by the Metropolitan Museum of Art and the Los Angeles County Museum of Art.

Using essays, catalogue entries, and high-quality photographs of 173 artifacts, Heckscher and Bowman open some new doors for the reader and offer fascinating insights into the origin and meaning of the rococo style in America. They tap into several little-used resources of information and gather together the facts from a number of earlier, widely scattered studies. Yet in their attempt to present a broad summary of this remarkably diverse subject, the authors fail in important ways as well.

In a brief introductory essay, Heckscher and Bowman recount the Italian and French origins of rococo ornament and its transferal into British design vocabularies via immigrant Huguenot craftsmen. Matthias Lock and Henry Copland are noted for their roles in developing the initial British interpretations of the style, and, of course, Thomas Chippendale, William Ince and John Mayhew, Robert Manwring, and their peers are appraised as disseminators of the rococo through Britain's trade shops and great houses.

Heckscher and Bowman next trace the movement of rococo taste to the colonies by means of published designs, imported goods, and migrating tradesmen. In America, they note that the "adoption of the rococo focused almost exclusively on the style's ornamental motifs—shells and rocaille, scrollwork, acanthus leaves, and other flora and fauna, often in asymmetrical compositions." Moreover, we are told, "only in and around the major cities were the necessary ingredients in place to cultivate [its] development," the most fertile areas being Boston, New York, Philadelphia, Charleston, and their environs.

The balance of the book is devoted to catalogue entries for the various media produced in the rococo taste, with chapters dedicated to architecture, engraving, silver, furniture, and a final section on iron, glass, and porcelain. These efforts are, in many instances, filled with valuable observations. For example, Bowman's remarks on engraving illuminate the topic and clearly demonstrate the importance of trade cards, bookplates, and other printed ephemera to an early distribution of the rococo in America. Similarly, her remarks on American rococo silver, its inspiration via British imports, and its regional variations are thought provoking. She also convincingly argues for the seminal role of immigrant British journeymen in the sudden appearance of sophisticated rococo ornament on silver from some long-established American shops and points out that in many instances newly arrived journeymen were more accomplished at the craft than their colonial masters.

The furniture entries, written by Heckscher, account for more than one-third of the text and nearly half of the book's illustrations. Broken into regional groups, each with its own preliminary essay, the material is further subdivided by function. Among the forms Heckscher explores in this part of the work is the portrait frame, a natural vehicle for the carved confections of the rococo movement, and one that has been too little studied in the past. Using surviving bills and other evidence, Heckscher is able to document the carvers of several important frames from Boston, New York, and Philadelphia, and his observations will almost certainly lead to further carving attributions for works produced in those cities. An exploration of the carving and gilding trades in late colonial Philadelphia is also useful and, as in the discussion of silversmithing, makes clear the importance of immigrant British craftsmen to the development of the city's unusually florid rococo furniture.

These and other important contributions aside, it must be noted that *American Rococo* suffers from several important defects, not the least of which is its narrow definition of the term "rococo." The authors note early in the book that Chippendale described his own designs as a mixture of the Chinese, Gothic, and French or Modern tastes, but the first two components are rarely mentioned in the present work. Although the French taste dominated American rococo productions, there were important passages of Chinese and Gothic ornament as well. Yet even when an object with blatantly Chinese or Gothic decoration, such as the Chew family sofa (cat. no. 150), is included in the catalogue—and there are few such inclusions—those elements, their design sources, and their place in the overall scheme generally go unnoted. A more balanced approach that acknowledged these aspects of the rococo style would have strengthened the work, especially with regard to furniture.

Along the same lines, any consideration of rural furniture in the rococo style was omitted. The impressive (if less academic) carved furniture of backcountry Pennsylvania, the Connecticut River valley, and other rural centers was inspired directly by the urban American rococo movement, and these objects need to be considered alongside their city-made counterparts if we are to understand the whole. Indeed, one also wonders about the less heavily ornamented furniture that was made in the larger cities by the same craftsmen who produced the most lavishly decorated goods. Are these pieces not rococo as well, and where do they fit into the overall picture?

A more serious lapse involves the entire section on southern furniture, which is peppered with both minor factual errors and large misconceptions. Among the former, for instance, note that the population of Williamsburg at 1775 was not 3,000, as stated, but about 1,800, and the town was by no means the "largest city" in the colony. Virginia's government did not move to Richmond in 1779, but in 1780. Nor was cypress the "favorite secondary wood" of the South, as it was used only sporadically in Maryland, Virginia, and North Carolina, where yellow pine and poplar were the secondary woods of choice during the colonial period. And the author reports that the shop of Charleston cabinetmaker Thomas Elfe produced "only two" easy chairs between 1768–1775, although Elfe's account book lists at least nine examples and possibly more.

These sorts of inaccuracies are small in scale, and, although there are a number of them, they might be overlooked. Of more central concern is Heckscher's decision to combine the furniture of Williamsburg and that of Charleston under one broad heading, even though two more dissimilar cities could hardly be found. Charleston, one of the richest urban centers in colonial America, was a great seaport with a population of nearly 40,000; Williamsburg was a small, inland governmental town, perhaps one-twentieth as large, with little commerce and no direct access to shipping. Although the cabinet industries in each place were grounded firmly in British tradition and technology, the furniture they produced had relatively little in common, aside from structural sophistication. To group the products of Charleston and Williamsburg together in a study of this kind is akin to pairing the cabinet trade of Annapolis with that of New York City.

More disturbing still is the manner in which important pieces of southern furniture are trivialized and misinterpreted. Text that likens a significant Virginia Masonic chair (cat. no. 123) to a group of "tools . . . tossed into a magnetized box," the whole having "aesthetic shortcomings," is simply uninformed. A ceremonial armchair covered with symbolic Masonic regalia—this one arguably the finest colonial example known—is not a piece of parlor furniture and cannot be judged as such. When Heckscher writes, "it must be admitted that [the craftsman's] great effort lacks total coherence," he is assessing the chair from the standpoint of personal, twentieth-century aesthetics, with no attempt to place the object in its logical, cultural context. Although the chair might have looked odd in a Virginia planter's home, it must have had a commanding presence on a platform in a Masonic hall.

Likewise, an exceptionally fine Charleston easy chair (cat. no. 122) is described as "much in the Philadelphia idiom," when, in fact, it is purely English in design and execution. There is no evidence to indicate that either Charleston tradesmen or their clients had the slightest interest in Philadelphia furniture or its design. To suggest that high-style South Carolina furniture was derived from or can be measured by Pennsylvania standards again reveals an unfortunate cultural bias.

In fact, the author's implicit decision to judge all American rococo cabinet wares against those of Philadelphia is one of the most troubling aspects of the furniture section. No one would argue that Philadelphia's rococo furniture is not remarkable for its virtuosity and aesthetic appeal, but it did not guide American taste in the eighteenth century, nor was it necessarily better or more appealing than furniture from other American centers. There can be little doubt that furniture from any large city looks the way it does primarily (though not entirely) because the taste of the wealthy local clientele dictated that it do so. Even London-trained, immigrant British cabinetmakers eventually conformed to local American tastes. In short, if the citizens of Boston, Newport, Charleston, or any other major urban center had desired to own furniture in the Philadelphia style, they certainly could have done so, as talented carvers and cabinetmakers were working in all of those places. But clearly, Philadelphia rococo did not suit affluent Bostonians or their counterparts in Newport or Charleston. To assume that the most heavily ornamented furniture was also the most desirable once again measures eighteenth-century objects by wholly modern, acultural standards and robs them of their inherent meaning.

It must be acknowledged that a broad-based study of American decorative arts in the rococo style is a daunting assignment, as the volume, variety, and complexity of such goods is almost overwhelming. Unfortunately, by failing to place the noteworthy material it explores into a cultural context, *American Rococo* has fallen short of the mark. In its restricted definition of the style, its failure to explore any but the most lavishly decorated objects, its inadequate scholarship on southern furniture, and its elevation of Philadelphia forms above all others, the work has left a great many questions unanswered and a number of useful resources untapped.

Despite such shortcomings, the book does present new and carefully synthesized material on several subjects, including silver and engravings, and it offers a convenient and ready reference to basic information on some of colonial America's most elaborately and artistically crafted decorative arts.

Ronald L. Hurst
Colonial Williamsburg Foundation

Graham Hood. *The Governor's Palace in Williamsburg: A Cultural Study.* Williamsburg: The Colonial Williamsburg Foundation, 1991. Distributed by University of North Carolina Press. 343 pp.; 207 bw and color illus., index. $59.95.

Few aspects of eighteenth-century American history are more elusive than the intimate patterns of daily life. Unlike the momentous events and important figures of the past, the nuances of domestic life, public ritual, purposeful thought, and expressive behavior are rarely mentioned in either public or private documents. Yet, as John Demos suggested in *A*

Little Commonwealth: Family Life in the Plymouth Colony, the structure and character of fundamental institutions and patterns of behavior are common denominators for understanding community and culture.

Graham Hood's *Governor's Palace in Williamsburg: A Cultural Study* is the most vivid and accurate depiction to date of life in an American house. Built in 1710 and enlarged around mid-century, the palace served as the official residence of five lieutenant governors and two royal governors between 1715 and 1775. In their official capacity, the governors enforced British law and protected the crown's interests. As personal representatives of the king, they also personified the political, social, and cultural values of the English aristocracy—the segment of British society with which affluent Virginians identified. Hood argues convincingly that the governors' position in the social hierarchy and their interaction with all levels of society fostered a two-way exchange of values that had a profound effect on eighteenth-century Virginia culture.

As the residence and office of the governor, the palace was central to this cultural exchange. Hood's chapter titled "The Setting" is a concise architectural history of the palace (from Spotswood's involvement in the design of the building and gardens to Colonial Williamsburg's reconstruction during the early 1930s) and an excellent survey of the lives of the governors in residence. References to international art movements (that is, dissemination of the baroque style during the late seventeenth century and the advent of Palladianism in England during the second decade of the eighteenth century), contemporary buildings in London and Williamsburg, and historical events during the tenures of the governors provide a rich context for subsequent chapters.

Hood's atmospheric prologue establishes the time, place, and several underlying themes of his study. It opens on October 15, 1770, with the death of Norburne Berekley, baron de Botetourt, perhaps the most widely admired and respected of Virginia's governors. Public and private expressions of affection and grief are quoted to show how expressive behavior in the eighteenth century often had multiple layers of meaning. Botetourt's elaborate funeral procession, as Hood points out, was a formal ceremony with a prescribed hierarchy that not only recognized the governor's rank and title, but acknowledged his relationship with the community and colony. It was an event with prescribed gestures and rituals as well as genuine expressions of feeling.

Shortly after the funeral, an "exact and perfect inventory" was taken of Botetourt's personal effects. The author's meticulous analysis of this inventory and such related documents as cash books and account books (discovered by Hood in England) animates for the reader the daily life of the governor and those around him. The rooms and groups of objects in them were symbolic of the governor's office and social status, and they either expressly or implicitly suggested specific patterns of behavior and thought.

Chapters on the entrance hall and middle room of the second story illustrate the importance of ceremony, hierarchy, and protocol in the governors' public and private lives. With its ornamental display of weapons, flags, and royal coats of arms—conspicuous symbols of power and order— the entrance hall was the most imposing formal room in the palace. Quoting numerous individuals who commented on the weapons, Hood traces the display and attitudes toward it from the administration of Lieutenant Governor Alexander Spotswood (1710–1722), who planned and supervised the installation, to the removal of the arms following the flight of Governor Dunmore in 1775. The sense of formality and ceremony created by the furnishings was reinforced by the retinue (hierarchy of servants) that distanced the governor from visitors who were not his equals. An amusing altercation involving Governor Fauquier, several of his servants, and the Reverend John Camm is cited to document this aspect of public life at the palace.

The chapter on the middle room upstairs charts changing attitudes in the social use of spaces from Spotswood's tenure to Botetourt's. Derived from the great chambers of medieval country houses, the middle room was originally reserved for important ceremonial functions. During Spotswood's time it had gilt leather wall hangings, sixteen gilt leather chairs, two pier tables, and two large looking glasses with the arms of the colony. By mid-century such chambers were referred to as salons, and they were used for both formal and casual gatherings. Hood's analysis of the furnishings in Fauquier's inventory, which included a settee, ten pictures in gilt frames, and a pair of gaming tables, suggests occasional informal usage. By tracking the same items in Botetourt's inventory, several of which appear in the front parlor adjoining the middle room, the author demonstrates a return to formality, possibly owing to the governor's noble rank and bachelor status. Botetourt's use of the middle room as a dressing chamber is confirmed by the presence of clothespresses and a basin stand; however, Hood interprets much more from these furnishings. They suggest that Botetourt (and probably other governors and members of the gentry) practiced the levee, an informal ritual during which the governor dressed and conducted business.

Public life is examined in chapters titled "The Dining Room and Parlor: Apartments of Conversation" and "The Ballroom and Supper Room: Fashionable Gatherings." Hospitality, as Hood notes, was a fundamental aspect of eighteenth-century life. Using quotations from Robert Adam's *Works of Architecture*, the author shows how parlors and dining rooms worked in tandem during entertainments. The parlor was a place for guests to gather before dinner and a refuge for the ladies, who customarily left the dining room after dessert and avoided the male-oriented conversation, drinking, and smoking that followed. For comfort and the stimulation of polite conversation, the parlor was furnished with an elegant canopied couch, side chairs covered in leather (a durable, practical covering), gaming tables, maps, and scriptural prints.

Hood's discussion of dining again underscores the importance of ritual and protocol in eighteenth-century life. Virtually every aspect of this "entertainment"—from the choice and arrangement of accoutrements and decorations to the service and consumption of food and drink—embodied the principles of balance, harmony, and order (hierarchy) that were the philosophical foundations of eighteenth-century British culture. The author also asserts that the dining room was the intellectual center of the house and that meals were occasions for lobbying, conducting business, and engaging in philosophical and political discussions. Central to this argument are the furnishings, which included a library table, a mahogany desk, a writing table, a reading desk, and a map of Virginia in addition to a large dining table, a smaller table, a wine cooler, and twelve chairs. The author's interpretation of the material evidence is supported by period accounts, such as Thomas Jefferson's recollection that "at these dinners [with Governor Fauquier, William Small, and George Wythe] I . . . heard more good sense, more rational and philosophical conversations, than in all my life beside."

Jefferson was but one of many who benefited from the paternalism of such conscientious governors as Fauquier and Botetourt. In addition to sponsoring promising young men, the governors also patronized such institutions as The College of William and Mary and the Public Hospital for the Insane and encouraged talented artists and tradesmen. Citing many other examples of beneficence, Hood demonstrates that patronage was a primary avenue for cultural exchange. The author acknowledges that the full extent of the governors' influence on colonial society may never be completely understood, but that without their paternalism and beneficence "the history of the colonies would have to be rewritten."

The private lives of the governors and the extended "family" of servants and slaves required to maintain the palace are examined in the final chapters, "The Bedchambers and Study: The Person of the Governor" and "The Family." Particularly engaging is the author's analysis of the pyramidal structure of servants and slaves who worked in the palace, their attendant responsibilities, and their attitudes toward each other. A considerable portion of "The Family" explores the many paradoxes of slavery in eighteenth-century Virginia. Hood shows how "enlightened" Virginia planters such as Robert Beverley abhorred slavery but were either unable (because of financial and social constraints) or unwilling to make the adjustments required to abolish the institution.

Graham Hood's remarkable proficiency in interpreting the material past has enabled him to reconstruct patterns of daily life, behavior, and thought that often elude traditional historians. In its use of material culture, *The Governor's Palace* reaches beyond the traditional boundaries of social history and art history. If other scholars follow in Hood's path, certain aspects of colonial history may indeed have to be rewritten.

Luke Beckerdite
The Chipstone Foundation

Of American Kasten and the Mythology of "Pure Dutchness": A Review Article

Peter M. Kenny, Frances Gruber Safford, and Gilbert T. Vincent. *American Kasten: The Dutch-Style Cupboards of New York and New Jersey, 1650–1800*. New York: The Metropolitan Museum of Art, 1991. viii + 80 pp.; 65 illus., line drawings, appendices, glossary, bibliography. $16.95.

Scholars concerned that the rapidly expanding historiography of American regional furniture might somehow pass over traditionally neglected New York Colony while questing new territories south and west of southeastern Massachusetts will welcome the appearance of this handsome new exhibition catalogue. To be sure, *American Kasten* will find a secure place on the shelf beside Roderic H. Blackburn and Ruth Piwonka's more general *Remembrance of Patria: Dutch Arts and Culture in Colonial America, 1609–1776* (1988) and Dean F. Failey's still very useful *Long Island Is My Nation: The Decorative Arts & Craftsmen, 1640–1830* (1976).[1]

The American kas (or "kast," as the authors pointedly prefer) has been perceived as synonymous, indeed almost inextricably intertwined, with the material life of early New York since at least the year 1900 when the influential antiquarian Esther Singleton first published a few well-documented examples in *Furniture of Our Forefathers*. Such an enduring relation has only served to exacerbate a curious process of mystification about the "Dutchness" of New York "Dutch-Style" furniture, which probably finds its ultimate textual origin in the nostalgic and ideological ethnic mythologies popularized by Washington Irving (1783–1859), particularly in *Dietrich Knickerbocker's A History of New York* (1809). But it was that moralistic entrepreneur and relentless promoter—a fortiori, the P. T. Barnum of seventeenth-century New England furniture—Wallace Nutting who, in his seminal *Furniture of the Pilgrim Century* (1924), conventionalized kasten as "striking example[s] of Knickerbocker work," while hastening to add dismissively, "we believe as a rule very large pieces are less sought for."[2] Nutting knew what was really important. If, as the minister from Framingham preached in his dedication to Henry Wood Erving, "the strength and beauty of Pilgrim furniture was an expression of Pilgrim character," then New York furniture as embodied by Nutting's unprofitable (and therefore trivial) Knickerbocker kasten could only have been an expression of Dutch corpulence, stolidity, closed and self-satisfied conservatism, and inertia. In short, everything his didactic, colonial revival Puritans were not.

The endurance of such self-serving ethnic stereotypes seems all the more anachronistic when confronted with important recent scholarship based on quantitative analysis compiled for extended time frames by folklorist David S. Cohen and historian Thomas L. Purvis, who argue persuasively that although New Amsterdam/New York came into being as a monopoly chartered under the auspices of the Dutch West India Company, from its very inception the colony did not seem to possess an effective ethnic Dutch majority. Indeed, many of the earliest colonists were French-speaking Huguenots and Walloons who, together with a large and steadily increasing population of African slaves, joined immigrants from all over Europe (especially the Germanic regions) to inhabit a profoundly pluralistic port town and its hinterland. This fact has enormous implications for the fluid history and culture of New York Colony. It suggests, for example, at least one reason why its "Dutch" citizens failed to mount serious opposition to the English invaders in 1664, choosing instead to cohere behind Frankfurt-born Jacob Leisler in 1689 when he launched his bloody, quixotic rebellion against the then-dominant Anglo-French (and anglicized Dutch) elites in the highly charged atmosphere that surged through the colonies following the Glorious Revolution.[3] Significantly, disaffected Dutch as well as many other groups of northern European woodworking artisans were among Leisler's most fervent political supporters, perhaps partially in response to their systematic displacement in the luxury trades (and hence removal from access to elite patronage) by Anglo-French artisans, their numbers bolstered by a massive influx of highly skilled Huguenot woodworkers who flooded into New York after Louis XIV's revocation of the Edict of Nantes in 1685.

It is therefore surprising, despite having made at least passing reference to the empirical work of Cohen and Purvis (p. 1), that the authors should then choose to align themselves so closely with the moribund Knickerbocker tradition by questing ceaselessly after what they consistently call, most unfortunately, "pure" Dutchness, with the venerable kas[t] as their Rosetta stone. Thus in his essay "Origins and Uses," Gilbert T. Vincent states unequivocally (but without specific evidence) that "most colonists acceded to Dutch cultural dominance"; and although after 1664 "direct contact with the Netherlands was increasingly cut off . . . many settlers of Flemish, French, or German heritage . . . tended to reject changes that came from the outside and sought to preserve much of the past. This was especially the case with rural inhabitants. . . . They were more than content with their daily lives" (pp. 1–3). Generalizations such as these are by their very nature basically fruitless and condescending and are especially vulnerable to criticism using evidence from specific, everyday, face-to-face interaction; evidence that the authors consistently ignore in favor of rudimentary formal analysis that fails to consider, in more than a perfunctory way, the perspective of either artisans or consumers of kasten. Yet arguably, this is precisely the level upon which analysis of domestic artifacts might yield important evidence supporting more complex, alternative interpretations. That is why it would seem inappropriate to summarily banish "kas" from this text even though we learn it was commonly used "interchangeably" with "kast" by appraisers of colonial New York inventories, simply because it apparently bears the heresy of "English mutations" (p. vii). By so doing, a crucial sociolinguistic link to the past—one that should have supplied the authors with an important insight—is also arbitrarily erased. As J.G.A. Pocock, Nancy S. Struever, and Quentin Skinner have amply demonstrated for early modern Europe, the intimate relation of language and culture is retrospectively riven for the sake of conceptual purity only at the historian's peril.[4] Ironically, for many scholars concerned with the development of mid-Atlantic regional material culture, it is *precisely* this problem of sorting out the historical meaning of such "mutations"—what anthropologists term "creolization"—that now seems most fascinating and is currently the subject of much fruitful inquiry.

Part of the difficulty lies in the authors' heavy reliance on traditional, idealistic art historical methodology that tends to worship too lovingly at the altar of what Marc Bloch called the "idol of origins." Kasten are therefore lined up serially in a highly dubious chronological order bracketed arbitrarily by the years 1650 and 1800. But even so the authors might have profited from assimilating ideas expressed by the numerous American followers of the influential French art historian Henri Focillon, who argues in his important essay *Vie des formes* (Paris, 1934) that it can be empirically useful to submit artifacts placed in a series to formal analysis, so long as such an analysis simultaneously is embedded in the specific, *mutable*, and above all *human* contexts of each of the artifacts placed therein. Instead, we are confronted here with an elitist rehearsal of nineteenth-century diffusion theory from the top down. Thus, although Vincent is particularly good at elucidating competition between the "older," "idiosyncratic" mannerist style associated with the influential design books of Hans Vredeman de Vries (1527–1604) and the "modern," "soberer" classical Italianate models—disseminated by printmaker Crispin de Passe the Younger (1593–1670) and especially Jacob van Campen (1595–1657), architect of the paradigmatic Amsterdam Town Hall (ca. 1648)—the text proceeds to employ these models—as well as that of the subsequent monumental Amsterdam "baroque" kussen (or cushion, to indicate projecting beveled door panels) kast—to signify the "pure" origin of and prototypes for *all* "Dutch-Style" American kasten. The logic of this method therefore leads the authors to place their series in a hoary (and ahistorical) organic framework of growth and inevitable decline that maintains the "original," "pure," and idealized seventeenth-century Amsterdam design as the ever-present context and standard for American kasten produced in New York and New Jersey, often nearly two centuries hence. We are told, for example, that by 1790, "Bergen County makers seized the kast form as their own and, taking a neoclassical perspective, attempted to breathe some new life into it before its final demise" (p. 28). One of the great glories of the best recent scholarship in regional furniture history lies in its success in escaping the self-limiting structures of such conventional narrative paths by hewing close to specific contexts provided by local artisans personally *engaged* with their mental and material worlds. The pursuit of such specificity would almost surely lead us far afield from Vincent's international pattern books and *haut bourgeois* Amsterdam kasten, to poor, relatively unregulated rural woodworking shops located all over Europe and Britain producing cheap, often crudely constructed painted softwood furniture made in what T. H. Lunsingh Scheurleer has called the *witwerker* tradition.[5] Only by following pathways taken by the craftsmen themselves can surviving artifacts produced by New York's pluralistic artisans be understood in terms of their own, decidedly multiple (and from the perspective of the little we currently know about early modern European regional woodworking traditions, still mostly painfully obscure) origins.

The limitations of the monolithic Amsterdam model for understanding American kasten is ironically laid bare the few times the artisanal context is actually addressed (albeit too generally) from an archival perspective. When we finally encounter a New York joiner engaged in "amaking" "the new cupboard" for Evert Van Hook in 1711 (p. 9), we are perhaps surprised to discover he is one Jean Le Chevalier. We are not told, however, that Le Chevalier, an exiled Huguenot and one of New York's leading joiners by 1711, found refuge in the colonies after having escaped from Saintonge in southwestern France by way of London, where along with other family members, he was naturalized on April 9, 1687. Following in the footsteps of his paternal grandfather Jean, who arrived in New York by way of Martinique by 1671, Le Chevalier was to be declared a freeman of the city no earlier than October 12, 1695. Le Chevalier, although married in the Dutch Reformed Church on June 17, 1692, was also an active, well-documented member of the local *French* Church (although we are told on page 1 that "most French—as well as German and Flemish —colonists simply "acknowledg[ed] the leadership of the Dutch Reformed Church"), where, in a most significant insight into hidden family allegiance, he and his wife Marie de la Plaine (the daughter of another prominent New York Huguenot joiner) chose to have their two daughters baptised in 1693 and 1695. Given the ethnic complexity of Le Chevalier's biography and the documentary evidence that strongly suggests that he was busily engaged in producing not only kasten but also a great variety of joined and carved work for whomever could afford to employ him—in addition to Van Hook, mostly by the 1690s, the city's Anglo-French elites including in one case a contract to repair and frame the English royal arms on the front of city hall—it would seem difficult to understand how this particular figure fits neatly into the authors' Dutch Gestalt.[6]

On another occasion, Peter M. Kenny diminishes an otherwise competent contribution to our understanding of the taxonomy of regional types by holding onto the pure Dutchness of Ulster County kasten (his particular area of research) so that he can ultimately attribute the bulk of Kingston's production to the Dutch "Elting-Beekman Shops." He asserts this conclusion even while acknowledging that the most salient construction features of this group (usually, as the folklorists rightly remind us, a far more reliable indicator of ethnicity than exterior design)—including the anomalous use of wedged tenon joinery in lieu of pegs for framing combined with the wholesale substitution of wooden pins for nails—"have been cited as hallmarks of *German* (italics mine) joinery when they occur in Pennsylvania furniture" (p. 26). Kenny tenuously stretches his explanation to fit the catalogue's schema by suggesting that "Jan Elting's native province of Drenthe was on the German border; it is possible that these techniques were well known there and that he brought them to Flatbush and Kingston." But it is also equally possible (and far more likely) that any number of unnamed artisans with other than Dutch genealogies were capable of producing kasten with Germanic construction in busy Kingston by the eighteenth century; especially if one considers Kenny's undocumented early dating primarily on the basis of style to be, as the authors themselves admit, mere guesswork at best. It would not be surprising if the two Kingston kasten attributed to the Elting-Beekman shops and subjectively dated circa 1700–1730 (numbers 10 and 11) were in fact made as late as circa 1760–1790 at the earliest. Inasmuch as templates and tools were valuable, enduring commodities passed down from father to son, transferred from master to apprentice through apprenticeship contracts, sold at public vendue, and in general circulated from town to town to be used, repaired, and reused by many hands over the course, sometimes, of generations, it would seem most difficult to reach conclusions about dating on the basis of molding patterns and the shape of door panels. One also wonders why Kenny ignores possible Huguenot influence in Ulster County kasten. Kingston's proximity to New Paltz and the fact that by Kenny's own reckoning two of the three "Kingston" kasten illustrated have strong histories of ownership in prominent local French families is suggestive in itself, but especially so when one considers that New Paltz appears to have been settled by a number of Huguenots who first fled the wars of religion to die Pfaltz (the German Palatinate), settling there for some time before coming belatedly to the Hudson Valley, and then only after having again been forced to flee the resurgence of similar confessional violence in Germany.

But overall, Kenny's attempt to classify eighteenth-century kasten by locality—New York City; Kings County; Queens County; the Upper Hudson Valley; and Bergen County—is useful, if often also arbitrary, speculative, and, when discussing Long Island, heavily in debt to Failey. Building on Failey's work on western Long Island, Kenny has done a particularly good job synthesizing prior scholarship to make a convincing argument for a coherent group of artifacts attributable to Kings County. Here formal analysis is finally effective because he has the advantage of proceeding from the Metropolitan Museum's crucial gumwood desk-on-frame, collected in 1922 from a house on Cortelyou Road in the Flatbush section of Brooklyn. With its applied, inset mahogany panels, this artifact also carries the date 1695 in a Dutch inscription under its lid. Kenny makes the key observation that the desk's upper section is related by construction to a group of Kings County kasten that all share a specific sort of dovetailed cabinetwork in the base that is arguably peculiar to the New York City area: "In both, the joints, precisely cut, have steeply pitched end-grain pins with thin necks. Even stronger evidence . . . of a common shop tradition is the dovetailing in each instance of the front boards to the sides and the sides to the back. The result is the same pattern of face-grain tails and end-grain pins on the facades of the desk and the kast[en] as on their exposed back corners" (p. 20). Having made this most important observation, however, Kenny should have reported that one of the two other paradigmatic artifacts for identifying all early New York furniture (the Lawrence family dressing table probably made to accompany Winterthur's chest of drawers-on-frame signed by Samuel Clement of Flushing and dated 1726) shares this idiosyncratic articulation of the dovetails, albeit here limited only to the front corners of its frame.[7] Still, one can only wonder how this provocative relationship between the Metropolitan's desk, Kings County kasten, and a dressing table made in the dominant Anglo-French style for an Anglo-American merchant by a second-generation Flushing Quaker trained by his father in a town comprised mainly of Friends from the English Midlands can be reconciled with Kenny's notion of a presumably Dutch "common shop tradition." Future research, however, may well reveal an important affinity between continental furniture craftsmen who migrated to England, Scotland, and Wales as well as the Middle Colonies in great numbers during the sixteenth and seventeenth centuries and Midlands and West County craftsmen who may have influenced the development of the one-part Queens County kas that appears to be something of an attenuated version of the distinctive western and west central Long Island two-panel, ball-foot chest (long associated by tradition with the Quaker towns). One curious clue that may be worth pursuing is that both a number of western Long Island kasten and many two-panel ball-foot chests have components that are connected by the relatively laborious method of nailing with deeply countersunk nails then neatly plugged with large round plugs for the sake of sturdiness, or perhaps for camouflage, or to give the appearance of wooden pegs. Is this a transplanted, creolized survival of construction common to a specific, regional *witwerker* tradition? Perhaps time and future fieldwork will tell. Meanwhile, for structural analysis to pay dividends, much clearly remains to be learned about local New York shop traditions and the artisans who embodied them before any truly meaningful conclusions about cultural interaction can be ventured.

The most significant new contribution to the literature is made by Frances Gruber Safford in her section titled "Joined Oak Kasten of the Seventeenth Century," as to my knowledge this is the first time that four of the five surviving oak kasten have been published together and rigorously compared. The fifth, Winterthur's massive Hewlett family oak kas with inlay and applied softwood door panels, has been deleted, again presumably for the sake of purity, because it would appear to relate more to Germanic than Dutch sources. It might have been wise to reconsider this decision. Much can be learned by allowing the Hewlett cupboard to enter freely into the comparison, as its construction and decorative schema share interesting similarities and differences with not only the other oak kasten but also some Pennsylvania German cupboards and the far more numerous "later" gumwood kasten. More than that, its strong history of ownership in a Long Island family possessed of an impeccable English ancestry that its genealogists like to trace back to service in Cromwell's army, vividly demonstrates how easily the popular kasten form traversed New York's multiple cultures. A comprehensive survey of the available inventories might also have given us some further insight into such patterns of ownership. Although Safford is indeed able to posit the existence of a discreet group of oak kasten related by similar construction techniques but obviously the work of different hands, only one, the extraordinary example from the Art Institute of Chicago (number 4), is arguably produced in the urban hardwood tradition and related to a known seventeenth-century Amsterdam design source. The others could have been made by opportunistic *witwerkers* freely taking advantage of an abundance of oak in their New World environment. Certainly, the possibility that the Metropolitan's recently acquired oak kas (number 3) retains its original decorative paint surface would support this hypothesis. And dating is again deeply problematic. If, for the sake of argument, we were to allow the overall assertion of Dutch origins, and if Lunsingh Scheurleer is correct in his widely accepted hypothesis that hardwood and softwood kasten were being produced simultaneously in the Netherlands, then why, in the absence of other evidence, should Safford assume a seventeenth-century date for colonial New York oak kasten and an eighteenth-century date for all the rest? Perhaps the time-honored association of oak with New England's "Pilgrim Century" remains steadfastly ingrained. But again, in the absence of evidence to the contrary, one might just as reasonably speculate that kasten made of every available wood were being produced concurrently throughout New York and New Jersey and that they can probably be dated quite a bit later than the authors would suppose.

Safford also includes a final section on grisaille-painted kasten that summarizes past research but does not advance far beyond what is already known. It is interesting, however, to observe an apparent conceptual continuity here between the protruding opulence of the *kussenkast* hardwood door panels and the overripe, burst, or distended fertility of the fruit and other naturalistic motifs conventionally painted on the doors of softwood kasten. Vincent rightly points out the association between kasten and the woman's domestic sphere and develops (borrowing substantially from Simon Schama's *Embarrassment of Riches*) the complex interplay between the competent storage of valuable, labor-intensive textiles, feminine virtue, war, ecology, and cleanliness.[8] But much still remains to be learned about the place of the kas in domestic space, its role in the ritual of engagement and marriage, and especially its association with family labor; by this I mean labor in the conventional sense of work as value and commodity but also in the primordial sense of fertility, birth, and succession.

In the end, *American Kasten* remains unconvincing in its rather forced assertion that the kas is simply a quixotic artifact reflecting specifically a one-dimensional, "conservative" culture. Rather, perhaps not unlike its close colonial relations—the Germanic schrank, French armoire, and Spanish armario—the kas may have endured in its various forms precisely because it conveyed certain universal early modern capitalist values associated with accumulation and the subtle comportment of domestic display and concealment, which would have been familiar to the many non-Dutch inhabitants of the New York region and, as such, was inclusive and adaptable to change.

Neil Duff Kamil
The University of Texas at Austin

1. Published by the Albany Institute of History and Art and the Society for the Preservation of Long Island Antiquities, respectively.

2. Esther Singleton, *Furniture of Our Forefathers* (New York: Doubleday, Page, 1900–1901), see especially pp. 234–311. The 1809 or first edition of Irving's *History* may be found in Washington Irving, *Dietrich Knickerbocker's A History of New York*, ed. Stanley Williams and Tremayne McDowell (New York: Harcourt Brace, & Co., 1927). Wallace Nutting, *Furniture of the Pilgrim Century* (Boston: Marshall Jones Co., 1921), p. 270.

3. See David S. Cohen, "How Dutch Were the Dutch of New Netherland?," *New York History* 62, no. 1 (January 1981): 43–60; and Thomas L. Purvis, "The National Origins of New Yorkers in 1790," *New York History* 67, no. 2 (April 1986): 133–53. For a succinct analysis of the ethnic component of Leisler's Rebellion, see Thomas J. Archdeacon, *New York City, 1664–1710: Conquest and Change* (Ithaca, N.Y.: Cornell University Press, 1976), esp. pp. 97–146.

4. See Quentin Skinner, "Meaning and Understanding in the History of Ideas," *History and Theory* 8, no. 1 (1969): 45; J.G.A. Pocock, *Politics, Language, and Time: Essays on Political Thought and History* (N.Y.: Atheneum, 1971); and Nancy S. Struever, "Historiography and Linguistics," in George G. Iggers and Harold T. Parker, eds., *International Handbook of Historical Studies: Contemporary Research and Theory* (Westport, Conn.: Greenwood Press, 1979), pp. 127–50.

5. Marc Bloch, *The Historian's Craft* (Manchester, England: Manchester University Press, 1954), pp. 29–35. T. H. Lunsingh Scheurleer, "The Dutch and Their Homes in the Seventeenth Century," in Ian M. G. Quimby, ed., *Arts of the Anglo-American Community in the Seventeenth Century* (Charlottesville: University Press of Virginia, 1975), pp. 14–21.

6. See Charles W. Baird, *History of the Huguenot Emigration to America*, 2 vols. (Baltimore: Regional Publishing Company, 1966), 2: 80–81, and 1: 210, note 2; see also E. B. O'Callaghan, Kenneth Scott, and Kenneth Stryker-Rodda, *New York Manuscripts Dutch: The Register of Salomon Lachaire Notary Public of New Amsterdam, 1661–1662* (Baltimore: The Genealogical Publishing Company, 1978), pp. xii, xvi; and I. N. Phelps Stokes, *The Iconography of Manhattan Island, 1498–1909* (New York: Dodd, Mead & Co., 1922), 4: 305. Baird argues incorrectly on the basis of his family's coat of arms that Le Chevalier originated in Normandy. I have discovered direct archival evidence that strongly suggests a Saintongeais origin. See Neil D. Kamil,"War, Natural Philosophy, and the Metaphysical Foundations of Artisanal Thought in American Mid-Atlantic Colony: La Rochelle, New York City, and the Southwestern Huguenot Paradigm, 1517–1730" (Ph.D., dissertation, The Johns Hopkins University, 1988), pp. 563–68.

7. The sides are attached to the back with blind dovetails on Winterthur's Flushing dressing table. In recent years, an early (ca. 1695) stretcher-based table with one drawer was deaccessioned from Colonial Williamsburg (accession number 1930-17) and has resurfaced in a private collection. This table arguably originated in Flushing—or even New York City (due to the presence of cedrela and other exotic woods)—and it also shares a similar dovetailing technique with the Metropolitan's desk-on-frame. The remarkable thinness of its drawer linings would seem to indicate a closer affinity to the wood starvation mentality usually associated with seventeenth-century English and especially London craftsmanship, than with what we currently know of continental construction techniques.

8. See Simon Schama, *Embarrassment of Riches: An Interpretation of Dutch Culture in the Golden Age* (N.Y.: Knopf, 1987).

Compiled by Gerald W. R. Ward

Bibliography of Works on American Furniture Published in 1991 and 1992

▼ THE FOLLOWING list includes more than 160 books, articles, and catalogues published in 1991 and 1992 about the history of American furniture and related objects. The titles included have been selected, somewhat subjectively, on the basis of their relevance to the editorial stance of *American Furniture* and its emphasis on scholarship.

This list could easily have been expanded greatly with the addition of titles on tangential subjects or articles of a popular or derivative nature. Although I am certain that some worthy titles have been omitted inadvertently, and although some books written for a popular audience have been included, my primary goal has been to provide scholars and students with a manageable guide to recent literature in a serious vein. A perusal of this list, ideally, should indicate to the reader the avenues that scholars are currently pursuing, bring to his or her attention important discoveries of objects and information, and provide an overview of the direction of the study of American furniture from an historical perspective.

With a few exceptions, this list does not contain articles about the antiques trade (such as auction notices and reports on sales that appear regularly in *Antiques and the Arts Weekly* and *Maine Antique Digest*); most technical works on conservation; articles about contemporary woodworking techniques or adaptations of old techniques (for example, those that appear in *Fine Woodworking*); articles about current trends in the making and marketing of furniture; articles in the popular press; and articles on contemporary woodworking (such as those in *American Craft*). References to articles on these subjects can be found in the *Art Index* and other reference guides to periodical literature, both in printed form and in various computer formats.

I hope this bibliography will be a regular component of *American Furniture*. Its purpose is to provide a service to the reader; thus readers are encouraged to help shape its format and content by contacting me with suggestions, corrections, comments, and references to titles that have been overlooked here. References to articles in museum newsletters, journals, bulletins, and ephemeral publications are especially welcomed.

I am grateful for the assistance of Greg Colati, librarian/archivist of Strawbery Banke Museum; the staffs of the Portsmouth Public Library and the University of New Hampshire; and, especially, to Neville Thompson of the Winterthur Museum Library. I have made an attempt to examine personally each title cited and have been reasonably successful in doing so. Any errors that remain are my responsibility.

1991 TITLES

Anscombe, Isabelle. *Arts and Crafts Style*. New York: Rizzoli, 1991. 232 pp.; numerous color and bw illus., bibliography, index.

Ball, Edward. *When Matter Speaks*. Cambridge, Mass.: List Visual Arts Center, MIT, 1991. Color and bw illus. (Pamphlet accompanying exhibition, Feb. 23–Apr. 14, of "Storytelling Chairs," made by Barbara Broughel.)

Banham, Joanna, Sally MacDonald, and Julia Porter. *Victorian Interior Design*. New York: Crescent Books, 1991. 224 pp.; 226 color and bw illus., bibliography, selected biographies, index.

Barquist, David L. "Imported Looking Glasses in Colonial America." *Antiques* 139, no. 6 (June 1991): 1108–17. 14 color and 2 bw illus.

Bigelow, Deborah, Elizabeth Cornu, Gregory J. Landrey, and Cornelius Van Horne, gen. eds. *Gilded Wood: Conservation and History*. Madison, Conn.: Sound View Press, 1991. 432 pp.; 32 color and 248 bw illus.

Bivins, John, Jr., and Forsyth Alexander. *The Regional Arts of the Early South: A Sampling from the Collection of the Museum of Early Southern Decorative Arts*. Winston-Salem, N.C.: Museum of Early Southern Decorative Arts, 1991. Distributed by University of North Carolina Press. 170 pp.; numerous color and bw illus., map.

Booth, Robert E., Jr., and Katharine Booth. "Divine Design: A Shaker Legacy." *The 1991 Philadelphia Antiques Show*. Philadelphia, 1991, pp. 25–47. Color illus.

Buck, Susan L. "Variations in 'Boston State House Chairs.'" American Classics No. 25. *Maine Antique Digest* 19, no. 4 (April 1991): 6D–7D. Bw illus.

Burchell, Sam. *A History of Furniture: Celebrating Baker Furniture, 100 Years of Fine Reproductions*. New York: Harry N. Abrams, 1991. 176 pp.; 175 color and bw illus., bibliography, index.

Callahan, Carol J. "Glessner House, Chicago, Illinois." *Antiques* 139, no. 5 (May 1991): 970–81. 13 color and 6 bw illus.

Celebrating Vermont: Myths and Realities. Richard H. Saunders and Virginia M. Westbrook, exhibition curators; ed. by Nancy Price Graff; with essays by Nancy Price Graff and William N. Hosley, Jr., J. Kevin Graffagnino, and William C. Lipke. Middlebury, Vt.: The Christian A. Johnson Memorial Gallery, Middlebury College, 1991. Distributed by University Press of New England. 245 pp.; numerous color and bw illus., catalogue of the exhibition, time line, bibliography.

The Chair, from Artifact to Object: October 6th–November 10th, 1991. Text by Trevor Richardson. Greensboro, N.C.: Weatherspoon Art Gallery, University of North Carolina at Greensboro, 1991. 59 pp.; color and bw illus.

Churchill, Edwin. "A New Look at Maine Furniture." *Decorative Arts Society Newsletter* 16, nos. 3/4 (Fall/Winter 1990–91): 2. (Abstract of paper presented at DAS session of SAH annual meeting, Boston, Mar. 31, 1990.)

Churchill, Edwin. "Thomas Jackson, Clockmaker: Now There are Two." *Maine Antique Digest* 19, no. 4 (April 1991): 12B–13B. Bw illus.

Conger, Clement E., and Mary K. Itsell; Alexandra W. Rollins, ed.; Will Brown photographer. *Treasures of State: Fine and Decorative Arts in the Diplomatic Reception Rooms of the U.S. Department of State*. New York: Harry N. Abrams, 1991. 497 pp.; 422 color and 8 bw illus., bibliography, index. (See esp. "The Furniture," 66–245.)

Cooke, Edward S., Jr. "The Legacy of Sam Maloof in New England." *Stuff Magazine*, no. 100 (May 1991): 58–60. 7 bw illus.

Copeley, William. "Musical Instrument Makers of New Hampshire, 1800–1960." *Historical New Hampshire* 46, no. 4 (Winter 1991): 231–48. 6 bw illus.

Crossman, Carl L. "The Export Furniture, 1730–1860." In *The Decorative Arts of the China Trade: Paintings, Furnishings, and Exotic Curiosities*. Woodbridge, England: Antique Collectors' Club, 1991, chap. 9, pp. 220–62.

Cumming, Elizabeth, and Wendy Kaplan. *The Arts and Crafts Movement*. London and New York: Thames and Hudson, 1991. Distributed by W. W. Norton. 216 pp.; 31 color and 136 bw illus., bibliography, index.

Davis, Lee H. "The Greek Revival Influence on American Clock Case Design and Empire Clock Case Development." *NAWCC Bulletin*. Supplement 18, Spring 1991. 112 pp.; numerous bw illus., bibliography.

Dilworth, Tim G. "The Labels of Thomas Nisbet." *Material History Review* 34 (Fall 1991): 70–72. 5 bw illus.

Ducoff-Barone, Deborah. "Philadelphia Furniture Makers, 1800–1815." *Antiques* 139, no. 5 (May 1991): 982–95. 6 color and 15 bw illus., checklist.

The Encyclopedia of Antiques. Introduction by David Battie. New York: Crescent Books, 1991. See Leigh Keno, "American Chippendale Furniture," pp. 17–21; and "Shaker Furniture," pp. 22–23. Color illus.

Eidelberg, Martin, ed. *Design 1935–1965: What Modern Was, Selections from the Liliane and David M. Stewart Collection*. New York: Le Musee des Arts Decoratifs de Montreal in association with Harry N. Abrams, 1991. 424 pp.; 530 color and bw illus., biographies and corporate histories, index.

Fairbanks, Jonathan L. "A Natural Devotion: Studio Furniture Maker, Sam Maloof." *Antiques and Fine Art* 8, no. 3 (May–June 1991): 65–69.

Fairbanks, Jonathan L. "Sam Maloof: Celebrating Forty-Four Years in the Fine Art of Furniture Making." *Stuff Magazine*, no. 100 (May 1991): 51–55. 5 bw illus.

Fairbanks, Jonathan L., et al. *Collecting American Decorative Arts and Sculpture, 1971–1991*. Boston: Museum of Fine Arts, Boston, 1991. 100 pp.; color and bw illus., checklist of 126 objects.

Fennimore, Donald L. "Brass Hardware on American Furniture: Part I, Cast Hardware, 1700–1850." *Antiques* 139, no. 5 (May 1991): 948–55. 9 color and 10 bw illus. Part II, "Stamped Hardware, 1750–1850." *Antiques* 140, no. 1 (July 1991): 80–91. 17 color and 3 bw illus.

Fidler, Patricia J. *Art with a Mission: Objects of the Arts and Crafts Movement*. Lawrence, Kans.: Spencer Museum of Art, 1991. Distributed by the University of Washington Press. 111 pp.; numerous color and bw illus., bibliography, index.

Fiell, Charlotte, and Peter Fiell. *Modern Furniture Classics Since 1945*. Washington, D.C.: American Institute of Architects Press, 1991. 192 pp.; 144 color and 191 bw illus., biographies, bibliography, index.

Flynt, Suzanne L., Susan McGowen, and Amelia F. Miller. *Gathered and Preserved*. Deerfield, Mass.: Memorial Hall, Pocumtuck Valley Memorial Association, 1991. 56 pp.; 90 color and bw illus.

Garrett, Wendell. "Thomas Willing's Card Table." In *Sotheby's Art at Auction, 1990–91*. New York: Sotheby's Publications, 1991, pp. 314–15. 1 color and 1 bw illus.

Gilbert, Christopher. *English Vernacular Furniture, 1750–1900*. New Haven and London: Yale University Press for the Paul Mellon Centre for Studies in British Art, 1991. viii + 294 pp.; 417 color and bw illus., appendixes, glossary, bibliography, index.

Gilliam, Jan Kirsten, and Betty Crowe Leviner. *Furnishing Williamsburg's Historic Buildings*. Williamsburg, Va.: Colonial Williamsburg Foundation, 1991. xii + 95 pp.; 111 color and bw illus., glossary, bibliography, index.

Gloag, John. *A Complete Dictionary of Furniture*. 1952. Revised and expanded by Clive Edwards. Woodstock, N.Y.: The Overlook Press, 1991. 828 pp.; line drawings, appendix.

Gustafson, Eleanor H. "Collectors' Notes." *Antiques* 139, no. 5 (May 1989): 856, 858. Bw illus. (Re chest of drawers made by Birdsall Salmon at the shop of Hugh Spier, Newburgh, New York, 1809, and relic furniture made by George J. Henkels, Philadelphia, 1876.)

Gustafson, Eleanor H. "Museum Accessions." *Antiques* 139, no. 5 (May 1991): 876, 878, 902. Color and bw illus. (Re chest of drawers made by Herter Brothers, New York, ca. 1880, and cabinet, Daniel Pabst, Philadelphia, ca. 1875 [Brooklyn Museum]; high chest, attributed to Samuel Sewall, York, Maine, ca. 1750 [Maine State Museum]; music cabinet, attributed to Herter Brothers, New York, 1870–1875 [Munson Williams Procter Institute Museum of Art]; chest, Wythe County, Virginia, 1820–1830, and side table, Williamsburg, Virginia, ca. 1745 [MESDA].)

Hawes, Elaine. *Charles Koones and the Alexandria Furniture Trade, 1820–1860*. Alexandria, Va.: Alexandria Historical Society, 1991. 87 pp.; bw illus.

Hays, John. "*Vive L'Antique*." *Auction News From Christie's* 12, no. 5 (January–February 1991): 4. 1 color and 1 bw illus. (Re pier table branded by Charles-Honore Lannuier, ca. 1815.)

Herdeg, J. A. "A Lower Housatonic River Valley Shop Tradition: An Analysis of Six Related Dressing Tables." *Connecticut Historical Society Bulletin* 56, nos. 1–2 (Winter–Spring 1991): 39–56. 10 bw illus., chart.

Hood, Graham. "Early Neoclassicism in America." *Antiques* 140, no. 6 (December 1991): 978–85. 8 color and 2 bw illus.

Hood, Graham. *The Governor's Palace in Williamsburg: A Cultural Study*. Williamsburg, Va.: Colonial Williamsburg Foundation, 1991. Distributed by the University of North Carolina Press. 343 pp.; numerous color and bw illus., appendixes, index.

Hosley, William. "The Wetmore Parlor and Eighteenth-Century Middletown, Connecticut." *Antiques* 139, no. 3 (March 1991): 586–97. 14 color and 2 bw illus.

Hurst, Ronald L. "Nota Bene: New in the Collection." *The Colonial Williamsburg Foundation Research Review* 2, no. 1 (Winter 1991): 22. 1 bw illus. (Re cupboard, Amherst Co., Va., possibly eighteenth century [1990.249]. See also *Regional Furniture Society Newsletter*, no. 14 [Summer 1991]: 10.)

In the Most Fashionable Style: Making a Home in the Federal City. Checklist for the exhibition, The Octagon, October 2, 1991–January 5, 1992. Washington, D.C.: The Octagon, 1991. 28 pp.; bw illus.

Janzen, Reinhild Kauenhoven, and John M. Janzen. *Mennonite Furniture: A Migrant Tradition (1766–1910)*. Intercourse, Pa.: Good Books, 1991. 231 pp.; 241 color and bw illus., line drawings, maps, appendixes, bibliography, glossary-index.

Jenkins, Emyl, with Joe E. A. Wilkinson. *Emyl Jenkins' Guide to Buying and Collecting Early American Furniture*. New York: Crown Publishers, 1991. xii + 148 pp.; numerous bw illus., line drawings, bibliography, index.

Jobe, Brock. "A Boston Desk-and-Bookcase at the Milwaukee Art Museum." *Antiques* 140, no. 3 (September 1991): 412–19. 6 color and 5 bw illus.

Jobe, Brock. "A Comparison of 18th Century Furniture of Boston, Portsmouth, and Newport." *The Forum* 5, no. 3 (July 1991). A Publication of the Antiques Dealers' Association of America, Inc. Published in *Antiques and the Arts Weekly* (July 12, 1991): 79–82. 21 bw illus.

Keller, Patricia J. "Black-Unicorn Chests of Berks County, Pennsylvania." *Antiques* 140, no. 4 (October 1991): 592–605. 15 color and 4 bw illus.

Kenny, Peter M., Frances Gruber Safford, and Gilbert T. Vincent. *American Kasten: The Dutch-Style Cupboards of New York and New Jersey, 1650–1800*. New York: Metropolitan Museum of Art, 1991. viii + 80 pp.; bw and color illustrations, line drawings, appendices, glossary, bibliography.

Kenny, Peter M., Frances Gruber Safford, and Gilbert T. Vincent. "The Eighteenth-Century American *Kast*." *Antiques* 139, no. 2 (February 1991): 398–411. 13 color and 4 bw illus.

Komanecky, Michael. "Screens of the Arts and Crafts Movement." *New England Antiques Journal* 9, no. 7 (January 1991): 4, 26, 36. Bw illus.

Kramer, Fran. "Groveland Shaker." *Maine Antique Digest* 19, no. 5 (May 1991): 32C–33C. Bw illus.

Kramer, Fran. "The Shakers of Groveland, New York." *Antiques* 140, no. 2 (August 1991): 228–41. 16 color and 4 bw illus.

Kramer, Fran. *Simply Shaker: Groveland and the New York Communities.* Rochester, N.Y.: Rochester Museum and Science Center, 1991. 88 pp.; 68 bw illus., 4 line drawings, bibliography, illustrated catalogue of selected objects.

Leopold, Allison Kyle. *Cherished Objects: Living with and Collecting Victoriana.* New York: Clarkson N. Potter, 1991. 240 pp.; numerous color plates, Victoriana directory, selected bibliography and notes, index.

Lindsey, Jack L. "An Early Latrobe Furniture Commission." *Antiques* 139, no. 1 (January 1991): 208–19. 8 color and 5 bw illus.

Linoff, Victor M., ed. *Illustrated Mission Furniture Catalog, 1912–13: Come-Packt Furniture Company.* New York: Dover Publications, 1991. 183 pp.; bw illus.

Liverant, Arthur. "New London County Furniture: Distinguishing Elements." *The Forum* 5. no. 4 (December 1991). A Publication of the Antiques Dealers' Association of America, Inc. Published in *Antiques and the Arts Weekly* (Dec. 6, 1991): 91–94. Bw illus.

Livingston, Thomas W., and Karel F. Wessel. *American Writing Furniture, 1760–1830: An Exhibition of Six American Desks from the Collection of Thomas Livingston Antiques.* San Francisco: The Firm, 1991. 16 pp.; color illus.

Lovell, Margaretta M. "'Such Furniture as Will Be Most Profitable': The Business of Cabinetmaking in Eighteenth-Century Newport." *Winterthur Portfolio* 26, no. 1 (Spring 1991): 27–62. 14 bw illus., 4 charts.

Mallalieu, Huon, ed. *The Illustrated History of Antiques: The Essential Reference for All Antique Lovers and Collectors.* Philadelphia: Running Press, 1991. (See "Furniture: America," pp. 126–37.)

Mayer, Lance, and Gay Myers, eds. *The Devotion Family: The Lives and Possessions of Three Generations in Eighteenth-Century Connecticut.* New London, Conn.: Lyman Allyn Art Museum, 1991. 64 pp.; 25 bw illus., checklist of 75 objects.

Miller, Judith, and Martin Miller, eds. *Miller's Antiques Checklist: Furniture.* New York: Viking Studio, 1991. 192 pp.; numerous color and bw illus., glossary, list of makers, bibliography, index.

Mo, Charles L. *Splendors of the New World: Spanish Colonial Masterworks from the Viceroyalty of Peru.* Charlotte, N.C.: Mint Museum of Art, 1992. 104 pp.; numerous color and bw illus., index.

"Museum Acquires Set of Signed Cottage Furniture." *Maine State Museum Broadside* 14, no. 1 (Fall 1991): 4. Bw illus. (Re objects made by Arad Evans and William H. Josselyn of Portland, active 1868–1872.)

Neo-classicism in America: Inspiration and Innovation, 1810–1840. Introduction by Stuart P. Feld, essay by Wendell Garrett. New York: Hirschl & Adler Galleries, Inc., 1991. 136 pp.; numerous color and bw illus., index.

Palmer, Gabrielle, and Donna Pierce. *Cambios: The Spirit of Transformation in Spanish Colonial Art.* Albuquerque, N.M.: Santa Barbara Museum of Art in cooperation with the University of New Mexico Press, 1992. 142 pp.; numerous color and bw illus., bibliography, index.

Peddle, Walter W. "Recent Acquisitions, Newfoundland Museum, St. John's." *Material History Review* 34 (Fall 1991): 76–77. 2 bw illus. (Re nineteenth-century games table and ca. 1900 picture frame.)

Prown, Jonathan, Ronald Hurst, and Sumpter Priddy III. "Fredericksburg Clock Cases, 1765–1825." *Journal of Early Southern Decorative Arts* 17, no. 2 (November 1992): 54–119. 43 bw illus., appendixes.

"A Philadelphia Card Table." *Sotheby's Newsletter* (January 1991): 1. 2 color illus. (Re rococo example owned originally by Thomas Willing.)

"Recent Study Examines Early Finishing Techniques." *SPNEA Conservation Center Bulletin* 2, no. 1 (Winter 1991). 1 bw illus., line drawings, bibliography. (Summary of unpublished research paper by Joseph Godla entitled "The Use of Wax Finishes on Pre-Industrial American Furniture.")

Sack, Harold, and Deanne Levison. "American Roundabout Chairs." *Antiques* 139, no. 5 (May 1991): 934–47. 13 color and 6 bw illus.

St. German, Priscilla. "A New Belter Discovery." *Maine Antique Digest* 19, no. 2 (February 1991): 34B. Bw illus.

The Saint Louis Art Museum: Handbook of the Collections. St. Louis: The Museum, 1991. 223 pp.; numerous color illus., index. (See "Decorative Arts," pp. 102–30.)

Schlereth, Thomas J. *Victorian America: Tranformations in Everyday Life, 1876–1915.* New York: HarperCollins, 1991. (See esp. chap. 3, "Housing," pp. 83–140.)

[Schorsch, David A.] *Catalogue VIII: Excellence in American Design, Current Offerings from the Collection of David A. Schorsch, Inc.* New York: David A. Schorsch, Inc., 1991. 66 pp.; numerous color and bw illus.

Schorsch, David A. "Frames Used on American Folk Paintings and Needlework, 1760–1880." *Antiques* 140, no. 4 (October 1991): 568–79. 26 color illus.

Schwenke, Thomas G. "The 'Seat' of Federalism: Styles and Trends in New York Chairs, 1788–1815." *The Forum* 5, no. 2 (April 1991). A Publication of the Antiques Dealers' Association of America, Inc. Published in *Antiques and the Arts Weekly* (April 5, 1991), pp. 99–102. 17 bw illus.

Short, William H. "New Additions to a Group of Federal Furniture." *Antiques* 140, no. 6 (December 1991): 960–65. 8 color and 2 bw illus.

Siefke, Madeline. "Philadelphia Chippendale: The Top Drawer of American Furniture." *Auction News from Christie's* 12, no. 8 (June 1991): 1–2. 1 color and 1 bw illus. (Re high chest labeled by Thomas Tufft [ca. 1745–1788] and owned by the Lewis family.)

Siegel, Jeanne B. *How to Speak Furniture with an Antique American Accent: Buying, Selling, and Appraisal Tips plus Price Guides*. Chicago: Bonus Books, Inc., 1991. 213 pp.; bibliography, index.

Siegel, Jeanne B. *How to Speak Furniture with an Antique Victorian Accent: Buying, Selling, and Appraisal Tips plus Price Guides*. Chicago: Bonus Books, Inc., 1991. xii + 171 pp.; bibliography, index.

Smith, Nancy A. *Old Furniture: Understanding the Craftsman's Art*. 2d rev. ed. New York, Dover Publications, 1991. 186 pp.; illus., bibliography, index.

Smith, Nancy A. "Understanding Historic Upholstery." *The Thirty-Second Ellis Memorial Antiques Show* (Boston, 1991), pp. 73–82. Bw illus., line drawings.

Solis-Cohen, Lita. "Neoclassic Furniture: Some Surprises." *Maine Antique Digest* 19, no. 6 (June 1991): 14A. Bw illus.

Solis-Cohen, Lita. "Virginia MFA Buys Japanned High Chest: Will Pay $1.5 Million for Ex-Kaufman Piece That Had Been Offered for $2.75 Million." *Maine Antique Digest* 19, no. 5 (May 1991): 18A. Bw illus.

Stickley, Gustav. *The 1912 and 1915 Gustav Stickley Craftsman Furniture Catalogs*. New York: The Athenaeum of Philadelphia and Dover Publications, 1991. 112 pp., 205 bw illus., 7 line drawings.

[Stokes, Jayne E.] *The Seat of Elegance: An Insider's Guide to the Chair, 1720–1760*. Milwaukee, Wis.: Milwaukee Art Museum, 1991. Unpaged; bw illus., checklist.

Swedberg, Robert W., and Harriett Swedberg. *Collector's Encyclopedia of American Furniture*. Vol. I, *The Dark Woods of the Nineteenth Century: Cherry, Mahogany, Rosewood, and Walnut*. Paducah, Ky.: Collector Books, 1991. 125 pp.; numerous color illus., bibliography, price guide.

Talbott, Page. "Seating Furniture in Boston, 1810–1835." *Antiques* 139, no. 5 (May 1991): 956–69. 25 color and 2 bw illus.

Thornton, Peter. *The Italian Renaissance Interior, 1400–1600*. New York: Harry N. Abrams, 1991. 407 pp.; 410 color and bw illus., 40 line drawings, index.

Trent, Robert F. "The Wendell Couch." American Classics No. 24. *Maine Antique Digest* 19, no. 2 (February 1991): 34D–37D. 10 bw illus.

Ward, Gerald W. R. "An American Tavern Table?" *Regional Furniture* 5 (1991): 108–9. 1 bw illus.

Ward, Gerald W. R. "New Hampshire Begins: Planning for the Sherburne House Exhibition at Strawbery Banke Museum." *New England Antiques Journal* 9, no. 9 (March 1991): 14, 59. Bw illus.

Ward, Gerald W. R., ed. *American Furniture with Related Decorative Arts, 1660–1830: The Milwaukee Art Museum and the Layton Art Collection*. New York: Hudson Hills, 1991. 315 pp.; 25 color and 164 bw illus., appendixes, bibliography, index.

Wiencek, Henry. *The Moody Mansion and Museum*. Galveston, Tex.: Mary Moody Northern, Inc., 1991. Unpaged; bw and color illus.

1992 TITLES

"A New Settee: Made, Sold, and Decorated in Maine." *Broadside* 15, no. 1 (Summer 1992): 2. Bw illus. (Re rocking settee/cradle, probably made by Moses Wells, Augusta, Maine, ca. 1829–1850, and stenciled by Chester A. Pierce, Portland, after 1911.)

Adamson, Jeremy Elwell. "The Wakefield Rattan Company." *Antiques* 142, no. 2 (August 1992): 214–21. 10 color and 6 bw illus.

American Antiques from Israel Sack Collection. Vol. 10. Old Town Alexandria, Va.: Highland House, 1992. Numerous color and bw illus., index.

Ames, Kenneth L. *Death in the Dining Room and Other Tales of Victorian Culture*. Philadelphia: Temple University Press, 1992. 265 pp.; numerous bw illus., index.

Austin, Bruce A. *The Arts and Crafts Movement in Western New York, 1900–1920*. Rochester, N.Y.: Rochester Institute of Technology, 1992. 40 pp.; illus., index.

Ball, Robert W. D. *American Shelf and Wall Clocks: A Pictorial History for Collectors*. Atglen, Pa.: Schiffer Publishing, 1992. 288 pp.; 1,250 illus., value guide, index.

Barquist, David. "American Looking Glasses in the Neoclassical Style, 1780–1815." *Antiques* 141, no. 2 (February 1992): 320–31. 14 color and 2 bw illus.

Barquist, David. *American Tables and Looking Glasses in the Mabel Brady Garvan and Other Collections at Yale University*. New Haven, Conn.: Yale University Art Gallery, 1992. 423 pp.; 30 color and numerous bw illus., appendixes, index.

Bartinique, A. Patricia. *Gustav Stickley, His Craft: A Daily Vision and a Dream*. Parsippany, N.J.: Craftsman Farms Foundation, 1992. 120 pp.; 128 bw illus., bibliography, checklist of exhibition.

Bartinique, A. Patricia. "Gustav Stickley, His Craft: Furniture, Textiles and Metalwork, Lighting, Documents, and Photographs." *Antiques and the Arts Weekly* (December 11, 1992): 1, 72–73. Bw illus.

Bowman, Leslie Greene, and Morrison H. Heckscher. "American Rococo: Lately from London." *Antiques* 141, no. 1 (January 1992): 162–71. 15 color illus.

Bushman, Richard L. *The Refinement of America: Persons, Houses, Cities*. New York: Alfred A. Knopf, 1992. xix + 504 pp.; bw illus., index.

Crossman, Carl L. "China Trade Furniture." *Antiques* 141, no. 2 (February 1992): 332–43. 21 color and 1 bw illus.

Deitz, Paula. "Sitting in the Garden." *Antiques* 141, no. 6 (June 1992): 978–89. 13 color and 3 bw illus.

Devanney, Joseph J. "The American 'Dutch Cupboard': Our First Status Symbol." *Antiques Journal* 11, no. 1 (July 1992): 64, 66. 2 bw illus.

"Edwards Tall Case Clock." *Concord Museum Newsletter* (Fall 1992): 7. (Re tall clock, ca. 1815, by Nathaniel Edwards [b. 1770] of Acton, Mass., donated to the museum.)

Ehrenpreis, Diane Carlberg, and Brock Jobe. *Portsmouth Furniture: Masterworks from the New Hampshire Seacoast: An Introduction*. Boston: Society for the Preservation of New England Antiquities, 1992. 20 pp.; 14 color and 13 bw illus. (See also a gallery guide accompanying the exhibition, 12 pp., with 11 bw illus.)

Elder, William Voss, III. "Living with Antiques: A Collection of American Furniture in Baltimore." *Antiques* 141, no. 5 (May 1992): 834–41. Color illus.

Field, Richard Henning. "Claiming Rank: The Display of Wealth and Status by Eighteenth-Century Lunenburg, Nova Scotia, Merchants." *Material History Review* 35 (Spring 1992): 1–20. 6 bw illus., appendixes.

Fine Woodworking Design Book Six: 266 Photographs of the Best Work in Wood. Introduction by Sandor Nagyszalanczy, with an essay on apprenticeship by Scott Landis. Newtown, Conn.: Taunton Press, 1992. 185 pp.; numerous color illus., index.

Garrett, Wendell. *Classic America: The Federal Style and Beyond*. New York: Rizzoli, 1992. 300 pp.; numerous color illus., bibliography, index of places of interest.

Gustafson, Eleanor H. "Museum Accessions." *Antiques* 141, no. 5 (May 1992): 734, 736. 3 color and 1 bw illus. (Re late nineteenth- and early twentieth-century furniture acquired by the Metropolitan Museum of Art: screen by Lockwood de Forest, cabinet by Kimbel and Cabus, table by William Lightfoot Price, and étagère by Kimbel and Sons.)

Hays, John. "Chippendale Table Recalls Old Philadelphia: The Bispham Family." *Auction News From Christie's* 13, no. 6 (May–June 1992): 4. Color illus.

Heckscher, Morrison H., and Leslie Greene Bowman. *American Rococo, 1750–1775: Elegance in Ornament*. New York: Metropolitan Museum of Art and Los Angeles County Museum of Art, 1992. Distributed by Harry N. Abrams. xv + 288 pp.; 82 color and 168 bw illus., bibliography, exhibition checklist, index. (See especially "Furniture," pp. 133–217.)

Hewett, David. "First Look at a Shaker Treasure Trove." *Maine Antique Digest* 20, no. 2 (February 1992): 8B–13B. Numerous bw illus.

Hewett, David. "Stephen Huneck: America's Hottest New Artist Has a Secret." *Maine Antique Digest* 20, no. 2 (February 1992): 1B–3B. Numerous bw illus.

Kirk, John T. "An Awareness of Perfection." *Design Quarterly* (Winter 1992): 14–19. Illus.

Kleckner, Susan D. "A Rare Queen Anne Walnut Slab Table." *Auction News from Christie's* 14, no. 2 (November 1992): 6. 1 color illus.

Knell, David. *English Country Furniture: The National and Regional Vernacular, 1500–1900*. New York: Cross River Press, 1992. 240 pp.; 28 color and 353 bw illus., bibliography, index.

Kuronen, Darcy. "The Musical Instruments of Benjamin Crehore." *Journal of the Museum of Fine Arts, Boston* 4 (1992): 52–79. 27 bw illus.

Lahikainen, Elizabeth, and Alexandra W. Rollins. "Upholstery Conservation in the Diplomatic Reception Rooms of the United States Department of State." *Antiques* 141, no. 5 (May 1992): 808–19. 23 color illus.

Ledes, Allison E. "Living with Antiques: Quaker Hill near Dayton, Ohio." *Antiques* 141, no. 1 (January 1992): 180–89. 14 color illus.

Levison, Deanne, and Harold Sack. "Identifying Regionalism in Sideboards: A Study of Documented Tapered-leg Examples." *Antiques* 141, no. 5 (May 1992): 820–33. 16 color and 5 bw illus.

[Levy, Frank M.] *Vanity and Elegance: An Exhibition of the Dressing Table and Tall Chest in America, 1685–1785*. New York: Bernard & S. Dean Levy, Inc. 1992. 48 bw illus.

Limbert, Charles P., and Company. *Limbert Arts and Crafts Furniture: The Complete 1903 Catalogue*. Introduction by Christian G. Carron. New York: Dover Publications, 1992. xi + 67 pp.; 188 bw illus.

Lindquist, David. "Colonial Revival Furniture: Is It Any Good?" *Antiques Journal* 11, no. 1 (July 1992): 28, 47. 3 bw illus.

Ly, Tran Duy. *American Clocks: A Guide to Identification and Prices*. 2 vols. Fairfax, Va.: Arlington Book Co., 1992. Vol. 1: 320 pp.; 1,159 illus., index. Vol 2: 320 pp.; 1,032 illus., index.

Mayer, Barbara. *In the Arts and Crafts Style*. Photographs by Rob Gray. San Francisco: Chronicle Books, 1992. 224 pp.; numerous color illus., bibliography, sources, index.

Nutting, Wallace. *Wallace Nutting . . . The Great American Idea*. 1921. Reprint. Doylestown, Pa.: Diamond Press, 1992. 40 pp.; illus.

Nutting, Wallace. *Wallace Nutting Windsors: Correct Windsor Furniture*. 1918. Reprint. Doylestown, Pa.: Diamond Press, 1992. 48 pp.; illus.

Petraglia, Patricia. *American Antique Furniture: Styles and Origins*. New York: Smithmark Publishers, 1992. 176 pp.; 150 + color and bw illus., line drawings, appendix, glossary, index.

Petraglia, Patricia. "Portsmouth Furniture: Masterworks from the New Hampshire Seacoast." *Antiques and the Arts Weekly* (Oct. 9, 1992): 1, 64–66. Bw illus.

Philp, Peter, and Gilliian Walkling, eds. *Field Guide to Antique Furniture*. Boston: Houghton Mifflin, 1992. 336 pp.; numerous color and bw illus., glossary, price list, index.

Prown, Jonathan. "A Cultural Analysis of Furniture-Making in Petersburg,

Virginia, 1760–1820." *Journal of Early Southern Decorative Arts* 18, no. 1 (May 1992): 1–179. 74 bw illus., appendixes.

Riccardi-Cubitt, Monique. *The Art of the Cabinet Including a Chronological Guide to Styles*. New York: Thames and Hudson, 1992. 224 pp.; numerous color and bw illus.; biographies of cabinetmakers, craftsmen, and designers; glossary; bibliography; index.

Safran, Rose. "Portsmouth Furniture." *Maine Antique Digest* 20, no. 11 (November 1992): 6D–7D. 11 bw illus.

Saunders, Richard, and Paula Olsson. *Living with Wicker*. New York: Crown Publishers, 1992. 159 pp.; numerous color illus., directory of antique wicker specialty shops and wicker restoration specialists, index.

Schorsch, David A. "Living with Antiques: The Gail Oxford Collection of American Antiques in Southern California." *Antiques* 142, no. 3 (September 1992): 352–59. 14 color illus.

Schwind, Arlene Palmer. "A Herter Discovery." *Victoria Society of Maine Newsletter*, n.s., 2, no. 1 (Summer 1992): n.p. 2 bw illus.

Smith, Mary Ann. *Gustav Stickley: The Craftsman*. 1983. Reprint. New York: Dover Publications, 1992. 208 pp.; 86 bw illus., 31 line drawings, index.

Solis-Cohen, Lita. "Rolling the Dice: How the Market Works." *Maine Antique Digest* 20, no. 11 (November 1992): 10A. 1 bw illus. (Re Boston bombé desk with history in the Griggs family.)

Sposato, Kenneth A. "The Watch and Clock Museum." *Antiques and the Arts Weekly* (July 17, 1992): 1, 64–66. (See also, "Museum Agenda Includes New Book on The Willards," p. 65.)

Steinbaum, Bernice. *The Rocker: An American Design Tradition*. New York: Rizzoli, 1992. 160 pp.; numerous color illus.

Stickley, L., and J. G. *Early L. & J. G. Stickley Furniture from Onondaga Shops to Handcraft*. Ed. Donald A. Davidoff and Robert L. Zarrow. New York: Dover Publications, 1992. xix + 187 pp.; 260 bw illus.

Stillinger, Elizabeth. *Historic Deerfield: A Portrait of Early America*. New York: Dutton Studio Books, 1992. vii + 206 pp.; numerous color and bw illus., bibliography, index.

Swedberg, Robert, and Harriet Swedberg. *Collector's Encyclopedia of American Furniture*. Vol. 2, *Furniture of the Twentieth Century*. Paducah, Ky.: Collector Books, 1992. 144 pp.; numerous color and bw illus.

Talbott, Page. "European Precedents for American Classical Furniture: Part I." *The Decorative Arts Trust Publication* 12, no. 1 (Winter 1992): 1–4. 10 bw illus. "Part II." 12, no. 2 (Spring 1992): 2, 4–5. 12 bw illus.

Talbott, Page. "The Furniture Trade in Boston, 1810–1835." *Antiques* 141, no. 5 (May 1992): 842–55. 7 color and 12 bw illus., checklist of Boston cabinetmakers, 1810–1835.

Theobald, Mary Miley. "Baker's Passion for Fine Furniture." *Colonial Williamsburg Today* 14, no. 3 (Spring 1992): 56–61. Color illus.

"Treating Portsmouth Furniture" and "From Drab to Brilliant." *SPNEA News*, series 58 (Fall 1992): 7–8. 2 bw illus. (In "Update" from SPNEA Conservation Center, re conservation for "Portsmouth Furniture" exhibition and of the Hannah Barnard cupboard at the Henry Ford Museum.)

Trent, Robert F. "Rediscovering French America." *Winterthur Magazine* 39, no. 1 (Winter 1992–1993): 6–7. 3 bw illus.

Ward, Gerald W. R. "Avarice and Conviviality: Card Playing in Federal America." *Antiques* 141, no. 5 (May 1992): 794–807. 16 color and 1 bw illus.

Ward, Gerald W. R., and Karin E. Cullity. "The Furniture [at Strawbery Banke Museum]." *Antiques* 142, no. 1 (July 1992): 94–103. 20 color illus.

Warren, Elizabeth V. "Living with Antiques: The Collection of Helaine and Burton Fendelman." *Antiques* 142, no. 4 (October 1992): 530–39. 17 color illus.

Warren, Velma Susanne. *Golden Oak Furniture*. West Chester, Pa.: Schiffer Publishing, 1992. 192 pp.; 670+ color illus., glossary, list of manufacturers, bibliography, index, price guide.

"What's New in the Collection." *Bennington Museum Notes* 13, no. 4 (Fall 1992): 4. 1 bw illus. (Re chest of drawers made by Daniel Loomis of Shaftsbury, Vermont, in 1817.)

Zea, Philip. "The Emergence of Neoclassical Furniture Making in Rural Western Massachusetts." *Antiques* 142, no. 6 (December 1992): 842–51. 17 color illus.

Zea, Philip, and Robert C. Cheney. *Clock Making in New England, 1725–1825: An Interpretation of the Old Sturbridge Village Collection*. Ed. Caroline F. Sloat. Sturbridge, Mass.: Old Sturbridge Village, 1992. 173 pp.; numerous color and bw illus., line drawings, appendixes.

Zea, Philip, and Suzanne L. Flynt. *Hadley Chests*. Deerfield, Mass.: Pocumtuck Valley Memorial Association, 1992. 31 pp.; 16 color and bw illus., exhibition checklist.

Zimmerman, Philip D. *Seeing Things Differently*. Winterthur, Del.: Winterthur Museum, 1992. 80 pp.; 108 color and bw illus.

Zogry, Kenneth Joel. "Anatomy of a Fraud." *Bennington Museum Notes* 13, nos. 2–3 (Spring–Summer 1992): 1. bw illus.

Zogry, Kenneth Joel. "Anatomy of a Fraud: The Bennington Museum." *Maine Antique Digest* 20, no. 7 (July 1992): 22A–23A. 5 bw illus.

Index